Economics, Aid and Education

THE WORLD COUNCIL OF COMPARATIVE EDUCATION SOCIETIES

The WCCES is an international organization of comparative education societies worldwide and is an NGO in consultative partnership with UNESCO. The WCCES was created in 1970 to advance the field of comparative education. Members usually meet every three years for a World Congress in which scholars, researchers, and administrators interact with colleagues and counterparts from around the globe on international issues of education.

The WCCES also promotes research in various countries. Foci include theory and methods in comparative education, gender discourses in education, teacher education, education for peace and justice, education in post-conflict countries, language of instruction issues, Education for All. Such topics are usually represented in thematic groups organized for the World Congresses.

Besides organizing the World Congresses, the WCCES has a section in *CERCular*, the newsletter of the Comparative Education Research Centre at the University of Hong Kong, to keep individual societies and their members abreast of activities around the world. The WCCES comprehensive web site is http://www.wcces.com.

As a result of these efforts under the auspices of the global organization, WCCES and its member societies have become better organized and identified in terms of research and other scholarly activities. They are also more effective in viewing problems and applying skills from different perspectives, and in disseminating information. A major objective is advancement of education for international understanding in the interests of peace, intercultural cooperation, observance of human rights and mutual respect among peoples.

CAIE 27
The WCCES Series Post-Instanbul, Volume 4
Series Editors:
Suzanne Majhanovich and Allan Pitman

The WCCES Series was established to provide for the broader dissemination of discourses between scholars in its member societies. Representing as it does Societies and their members from all continents, the organization provides a special forum for the discussion of issues of interest and concern among comparativists and those working in international education.

The first series of volumes was produced from the proceedings of the World Council of Comparative Education Societies XIII World Congress, which met in Sarajevo, Bosnia and Herzegovina, 3–7 September, 2007 with the theme of *Living Together: Education and Intercultural Dialogue*. The series included the following titles:

Volume 1: Tatto, M. & Mincu, M. (Eds.), *Reforming Teaching and Learning*
Volume 2: Geo JaJa, M. A. & Majhanovich, S. (Eds.), *Education, Language and Economics: Growing National and Global Dilemmas*
Volume 3: Pampanini, G., Adly, F. & Napier, D. (Eds.), *Interculturalism, Society and Education*
Volume 4: Masemann, V., Majhanovich, S., Truong, N., & Janigan, K. (Eds.), *A Tribute to David N. Wilson. Clamoring for a Better World.*

The second series of volumes has been developed from the proceedings of the World Council of Comparative Education Societies XIV World Congress, which met in Istanbul, Turkey, 14–18 June, 2010 with the theme of *Bordering, Re-Bordering and new Possibilities in Education and Society*. This series includes the following titles, with further volumes under preparation:

Volume 1: Napier, D.B. & Majhanovich, S. (Eds.) *Education, Dominance and Identity*
Volume 2: Biseth, H. & Holmarsdottir, H. (Eds.) *Human Rights in the Field of Comparative Education*
Volume 3: Ginsburg, M. (Ed.) *Preparation, Practice & and Politics of Teachers*
Volume 4: Majhanovich, S. & Geo-JaJa, M.A. (Eds.) *Economics, Aid and Education*

Economics, Aid and Education

Implications for Development

Edited by

Suzanne Majhanovich
The University of Western Ontario, Canada

and

Macleans A. Geo-JaJa
Brigham Young University, USA

SENSE PUBLISHERS
ROTTERDAM/BOSTON/TAIPEI

A C.I.P. record for this book is available from the Library of Congress.

ISBN: 978-94-6209-363-8 (paperback)
ISBN: 978-94-6209-364-5 (hardback)
ISBN: 978-94-6209-365-2 (e-book)

Published by: Sense Publishers,
P.O. Box 21858,
3001 AW Rotterdam,
The Netherlands
https://www.sensepublishers.com/

Printed on acid-free paper

TABLE OF CONTENTS

ACKNOWLEDGEMENTS

The development of a book is an involved process and its success depends on the cooperation of many parties. As editors, we would like to thank those who have contributed to this project. This publication would not be possible without the assistance of those who organized the WCCES XIVth World Congress at Boğaziçi University in Instanbul, Turkey, June 24–28, 2010. We are very grateful to Professor Fatma Gök from Boğaziçi University and from the Turkish Comparative Education Society (TÜKED) which hosted the Congress on behalf of the WCCES, and to her very able colleagues from the local organizing committee, Meral Apak and Soner Şimşek for their help in providing contact information of presenters enabling us to invite them to submit papers to be developed into chapters for this volume.

We would also like to thank the contributors of chapters that appear in the book for their willingness to submit their manuscript, and for their careful attention to suggestions made by the editors and reviewers to strengthen each paper. *Economics, Aid and Education: Implications for Development* has taken many months to bring to completion as we worked through each chapter with the authors. We thank our authors for their patience and academic integrity while working on the chapters. We are proud to be able to present a volume that includes research reports, opinion pieces and case studies by authors from countries worldwide—from Africa, North and South America, Europe, Asia and Australia. The different conceptual perspectives presented in this volume reflect scholarship in the area of comparative and international education, and complement the mission of the World Council of Comparative Education Societies to promote research in countries around the world.

Finally our gratitude is due to the reviewers who carefully read through the manuscripts and offered constructive feedback to authors and to the editors to help improve each chapter: thanks to Zehlia Babaci-Wilhite, Andres A. Chavez, Alyson Larkin, Donna Hazel Swapp, Paul Tarc and Aniko Varpalotai. We are grateful as well to the editors and their staff at Sense Publishing, in particular Michel Lokhorst, who took responsibility for bringing the publication to completion. Thank you as well to Allan Pitman, senior editor of the series of publications derived from World Congresses.

SUZANNE MAJHANOVICH & MACLEANS A. GEO-JAJA

ECONOMICS, AID AND EDUCATION: IMPLICATIONS FOR DEVELOPMENT

INTRODUCTION

The XIVth Congress of the World Council of Comparative Education Societies met in Istanbul in June, 2010. The theme of the Congress was "Bordering, Re-bordering and New Possibilities in Education and Society". There were fourteen thematic groups with papers addressing various aspects of the over-arching theme; many papers were concerned with the impact of economics and education on development. This volume features fourteen articles drawn from the thematic groups related to issues of economics, aid and development. Although versions of all papers were first presented at the World Congress in 2010, for the purposes of this collection the authors have reworked them to bring them up to date to reflect the evolution of the issues expressed in the original papers.

It is impossible to discuss economics, development or education in a world-wide context without considering the effects globalization has had on these issues. Globalization has had profound consequences for education worldwide, particularly in the developing world. Although we can celebrate the fact that through technological development the world has become a much smaller place, a 'global village' as it were, in which instant communication across the world, even to the most remote regions is possible, yet concerns have been growing regarding the effects of world interconnectedness on the ability of sovereign states to meet the needs of their citizens in such areas as education and health. As Bray (2005) has noted, globalization can mean different things to different people (p. 35). He refers to the work of Held et al (1999) which identifies three camps with different views on globalization: of these camps, the first deemed *hyperglobalists,* sees globalization as subjugating people and nations to the global marketplace; the second, or the *sceptics* see current manifestations of globalization as merely the latest incarnation in a history going back centuries, of attempts to bring about economic integration; and finally, the *transformationalists,* similar to *hyperglobalists,* view globalization as bringing about changes of a social, political and economic nature with a goal of reshaping societies. Transformationalists are also concerned about stratification and inequalities across the globe driven by globalisation (Held et al, 1999, cited in Bray, 2005, p. 36). Accordingly, it can be considered a process of reinvigorating colonialism or a colollary of global capitalism's self-interest.

S. Majhanovich and M.A. Geo-JaJa (Eds.), Economics, Aid and Education:
Implications for Development, 1–12.

Holger Daun (2005) notes that globalization has reduced the power of states to manage their own resources and exert any control over economic processes (p. 96, see also Castells, 1995). The cultural effects of globalization that tend to homogenize and standardize in favour of dominant powers to the detriment of indigenous cultures is also problematic. He remarked that, "economic imperatives dominate over all others; there is a universal commodification of life and pricing is extended to more and more services and activities...Also with the spread of the market model, a consumer culture is disseminated" (p. 96). A further consequence has been the tendency of governments to formulate alien educational policies to make their populace competitive on the world market (p. 96). This involves a constraint on curriculum to favour those subjects considered appropriate for creating global workplace skills with attendant downplaying of skills relevant to the local economy and human values.

Overall, this process of transferring, and adaptation of values, knowledge, technology and behavioural norms across countries and societies in different parts of the world, driven as it is by a neoliberal capitalism agenda has resulted in great advances for some—mostly in the developed world and disaster and down grading of all aspects of indigenous knowledge and innovation. Indeed, as contended by Geo-JaJa in his chapter, socio-economic insecurity and deprivation predominates in numerous standardization packaged international recommendations and policies that outline the market-logic of globalization. As Chomsky stated in an interview with Toni Gabric:

> The term "globalization" has been appropriated by the powerful to refer to
> a specific form of international economic integration, one based on investor
> rights, with the interests of people incidental (May 7, 2002).

The chapters in this volume reflect the concerns about globalization on matters of equity, impoverishment, and the opportunity to localize both education and development. They also analyse globalization as accelerating compression of the contemporary world and the intensification of consciousness of the world as a singular entity (Robertson 1992, p. 132). Papers include both case studies on specific countries or regions as well as reflections on economic priorities in a globalized world and the effects on education. The issue of aid, how it is delivered and conditions of its provision is debated in several papers. Similarly, development is conceived in a number of ways depending on the context. In addition, the issue of what quality education has come to mean in a globalized age is also taken up in several papers. The contrasts between discourses of humanistic approaches to education (Freire, 2000, Sen, 1999, 2002, Nussbaum, 1997, 2000), human capital theory (Bourdieu, 1986, Georgialis, 2007) and those of the Washington Consensus as propounded by the documents of the World Bank form a basis of discussion throughout the volume. The book is divided into three sections: The Politics of Aid and Development; Education and Development in a Neoliberal World; and the African Context.

2

The first section contains chapters that look critically at the issue of aid and unpack conceptions of development from the perspective of economic theory. Steven Klees & Omar Qargha in *The Economics of Aid: Implications for Education and Development* review the alarming data regarding the growing gap between rich and poor, the disturbing numbers of people subsisting on less than $1.25US a day, starving and malnourished children and children denied access to school—this in the face of billions of dollars of aid given or loaned to developing countries. They ask whether the aid has helped at all. The answer is quite clear: there are serious problems with the way aid is delivered and the conditions under which it is awarded. To buttress their arguments, they review five recent studies on problems with international aid written from both neoliberal and liberal and progressive perspectives. Not surprisingly the neoliberal authors, Dichter, Easterly and Mayo support the notion that the market holds the solution to effective aid transfers. The liberal and progressive side proposed by Riddell and Ellerman suggests an overhaul of the current system with more attention to a rights-based approach and development of autonomy of the aid recipients. Klees and Qargha observe that today in discussions about problems with aid, neoliberal discourse seems to prevail with fewer voices from the progressive side. As self-declared members of the progressive side, they counter with a series of suggestions that they contend would ameliorate the situation. They conclude on the relatively hopeful note that it would not take that much to address the problems of the world's impoverished masses in a just and humane way.

In *The New Geopolitics of Educational Aid: From Cold War to 'Holy Wars'* Mario Novelli looks at the shifts in the nature, volume, trajectory and content of aid to education post 9/11 when the West has become concerned with the rise of radical Islamism. The chapter focuses in particular on Afghanistan and Iraq as conflict and post-conflict countries. Furthermore the chapter looks at how the political situation has affected the educational aid they receive. He sees a dangerous trend towards 'militarization of development' which has implications for educational aid in post conflict and fragile regions. He is most concerned that military and security considerations will outweigh the needs to address issues of widespread deprivation and development. A further worry is the dangers aid workers face in a hostile environment where the locals view those trying to bring aid and development with mistrust. The tragic death of Jackie Kirk provides a striking example of the position aid workers are placed in when their humanitarian goals are seen as mere fronts for the military agenda.

Rukhsana Zia in *Aid in Education: A Perspective from Punjab Pakistan* presents a case study on aid from the World Bank to the Government of Pakistan for the purpose of education reforms and teacher development and training. Her paper provides a nice companion piece to the Novelli chapter in its acknowledgement that aid to fragile, unstable countries like Pakistan may have more to do with political and strategic interests than with actual development needs. Her study however focuses more on the mismatch between the conditions of aid provision and the actual situation of the

3

organizations expected to carry out the reforms and develop the programs to train teachers. Among the problems she identifies are: lack of consensus on the indicators for key objectives of the reforms; disregard of the need for institutional development and capacity building; lack of synchronization of activities preventing an integrated process; frequent changes of leadership in the government sector; different agendas of various aid donors, and different strategies by them to meet objectives; loopholes in governance style; and biases of the Punjab government favouring certain donors. Zia is concerned that owing to competing agendas with the Punjab government, opportunities were lost for the educational organizations to effect needed reforms. She argues that as a result the country was not really able to manage the aid it received, thus allowing donors to step into the gap to promote their own objectives. She is of the opinion that despite all, more aid is needed in countries like Pakistan, echoing a conclusion expressed by Klees & Qargha, but she also bemoans the fact that the largest donors are not meeting their commitments to aid nor have they directed the aid they do supply to the neediest recipients.

The final paper in this section, *Critical Analysis of Economics of Education Theories with Regard to the Quality of Education* by Aksoy et al considers the economic theories that drive aid and development today and link them to the current definitions of 'quality' education. Theirs is a historical overview of the evolution of thoughts on quality education. They comment on the neoliberal perspective where quality education implies a view of human capital theory in which the goal of education is to provide skills and knowledge for the global market. These authors decry market driven indicators to define quality education along with the role of the World Bank, the IMF and WTO in imposing their neoliberal ideology on education systems. Instead their notion of quality education is a humanistic one that tries to overcome inequalities and injustices of society and seeks human emancipation in the Freirian sense (Freire, 2000).

The papers in the first section present potent examples of negative feedbacks, indeed wasteful results of aid delivered under the constraints of neoliberal market ideology. The economic theories that guide approaches to education can result in more harm than good if the humanistic element is ignored. In the next section of the book, the five papers explore what has happened to education and development in a neoliberal world.

The paper by Majhanovich *How the English Language Contributes to Sustaining the Neoliberal Agenda: Another Take on the Strange Non-demise of Neoliberalism,* includes a discussion of economic conditions in the emerging countries that have been subjected to the ruinous structural adjustment programs (SAPs) imposed by the World Bank. The author speculates on the extent to which neoliberal practices represent a new type of colonialism. She compares past colonial times in North America with the destruction of indigenous languages and cultures to current times where European education systems are chosen by developing countries in the hopes of preparing their youth for participation in world markets. Now as in the past local languages and cultures are devalued or even lost. Majhanovich looks at the changes to higher education in the developed North all in the service of neoliberalism. The English language as the *lingua franca* of business and commerce contributes to validating the tenets of neoliberalism, she contends. As nuances of language shift to reflect neoliberal connotations, those meaning become accepted as the norm and are more difficult to dislodge. This contributes to the continuing acceptance of neoliberalism despite the demonstrable failures of a market approach to correcting the problems of the world economy. The paper concludes with the observation that the brutality of neoliberalism may ultimately lead it to self-destruct especially now that its nefarious results are undermining the developed world and the middle class.

In the second paper in this section, *The Economic Capture of Criticality and the Changing University in Australia and the UK,* Christine Daymon and Kathy Durkin investigate how the neoliberal agenda plays out in higher education to change the kind of programs taught. They argue that neoliberalism has influenced universities to move away from the kind of courses that would teach critical thinking skills to focus instead on areas that prepare students to work in the global market. To test their hypothesis they interviewed professors and post-graduate students in two universities, one in Australia and the other in the UK. They found that many of both international and home students were unsure of what criticality actually was, and in many cases did not see it as a necessary skill for their future endeavors. Similarly, some instructors did not see the need to engage their students in critical thinking. Only a minority of students and instructors in the targeted courses appreciated the value of critical thinking for their courses; most preferred to engage in a more instrumental approach. Although Daymon and Durkin admit the limitations of their study to only two universities in two countries in a particular business area of study, still the authors find it alarming the extent to which universities buy into neoliberal business and consumer approaches that support economic imperatives and undermine the traditional role of universities to foster critical thinking necessary to maintain and develop democratic society. In this they echo Giroux's (2004, 2009) warning that democracy is threatened by the corporatization of universities.

Bethsaida Nieves in *Systems of Reason(ing) in the Idea of Education Reforms for Economic Development: the Puerto Rican Context* examines how the globalization discourse plays out in the context of Puerto Rico. Although education reforms are ostensibly carried out to enable Puerto Rico to be competitive in the knowledge based economy, Nieves contends that ultimately political reasons are driving the changes more than purely economic ones. In other words, she sees the move to the internationalization of higher education and research as another tool of governmentality—or control. Language policies have obviously been influenced by Puerto Rico's status as a US territory and at various times English or Spanish have been designated as the main medium of instruction. Currently bilingual education, Spanish and English is the policy but knowledge of English has always been seen as necessary for economic advancement she notes.

In seeking to understand education reform and economic development in Puerto Rico, Nieves draws on Foucault's notion of biopolitics as a way the state can govern its population. She contends that 'the biopolitical will of the state is driving education reform for economic growth in Puerto Ricos's education system today but the state is also at the mercy of biopolitical development driven by the market'. Nieves concludes that as a part of the global economy, Puerto Rico tailors its education reforms to match requirements of the world knowledge economy. Language policies reflect the conviction that mastery of both English and Spanish is necessary to secure Puerto Rico's economic, political and cultural place in the world.

The majority of papers in this volume are critical of the effects of neoliberalism on education and development. However, in *Decentralization, Marketization and Quality Orientation,* Hu Rongkun, Qian Haiyan and Allan Walker express a different perspective. They note that in China, the move to neoliberalism has prompted much needed reforms to the Chinese education system. The authors argue that after years of isolation, China saw the need to become more open to world markets. The Party recognized the significance of market and free enterprise and so began to enact reforms in agriculture and industry that allowed them to enter the World Trade Organization. Such reforms champion performance and competition in line with neoliberal ideology rather than continuing with an economy planned and controlled from the centre. This move to embrace neoliberal ideas necessitated reform in the education system. The paper details a series of reforms carried out from 1985 to 2010 with the goal of providing quality education and linking education to economic development. The reforms have entailed much decentralization—a devolution of authority for education from rigid central government control to local levels. Reforms to create 'quality' education have included measures to develop an exemplary school system, reforms to curriculum and examinations and personnel reforms.

It is interesting that in the Western world as well as in developing areas such as Africa, the influences of neoliberalism and market fundamentalism have been decried as harmful to education systems (See Giroux, 2009, Burbules & Torres, 2000 among others). In China, however, at least according to the authors of this article, neoliberal ideology has resulted in needed reform and development to an education system that was overly restricted. One might question this development in a tightly controlled society such as China's. However, perhaps as Giroux (2009) has pointed out, under neoliberalism the state gains more powers as long as it controls the market since when education reforms are carried out to promote economic development, the market dictates what will be learned. So despite the changes to the education system in China, the mechanism and process of reform are not ultimately inimical to Chinese traditions and party control. This resonates with Nieves' paper on Puerto Rico where the argument was also made that education reforms for economic development are connected to tools of governmentality.

The final paper in this section, *Narrative as an Educational Tool for Human Development and Autonomy* by Helena Modzelewski focuses on human development as a means to personal economic betterment. Modzelewski reports on work she carried out with disadvantaged and homeless women at a daytime activity centre in Montevideo. She uses Amartya Sens' capability approach as the theoretical framework and Martha Nussbaum's narrative method as a basis for interventions with the women. She wished to bring them to the point where they would overcome their adaptive preferences, that is, their unrealistic expectations for themselves, expectations that were constantly frustrated. Instead she wanted them to come to the realization that there were other options open to them to change their lives for the better and perhaps overcome their homeless situation. Her hypothesis was that the way to help the women give up their adaptive preferences involved giving them a chance to narrate their own stories, to trace the events that had resulted in their current situation. By claiming ownership of their life story, in the presence of others in similar situations, she believed the women could see other more workable possibilities that would enable them to turn their lives around. She gives several examples from the literacy workshop she led, and showed that given the chance to write their life stories and share with others, some of the women indeed found new ways to make a more stable life for themselves and their children.

The final section of this volume includes five chapters that look at economics, aid and education in the context of Africa. MacLeans A. Geo-JaJa in *Education Localization for Optimizing Globalization's Opportunities and Challenges in Africa,* makes a powerful case for valuing indigenous knowledge as a vehicle for self-development and autonomy. He reviews the problems globalization practices have wrought for Africa, not the least of which has been suppression of indigenous languages and cultural ways of knowing. He sees indigenous languages and cultures as dynamic factors that should be allowed to flourish to foster rights-based educational development and social justice. In his comprehensive paper, Geo-JaJa discusses what globalization means for effectiveness of learning in schools; he outlines the dimensions and characteristics of globalization arguing that Africa should not have to accept economic and education openness in order to participate in the globalized world. Next he criticises the influence of neoliberalism in incorporating economism into education. Finally he questions whether globalization in the context of Africa is enabling choice for enlarging capabilities. The chapter contributes to the ongoing debates over impediments to learning in school systems caused by globalization. He closes with suggestion for new strategies to ensure rights in education over right to education and responsibility in development. Geo-JaJa sees globalization as providing both opportunities and threats to national development. He argues for a 'localized' path in globalization that will allow for freedom and sustainable socio-economic rights where both the instrumental and the intrinsic have a place in education. He contends that the non-reliance on the role of indigenous knowledge in the development of local sustainability or the facilitation of a culturally appropriate development program is a core drawback of globalization.

Tingting Yuan in *The Rising 'China Model' of Educational Cooperation with Africa: Features, Discourses and Perceptions* presents a different model of aid to the developing world than the much criticized versions embodied by the structural adjustment programs (SAPs). The China Model as she describes it represents more of a collaboration between partners and more reciprocity, unlike the Western models

7

where aid is awarded conditionally provided that certain economic measures are met involving plans to repay debt, balance budgets, privatize and deregulate, all tenets of neoliberalism. In this volume and elsewhere it has been argued that the imposition of the Western (or World Bank) kind of aid has not worked and has left the countries far worse off than they were before. The school systems have also been negatively affected since Western/Northern models of schooling have been adopted often employing colonial languages of English and French as the medium of instruction with the resulting elimination of traditional forms of schooling. The model Yuan describes in her case study of Tanzania seems to respect more the needs of the developing country. She outlines the main approaches of Chinese educational aid as including: Chinese government scholarships; short-term training; cultural exchanges; the setting up of Confucius institutes; school building or training; teacher secondment and university cooperation. While admitting that this model reflects in some ways that of other educational agencies such as the British Council, she maintains that the donor-recipient relationship differs from previous colonial relations. The latter is due to the fact that the Chinese are committed to delivering knowledge in a practical and diplomatic way. For her study, she spent time in Tanzania and interviewed participants in the program. Overall, reactions were positive to the program although it was not without problems. The most positive distinguishing feature between the China model and Western aid is that the purpose of China aid was not to make recipients over in the likeness of the donors as is often the case with Western aid, but rather was seen as an exchange of benefits through mutual support. The fact that China had never been in a colonial relationship with Africa was a positive element to the program. Despite some issues with providing higher education opportunities for Tanzanians—language issues, length of program and so on, it was hoped that the China aid model could still provide an improved version of foreign aid. She closes with comments that if China can follow King's (2007) eight principles of foreign aid, there would be a potential to build upon foundations of mutuality, equal benefit and self-reliant development.

Jonah Nyaga Kindiki in his paper *Educational Policy Reforms in Africa for National Cohesion* highlights several discourses of education, the first, a positive one in his opinion, where education advances global partnerships and can result in economic benefits for the state. He is however more concerned with the negative roles education can play in which as a force for reproduction of what already is the norm in society. He remarked that education does not serve to advance the poor and disadvantaged but can make their situations even worse. He is concerned at the way schools can reproduce and cause violence. The study he conducted involved both a review of literature in the area as well as interviews with students, teachers and parents to sound them out for ways to overcome the negative consequences in the current education system. His focus is mainly on Kenya, but he also draws on examples from other African countries. He concludes his paper with a series of recommendations for changes to the education system that he hopes will end the cycle of violence reproduced in schools. He believes that the incorporation of peace education, political education, human rights education, and conflict resolution skills education among others will offer the potential to ensure that education in Kenya and elsewhere in Africa represents a positive force leading to national cohesion. This he sees by extension could also contribute to economic development.

In *Breaking Down Borders in Development Education. Something's gotta give,* Beth Packer presents a case study of an aid program that took place in Senegal under the auspices of an NGO. The plan offered an alternative paradigm to the usual manner of aid delivery. Packer argues that the traditional provision of aid to the developing world has not worked and cites at the beginning of her paper the dismal indicators of poverty and illiteracy worldwide despite the vast amounts of money spent on aid. In this she reflects the same message that Klees and Qargha delivered in the first chapter of this volume.

Packer's suggestion for improvement of aid provision involves re-localization (much as Geo-JaJa articulates in his paper). Re-location involves local input rather that the top-down approach to aid delivery generally used worldwide. In the Senegalese case she describes a program that was developed involving an equal number of American and Senegalese students in a type of action plan that incorporated collaborative research and project design. The program included both instruction in development theories intended to result in sustainable development paradigms. The field based part of the program involved the students working with locals in a rural area. The idea was to encourage the local people to assess their own development needs and then with the help of the international development students, realize a solution. Once students had met with community members and had mapped out community needs, they began to develop projects to meet the development goals.

This promising approach to aid in development enjoyed some measure of success but ultimately failed to deliver the expected transformation. The goal had been for the local villagers to take ownership of the projects making use of the outsiders' expertise and turn the projects into sustainable development. Since the projects essentially were developed by the outsiders and imported to the village, there were misunderstandings as to what exactly was envisaged. As Packer comments: "Students envisioned implementing projects that would contribute to long term improvement of the living conditions in the community and were disappointed when they discovered that many villagers were unclear why they were even there." Villagers too had different expectations for the program hoping for funding for large-scale development. Certainly funding was a problem as was the lack of long-term commitment. Packer reports that the NGO was disbanded in 2012 probably due to insufficient financial support.

Although the program did not meet anticipated success, Packer maintains that the notion of re-localization is the right way to go with international aid if only new partnerships between North and South can be forged. Also she maintained that the economic and symbolic borders that prevent the South from developing the necessary expertise for sustainability can be broken down.

9

The final paper in this collection, *Skills Management for Better School-to-work Transitions in Africa,* by Nora Alleki argues for an improved skills management system in Africa to facilitate school to work transitions. Although world economies are in a fragile state with high unemployment, especially among youth, Alleki points out that the situation in Africa is much worse and notes that key social and economic indicators there are quite alarming.

She refers to numerous UNESCO and ILO databases to support her claims. Mismatches occur between qualifications that African youth hold and the kind of skills needed if they are to enter the workforce. She contends that the situation could be improved if employment policies were related to recruitment and if employers were aware of the type of skills needed for the positions they offer. Further, young people need the opportunity to access life-long learning, and employers should be able to assess and pay accordingly when their employees have acquired new and needed skills.

In her review of the data bases on education, she asserts that progress has been made in minimizing illiteracy among youths aged 15–24 but adult illiteracy still persists in many African countries. Moreover, there are still far too many children not attending school and factors such as gender, language or location contribute to the problem. Overall youth are finding it more and more difficult to find work in the formal sector, and many resort to the informal sector to find work. Jobs in the informal sector do not usually require qualifications or certificates but do need certain skills that youth who work in those areas acquire.

Alleki offers some suggestions that she hopes will smooth out the transition from school to work. She believes legislative measures and collective agreements are needed to protect workers. Secondly employers should recognize skills acquired in the informal work market. She also believes it would be helpful to have employment intermediaries to help match workers to appropriate jobs. The problems with unemployment in her opinion result from poor or non-effective skills management because of malfunctioning human resources strategies and employment policies. These problems need to be addressed in order to give young people a chance to find gainful employment and fulfill their role in society.

The collection of papers in this volume addresses issues of development in its many forms in a globalized neoliberal world. As we have seen, some papers focus more on aid ineffectiveness; others are concerned with the neoliberal roadmap on development resulting in the commodification of education. Apprehension was expressed over the prominence of neoliberal capitalism as the only hope for Africa. Thus, it is argued that reactionary policies so costly to human beings, interpret power within the confines of aid distribution and consumption of knowledge in market driven conditions. Finally since the issues of economics, aid and education for development are particularly acute in Africa, a number of papers were selected from the Istanbul WCCES to mitigate challenges, problems and propose possible solutions. Although the tenor of the volume presents a rather negative picture of the current economic situation and concurrent effect on education in the world, still it is felt that frank discussion of the problems needs to be aired in order to come to possible improvements for the future.

REFERENCES

Bourdieu, P. (1986). The forms of capital. In Richardson, J. G. (Ed.) *Handbook of theory and research for the sociology of education.* New York: Greenwood.
Bray, M. (2005). Comparative education policy and globalization: Evolution, missions and roles. In Zajda, J. (Ed.), *International handbook on globalisation, education and policy research* (pp. 35–48). Dordrecht, The Netherlands: Springer
Burbules, N. C., & Torres, C. (2000). *Globalization and education. Critical perspectives.* New York: Routledge.
Castells, M. (1993). The informational economy and the new international division of labor. In Carnoy, M., Castells, M., Cohen, S. S., & Cardosa, F. H. (Eds.) *The new global economy in the information age* (pp. 15–44). University Park, Penn.: Pennsylvania State University.
Chomsky, N. (2002). Interview with Toni Gabric for *The Croatian feral tribune*, "On escalation of violence in the middle east". www.chomsky:info/interviews/20020507.htm.
Daun, H. (2005). Globalisation and the governance of national education systems. In Zajda, J. (Ed.), *International handbook on globalisation, education and policy research* (pp. 93–107). Dordrecht, The Netherlands: Springer.
Freire, P. (1970, reprinted 2000). *Pedagogy of the oppressed.* New York: Continuum International Publishing Group.
Georgialis, N. M. (2001). Educational reforms in Greece (1959–1997) and human capital theory. *Journal for Critical Education Policy Studies (JCEPS)* 5:2 http://www.jceps.com/?pageID=articles&articleID=105
Giroux, H. (2004). *The terror of neoliberalism: Authoritarianism and the eclipse of democracy.* Boulder CO: Paradigm Publications.
Giroux, H. (2009). Democracy's nemesis. The rise of the Corporate University. *Cultural Studies, Critical Methodologies* 9(5), 669–695.
Held, D., McGrew, A., Goldblatt, D., & Perraton, J. (1999) *Global transformations: politics, economics and culture.* Cambridge: Polity Press.
Nussbaum, M. (1997). *Cultivating humanity: A classical defense of reform in liberal education.* Cambridge, MA: Harvard University Press.
Nussbaum, M. (2000). *Women and human development.* Cambridge: CUP.
Robertson, R. (1992). *Globalization: Social theory and global culture.* California: Sage Publications
Sen, A. (1999). *Development as freedom.* New York: Anchor Books.
Sen, A. (2002). *Rationality and freedom.* Harvard: Harvard Belknap Press.

AFFILIATIONS

Suzanne Majhanovich
Faculty of Education
Western University, Canada

Macleans A. Geo-JaJa
David O. McKay School of Education
Brigham Young University, USA

PART I

THE POLITICS OF AID AND DEVELOPMENT

STEVEN J. KLEES & OMAR QARGHA

THE ECONOMICS OF AID: IMPLICATIONS
FOR EDUCATION AND DEVELOPMENT[1]

Our world faces pervasive poverty and inequality:

- the world's rich-poor gap has more than doubled since the 1960s;
- 1.4 billion people live on less than $1.25/day;
- hunger affects 963 million people worldwide;
- nearly 1 billion people lack access to safe drinking water;
- one in three children in developing countries suffers from malnutrition;
- about 75 million children who should be in primary school are not; and
- every year, nearly 10 million children under the age of 5 die from preventable causes.

(Bread for the World, 2009; UNESCO, 2009; Dichter, 2003, p. 1)

Hundreds of billions of dollars in international aid have been given or loaned to developing countries though bilateral and multilateral mechanisms, at least, ostensibly, in order to do something about these and other problems. Has such aid helped?

Debates around this question have been ongoing for decades, perhaps intensifying in recent years. This should not be a surprise. It is far from straightforward to even determine how to investigate the question. At first glance, a researcher might want to look before and after to observe how well indicators, such as of poverty and economic growth, improved over a specific time period, and link that to changes in aid, controlling for other factors that might affect poverty and economic growth. While some research along these lines exists, this approach is generally a non-starter, especially on a global level, but also even for specific countries. The question is just too complicated to be well specified because, among other reasons, there is a myriad of interactive factors that affect poverty and economic growth besides aid, and international aid serves many purposes other than these. Given that a supposedly 'scientific' approach cannot answer the question of the impact of aid, it is not surprising that many of the debates about it rely heavily on anecdotal and idiosyncratic evidence marshalled from particular ideological perspectives.

Periodic studies and international meetings, such as the World Bank sponsored Pearson Commission in 1970 and the Paris Declaration of 2005, have reviewed aid and development linkages and made recommendations. However, despite the fact that most of these official views of aid end up arguing that more is necessary, foreign aid has long had its critics from all sides of the political spectrum. For example,

S. Majhanovich and M.A. Geo-JaJa (Eds.), Economics, Aid and Education:
Implications for Development, 15–28.

from the right, Peter Bauer, an early neoliberal economist writing before the term "neoliberal" was popular, published in 1972 a book called *Dissent on Development* that summarized the critique he had been making for many years. He argued that rather than helping, "foreign aid...is likely to obstruct" development (p. 95) by creating dependency, distorting priorities, fostering corruption, and exacerbating market imperfections. His recommendation was to mostly eliminate foreign aid. This has also been a long-term political position of the neoconservative movement in the United States.

A strong critique of foreign aid has come from some on the left as well. For example, Andre Gunder Frank (1967) in his classic article on dependency entitled *The Development of underdevelopment* argues that foreign aid is a form of neocolonialism. Samir Amin (1980), in his book, *Delinking: Towards a Polycentric World*, argues the need for developing countries to delink from world trade and aid systems in order to focus on internal needs. Amin does not argue that trade and aid should be eliminated, just reduced.

It is not our purpose to do a historical analysis of the state of aid and development. We do, however, wish to give a sense of current debates on the topic and conclude by offering some of our own views. In our review of the literature on aid and development, five recent books stood out as repeatedly discussed and referenced. We therefore examine briefly each of these works, trying to provide a sense of each author's argument. The first three books mostly offer neoliberal perspectives, while the last two come from more liberal and progressive perspectives. We follow this examination with a discussion of their views and conclude with our own views on aid and development, including implications for education.[2] This paper spends more time on aid and development issues than on education, in part, because we found we could not sensibly discuss education issues without first examining the debates about aid and development and their broader implications.

CURRENT DEBATES

Thomas Dichter

Thomas Dichter's 2003 book is entitled *Despite Good Intentions: Why Development Assistance to the Third World Has Failed*. Dichter's main argument is "that aid has become a business whose main stake is its own survival" (p. 4) and that development is "staggeringly complex" (p. 191). This complexity makes control and engineering of change almost impossible. He argues that development should not be about "doing" things, but rather about institutions, attitudes, laws and human resources.... "[Rather than engineering], we could instead undertake more subtle and indirect interventions, stimulating, encouraging, and cajoling" (p. 185, 191). Dichter, like most of the other critics discussed below, does not deny that there are aid and development success stories such as in the areas of primary education, the elimination of smallpox, and the lowering of infant mortality rates (p. 2). But for

Dichter these are the exceptions and development strategy should not be based on such anomalies. Rather, he argues that "let's leave well enough alone, let them (the poor of developing nations) be. Let the forces of the international marketplace bring on development. Let globalization reign" (p. 10)

Dichter insists his conclusion is not "gloomy" (p. 10). His sources for hope are the potential for telecommunications, the migration of the poor towards better opportunities, and the overall workings of the market and the private sector in the interests of development. While acknowledging the continued need for humanitarian assistance, he nevertheless concludes: "It is time for us to entertain the serious possibility that development assistance is not necessary for development" (p. 293).

William Easterly

The title of William Easterly's 2006 book is *The White Man's Burden: Why the West's Efforts to Aid the Rest Have Done so Much Ill and So Little Good*. He offers a strong critique of international aid as a "tragedy in which the West spent $2.3 trillion on foreign aid over the last five decades and still had not managed to get twelve-cent (malaria) medicines to children" (2006, p. 4). Like Ditcher, Easterly sees the failure rooted in the inherent problems with planning and social engineering. He argues that the failure of aid is because it is left to "planners" who are unable to be as efficient as the market. However, he does not advocate that everything should be turned over to the free market because the poor don't have money to motivate the market to meet their needs. Easterly recommends a much reduced role and scope for foreign aid. He suggests that aid be oriented towards programs that seek to have a direct and concrete impact on the poor, and away from broad goals like development, broad policies like structural adjustment policies (SAPs), and the poverty reduction strategy process (PRSP). He recommends that "agents of assistance have to have incentives to search for what works to help the poor" and concludes with principles centered around individual accountability, individual freedom to search for what works, experimentation, and incentivizing aid based on the results of evaluation.

Dambisa Moyo

Dambisa Moyo's (2009) hotly debated book is entitled *Dead Aid: Why Aid is Not Working and How There is a Better Way for Africa*. Her essential argument is that "aid has helped make the poor poorer and growth slower." Moyo does make clear that she is talking about official development assistance (ODA) only, not humanitarian aid. Her argument that aid is not just "innocuous" but actually "malignant" (p. 47) rests on attributing to aid a host of ills: most especially, fostering corruption, but also diminishing social capital, increasing conflict, decreasing savings and investments, increasing inflation, hurting exports, and increasing bottlenecks (pp. 54–65). The result is a culture of "aid-dependency" or "addiction" (pp. 66, 75) that is fostered by what we might call an international aid complex employing half a million people.

This complex generates "pressure to lend" (p. 54) and "engenders laziness on the part of African policymakers...in remedying Africa's critical woes" (p. 66). Contrary to many researchers' calls for more democracy as part of a solution to these problems, Moyo further argues for a "decisive benevolent dictator to push through the reforms required to get the economy moving.... (p. 42)"

The evidence Moyo uses to support her arguments is almost wholly anecdotal and correlational, and the rationale is that of a neoliberal economist convinced of the necessity of market solutions.[3] Moyo concludes by calling for a complete phase-out of ODA over a 5 to 10 year period. A number of market-based prescriptions are offered as ways to replace, in a more productive manner, the capital that would be lost: borrowing on international capital markets; attracting more foreign direct investment; promoting trade; expanding microloans; facilitating remittances; incentivizing savings; and employing conditional cash transfers.

Roger Riddell

The title of Roger Riddell's 2007 book is *Does Foreign Aid Really Work?* This book differs from the others in a number of ways. First, in addition to a focus on ODA, it also looks closely at humanitarian and emergency aid and at aid provided by NGOs. Second, it considers providing aid within a human rights framework. Third, it offers the most detailed review of foreign aid and of studies of its impact.

After an exhaustive review of empirical studies, Riddell concludes that although there is evidence for both significant success and noticeable failures resulting from aid, we still don't know if most of official development aid has worked or failed. He attributes this uncertainty to the "inherent difficulties of tracing" the impact of aid.

Riddell summarizes that insufficient quantity, the lack of a systematic and efficient allocation, the volatile and unpredictable nature, the lack of coordination, and the lack of true recipient ownership of aid are the fundamental problems he sees with the current system (pp. 386–7). In his two concluding chapters, he recommends an overhaul of the entire aid architecture and proposes a new structure based on a human rights approach with recipient involvement and participation as the overarching indicators.

David Ellerman

David Ellerman's 2005 book, *Helping People Help Themselves: From the World Bank to an Alternative Philosophy of Development Assistance,* also critiques the 'big push' social engineering side of foreign aid and offers in its stead a model based on incrementalism and self-help. He says:

> After a half century on the path of official development assistance, we find ourselves lost....Development will not yield to social engineering no matter how much aid is provided. A fundamentally different philosophy of development assistance is needed... (p. 241)

That fundamentally different philosophy for Ellerman means rethinking the relations between 'helpers', those offering assistance, and 'doers', those receiving the assistance. Ellerman's (pp. 253–61) different philosophy is based on the view that the 'helpers' role should be to provide indirect, enabling, and autonomy respecting guidance to the 'doers' so that they can actually do the 'development' themselves.

DISCUSSION

So, what are we to make of all this? Clearly, all the authors offer some dismal analyses and depressing conclusions. Of course, this is not surprising given the current state of global poverty and inequality. One would have hoped that 60 years of international aid would have led to clear improvement. However, the best that anyone can say is that the situation could have been a lot worse than it is now had there been no aid. And only Riddell makes this argument explicitly.

However, these books do differ from one another. We find it useful to divide the world of political economy into three broad paradigms: neoliberal, liberal, and progressive. Neoliberalism, which predominates today, focuses on market solutions, criticizing the efficiency and equity of government interventions. A liberal perspective offers greater recognition of the inefficiencies and inequities of markets and puts more faith in government. Finally, a progressive perspective, focuses on the reproductive nature of both the market and the state under current world system structures like capitalism, patriarchy, and racism, and puts greater reliance on transformation from below through more participatory forms of democracy and collective action. It should be noted that these paradigms are, in some ways, more continuous and overlapping than mutually exclusive.

The predominant argument in these books– in particular, those by Dichter, Moyo and, to a large extent, Easterly – is neoliberal. Aid is seen as having been almost a complete waste at best, if not an unmitigated disaster, while the solution lies in minimizing government and maximizing free markets and trade. This is not surprising either, given that for the last three decades a neoliberal view has dominated in much of the world. However, what is interesting is that while Dichter, Moyo, Easterly, and other neoliberal commentators on the problems of aid have received a lot of attention, it is well to remember that neoliberals have generally been in charge for the last three decades during the biggest build-up in international aid the world has ever seen. Neoliberals have been in charge while the Millennium Development Goals (MDGs) – perhaps the most sweeping call for aid and social engineering in history – were instituted. At least on the surface, this implies that many neoliberals have maintained some belief in the efficacy of aid – or perhaps it is a result of neoliberal guilt given the worsening of poverty and inequality caused by their policies.

Or perhaps there is something else operating here. As progressive political economists, critical of both neoliberals and liberals, we see the neocolonial dimensions of aid in the world system, as Frank (1967) pointed out. From this perspective, international aid and the MDGs are a form of what Weiler (1984) called compensatory legitimation; more colloquially, we see it as a form of "good cop, bad cop." International crises, shaky and poorly-performing economies, increasing poverty and inequality, widespread conflicts, and the equivalent of structural adjustment policies everywhere, all call into question the legitimacy of the neoliberal social order – this is the bad cop. To compensate for this, actors in the world system of neoliberal globalization must introduce polices related to aid and the MDGs that are aimed at ameliorating some problematic conditions and thus restoring system legitimacy – this is the good cop.

This argument does not question the good intentions of the proponents of these policies, but it does question their effects.[4] Simply the existence of these policies may be sufficient for compensatory legitimation; whether they are effective seems to be less important. All of the books reviewed were written before the current economic crisis. This crisis changes things in that it calls into more serious question the neoliberal regime and poses a global challenge to its legitimacy. For the first time in three decades, whether neoliberalism will survive is not clear. If it does, however, it will probably not be a time for policymakers to heed the calls of people like Dichter, Moyo, and Easterly, as even greater compensatory legitimation will be needed. The world system must look like something is being done to improve the situation even if it is not.

We do not mean to argue that all policies are the result of systemic forces that reproduce and legitimate the unequal world order. We are firm believers that neoliberal policies are continually challenged by individuals, organizations, social movements, and left-of-center governments. The existence of aid and the MDGs represents real gains for the world's disenfranchised, as does, for example, the more participatory processes called for in PRSPs. However, in this neoliberal era, these policies unfortunately bear little fruit.

It is interesting to note that one could make the argument that aid was more successful in the liberal era of the 1960s and 1970s than it has been in the neoliberal era that followed. Even Moyo (2009, p. 5) admits that Africa was doing much better in the 1970s than today, and it was "awash" with aid then. A big difference is that the 1980s introduced neoliberal Structural Adjustment Programs (SAPs) throughout Africa, cutting government and liberalizing trade. Even many neoliberal economists admitted these policies had harmful, if not devastating, consequences. Yet current-day mechanisms such as the PRSP and the Poverty Reduction and Growth Facility (PRGF) continue to produce results that look very similar to those produced by the bankrupt SAPs.

Riddell and Ellerman proceed from a predominantly liberal perspective, although both have some progressive elements. Riddell is very critical of aid and its ties to commercial and political interests, but he recognizes that much aid has had a positive impact. His conclusion for increasing aid and restructuring aid architecture offers some progressive alternatives worth considering. Ellerman also critiques the structure of aid and the ability of bilateral and multilateral aid agencies like the World Bank to socially engineer a better world. His solution, to rely more on respecting the autonomous efforts of the "doers," especially at the grassroots level, fits with a more progressive perspective.

Our reading of additional literature related to aid and development indicates to us that these five books are representative of the debate. A neoliberal perspective predominates. Liberal views are reasonably represented, especially if you include works that are indirectly about aid and development (e.g., Collier, 2007; Sachs, 2005). Scarcer are works from a progressive perspective. In an excellent paper from this point of view, Samoff (2009, p. 24) comes to quite different conclusions than all the authors above: the aid system "is in fact working very well. Its essential role is not to achieve publicly stated objectives but rather to maintain a global political economy of inequality."

We agree with Samoff. But, as we are sure he would agree, this is not a call for despair. It is a call for transformation. We believe, as do many who share a progressive perspective, that that transformation will have to come from widespread collective action. Part of that action is thinking about and discussing what such transformation might entail. In what follows, we offer our own perspectives on certain key steps that need to be taken with regard to aid, development, and education.[5]

IMPLICATIONS FOR AID, DEVELOPMENT, AND EDUCATION

Much More Money Is Needed

In today's world, it has become fashionable to say 'better management and stronger accountability, not money, is what is needed to fix development problems.' This mentality has been an excuse for inaction. Of course more money is needed, much more. Rich countries spend less than 1% of their GDP on ODA. In 2008, ODA to all of Africa was about $35 billion, less than the U.S. bailout of the auto industry. It is worth noting that the Marshall Plan for reconstruction after WWII spent as much on Europe as the rich countries do on total ODA for all developing countries now (Moyo, 2009, p. 12). On a per capita basis, the Marshall Plan received about 8 times as much money as ODA receives now. And for Europe the development problem was much easier than that faced by developing countries today: Europe was already industrialized with an educated workforce; it only needed to rebuild the physical infrastructure damaged in the war. Developing countries need a much more intense effort than the Marshall Plan. The point is that we haven't been throwing money at our social problems; instead we've been miserly.

Education, like other social sectors, has been a victim of the neoliberal onslaught that has argued that schools generally do not need more money but need to spend it more wisely (Klees, 2008a). This is simply not true! Of course, spending wisely is important, but more money is desperately needed. We have 75 million children of primary school age out of school (UNESCO, 2009). They need teachers, classrooms, and learning materials. Moreover, we have many more millions of students receiving a very low quality primary education who need more and better educated teachers, improved facilities, and better learning materials. This does not include the huge secondary school coverage deficit.

Disburse some of that Money Directly to the Poor

One example of this is the idea of conditional cash transfers, which has recently gained quite a bit of support. Even people like Moyo (2009) and agencies like the Bank are touting these programs. However, as Riddle points out, these programs still shy away from giving directly to the poor because of the belief that they will spend it unwisely.

The idea of conditional cash transfers has shown promising results in the area of education. There are small- and large-scale programs in developing countries (e.g., Brazil and Mexico) that pay poor children to go to school, conditional on attendance and passing. Given the persistence of user fees and the very large opportunity costs of child labor faced by poor parents, offering scholarships such as these on a very large scale will be the only way to achieve UPE. Giving all aid money directly to the poor is not the answer. However, more programs that empower the poor by trusting them and believing that they know best how to achieve their immediate goals will go a long way.

Real and Strong Participation should be the Fundamental Basis for Governance

Who or what directs and should direct the aid system? There is much talk of "country ownership." The bilateral and multilateral aid agencies all claim that the country is in charge and that the agencies only have an advisory role. But that is simply not true. The aid agencies have overwhelming power in the aid relationship, specifically through the conditionalities they require, and generally through the power to withhold and direct aid. This power is even greater under the currently fashionable SWAps (sector wide approaches) through which the gang of donors effectively makes country policy. For aid to be effective, we must curtail the power of aid agencies and move beyond country ownership to rely on direct and widespread participation by beneficiaries and other stakeholders.

Participation in aid processes by the disadvantaged themselves and their advocates in civil society has long been discussed. Instrumental, idiosyncratic, and sporadic uses of participation have been common. But it is rare that participation takes on real and strong roles in governance (Edwards and Klees, 2012).[6] The rhetoric is often lofty, but the reality is weak. For example, the formulation of PSRPs that are supposed to guide all World Bank and IMF aid to a country require, in principle, extensive participation by civil society. In practice, consultation replaces participation, and the consultation is hurried and superficial, with civil society having hardly any say in the final product. As mentioned earlier, the final results are policies that bear strong similarities to the draconian and unsuccessful SAPs.

This call for serious participation in the governance of public policies and programs is a call for reform in rich countries as much as for reform in poor countries, as well as with global actors.[7] Representative democracy has had many positive features, but it has led to a system that is strongly reproductive, protecting the interests of the advantaged at the expense of the disadvantaged.

Neoliberals consider relying on the market as a form of participation. Of course that is true but only in a very limited sense. The market only provides participation to those with resources and does so individually, not collectively. As in all development endeavours, education needs much deeper and more widespread forms of participation. A good example is the effort to connect a broad approach to critical pedagogy in the administration, content, and process of education, such as with the Citizen School movement in Brazil (Fischman and Gandin, 2007; Gandin and Apple, 2002).

Replace the World Bank and the IMF

The Bank and the Fund are completely ideological institutions. Even insiders point to the internal "thought police" who reinforce orthodoxy and suppress dissent (Broad, 2006). For the last three decades, that ideology has been neoliberalism. Neoliberalism has been a total failure in terms of development and has resulted in the most incredible concentration of wealth the world has ever seen. It was a failure before the current economic crisis, and now that failure is even more apparent. Liberal and progressive economists have had hardly any voice in the Bank or the Fund since the 1970s.[8] Neither have non-economists, civil society, or developing countries. The result has been three decades of bad, one-sided advice (Klees, Samoff, and Stromquist, 2012).

Clearly the Bank and the Fund have functions that need to be fulfilled, in particular, giving grants and loans for development and for economic crises. But we need an entirely new architecture for doing so. Given the fundamental debates among economists, one school of economic thought should not dominate as it does now. Moreover, given that economic issues shade into all sorts of other social issues, economists should not be in charge. In keeping with our previous point, governance should be participatory, with developing countries and civil society having a considerable say. The Global Fund for Aids, Tuberculosis, and Malaria and the new Global Partnership for Education,[9] even though both are partially housed within the Bank and have other limitations, offer examples of attempts to develop a more participatory and consensus-based process.

We believe future historians will shake their collective head in wonder that the world today allowed a bank to be the global leader in developing and enforcing educational policy. We need an alternative architecture for ODA funds for education and the Bank's ideological role as global education cop must end.

Focus Aid on the Attainment of Human Rights

Instead of focusing development efforts on instrumental goals like promoting economic growth, at which we have been miserable failures, focus more directly

23

on attaining the human rights that so many are denied: the right to food, health, employment, housing, and education, to name a few. Of fundamental importance is to base education policy on the right to education. UNESCO and UNICEF have already moved in this direction, but the Bank and the Fund resist. In part, that is because such a change would wreak havoc with an instrumental human capital framework where education is only valued for its impact on earnings and economic growth, but not seen as an end in itself or as a means to alternative ends.

More of the Same Research Is Not Needed

Most studies end with a call for further research. Unfortunately, most research offers little guidance about what to do. As Easterly (2008) argues, the literature on aid and growth is so full of contradictory results that one can find support for almost any claim. This is because much of the research is ideologically driven and prone to data mining. Even more to the point, the lack of agreed upon findings is inherent in quantitative research. As argued elsewhere (Klees, 2008b), for quantitative research methods to yield reliable cause-effect information requires fulfilling impossible conditions. Regression analysis, the most frequently used methodology, requires three conditions: all independent variables that affect the dependent variable are in the equation, all variables are measured correctly, and the correct functional form is specified. In practice, these conditions are never fulfilled and can never be fulfilled. Regression analysis studies thus become a battleground over model specification. It is currently fashionable to call for an alternative to regression analysis – randomized experiments (Duflo and Kremer, 2008). In theory, well-controlled experiments are supposed to make it easy to make cause-effect inferences. In practice, real world experiments, outside the laboratory, are never well controlled. Researchers acknowledge this and try to make compensatory statistical adjustments, but they are always ad hoc and easily contestable. Basically, real world experiments revert right back to the problematic need for proper regression analysis specification to untangle cause-effect relationships.

This is a major conundrum.[10] We do need research and evaluation to help figure out what works, yet research and evaluation results are always contested and contestable. Our only answer is to return to the centrality of participation.[11] Participatory research and evaluation – with participation by beneficiaries and other stakeholders as well as by analysts who depart from different frameworks – may not yield definitive answers, but it can put our debates on the table. Drawing on quantitative, qualitative, and critical research and evaluation methodologies (Mertens, 2004; Denzin and Lincoln, 2000), the resulting information and arguments should become part of participatory decision-making processes. When truth becomes a problematic goal, the legitimacy of political processes becomes paramount.[12]

The indicators that we began this paper with are horrendous. Right now millions are dying and dying needlessly; millions more are barely surviving at the margins. Relatively few resources are needed to change this. The market mechanism does not work for billions of people and aid is insufficient and misdirected. Transformation is possible. We can turn this around and make the 21st century the first one that is just and humane.

NOTES

[1] An earlier version of this paper was presented at the World Congress of Comparative Education Societies held in Istanbul, June 13–17, 2010 and published in *Current Issues in Comparative Education*.

[2] Aid is a hot topic in education as well as in the development literature. See Benavot, Archer, Moseley, Mundy, Phiri, Steer & Wiking (2010, and King (2009).

[3] In a critique of Moyo's reliance on the correlation between aid and difficult development situations, Watkins (2009, p. 20) calls it "guilt by association: there's an awful lot of aid sloshing around in countries that are doing badly. Using the same logic you could argue that fire engines are best avoided because you tend to find them clustered around burning buildings."

[4] See also Samoff (2009, p. 4): "It is important to note here that a critical approach to foreign aid does not require a conspiracy theory. At issue are not the intentions or attitudes or good will of aid agency staff."

[5] We do not pretend that all progressives will agree on all points. For example, although we believe the need for more spending by the North on education and development in the South is essential, some progressive perspectives, such as delinking, might disagree (Amin, 1985). Relatedly, with more money comes more threats to sovereignty (Samoff, 2009)

[6] Waisbord (2008) offers a good analysis of three barriers to strong participation: the bureaucratic nature of aid agencies; their technical, expert-dominated model; and their pretense to be apolitical.

[7] Ellerman's call for encouraging self-help and respecting autonomy is, in part, a call for greater participation.

[8] Liberal or progressive economists in these institutions who have been vocal have been marginalized or fired. It is not only the Fund and the Bank that have been shaped strongly by neoliberal economists but universities, think tanks, bilateral aid agencies, and governments as well. It is interesting to note that even in the liberal Obama administration, despite the serious on-going economic crisis, critical voices get excluded. Paul Krugman and Joseph Stiglitz, both Nobel Prize-winning economists, have not been part of White House efforts because "an entire economics perspective…a progressive economist wing" has been excluded from policymaking (Krugman, 2009).

[9] The Global Partnership for Education is a more democratically structured successor to the Fast Track Initiative, although still limited in many ways.

[10] The ubiquitous call for "evidence-based decision-making" or "outcomes-based aid," while understandable in the abstract, in practice becomes a fetish, another way of privileging the research of those with power, dismissing challenges, and avoiding taking needed actions.

[11] A discussion of more qualitative approaches to research is beyond the scope of this paper. While qualitative research has its problems, we certainly see it as an improvement over a single dominant quantitative approach. Nonetheless, the bottom line is that since all research reflects the perspectives of the researcher, all research needs to be broadened by making participation central.

[12] There has been a call for "smarter aid," but this assumes that research and evaluation methods can tell you which are the best aid policies and programs. Unfortunately that is simply not possible, as decades of experience should have made clear.

REFERENCES

Amin, S. (1985). *Delinking: Towards a polycentric world*. London and New Jersey: Zed Books.

Bauer, P. (1972). *Dissent on development: Studies and debates in development economics*. Cambridge, MA: Harvard University Press.

Benavot, A., Archer, D., Moseley, S., Mundy, K., Phiri, F., Steer, L., & Wiking, D. (2010). International aid to education. *Comparative Education Review 54*(1), 105–24.

Bread for the World (2009). Hunger and poverty facts. (http://www.offeringofletters.org/foreign-aid-basics/facts and figures, accessed 9/30/09)

Broad, R. (2006, August). Research, knowledge, and the art of 'paradigm maintenance:" the World Bank's development economics vice-presidency." *Review of International Political Economy, 13*(3), 387–419.

Collier, P. (2007). *The bottom billion: Why the poorest countries are failing and what can be done about it.* New York: Oxford University Press.

Denzin, N., & Lincoln, Y. (2000). The discipline and practice of qualitative research. In N. Denzin & Y. Lincoln (Eds.) *Handbook of qualitative research* (2nd ed.) (pp. 1–28). Thousand Oaks, CA: Sage Publications.

Dichter, T. (2003). *Despite good intentions: Why development assistance to the third world has failed.* Amherst & Boston: University of Massachusetts Press.

Duflo, E., & Kremer, M. (2008). Use of randomization in the evaluation of development effectiveness. In W. Easterly (Ed.), *Reinventing foreign aid* (pp. 93–120). Cambridge, MA: MIT Press.

Easterly, W. (2006). *The white man's burden: Why the West's efforts to aid the rest have done so much ill and so little good.* New York: Penguin Press.

Easterly, W. (Ed.). (2008). *Reinventing foreign aid.* Cambridge, MA: MIT Press.

Edwards Jr., Brent D., & Steven K. (2012). Participation in development and education governance. In A. Verger, M. Novelli & H. Kosar-Altinyelken (Eds.) *Global education policy and international development: New agendas, issues and programmes.* New York: Continuum.

Ellerman, D. (2005). *Helping people help themselves: From the world bank to an alternative philosophy of development assistance.* Ann Arbor: University of Michigan Press.

Fischman, G., & Gandn, L. (2007). Escola cidada and critical discourses of educational ope. In P. McLaren & J. Kincheloe (Eds.) *Critical pedagogy: Where are we now?* New York: Peter Lang.

Frank, A. (1967, September). *The Development of underdevelopment,* Monthly Review, XVIII: *4*, 17–31.

Gandin, L., & Apple, M. (2002). Challenging neoliberalism, building democracy: Creating the citizen school in Porto Alegre, Brazil. *Journal of Education Policy 17*(2), 259–279.

King, K. (Ed.) (2009) A safari towards aid effectiveness? A critical look at the Paris Declaration and the Accra Agenda for Action as part of the new aid reform architecture. *Norrag News, 42*(Special Issue).

Klees, S. (2008a). A quarter century of neoliberal thinking in education: Misleading analyses and failed policies. *Globalisation, Societies and Education 6*(4), 311–348.

Klees, S. (2008b). Reflections on theory, method, and practice in comparative and international education. *Comparative Education Review 52*(3), 301–328.

Klees, S., Samoff, J., & Stromquist, N. (Eds.) (2012). W*orld bank and education: Critiques and alternatives.* Rotterdam: Sense.

Krugman, P. (2009). http://www.huffingtonpost.com/2009/07/19/krugman-white-house-exclu_n_240032.html

Mertens, D. (2004). *Research methods in education and psychology: Integrating diversity with quantitative and qualitative Approaches* (2nd ed.). Thousand Oaks, CA: Sage.

Moyo, D. (2009). Dead aid: Why aid is not working and how there is a better way for Africa. *Is not working and how there is a better way for Africa.* New York: Farrar, Straus, and Giroux.

Riddell, R. (2007). *Does foreign aid really work?* New York: Oxford University Press.

Sachs, J. (2005). *The end of poverty: Economic possibilities for our time.* New York: Penguin.

Samoff, J. (2009). The fast track to planned dependence: Education aid to Africa. Paper presented at the *International political science association XXI world congress,* Santiago, Chile, 12–16 July.

UNESCO (2009). *Education for all global monitoring report 2009: Overcoming inequality.* Paris: UNESCO.

Waisbord, S. (2008, November 1). Are international aid and community participation inevitably at Oodds? *The communication initiative network.* (http://www.comminit.com/en/print)

Watkins, K. (2009, June). Missing the point with Moyo. In K. King (Ed.) *A safari towards aid effectiveness? A critical look at the Paris declaration and the accra agenda for action as part of the new aid reform architecture.* Norrag News *42*(Special Issue), 19–22.

Weiler, H. (1984). The political economy of education and development. *Prospects, 19*(4), 468–477.

AFFILIATIONS

Steven J. Klees
Harold R. W. Benjamin Professor of International and Comparative Education
University of Maryland

Omar Qargha
University of Maryland

MARIO NOVELLI

THE NEW GEOPOLITICS OF EDUCATIONAL AID:
FROM COLD WARS TO HOLY WARS?

INTRODUCTION

Throughout the 1980s and early 1990s development aid to education in low-income countries was often provided on condition that recipient governments implemented a string of neo-liberal education reforms linked to structural adjustment policies and fiscal austerity. Many critics challenged the overemphasis on economics that was driving these reforms, both in terms of the effects of fiscal austerity on already under-funded education systems and also the reliance on human capital theory to calculate estimated rates of return to education (Adams, 1989; Bonal, 2002; Bonal, 2004a; Bonal, 2004b; Carnoy, 1995; Reimers, 1989, 1990; Samoff & Unesco., 1994; Torres, 2002). They argued that education was much more than 'human capital' development and that the World Bank and others driving these reforms should go beyond this narrow 'economism' and conception of the value of education, and recognize the positive social, political and cultural effects that education can potentially produce.

Today, that narrow economic approach of the major international donors and multilaterals on education appears to have been superseded by a much broader recognition of the role of education which emphasizes its central importance in the socialization, citizenship and nation building process – both at home and abroad. One area where this switch of focus is manifestly clear is with aid to education in conflict and post-conflict countries, particularly those countries with large Islamic populations. While the economic justifications of education as human capital have not disappeared, it is increasingly recognized that economic growth is undermined by conflict and that a broader understanding of education's role in promoting tolerance, peace and prosperity needs to be examined, and that a variety of interventions might be appropriate (Davies, 2004; DFID, 2003; Novelli & Cardozo, 2008). Furthermore, there has been a growing recognition since the tragic events of 9/11 in the USA and subsequent events in London, Mumbai, Bali, Istanbul and elsewhere that development policy 'abroad' and security at 'home' are directly linked. While the renewed interest and commitment to development, and the broader understanding of education, may be seen as a positive step forward and a welcome retreat from the harsh economism of the past, there are also dangers.

The argument of this paper is that this security agenda is increasingly influencing development policy and practice, that education is emerging as a central component

S. Majhanovich and M.A. Geo-JaJa (Eds.), Economics, Aid and Education:
Implications for Development, 29–46.

of this, and that it is producing a range of challenges and dilemmas for development agencies, NGOs, practitioners and academics working in the field which we need to open up to discussion and critical debate.[1] In reappraising the importance of development and moving beyond economism within the education debate, I would argue that we are also moving back to some of the issues, albeit in a very different form, that shaped the terrain of education and development during the Cold War period, when development aid, policy and practice was utilized in the interests of containing, and later rolling back the Soviet Union and its allies: issues such as supporting dictatorships under the principle that my enemy's enemy is my friend, turning a blind eye to widespread corruption, using aid as a political weapon to induce policy change and using education as a means of socializing target populations towards accepting Western and 'capitalist' hegemony' (Altbach & Kelly, 1978; Carnoy, 1974; King, 1991; Watson, 1982). This is particularly worrying as it comes at a time when the effectiveness and utility of international aid is being questioned from a range of different perspectives (Moyo, 2009; Riddell, 2008) and in a period where the high costs of the global financial crisis are leading to a careful reassessment of budgetary priorities amongst the major bi-lateral donors (IMF/World Bank, 2009).

This paper is linked to several other recent publications, which seek to develop and apply a critical globalisation approach to aspects of the field of education and conflict (Novelli, 2009a, 2009b); Novelli & Cardozo, 2008).[2] This piece focuses on the newly emergent tendencies within the geographies of aid to education and their links to post-cold war security governance concerns, moving from a Cold War state-centric cartography of East and West, to a much more complex, fluid, multi-scalar and transnational picture, where 'terror suspects' (often linked to radical Islam) reside between borders, exist within our own states, 'friendly' states as well as 'rogue' states. A place where the US led Western alliance has reconfigured the world away from East-West and North-South binaries to a new language of 'fragility' which draws a map of the world linked to 'conflict' and 'state failure' and where for some, national sovereignty and national frontiers are now porous, conditional, and subject to the increased intervention by Western states, often under the banner of humanitarianism (Duffield, 2008; Duffield, 2001, 2007).

FROM 'COLD WAR' TO 'NEW WARS' TO THE 'WAR ON TERROR':
THE NEW GEOPOLITICS OF DEVELOPMENT

In many ways development aid has always been political and the 'politicization of development' should come as no surprise. During the colonial period, education was a key mechanism through which foreign rule was maintained, and during the Post World War II period aid appears to have been allotted largely on the basis of where a country stood in the great Cold War confrontation (Christian Aid, 2004; Lundborg, 1998; Wang, 1999). Crucially, the geography of aid was based less on perceived humanitarian need and more on political alliances that often led to a blind eye being turned to human rights violations and repression in 'friendly' states.

Since the end of the Cold War we began to see the effects of the end of bi-polarism in international relations with first a drop in overall development aid, and then a shift of focus in development policy and education policy towards the least developed countries and population groups. This shift led to an increasing focus on Sub-Saharan Africa and increased effort to improve the coordination of international development policy between major donors. These efforts culminated in the Millennium Development Goals – and the Education for All objectives therein, sector wide approaches to education, the Paris Declaration etc. (King, 2007; Mundy, 2006; Mundy, 2002). While not without its critiques, there was a sense that at least the rhetoric of development policy was heading in the right direction (Cosgrave, 2005), even if the financing wasn't always forthcoming (GCE, 2009).

Parallel to these Post Cold War developments, we also witnessed an increased capacity and interest by Western nations, generally under the leadership of the United States, to engage and intervene in a wide range of high profile conflicts from the Balkans to Rwanda, Somalia, Sudan, Iraq and Afghanistan. Importantly for us, these interventions were also discursively framed as 'humanitarian interventions' (Fearon, 2008:52), drawing on issues of human rights, democracy and freedom for their justification, paralleling the intentions and objectives and discourses of many of the international humanitarian and development organisations. On occasions they were also preceded by calls from some humanitarian organisations themselves for armed intervention (Roberts, 2000). This newfound willingness to directly intervene into sovereign states reflected a real shift in the Post Cold War balance of power. During the Cold War the threat of retaliation or the UN Security Council veto, would have blocked this type of direct intervention by either side across the Cold War divide.

This new 'humanitarian interventionism' was accompanied by a massive increase in the number of humanitarian and development actors operating in conflict situations. By 1995, humanitarian agencies were responding to a total of 28 complex emergencies around the world, increasing from just five in 1985 (Bradbury, 1995; Slim, 1996). By the mid 1990s emergency spending had increased by over 600% from its mid 1980s point to over $3.5 billion and has continued to rise as Figure 1 demonstrates (Fearon 2008). According to the 2008 Reality of Aid Report (2008:8) "aid allocations to the most severely conflict-affected countries....increased from 9.3% of total ODA in 2000 (for 12 countries) to 20.4% (for 10 countries) in 2006. Coupled with the general increase in ODA during the same period, aid to conflict affected countries has nearly tripled in real terms between 2000–2006. In 2007, according to a recent OECD/DAC report (2008:8) 38.4 % of total ODA (USD 37.2 billion) went to conflict and fragile states.

In a similar manner, military peacekeeping, which comes under a different non-DAC budget, has increased massively over the last two decades. By 1994 total UN peacekeeping expenditure was estimated to be in the region of $3.2 billion per year (Duffield, 1997:539). In its most recent report the OECD/DAC (2008:11) stated that UN peacekeeping expenditures were at an historic high with twenty ongoing

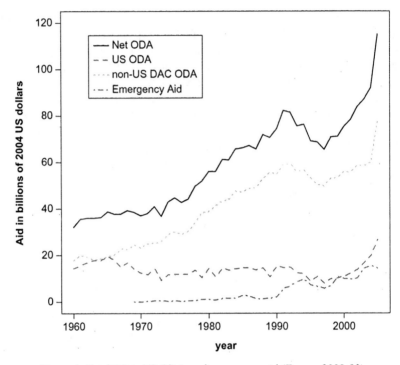

Figure 1. Total ODA, US ODA, and emergency aid (Fearon 2008:53).

missions. They also noted that personnel had increased by over 700% since 1999 to 110,000 personnel with a budget of 7 USD billion.

What is also clear from the literature is that the distribution of aid among severely- conflict-affected countries was, and remains, highly unequal. In 2006 Iraq and Afghanistan accounted for over 60% of all aid to severely conflict-affected countries. The other eight countries shared the remaining 36.7% (Reality of Aid 2008: 217). In 2007, (OECD/DAC, 2008:8) of the 38.4 percent of total ODA (USD 37.2 billion) that went to conflict and fragile states, over half was directed to just five countries: Iraq (23 percent), Afghanistan (9.9 percent), and Ethiopia, Pakistan and Sudan (sharing 17% of the total). Most strikingly, the almost US$50 billion of new resources for Iraq, Afghanistan and Pakistan since 2000 "represent the largest ever donor country commitments for aid." (Reality of Aid, 2008: 207)

In summing up this section we can say that post Cold War Western interventionism has led to a massive increase in both peacekeeping and development assistance directed to conflict and post conflict countries resulting in a massive expansion of humanitarian and development personnel and an expansion of the nature of the activities that these organisations engage in. Furthermore, rather than the steady flows of funds towards key allies during the Cold War, resources appear to shift

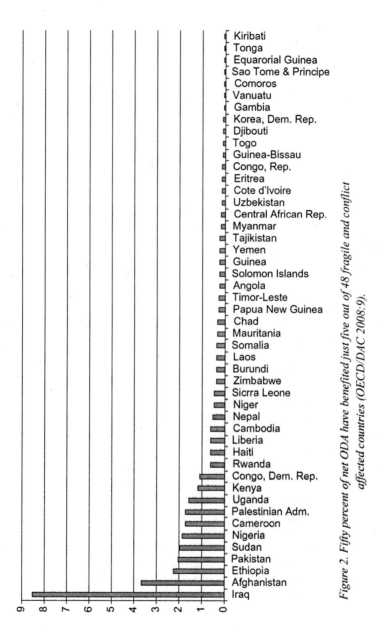

Figure 2. Fifty percent of net ODA have benefited just five out of 48 fragile and conflict affected countries (OECD/DAC 2008:9).

and flow swiftly to key conjunctural conflicts or potential conflicts. A form of 'geopolitical fire fighting' might be an apt metaphor for this process, which is a sign perhaps that development aid, and perhaps development itself, is now increasingly concerned with containing, managing and engaging with conflicts rather than acting as a catalyst for sustainable growth (Duffield 2007).

UNDERSTANDING THE RISE IN AID TO EDUCATION IN CONFLICT ZONES

Since the late 1990s and in tandem with the expansion of development and humanitarian intervention in conflict zones, there has been a parallel increase in interest and recognition of the importance of education delivery in conflict and post conflict zones. Education, like food and shelter, has come to be seen as part of the core building blocks of human development and a necessary and vital part of humanitarian response in conflict situations in particular (Johnson and Van Kalmthout 2006:3, UNDP 2005:159). Since 2008, there has also been a Global Education Cluster, headed by UNICEF and the International Save the Children Alliance that coordinates the educational response in emergency situations, as part of the Inter-Agency Standing Committee (IASC) that assumes overall coordination, and develops policy involving UN and non-UN humanitarian partners operating in conflict zones. Central to the rise in prominence of education within conflict situations has been the actions of the *Inter-Agency Network on Education in Emergencies*, which emerged out of the World Education Forum in Dakar and is a network created to improve inter-agency communication and collaboration within the context of education in emergencies, and which has proved an effective lobbying, advocacy and policy coordination and development institution.

As with the more general increases in development aid to conflict effected zones (Fearon, 2008–72) , increases in aid to education are at least partly due to the success of organizations like Save the Children, INEE, and UNICEF to successfully lobby for an expansion their own mandates and activities in education...that is, to justify why education service delivery should be at the heart of humanitarian and development responses to conflict and post conflict situations. Furthermore, over the years practitioners and the agencies they represent have developed a variety of approaches to address the particular needs of children in conflict and post conflict situations that can deal with the often deep and long lasting psychological effects of war and conflict (Aguilar and Retamal 2009).

The success of these linked organizations and practitioners in placing education and conflict firmly on the international development agenda has been aided, at least in part, by a general recognition from bi-lateral donors that most of the world's out of school children are located in conflict and post conflict countries (SavetheChildren, 2007) and therefore if the international community are serious about achieving the educational Millennium Development Goals then conflict and post conflict educational delivery needs to be addressed (Stewart, 2003). It has also been influenced by the growing awareness of the relationship between education and conflict, and its potentially catalytic and preventative roles (Bush & Saltarelli, 2000; DFID, 2003). The general push for attention to the Education For all objectives appears to have increased markedly the amount of resources that the international community now direct towards basic education. The Reality of Aid 2008 report notes that aid to basic education increased from US$747 million in 2000 to US$2.8 billion by 2006 (Reality of Aid, 2008: 209). However, there is a debate as to whether conflict affected countries are receiving their fair share of educational resources. The Save the Children's (2007) *Last in Line, Last in School: How donors are failing children in conflict-affected fragile states*, recent report, set up to monitor flows of educational resources to conflict affected states argues that "donors do not prioritise education in their aid programmes to CAFS (Conflict Affected States), despite the educational needs of these countries. Even when compared to other LICs, education is prioritised less in CAFS. On average only 4 per cent of total ODA to CAFS was used to support education, compared to 13 per cent of total ODA in other LICs" (Save the Children, 2007:12). They note that while just under 70% (39 million) of the 56 million out of school children live in conflict affected countries only 33% of funding was allocated to them in 2006. However, while this might be the average case of the 28 conflict affected countries selected for their report, they do not analyse the distribution of resources between countries, which as we have seen in the earlier section on development aid is highly focused on a very select number of countries (Iraq, Afghanistan, Pakistan etc). Disaggregating this data would likely reveal a similar concentration of educational resources in certain key conflict countries.

What this section has hopefully managed to demonstrate is that aid to conflict zones generally, and aid to education as a subcomponent of that, has increased substantially over the last decade and more. Rather than working around wars and conflicts, international development organizations have learnt how to work within them, and alongside them. As Duffield notes:

> During the Cold War, although UN intervention was relatively uncommon, when it did take place it was on the basis of agreed ceasefire or clear peacekeeping arrangements. UN agencies did not attempt to operate in the context of an ongoing conflict. The *ad hoc* UN resolutions that have made negotiated access possible, however, send a different signal. The new paradigm, while not condoning conflict, now appears to accept that political instability is an unfortunate reality in the South. Unable to prevent internal war, the West has resigned itself to finding ways of working within ongoing crises and managing their symptoms (Duffield, 1997:534).

As a result of this engagement international organisations and NGOs working inside ongoing conflicts face particular problems and issues that challenge their humanitarian credentials, test their autonomy and independence and put pressure on their security. This tension has been exacerbated since 9/11 with US-led attempts to divide the world into those that are 'with' or 'against' them in the war on terror.

ARE WE ALL SOLDIERS NOW?: EDUCATION AS COUNTERINSURGENCY

As I speak, just as surely as our diplomats and military, American NGOs are out there serving and sacrificing on the front lines of freedom . . . . I am serious about making sure we have the best relationship with the NGOs who are such a force multiplier for us, such an important part of our combat team. [We are] all committed to the same, singular purpose to help every man and woman in the world who is in need, who is hungry, who is without hope, to help every one of them fill a belly, get a roof over their heads, educate their children, have hope.

US Secretary of State Colin Powell, Remarks to the National Foreign Policy Conference for Leaders of Nongovernmental Organizations, at http://www. state.gov/secretary/rm/2001/5762.htm

The speech by Colin Powell has become an oft-cited example of the growing concern of many within the development community that the last decades have seen the increasing militarization of development. That is, that the agendas of humanitarian and development organizations have been taken over – for some hijacked – for others in willing complicity, by powerful western militaries. In this section I will argue that the price for increased funding for humanitarian and development operations in conflict and post conflict zones has been a political one. Furthermore, this political price – to line up policy and practice with the security objectives of western powers – brings a range of problems in its wake for educators in terms of ethical, moral, political and security issues.

The post-Cold war capacity of Western states to intervene for humanitarian objectives, outlined above, was for many a welcome advance marking a shift from the bi-partisan politics of the Cold War to a potentially more humanitarian rationale for intervention. However, its application in practice was highly selective, with the West intervening in some conflicts whilst turning away from others. It also brought with it its own dangers and risks. Hilhorst (2004:9) notes that:

Humanitarian aid has increasingly been incorporated as an instrument of foreign policy, and policy is increasingly expressed in terms of International Humanitarian Law and Human Rights. Although it could be welcomed that foreign policy increasingly coincides with NGO values, there are strong concerns too. NGOs fear the abuse of values for foreign policy interests, criticise the selective application of values by governments such as in addressing human rights abuses in some but not other parts of the world, and find it difficult to define their own identity and approach in relation to the political powers (Hilhorst, 2004:9).

The post 9/11 environment has increased this process of politicisation as the US and other Western powers have prioritised concerns over 'terrorism' and sought to integrate all other aspects of government policy under this overarching objective. During the Bush administration development and humanitarian organisations were often simplistically treated as 'force multipliers', and while the language has softened under the Obama administration, the central thrust of linking development aid to national security objectives has remained intact. In June 2008, USAID released their new 'civil military cooperation policy' (2008), explaining their 3-D approach, incorporating Defence, Diplomacy and Development and stating that: "Development is also recognized as a key element of any successful whole-of-government counterterrorism and counter-insurgency effort" (USAID, 2008:1).

Exploring the issue more broadly we can note that while the US, in the wake of 9/11 was the most active in initially promoting this merging of security interest and development, the EU also quickly followed suit:

> European assistance programmes, military and civilian capabilities from Member States and other instruments such as the European Development Fund. All of these can have an impact on our security and on that of third countries. Security is the first condition for development (EU, 2003:13).

For both the US and Europe then national security and international development have become increasingly intertwined and this extends to the policy documents of DFID and other major bi-lateral and multi-lateral institutions. As Duffield (2002:1067) notes:

> the security concerns of metropolitan states have merged with the social concerns of aid agencies; they have become one and the same thing. If poverty and institutional malaise in the borderlands encourage conflict and undermine international stability, then the promotion of development to eliminate these problems serves a security function; in the transition to a post-Cold War international system, aid and politics have been reunited.

In September 2009 the UK Prime Minister Gordon Brown, in a speech on Afghanistan made similar links between the need to be in Afghanistan and UK homeland security:

> The Director-General of our security service has said that three quarters of the most serious plots against the UK have had links that reach back into these mountains. At present the threat comes mainly from the Pakistan side, but if the insurgency succeeds in Afghanistan Al Qaeda and other terrorist groups will once again be able to use it as a sanctuary to train, plan and launch attacks on Britain and the rest of the world (Brown, 2009).

He also stressed that 'development' and within that 'education' were central planks in the UK strategy of both 'winning hearts and minds' (ibid) in Afghanistan and protecting the UK from attack:

> ....when the Taliban ran the country, only a million children were in school, all boys. Today there are 6.6 million – with more than 2 million girls. With the help of British development funding, 10,000 new teachers were recruited from 2007 to 2008, with more expected in 2009. This is an investment in the

future of Afghanistan, in its stability and its resilience against extremism – and therefore in our security (ibid).

While the renewed commitment of Western governments to the importance of development might be welcomed, this 'joined up' whole-of-government approach brings with it dangers for the development and humanitarian community of being taken over by the generally more powerful security wing of national governments. As the failure of both the Iraq and Afghanistan occupations is becoming increasingly evident, so it appears that there is an increased emphasis on the 'hearts and minds' strategies (read development) alongside the military activities. This raises questions as to how do these organisations working in conflict and post-conflict zones separate the 'military' and security 'interest' and their 'development' and 'humanitarian' activities? (Woods 2005). What might be the cost for these organisations of being seen as too close to certain belligerent forces? Will long term goals of development be subordinated to the short-term objectives of winning the hearts and minds of target population groups. Amongst humanitarian organizations this has provoked heated debate with some announcing the end of humanitarianism. One researcher from Médecins Sans Frontières raised the difficult question of the problem of carrying out humanitarian and development activities under the overarching rule of an occupying power, arguing that whether they directly engage with the occupying forces or not:

> over time, the resentment that often builds up within a population against foreign rule can lead to an equally violent rejection of all changes brought about by outside actors, their claimed neutrality notwithstanding." (Crombe, 2006).

The merging of security and development thus appears as a process of reinterpreting both the purposes and the practices of development – seeing activities as having potential 'security benefits'. An illustration of this is the prevalence of references to the role of education in the US's counter-terrorism strategies elaborated in *the Patterns of Global Terrorism Annual Reports* (since 2004 renamed *Country Reports on Terrorism*). As an example, the 2007 report, in Chapter 5, *Terrorist Safe Havens*, sub-section 7 focuses on Basic Education in Muslim Countries. In this section it notes that:

> The Department of State, USAID, and other U.S. agencies continued to support an increased focus on education in predominantly Muslim countries and those with significant Muslim populations. The United States' approach stresses mobilizing public and private resources as partners to improve access, quality, and the relevance of education, with a specific emphasis on developing civic-mindedness in young people. In many Muslim-majority countries, such as Afghanistan and Yemen, the challenge was to increase country capacity to provide universal access to primary education and literacy (USStateDepartment, 2008:243).

Similarly, as part of the US military's counterinsurgency strategy in places such as Iraq and Afghanistan 'humanitarian and civic assistance' "can include such non-emergency services as constructing schools, performing dental procedures, and even vaccinating the livestock of farmers" (Brigety, 2008). Crucially for us, it appears that educational provision (particularly for girls) became a key discursive justification for the military intervention in Afghanistan, and educational progress as a means of demonstrating the success of the occupation. As a result, attacking education seems to be a key strategy of the Taliban with attacks on education in Afghanistan both widespread and increasing. According to Human Rights Watch, education systems and personnel are attacked for three overlapping categories:

> first, opposition to the government and its international supporters by Taliban or other armed groups...; second, ideological opposition to education other than that offered in madrassas (Islamic schools), and in particular opposition to girls' education; and third, opposition to the authority of the central government and the rule of law by criminal groups (HumanRightsWatch, 2006:33).

Clearly in the case of Afghanistan, education has become a central battleground in the war and emphasizes the increasing dangers that all education personnel and students face there. This also appears to be occurring in Somalia (UN, 2008) and Iraq (Bonham Carter, 2007; O'Malley, 2007). Most problematically, education provision is increasingly becoming interpreted by both sides in these polarized contexts as a battle between Western secular education and Islamic madrassa education (McClure, 2009).

The dilemma for education aid workers is that the counterinsurgency and counter-terrorism strategies of the Western powers become the perceived major rationale for educational interventions and while activities may remain largely the same, their discursive representation means that they can be interpreted as part of the 'war effort': civilian modes of counterinsurgency, aimed at winning hearts and minds and producing certain types of subjectivities. In doing so they increase the danger for all involved.

In situations such as Iraq and Afghanistan it appears that humanitarian and development organisations have become overwhelmed by the counterinsurgency agenda, making it almost impossible to distance themselves form the occupying forces and present a picture of neutrality. As Torrente (Torrente, 2004:3) notes:

> the U.S. government failed to preserve space for the politically independent and principled role of humanitarian organizations. Instead, the United States sought to bring humanitarian aid efforts under its control and claimed that all assistance supports its cause... The U.S. efforts to associate assistance with its political objectives have jeopardized the ability of humanitarian organizations to distinguish themselves from all parties and to provide aid based solely on need during times of crisis.

One further aspect also exacerbates the risks for humanitarian and development workers is the prevalence in both Iraq and Afghanistan, but also other parts of the world of a large amount of civilian contractors carrying out work funded by the Western powers, and a large amount of private security contractors that also dress in civilian attire. This massive presence of these contractors makes it increasingly difficult for aid organisations to argue for the distinctiveness of their 'civilian' activity in increasingly complex conflicts.

This situation has been worsened with the establishment by the Western occupying countries in both Iraq and Afghanistan of Provisional Reconstruction Teams that under the control of the military also carry out development like activities such as the construction of schools. In 2009 an alliance of NGOs operating in Afghanistan produced a strong report condemning the behaviour of the Western occupying forces. They alleged that the military (particularly the US and France) were continuing to use "unmarked, white vehicles....conventionally used by the UN and aid agencies" and were carrying out infrastructure work traditionally done by development organisations as part of their counterinsurgency 'hearts and minds' strategies. All this, they argued, was "blurring of the civil-military distinction... (and) contributed to a diminution in the perceived independence of NGOs, increased the risk for aid workers, and reduced the areas in which NGOs can safely operate".(Waldman, 2009, p. 6:9)

They alleged that these activities were contributing to the causes of

a marked increase in violence against aid workers globally, which has a range of causes, however one important factor is military engagement in assistance activities. In Afghanistan, such engagement is extensive and wide-ranging, and has blurred the line between military and humanitarian actors. This has adversely affected NGO security, endangered the lives of NGO workers, and restricted their ability to operate. NGOs are being increasingly subject to direct threats and attacks, and in 2008, 31 NGO workers were killed, twice as many as in 2007. This is significantly decreasing humanitarian operating space: currently, large parts of the country are inaccessible to humanitarian actors, leaving many communities deprived of humanitarian assistance. NGOs regularly receive warnings that any perceived association with military forces will make them a target. In many areas, NGO offices and staff have been searched for links to the military, and threatened with severe consequences if such links are established. Likewise, NGO projects have been forced to close due to visits from PRTs or foreign donor agencies in heavily armed escorts. In the aftermath of such visits, communities have informed NGOs that they can no longer guarantee the safety of project staff (Waldman, 2009, p. 6:16).

In a further report Stoddard et al (2009) noted that in Afghanistan locals were no longer making a distinction between those organisations working with the military and those that were not. They suggested that for afghan locals "all Western-based international humanitarian organizations are judged as partisan" (Stoddard et al, 2009:6).This breakdown in trust in humanitarian and development organisations can only increase the dangers that aid workers face.

While the cases of Iraq and Afghanistan are extreme, it does appear that there is a growing tendency for humanitarian and development organisations, because of their largely 'western' nature, home location, and political orientation, to be targeted in locations where the 'West' is seen, at least by a substantial section of he population, as the enemy. That is that aid workers are not just being targeted because they are somehow collaborating with the occupying forces, but more so that they are seen as an integral part of that force. While attacks on aid workers is a war crime and can never be justified, what seems clear is that the increasing blurring of the lines between Western military objectives and the practices of humanitarian and development organisations seem to be increasing the danger for these organisations:

> When governments drape their military and political actions in the cloak of humanitarian concerns, they undermine humanitarian action's essential purpose: the unconditional provision of assistance to those in need. When all aid efforts are presented and perceived as being at the service of political and military objectives, it is more difficult and dangerous for independent humanitarian organizations to carry out their work (Torrente, 2004:29).

Furthermore, the relationship between education and the new geopolitics of the war on terror does not stop in the direct theatre of operations. Increasingly, as aid is being targeted at strategic locations in the post-Cold War world, education is seen as a vital mechanism in the battle of hearts and minds across the Muslim world (Indonesia, Yemen, the Philippines). Investment in low-income education systems can also serve as a sweetener for cooperation in other domains. The increase in aid flows to Kyrgstan in Central Asia, and Djibouti in Africa represent examples of flows of aid to education Post 9/11 that occur in parallel with the development of US military bases used as launching pads for military activities in Afghanistan and Somalia respectively.

CONCLUSIONS

There is a popular narrative over the history of aid to education that goes something like this: During the Cold War aid to education was seen as being highly politicized, often lacking development principles at its heart, and directed instead at allies in the war against communism. The post 1990 collapse of the Soviet Union led finally to the possibility of focusing aid on poverty and of pooling resources towards those objectives. However there is now a potential challenge/rupture to this narrative. The post Cold War, Post 9/11 world has also produced another common agenda to focus the concentration and attention of many Western powers. It remains to be seen whether the objectives of poverty eradication and counter-terror are mutually complementary, whether they will be given equal priority and focus, or whether the military and national security interests will, as in the Cold War, once again trump poverty and development objectives. I suggest that the signs are not good, but this clearly requires further research and investigation.

These tensions between 'humanitarian' concerns and 'military' objectives, between 'development' and 'security' have of course always been present in the post-WWII development discourse and reflect the schizophrenia of the development project itself – both a utopian idealism that postcolonial states would create independent, progressive and humane societies that would catch up with the west and break the chains of imperialism, and a US-led Cold War realism best encapsulated in a US State Department document, Policy Planning Study 23 (PPS23), written in 1948 by George Kennan (1948), a diplomat credited as the ideologue of US Cold War 'containment' policy:

> We have about 50 percent of the world's wealth, but only 6.3 percent of its population... In this situation, we cannot fail to be the object of envy and resentment. Our real task in the coming period is to devise a pattern of relationships which will permit us to maintain this position of disparity... We need not deceive ourselves that we can afford today the luxury of altruism and world-benefaction... We should cease to talk about vague and... unreal objectives such as human rights, the raising of living standards, and democratization. The day is not far off when we are going to have to deal in straight power concepts. The less we are then hampered by idealistic slogans, the better.

On August 13th, 2008, my friend and colleague Jackie Kirk was murdered by Taliban militants in Afghanistan along with three other aid workers from the International Rescue Committee (a US based NGO working on issues of refugees and internally displaced peoples). They were attacked whilst travelling on the road to Kabul in a clearly marked 'IRC' car. Jackie was a brilliant Canadian gender, education and conflict specialist. The Taliban argued that Jackie and her colleagues were part of the 'illegal occupation forces'. She saw herself as neither 'force multiplier' nor 'enemy combatant' and her tragic death, and that of many other humanitarian workers that have died in Afghanistan and elsewhere reflect the much deeper and ongoing problem of this increased blurring of the lines between military and humanitarian operations in contexts of war and conflict. As education and development academics, practitioners and policy makers maybe it is time for us to think through our own relationships and alliances, what we agree with and what we oppose, and to carve out alternative and independent development trajectories in our increasingly conflictual world.

NOTES

[1] This paper is a revised version of a journal article: Novelli, M (2010). The New Geopolitics of Aid to Education: From Cold Wars to Holy Wars. *International Journal of Educational Development*, *30*, 453–459. I wish to thank the journal for agreeing to its republication here.

[2] The approach is inspired by work carried out in the Centre for Studies of Globalization, Societies and Education at Bristol University led by Susan Robertson and Roger Dale. See for example Dale (2005). and explained in reference to education and conflict in Novelli & Lopes Cardozo (2008).

REFERENCES

Adams, J. D. (1989). The threat to education from structural adjustment – A realistic response. *IDS Bulletin-Institute of Development Studies, 20*(1), 50–54.

Aguilar, P., & Retamal, G. (2009). Protective environments and quality education in humanitarian contexts. *International Journal of Educational Development 29*(1), 3–16.

Altbach, P. G., & Kelly, G. P. (1978). *Education and colonialism.* New York: Longman.

Bonal, X. (2002). Plus ça change...The world bank global education policy and the post-Washington consensus. *International Studies in Sociology of Education, 12*(1).

Bonal, X. (2004a). Is the world bank education policy adequate for fighting poverty? Some evidence from Latin America. *International Journal of Educational Development, 24*(6), 649–666.

Bonal, X. (2004b). On Global Absences; some reflections on what is missing about the education and poverty relationship (DRAFT). Paper presented at the *European educational research association conference,* Crete.

Bonham Carter, R. (Producer). (2007). Five girls killed in mortar attack on school in Baghdad. [UNICEF Press Release] Retrieved from http://www.unicef.org/emerg/iraq_38180.html

Bradbury, M. (1995). Aid under fire: Redefining relief and development assistance in unstable situations. *Wilton Park Paper* (Vol. 104). London: HMSO.

Brigety, R. E. (2008). *Humanity as a weapon of war: Sustainable security and the role of the U.S. military.* Washington Centre for American Progress.

Brown, G. (2009). *Afghanistan – National security and regional stability.* Paper presented at the Speech by Rt Hon. Gordon Brown, UK Prime Minister, at the International Institute for Strategies Studies, London, Friday 4th September 2009.

Bush, J., & Saltarelli, D. (2000). *The two faces of education in ethnic conflict.* New York UNICEF

Carnoy, M. (1974). *Education as cultural imperialism.* New York: D. McKay Co.

Carnoy, M. (1995). Structural adjustment and the changing face of education. *International Labour Review, 134*(6), 653–673.

Christian Aid. (2004). *The politics of poverty: Aid in the new cold war* (p. 57). Christian Aid.

Cosgrave, J. (2005). *The impact of the war on terror on aid flows* (p. 35). Action Aid.

Crombe, X. (2006). Humanitarian action in situations of occupation: the view from MSF. *Humanitarian Exchange Magazine* (33).

Dale, R. (2005). Globalisation, knowledge economy and comparative education. *Comparative Education, 41*(2), 117–149.

Davies, L. (2004). *Education and conflict: Complexity and chaos.* London: RoutledgeFalmer.

DFID. (2003). *Education, Conflict and Development.* London: DFID.

Duffield, M. (1997). NGO relief in war zones: Towards an analysis of the new aid paradigm. *Third World Quarterly 18*(3), 527–542.

Duffield, M. (2002). Social reconstruction and the radicalization of development: Aid as a relation of global liberal governance. *Development and Change, 33*(5), 1049–1071.

Duffield, M. (2008). Global civil war: The non-insured, international containment and post-interventionary society. *Journal of Refugee Studies, 21*(2), 145–165.

Duffield, M. (2001). *Global governance and the new wars: The merging of development and security.* London: New York: Zed Books; Distributed in the USA exclusively by Palgrave.

Duffield, M. (2007). *Development, security and unending war: Governing the world of peoples.* Cambridge: Polity.

EU. (2003). *A secure Europe in a better world.* Brussels: European Union

Fearon, D. (2008). The rise of emergency relief aid. In M. N. Barnett & T. G. Weiss (Eds.) *Humanitarianism in question* (pp. 49–72). Ithaca: Cornell University Press.

GCE. (2009). *Education on the brink: Will the IMF's new lease on life ease or block progress towards education goals?* In G. C. F. Education (Ed.). Johannesburg.

Hilhorst, D. (2004). A living document? The code of conduct of the red cross and red crescent movement and NGOs in disaster relief. Research paper produced for the conference ten years code of conduct: principles in practice. Paper presented at the *Ten years code of conduct: Principles in practice disaster studies.* The Hague: Wageningen University.

HumanRightsWatch. (2006). *Lessons in terror: Attacks on education in Afghanistan* (Vol. 18). Washington.

IMFWorldBank. (2009). *Global monitoring report 2009: A development emergency.* Washington World Bank.

Johnson, D., & Van Kalmthout, E. (2006). 'Editorial', in: *Forged migration review supplement: Education and conflict: research, policy and practice,* Oxford: Refugees Studies Centre, UNICEF, Oxford University's Department of Educational Studies.

Kennan, G. (1948). U.S. State Department Policy Planning Staff Document PPS 23, Feb. 24, 1948. This document was published in Foreign Relations of the United States, Vol. 1, (pp. 509–29), and the full text is available online at www.geocities.com/rwvong/future/kennan/pps23.html.

King, K. (1991). *Aid and education in the developing world : The role of the donor agencies in educational analysis.* Harlow, Essex: Longman.

King, K. (2007). Multilateral agencies in the construction of the global agenda on education. *Comparative Education, 43*(3), 377–391.

Lundborg, P. (1998). Foreign aid and international support as a gift exchange. *Economics and Politics 10*(2).

McClure, K. R. (2009). Madrasas and Pakistan's education agenda: Western media misrepresentation and policy recommendations. *International Journal of Educational Development, 29*(4), 334–341.

Moyo, D. (2009). *Dead aid: Why aid is not working and how there is another way for Africa.* London: Allen Lane.

Mundy, K. (2006). Constructing education for development: International organizations and education for all. *Comparative Education Review, 50*(2), 296–298.

Mundy, K. E. (2002). Retrospect and prospect: Education in a reforming world bank. *International Journal of Educational Development, 22*(5), 483–508.

Novelli, M. (2009). *Colombia's classroom wars: Political violence against education sector trade unionists.* Brussels: Education International

Novelli, M. (2009a). *Political violence against education sector aid workers in conflict zones: A preliminary investigation.* Paris UNESCO.

Novelli, M., & Cardozo, M. T. A. L. (2008). Conflict, education and the global south: New critical directions. *International Journal of Educational Development, 28*(4), 473–488.

O'Malley, B. (2007). *Education under attack.* Paris: UNESCO.

OECD/DAC. (2008). *Resource flows to fragile and conflict-affected states annual report 2008.* Paris: OECD.

Powell, C. (2001). *Colin Powell, US secretary of state, remarks to the national foreign policy conference for leaders of nongovernmental organizations,* at http://www.state.gov/secretary/rm/2001/5762.html.)

Reimers, F. (1989). *Educational and structural adjustment in Latin America.* Cambridge, Mass.: Harvard Institute for International Development Harvard University.

Reimers, F. (1990). *Education for all in Latin America in the twenty-first century: The challenges of Jomtien.* Cambridge, Mass.: Harvard Institute for International Development Harvard University.

Riddell, R. (2008). *Does foreign aid really work?* (New ed.). Oxford: Oxford University Press.

Roberts, A. (2000). Humanitarian issues and agencies as triggers for international military action. *International Review of the Red Cross* (839), 673–698.

Samoff, J., & Unesco. (1994). *Coping with crisis: Austerity, adjustment and human resources.* London; New York: Cassell with UNESCO.

SavetheChildren. (2007). *Last in line, last in school: How donors are failing children in conflict-affected fragile states.* London: Save the Children.

Slim, H. (1996). Military humanitarianism and the new peacekeeping: An Agenda for Peace? *IDS Bulletin, 27*(3).

Stewart, F. (2003). Conflict and the millennium development goals. *Journal of Human Development, 4*(3), 326–350.

Stoddard, A., Harmer, A., DiDomenico, V., (2009). Providing aid in insecure environments: 2009 Update trends in violence against aid workers and the operational response. *HPG Policy Brief* (34), 1–12 Available online at http://www.odi.or- g.uk/resources/download/3250.pdf.

The Reality of Aid (2008). *Aid effectiveness: "Democratic ownership and human rights".* IBON Books, Philippines. Available at http://realityofaid.org/down- loads/RoAReports2008_full.pdf.

Torrente, N. (2004). Humanitarian action under attack: Reflections on the Iraq war *Harvard Human Rights Journal 17*, 1–29.

Torres, C. A. (2002). The state, privatisation and educational policy; a critique of neo-liberalism in Latin America and some ethical and political implications. *Comparative Education, 38*(4), 365–385.

UN (2008). UN and NGOs condemn attacks on Somali students, teachers and schools.

UNDP (2005). Human development report 2005: *International cooperation at a crossroads: Aid trade and Security in an unequal world*, New York: UNDP.

USAID, (2008). *Civilian-military cooperation policy*. Wahington:USAID. Availableathttp://www.usaid. gov/our_work/global_partnerships/ma/documents/Civ-Mil-PolicyJuly282008.pdf.

US State Department. (2008). *Country reports on terrorism 2007*. Washington United States Department of State Publication Office of the Coordinator for Counterterrorism.

Waldman, M. (2009). Caught in the conflict: Civilians and the international security strategy in Afghanistan: A briefing paper by *Eleven NGOs operating in Afghanistan for the NATO Heads of State and Government Summit*, 3–4, April 2009. London: Oxfam.

Wang, T. Y. (1999). US foreign aid and UN voting: An analysis of important issues. *International Studies Quarterly 43*.

Watson, K. (1982). *Education in the third world*. London: Croom Helm.

AFFLIATION

Mario Novelli
Centre for International Education
University of Sussex

RUKHSANA ZIA

AID IN EDUCATION: A PERSPECTIVE
FROM PAKISTAN

INTRODUCTION

Since Pakistan's inception in 1947, aid has been a regular feature of various development programs (Ellahi & Mahmood, 2012) in the country. In the 60s and 70s Pakistan was the largest recipient of aid in the South Asia region (Khan 2007). From 1961–88 alone, Pakistan received some $ 32 billion in aid (Cassen *et al,* 1970). The 80s saw aid turn in to loans rather than grants, bringing with it a sharp emphasis on aid which was tied to specific areas of development that were of interest to donors (Maizels & Nissanke, 1984) and aid conditionality. Aid in 1980s focused on market liberalization, while in 1990s donors linked aid to democracy, human rights and good governance (Stokke, 1995). This calls to question a very basic concern of whether the agenda of the donors /funders is aligned with that of the recipient country's. It is an important point that needs to be addressed, but has not been considered in this paper.

Much research explains aid allocation differences on the basis of bilateral or multilateral aid (Maizels & Nissanke, 1984) or claims that aid is dictated by political and strategic considerations much more than the economic needs and policy performance of the recipients (Alesina & Dollar 1998). Korb (2009), on the other hand, links the history of aid fluctuations in Pakistan with the changes in governments (dictatorship or democratic); to wars (1965 and 1971); to the country's nuclear program (1980s); to the war on terror from the 80s onwards with a drop from 1991–2000 due to the Pressler amendment with a surge again after Sept 2001. The War on Terror, from the late 1990s onwards, brought a manifold increase in aid that protected the political interests of the donors at the same time (Azam &Thelen, 2008, p. 393). History of aid to Pakistan shows changes in aid inflow with the change in the political sphere of the country or the world at large. The political motivation or political implications of aid, *per se*, are not the focus for this paper but need to be considered for further research. But the political context does have ramifications for the funder/donor agenda and as such is an important part of the discourse. Irrespective of the reasons, the magnitude of aid to Pakistan has been massive and hence the demand for aid management takes center stage, both, for the policy makers and implementers in Pakistan, and for the donors/funders.

With the recent rise in security concerns and the accompanying aid, the discourse on aid effectiveness is also on the rise within and across countries. Different studies

S. Majhanovich and M.A. Geo-JaJa (Eds.), Economics, Aid and Education:
Implications for Development, 47–60.

have cited different viewpoints for aid effectiveness (Easterly, 2006) and place the onus on various 'fitness' factors of the recipient country (Svensson, 1999; Burnside & Dollar, 2000; Dubarry et al, 1998, quoted in Ellahi & Mahmood, 2012, p 107). Others cite variations in aid effectiveness on the basis of periods of time of the aid in-flow (Malik, 2008, cited in Ellahi & Mahmood, 2012, p 108). Khan (1997) states several governance style factors that could neutralise the effectiveness of aid while Riddell (1987, p. 114) blames biased project selections. Cassen *et al* (1990), calls to question the aid utilization criteria and, points to an inherent bias in favour of the country providing the aid.

The literature, as shown above, by and large, neglects the issues inherent in the processes and procedures that effect policy making for aid, like, the capacity development of the institutions and the human resources involved in aid management and utilization; accountability of donor actions and personnel; politics of interaction among the stakeholders; effect of political process on aid; effect of governance style of the recipient country/organization; differences in working between funders and donors and so on and so forth.

Given the heavy influx of aid into the country, and given the limited literature on aid effectiveness, it is clear that further discourse is needed to share experiences of aid management at various levels of governance for maximizing aid effectiveness. The following pages do not try to evaluate the effectiveness of aid to Punjab education sector *per se*. Aid management is discussed here, through the lens of one institution that was one of the key implementers of aid to the educational reforms in a province of the country. The purpose is to broaden the scope of discourse on possible impediments to aid effectiveness and to share some practices that were used to counter the related issues in the process of improving aid management. The paper also delineates the issues inherent in partnership, be it between the province of Punjab and the funder/donor as well as issues of co-ordination among the various donor/funder agencies. This issue has been cited elsewhere (Cassen *et al*, 1990) but this is an area that needs to be further elaborated. The paper agrees that aid cannot be dismissed as irrelevant for needs of development (Prasad, 1997). Clearly, conditional on sound macro-economic policies, aid does have a positive impact on economic growth in the country (Javid & Qayyum, 2011, p. 2) contrary to argument put forward by Khan (1997) that aid is actually detrimental to economic growth in the country. Developing economies are heavily dependent upon aid (Killick, 2008), and hence Pakistan like others, welcomes international funding and donor agencies as partners for their development plans.

The following pages provide the context, explicitly for the non-Pakistani reader. Notwithstanding the fact that the context below is also crucial to appreciate the implications of the aid management in Punjab, from the perspective of an institution that was a key player in the reform program. Once the context has been established for the period 2004–2008, the paper will establish that aid management in the sector of education in Punjab, tended to suffer from lack of clarity of objectives and a common understanding of educational reform policy at the level of the department of education; that the concept of institutional capacity building in the planning process for implementation of the educational reform plans was neglected; and that there was a disconnect within the various educational organizations responsible for implementing the reform policy. I argue that, in this specific case, these factors, led to the advantage of funder/donors who found it easy to bypass accountability screening by the recipient countries/organizations/government departments, whatever the case may be. This by default allowed the funders/donors to promote their own agenda. Also, the government of Punjab, in this case, showed a clear bias in favor of the funder rather than the donors. The following pages show how the politics of interaction at the level of implementation affects the process of aid management and though not the objective of the present discourse, it is an area that needs to be further explored.

CONTEXTUAL BACKGROUND: EDUCATION REFORMS IN PUNJAB

Punjab (one of the four provinces of Pakistan) has over 85 million people (more than half the country's population). In 2000 the Government of Punjab (GoP) initiated plans for a major reform in Education. Massive resource allocations were made. As is mostly the case where political mileage is an angle, (Zia & McBride, 2008) the focus was mostly on infrastructure and other materials such as new buildings for schools, upgrade of civil works in existing schools, provision of free text books for primary school children and the like. The World Bank (WB) offered to support the program with an attractive repayment package in 2003 and, as a result, the Punjab Education Sector Reform Program (PESRP) was developed. Starting as a three year credit in 2003 with the support of the GoP, it was continued for later years. PERSP focused on education reforms but also put up plans for public finance reforms, and, reforms in fiduciary environment and governance, basically to develop an environment conducive to education reform.

During the implementation process (2001 onwards) the government's allocation for education steadily increased with every successive year. The WB joined in 2003 and it is interesting to note that by the year 2008 the WB contribution, at an average of approximately 100 million dollars per year (WB, 2005), stood at 7% of the Punjab government's yearly budget for education.

The WB, as a funder, is specified here for obvious reasons. This mention might raise ethical concerns. The WB was a major partner with the GoP in the planning and monitoring of the Punjab education reform agenda, i.e. the PESRP. The reference here is also notable on the basis of the author's "immersion" (Punch, 1994, p 86) in the situation. The Directorate of Staff Development (DSD) as the only organization of Punjab, entrusted with pre-service and in-service education of all public school teachers (350,000), played a key role in the PESRP. The author was the head of the DSD from 2004–2008 and, as such can offer a first hand account of aid management from the perspective of the institution. This paper is largely driven by social ethics, that is, to "enable community life to prosper" (Christians, 2000, p. 145). The "aim is not fulsome data *per se*, but community transformation" (Christians, 2000,

p. 148) with the primary intention to provide further knowledge to all concerned stakeholders, especially governments and funders/donors to rethink their strategies for the betterment of education in developing countries like Pakistan.

The DSD forms the test case for this paper. The following paragraphs provide a brief outline of the educational organization, basically to consolidate the necessary contextual information.

Established in 1961, the DSD Punjab has, over the years, undergone changes in name and area of administration although its functions have largely remained the same. In 2001, when the PERSP was launched it was incorporated into the newly established University of Education. Under the umbrella of the new university, the DSD was entrusted with the task of teacher training as a key partner in the PERSP.

The training of some 150,000 primary school teachers was conducted by the DSD in the first year of the PESRP i.e. 2003. The outcomes of the training were stated to be "disappointing" in a third party validation report sponsored by the Department for International Development (Agha Khan University-Institute of Educational Development and Society for Advancement of Education 2004, p. 3). This became the *raisin'd'etre* to de-link the DSD from the University of Education and establish it as a separate entity under the ambit of the Education Department of the GoP (July 2004). Within a year another organization in Punjab with functions similar to the DSD, the Provincial Institute for Teacher Education, and the 33 Colleges of Teacher Education providing pre-service education (B.Ed. and M.Ed.) were also taken away from the University of Education and placed under the umbrella of the DSD. This empowered the DSD to be the sole organization responsible for the professional development of the largest human resource of Punjab i.e., pre-service and in-service of public school teachers. Though not thought of at the time, by default, this provided the much needed policy and program continuum between pre-service and in-service areas of school teachers.

The author as a Director at the DSD, for the years 2004–2008, introduced major changes in the: the DSD's organizational structure and administrative posts; role and functions of the DSD; implementation /delivery structure for the in-service program; and governance patterns. More importantly, during the initial year, *training* was conceptually reshaped from the workshop mode towards a much closer form of *continuous professional development,* whereby support to teachers became an integral component of the program. It was also a first time ever that, a long term vision for the DSD's functioning was developed with a detailed implementation plan and program activities for the next 10 years. A comprehensive policy document for continuous professional development of serving primary school teachers (1,80,000) was developed by the DSD (2006), and got approved from government along with the needed resource allocations. The latter was a major move whereby the GoP committed some one billion rupees per year for this program. The policy was translated to a 'action-plan' document complete with specified objectives and tasks; expected outcomes with validation triggers and designated time frames by agencies responsible for the specified tasks These documents formed the basis for a consultative dialogue with all stake holders, specifically donor/funder agencies, and local civil society organizations. The detail and the clarity of the 'action-plan' minimized confusion among interacting partners and promoted the smooth operation of the policy developed for teacher development.

The above pages provide the contextual background that makes the discussion of the following pages comprehensible.

AID IN EDUCATION: SOME CONCERNS OF POLICY AND PRACTICE

Donor contribution to the educational process is particular to developing economies and here we look at the role of various funder/donors from the prism of the DSD experience and how it interacted with the policy and practice of the process. The following pages will delineate the various facets of policy, planning and implementation and see how education reform in Punjab, at times, has been impacted by or impacted upon, as the case may be, the role the funder/donors. This discourse is not inclusive, and, looks at areas where clear possibility for improvement is indicated.

Most international donor agencies, like UNICEF, UNESCO, GTZ, CIDA, DFID and some others have been, traditionally speaking, and still are active partners of Department of Education in Punjab. All are involved in the educational process with varying degrees of engagement and by different areas of interest/objectives. The DSD brought all these donors to a common platform. The regular six-monthly 'Donor Co-ordination' meetings held at the DSD, were basically held to apprise and develop consensus with all development partners about the DSD's policies and plans. It was during such meetings that donors in keeping with the big picture defined by the DSD's action-plan identified areas of program objectives they wanted to support in keeping with their own specific agendas. It forced the donors to be transparent, develop trust as partners, to consult with each other and, in some cases, collaborate with each other towards the common objectives. Though not intended, it came to be very much in keeping with the spirit of the Paris Declaration (OECD, 2005). It also provided a basis for avoidance of many issues that Killick (2008, pp. 3–4) also cites like: donor's pursuing their own objectives; poor harmonization and co-ordination of the programs; proliferation of aid sources leading to multiplicity of funds; multiplicity of administrative, reporting and monitoring mechanisms that tend to overburden the already weak systems of the recipient countries (in this case the DSD's); commitments not honored by donors; donor assistance tied to procurement of goods and services from their own countries; assistance programs not in sync with national in this case the DSD's priorities; lack of trust between donors and recipients; issues of technical assistance by donor at high costs inconsistent with domestic capacity; and excessive number of conditionalities by donors that tend to impinge upon national sovereignty. All the above except the last point were experienced by the author at the DSD, but not all have been addressed in this paper. Placed below are some concerns as encountered by the author in the specified years at the DSD, with measures to counter these in some cases. Examples are quoted where feasible.

1. Lack of consensus on the indicators for key concepts/objectives of the reform:

   The PESRP Log Frame Analysis issued as WB *Aide Memoire*, defined the education agenda for Punjab. All outputs were developed jointly by the WB and the government functionaries of the various partner departments/ organizations. The political leadership provided the political will for providing support to aid management (Killick 2008, p. 13). But, as is usually the case, political leadership tends to be uninformed of the technicalities involved in the process. For this, it depends upon the civil service bureaucrats to prepare the policies and implementation plans. These civil servants heading the education department and the related organizations, do not have the technical expertise in education either. Hence, the drafting of the Log Frame Analysis and the ensuing *Aide Memoire*, developed in separate consultations with the heads of various departments of the education sector, became a list of discrete activities without a common understanding of the basic objectives or concepts. It was a clear show of lack of co-ordination among the organizations that were partners towards the common goals of the PERSP. For example, the various departments dealing with teacher training (DSD) or text book formulation (Punjab Textbook Board) or the examination assessment system (Punjab Examination Commission) developed their own separate strategies to improve quality but without arriving at a common consensus on *quality,* and its possible indicators. The above example is perhaps similar to what Killick (2008, p. 8) cites as 'degree of fragmentation' in reference to case of Sierra Leone, whereby co-ordination might exist on paper among the development partners but not in practice. This confused situation hence was in a way, ideal for the various funder/donors, who found it flexible to pursue their own indicators for 'quality' in their plans.

2. Disregard of the need for institutional development and capacity building:

   That the 'triggers' of the Log Frame Analysis largely disregarded many necessary requisites of sustainable, effective reform was another issue. For example, the government notification to de-link the DSD from the University of Education was the **only** trigger required by the WB to verify achievement of successful "reorganization of the DSD" (WB *Aide Memoire*, 2005). Both the WB and Department of Education demanded that the DSD deliver 'training' to public school teachers as it was the pre-requisite to release the funds owed to the DSD. There was no fund allocation for the accompanying institutional reform and capacity building so crucial to the tasks of the newly re-established DSD. The support to the institution as the strategic policy maker, planner and implementer of teacher development activities was totally neglected. All the related issues of organizational structure, staffing requirements, governance style and various aspects of capacity building in both structures and processes of the DSD were not stated as inputs in the Log Frame Analysis developed by the WB for the expected outcomes for quality. Clearly, the PESRP did not pay sufficient attention to systemic reform, consolidation or to institutional development (Zia & McBride, 2009, p. 141). Also, the decision to de-link the DSD from the University of Education shows a 'reaction' to the validation report carried out by AKU-IED and SAHE in 2004. Perhaps, the move to de-link the DSD and other organizations from University should have happened after a well researched plan within a comprehensive framework.

The Provincial Institute of Teacher Education was established in Punjab, in 1982 as a separate entity, with the same roles and functions as the DSD. Under the reform agenda it was placed under the ambit of the DSD in 2005, but the Log Frame Analysis disregarded the need to rationalize and integrate the roles of both. Not only did this perpetuate the unnecessary administrative and financial burden on the government, it created a major disturbance in the smooth functioning of the DSD. The ensuing confusion was used by the staff of the Provincial Institute of Teacher Education to create an atmosphere of political and legal unrest on the DSD campus. They filed a court case etc. challenging their placement under DSD, which they eventually lost after a long convoluted struggle. This, *inter alia*, created an unstable climate whereby the credibility of the role of the DSD was questioned. Repeated initiatives by the author, as head of the DSD, for the restructuring of the DSD to rationalize the roles of its component institutions (Provincial Institute of Teacher Education and 33 Colleges of Education) were not considered by the Department of Education. This would have avoided overlapping of roles and resources; streamlined the systemic flaws, and, created a holistic continuum for professional development of teachers. The situation remains so to date.

3. Various planned activities not synchronized to fit as an integrated process:

The activities stated in the PESRP policy document were not scheduled in a reasonably logical order nor synchronized to fit together. This was the ultimate responsibility of the head (Secretary) of the Department of Education. This was a crucial issue since different organizations within the Department of Education were responsible for different specialized functions. And, instead of the Secretary as the head of the Department of Education who should have taken responsibility to coordinate the activities of various organizations under its umbrella, each organization was left to fend on its own to deal with other related organizations/officials as needed. For example, all education related activities at the field level have to be undertaken by the 35 different district governments. The delegation of governance from the Punjab provincial unit to the 35 sub-units of the districts is also a recent development (2001). It is clear that the capacity building and orientation of district staff is an important component and should be done in parallel with education reform initiatives at the district level. Unfortunately this part was overlooked in the earlier planning of the Log Frame Analysis and *Aide Memoire*, and the training/capacity building of the district education staff was a much later addition to the program. This led to the dissipation of efforts for educational reform at the field level. And so, in 2006, while the DSD was ready to provide the initial training to all primary school teachers in all the 35 districts of Punjab, the district government staff was disoriented and unprepared to facilitate this activity. In an environment where the district head of education department was not in the loop of the reform agenda, the efforts by the DSD to consult and liaise with stakeholders at the district level, at best produced lukewarm results. That the expertise level of the selected district education staff, specifically for teacher education and development is minimal, is another matter and, needs a separate discourse.

At other times, overlap in similar activities conducted by different organizations was a glaring issue leading to unnecessary wastage of government's meager resources. This oversight could have been easily avoided with a well-integrated plan (Leithwood, Jantzi & Mascall, 2002, p. 14), in this case the Log Frame Analysis document, finalized by the WB and Department of Education. For example, another organization under the Department of Education and generously funded by the government, the Punjab Education Foundation, is entrusted with training of private school teachers. Since both public and private schools were using the same curriculum, the DSD and the Punjab Education Foundation both could have collaborated with each other to train teachers in the public and private schools. This duplication of efforts and resources seems not to have been considered at the either the policy or the implementation level.

4. Frequent changes of leadership in the government sector:

More recently a feature of the Punjab, and indeed Pakistani landscape, is political instability. This resulted in frequent changes of leadership of the Punjab Department of Education. During the four year period from 2004 to 2008, there were two changes of political leadership and five Education Secretaries. Such changes create problems of expertise and necessary experience which can lead to serious lag in decision making and action. New appointees, understandably so, with poor prior knowledge and in a hurry to impress, are eager to attract providers who can be attributed to their office and become very 'flexible' at the opportunity to provide the service with more money/resources. In this situation we have seen some funders gain more influence. At other times, decisions that have already been approved, and even implemented earlier, are instantly reversed. For example, the professional development day for all primary teachers, approved by one education secretary was abruptly halted by the new one in his place without a well informed enquiry. Of course, this had repercussions on the quality of the teacher development program.

5. Different (rigid?) agendas of different funder/donors:

Most funder/donors offer support in specified areas. All have their own areas of specific objectives and tasks, and all make a bid to register themselves as the strongest ally in the competition to provide aid. For example, in the first meeting between the DSD and some six major funder/donors, head of one organization criticized the plan for lack of stated objectives for 'good governance' or 'gender-justice'. He pointed that the plans put up would not 'appeal to our taxpayers back home' and hence the support of the organization to the DSD's plans would be difficult to justify. Many donors pledged their support at the time, and later became key partners of the DSD like UNICEF, CIDA and GTZ.

Another problem was that once funder /donors had agreed upon a specific course of action and had their project plans approved at their end, they were by and large, unable to change course or adapt to new circumstances, if so required. In this specific case, when the organizational structure of the DSD was totally redefined in 2004, resources were needed for capacity building of the new organization. The only funding available to the DSD in that year (2004–2005) was conditional on the trigger of training activity of school teachers. Both the Funder and the education department understood the need, but refused the DSD's request on the basis that the planned triggers could not be changed. Had donors like UNICEF, GTZ and CIDA not come forward to support the program, no amount of effort by DSD's leadership could have managed to establish the basic structure/capacity that could deliver quality programs during the subsequent years. It is to be pointed, that during the four years under discussion here, donor support was so inclusive that the PESRP funds were not utilized by the DSD.

6. Same objectives, different strategies by funder/donors:

It is often the case that donors in the same sub sector have similar objectives but follow different strategies to achieve the required results. This contributes to differences in quality of work and different methods but, most of all, ends up by confusing recipients who receive different messages for the same objectives. For example, most donors are interested in teacher development, and specifically training for the same, but all tend to prefer their specific agenda/objectives as the focus of the training programs, which could be gender equality, human rights, environment, HIV/Aids so on and so forth. The materials developed and training have a strong bias towards funders'/donor's objectives. This is especially problematic in Punjab where the main issue is the teacher's mastery of content knowledge and basic pedagogical skills, and so the programs put up to develop teachers may not emphasize issues of gender, environment, and so on. To make it a win-win for all partners, the objectives of the different funders /donors can be aligned at the policy and plan implementation level. The Log Frame Analysis developed for the PERSP could pre-plan indicators/tasks with the consensus of all major stakeholders. The WB as the funder was the only partner of the Education Department in the development of the PESRP. The consultative dialogues that the DSD carried out with donors/funders during its program planning and implementation, is one possible model that can be further refined for such like situations.

7. Loopholes in governance style of recipient governments/organizations:

Most funders/donors work through a limitless stream of consultants and service providers. Consultants can be either national or international. They are prized for their sorely needed expertise but their selection and the use of their services is another issue. Mostly, funders/donors provide consultants based on a set terms of references, which are usually, jointly developed with the recipient organization. Issues can arise as organizations do not always have the opportunity to vet individuals before hiring or comment on the mission after completion. Validation of the consultants' work by the recipient country/ organization is not a standard procedure, thus leaving no possibility of ensuring quality work. Following some negative experiences, the DSD insisted on vetting the consultants. The DSD also ensured that final payments made to consultants and service providers, were on the basis of a validation report by the organization. This led to certain international consultants being taken off the consultants lists while, in other cases, it was ensured they did not return.

8. Consultant documents are often well presented and well written but the issue of fairness, accuracy or relevance of the reports is neither addressed nor questioned. A case in point is the Learning and Educational Achievements in Punjab Schools (LEAPS) study done in Punjab. It makes a strong case for support of private schooling as a stark contrast to stated issues in public schooling. Despite a disclaimer about the authors' affiliations, two revealed that they are affiliated with the major funder of the PESRP, i.e. the WB. The acknowledgements clarify that a number of people employed by the same funder, including Pakistanis and expats, were involved in initiating and supporting the writing of this report. That both the PESRP and the LEAPS report received substantial funds from the same major funder is surely not a coincidence. Based on the results of the report, the promotion of private schooling in Pakistan was aggressively pursued under the PERSP. The report was not questioned for appropriateness of the research employed to draw conclusions, nor was it put out to the educational community for discussion or analysis. It did create discontent and frustration among many in the education community. Such situations can be avoided if the governments/recipient organizations have clearer objectives and clear visioning of the contextual realities. Massive consultations would definitely be one way for consensus building for a smoother implementation process. In this specific case it gave opportunity to the funder to push its agenda of privatization of the schooling process. Possible bias of the Punjab government in favor of the funder:

Large sums of money are influential and tend to change the psyche on both sides. In general, the civil bureaucracy is more interested in funders because they have larger budgets than donors. The large funder is usually able to guard its interest, may even be aggressive and is likely to have greater freedom to influence decisions in countries that receive these funds. Large funders can have a major effect on policy and practice and this has become more pronounced during the recent periods of political instability in Pakistan. It was clear in this case where the donors, who had a long history of engagement in the education sector, were neglected in the PERSP planning and implementation. The WB remained the sole partner in this major reform initiative.

One funder in particular, in this specific case, gained influence early on when the sector program was just beginning. This funder worked to secure its supporters in some key positions. In fact, as the funder credibility developed, with long term commitment to the program, the funder actively worked to acquire the placement of its chosen personnel in the key positions to get a sympathetic and flexible connect with the direction and implementation of the program. This can work both ways. While it can ensure continuity of the program, it can on the flip side, *inter alia*, bring about a limited vision to the program.

The above cited concerns do not, of course, absolve the civil service leadership or the government of its responsibilities in policy-making and implementation. But they clearly show how the limitations of the policy making and the implementation process, allows more space to funders/donors to follow their own interests and agendas. And, within the aid providers, the bias in this specific case study was clearly in favor of the funder.

TO CONCLUDE: THE CONFUSION AND COUNTER MEASURES?

The Paris Declaration (OECD, 2005) has forced funders/donors to increase their reliance on government co-ordination and leadership. In paragraph 10, it talks about 'leadership of the partner country' and 'country level mechanisms' as vehicle for implementing aid commitments. It proposed the principle of country ownership, and alignment with country institutions, strategies, procedures, and mutual accountability of donors and recipient governments to each other. But evidence clearly shows limited implementation of these principles so far. OECD-DAC (2006, pp. 9–10) is also clear to point that more work needs to be done in this area. This has forced the governments to clarify their agenda and strategic plans. And as Killick (2008, p. 6) proposes, it is imperative that countries take control of aid management and maximize their negotiation by capitalizing on the Paris Declaration to take control of aid management. This has on the other hand, magnified the variance among strategies of the various funders/donors even when their objectives are similar.

Another recent development is that the big money of the funders has pushed the small donor monies out of the corridors of the policy makers and power brokers. Perhaps it was either, or both of the above, that led to the emergence of a 'One UN Program' for some selected developing countries of which Pakistan is one. It is to be hoped this will force the various international aid organizations onto a common platform. This will surely benefit the developing countries by bringing co-ordination in the funders/donors' objectives.

In the meantime, much of the damage has been done. The mayhem of funder/donor activity, alongside very weak/unstable federal and provincial leadership in Pakistan has created confusion which allowed funders /donors to use it to their advantage. This is not to say that the advantage of funders /donors is to the disadvantage of the recipient country, but is an issue that needs to be further researched Another outcome is that some heads of certain major government departments have very little idea what the uncoordinated factions or branches are doing, or what expertise they have. Given the neglect of institutional capacity building, the situation is further aggravated. The end result is that no one is completely sure what the policy is, how it is to be implemented or by which branch. This tends to be stoked up by the funders/ donors as they, too, vie for influence of their own specific agendas/objectives. It raises the concern that perhaps, the policy/planning and implementation process advertently or inadvertently *allows subversion of the educational process to the advantage of funders/donors*. This also enables funders/donors to by-pass the accountability procedures by the recipient government/organization. The paper clearly raises some concerns about the *modus operandi* of funders/donors, and these need to be examined to the minutest detail so that aid management provides optimal benefit to the recipient.

For educational aid/support to be effective there has to be a set of comprehensive and holistic policies, strategic planning and sequenced implementation. Killick (2008, pp. 14- 21) has recommended parameters of an aid management policy which can provide a firm basis for imposing aid effectiveness and is worth considering. Strong government leadership is missing. This, in turn, requires the capacity building of government departments, so that the resources funders/donor are effectively used and accounted for. Funders/donors simply have to learn to place more emphasis on preparing the ground before they rush in to disburse money. In such an environment it is crucial that the governments also do their homework with meticulous care. This includes strong co-ordination among the various arms of the government and, as is obvious in this case, within the different organizations of the Department of Education.

It is hoped that the identification of these issues and some suggested counter measures will encourage further discussion and debate for the benefit of educational betterment. They are equally applicable in other areas of economy, especially in developing countries, where funders and donors are a 'welcome' reality. In the larger context of a global world one reality that impacts aid effectiveness is the gap between the resources needed for the support of the developing/underdeveloped economies and the actual aid provided. It also needs to be questioned as to why even the largest bilateral donors (Japan and USA) have failed to meet the UN target of 0.7 percent of GNI that ought to be devoted to aid and have also failed to perform adequately in targeting aid needy recipients (Thiele, Nunnenkamp & Dreher, 2007, p. 622).

REFERENCES

Agha Khan University Institute of Educational Development (AKU-IED) and Society for Advancement of Education (SAHE) (2004). *Effectiveness of in-service teacher education programmes offered by the University of Education, Lahore.* Islamabad: DFID.

Allesina, A., & Dollar, D. (1998). *Who gives foreign aid to whom and why?* NBER working paper no 6612. Cambridge, MA: The National Bureau of Economic Research.

Azam, J-P., & Thelen, V. (2008). The roles of foreign aid and education in the war on terror. *Public Choice, 135*(3/4), 375–397.

Burnside, C., & Dollar, D. (2000). Aid, policies and growth. *The American Economic Review, 90*(4), 847–868.

Cassen, R. H., Duncan, A., Guisinger, S., Hooper, E., & Norman, O. (1990). *The effectiveness of aid to Pakistan: a report to UNDP/government of Pakistan* (2 volumes). Islamabad, Pakistan: Economic Affairs Division and Government of Geneva, Switzerland.

Christians, C. G. (2000). Ethics and politics in qualitative research. In Denzin K. D., & Lincoln, Y. S. (Eds.) *Handbook of qualitative research* (2nd ed.). London: Sage Publications.

Directorate of Staff Development (2006). *Transforming teacher development in Punjab: A conceptual framework for quality learning.* An unpublished blueprint developed by Rukhsana Zia and documented by UNICEF, Lahore.

Easterly, W. (2006). *The white man's burden: Why the west's effort to aid and the rest have done so much ill and so little good.* New York: Penguin.

Ellahi, N., & Mahmood, H. Z. (2012). Bounds testing approach to find the impact of capital inflow on real output growth of Pakistan. *International Journal of Economics and Finance, 4*(4), 106–113. Toronto: Canadian Center of Science and Education.

Javid, M., & Qayyum, A. (2011). *Foreign aid-growth Nexus in Pakistan: Role of macroeconomic policies.* Islamabad: Pakistan Institute of Development Economics.

Khan, S. R. (1997). Has aid helped in Pakistan? *Journal of Pakistan Institute of Development Economics, 36*(4). Islamabad: Pakistan Institute of Development Economics.

Khan, M. A. (2007). *Foreign direct investment and economic growth: The role of domestic financial sector,* Working paper number 18. Islamabad: Pakistan Institute of Development Economics.

Killick, T. (2008). *The least developed countries report 2008: Growth, poverty and terms of development partnership*: Background paper on, Taking Control: Aid Management policies in least developed countries. Geneva: UNCTAD.

Korb, L. (2009). *Reassessing foreign assistance to Pakistan: Recommendations for US engagement.* Washington: Center for American Progress.

Leithwood K., Jantzi, D., & Mascall, B. (2002). Large-scale reform: what works? *Journal of Educational Change, 3*(1), 7–33.

Maizels, A., & Nissanke, M. (1984). Motivations for aid to developing countries. *World Development, 12*(9), 879–900.

OECD (2005). *Paris declaration on aid effectiveness.* Accessed at http://www.oecd.org/dataoecd/11/41/34428351.pdf on May 2010.

OECD-DAC (2006). *Survey on monitoring of Paris declaration: Overview of the results.* Paris: OECD-Development Assistance committee.

Prasad, K. (1997). Some thoughts on development assistance. *Economic and Political Weekly, 32*(41), 2594–2598.

Punch, M. (1994). Politics and ethics in qualitative research. In Denzin K. D., & Lincoln, Y. S. (Eds.) *Handbook of qualitative research.* London: Sage: Publications.

Ridell, R. C. (1987). *Foreign aid reconsidered.* London: Johns Hopkins University Press.

Stokke, O. (1995). (Ed.). *Aid and political conditionality.* London: Frank Cass & Co.

Svensson, J. (1999). Aid, growth and democracy. *Economics and Politics, 11*(3), 215–291.

Thiele, R., Nunnenkamp, P., & Dreher, A. (2007). Do Donors target aid in line with the millennium Development Goals? A sector perspective of aid allocation. *Review of World Economics/ Weltwirtschaftliches Archiv, 143*(4), 596–630.

World Bank (2005). Aide memoire, PERSP. *World bank review mission and preparation mission for the proposed Punjab education development policy credit*, June 16–22.

Zia, R., & McBride, R. (2008). Education policy formation and the global grip: A case study from Punjab. Paper presented at 2008 conference of the *British association for international and comparative education*, Scotland, University of Glasgow.

Zia, R., & McBride, R. (2009). A support network for primary school teachers in the Punjab: Challenges of policy and practice. In Field M. H. & Fegan J. (Eds.). *Education across borders*. Tokyo: Springer Science and Business Media B.V.

AFFILIATION

Rukhsana Zia
Director of the Center of Learning and Teaching
Forman Christian College

HASAN HÜSEYIN AKSOY, HATICE ÖZDEN ARAS, AYGÜLEN
KAYAHAN & DILEK ÇANKAYA

CRITICAL ANALYSIS OF ECONOMICS
OF EDUCATION THEORIES WITH REGARD
TO THE QUALITY OF EDUCATION[1]

INTRODUCTION

The aim of this study is to analyze critically hegemonic discourses and to reveal critical approaches on "the quality of education". First, the conceptual and loaded meaning of the word of "quality" will be revealed. Then the relation between "quality" and "education", the quality indicators of education according to Human Capital Theory and other theories which are used as main references in the mainstream economics of education will be discussed. The criticisms about Human Capital Theory's vision on quality of education will be analyzed. Afterwards the meaning of education for critical pedagogy and admitted quality indicators for critical educators and the writers will be revealed by reviewing basic concepts and approaches of critical education theorists. The "conceptual object" that is analyzed in this study is education, which is the responsibility of the state. This type of analysis about education is significant as education has become one of the "products produced for the national economy and international competition" (Farenga, 2006/2008).

Definition of Quality Related to Education

Aside from the fact that the concept of quality is related to a dominant paradigm, it is relative and value-laden. It has different meanings according to socio-economical formation, production type, the development level of productive forces, relations between production or class position, government type, ideology, culture, gender, different belief systems etc. (Cheng & Tam, 1997; Abalı, 2007). On the other hand, the determination of the quality of service and the power to arrange it has led to the creation of organizations to measure standards such as the ISO (International Organization for Standardization), TSE (Standardization Organization of Turkey). Standards that are determined by these organizations are accepted as "quality indicators". Although quality is a relative construct, it now is being taken into consideration at a more "absolute" level depending on the perspectives of corporations that lead in assessment and evaluation (Aksoy, 2008).

The concept of "quality" from social perceptions about education shows an evolution that includes features ensuring success or advantage in the exams that

S. Majhanovich and M.A. Geo-JaJa (Eds.), Economics, Aid and Education:
Implications for Development, 61–76.

lead to positions which will be rewarded by the market in the long term. With the increasing effect of market capitalism on social environments, the concept of quality in education now is viewed as related to "standardization", "test success, performance, effectuality, choice, and perfection" rather than equality, value and social justice (Adams, 1993: Hanushek, et al., 1994; Aspin, et al., 1994; Carnoy, 1995; Berliner & Biddle, 1997; Cheng & Tam, 1997; Hanushek, 2005). Acceptance of the former notions of quality brings many indicators with it. Some of these are; expenses per student, repeating a grade level, graduation levels, education level of teachers, cognitive skills; books, residence fees, computers, laboratory and laboratory tools in schools, length of time that students are schooled, absenteeism and attendance, teacher-pupil ratio, and student success in class (Carnoy, 1995). In addition to these indicators of quality education in school, graduates' participation in production in the current market conditions and the individual incomes are accepted to be "measurable" indicators of quality in education.

When some indicators stated above regarding the functioning of education processes are analyzed, it is seen that there have been some changes in provisions about these indicators over time. For instance, Wasley (2003) proposes that differences in school size should be removed in order to prevent inequality in education and to give a more quality education to disadvantaged groups. On the other hand, Johnson (2003) emphasized that the amount of money needed to decrease differences in class size and schools is too high, but the difference in the level of education does not justify the cost. Additionally he stated that starting from the 1970s, the number of students per class and per teacher has been decreasing, but there has not been an increase in success levels parallel to this decrease; it is also not known if the source of increase in success is related to the size of schools. Another example is that, starting from the mid 1990s, the necessity of computer-based technology in schools has been emphasized everywhere. But there has also been some skepticism regarding the use of computers for basic educational goals as well as on the educational value of computer supported education programs overall (Apple, 1989, 2011; De Castell, et al., 2002; Postman, 2004). On the other hand, it is also possible to state that economics is the reason why quality in education is related to computer technology rather than to educational sciences. Distance learning's success has been discussed in terms of its close connection with the market besides decreasing the educators' close relationship with learners (Feenberg, 1999a;1999b; De Castell, et al., 2002).

While "participation" and "student centeredness" are generally accepted to be important for student success, the participation factor is changing and becoming generally based on sharing school expenses, namely, focusing more on the families' ability to pay. One example of this kind of participation is the relationship that is institutionalized through "school and parent associations" (Kılınçalp, 2007); another is the increasing role of market agents and companies in educational institutions both as marketing members and as "shareholders" (N. Aksoy, 2010). Companies' participation in education firstly starts with "social responsibility projects"; civil society organizations attend to education through projects such as supporting girls' participation in education, or giving material support to schools. Such company expenses point to the commercialization of education which is a hidden agenda, but are in fact a daily practice (Ball & Youdel, 2008; N. Aksoy, 2010).

According to a report from the World Bank (López, et al., 1998), if individuals do not use their knowledge in a competitive and open market, the effect of investment in human capital on economic development will be minimal. What is interesting here is that education is provided for the market that has open and competitive conditions. It is mentioned in the European Union that, "quality" in education and development is a highly political priority for all member countries (European Commission, 2000). High level of knowledge is accepted as very important in terms of "active citizenship", "employment" and "social cohesion". In the introduction of the European Commission's report on quality in education, it is stated that "quality in education" is necessary for labor markets and for workers to have required mobility (in terms of investing in human capital); this statement shows where the priorities lie.

In studies on the relationship between education and work, while positive theories are focused on the present relations between education and work, normative theories are focused on the relations that "must be" between education and work (Levin, 1995). The logic of the relationship between education and work is based on Human Capital Theory which argues that education "increases labor's production of quality and abilities" (Carnoy, 1995). Human Capital Theory is an important basis for discussions on quality in education as it sets the frame of reference for many prominent educational indicators as the basis of employment which is based on competition and profitability.

Human Capital Theory

The word "capital" was a word that described material objects until the second half of last century. In social science literature, some abstract values are now seen as "capital" in addition to concrete physical beings; examples that now appear include psychological capital, social capital, cultural capital, and human capital.

Although Smith (1723–1790) known as the founder of classical economics, Malthus (1766–1834) and Ricardo (1772–1823) dealt with the economic dimension of education, this interest have never reached the theoretical level. At the end of studies firstly by T. Schultz (1962, 1966), E. F. Denison (1962) and G. S. Becker (1962, 1993), it can be said that Human Capital Theory is the oldest and most commonly accepted concept in education economics. The concept of "Human Capital" which emerged in the theoretical framework of neoclassical development at the end of the 1950s and 1960s is considered a revolutionary definition (Ehrlich & Murphy, 2007). According to neoclassical economics, physical capital, labor, technical process and human capital which is added to labor, have roles in production. After the Second World War, Japan and Germany were countries that had lost physical assets but, these countries are among the most developed countries today. Their development is thought to result from the successful use of "human capital". This situation shows the importance of human capital's role in the production power of re-developed countries (Becker, 1964/1993; Schultz, 1966; Carlin, 1993; Broadberry & Wagner, 1996).

To "invest" in education is seen to be "profitable" for both individuals and society. Education has a significant effect on the increase of national income and economic development (Woodhall, 1995) and the theory is highly accepted by governments of under–developed and developing countries. The theory emerged in a period when the social state ruled and when the analyses of educational services, accepted among the basic duties of a state, were being carried out. There has been an increase in the "social" state's education expenses with the general acceptance of Human Capital Theory (Georgiadis, 2007).

According to Shultz (1966), activities directed at developing human capital are divided into five categories. These are medical services and facilities, in-service training that people get in the institutions where they are employed, formal training, the process of increasing capacity through individual research in order to get more knowledge and abilities, and mobility of individuals and families in order to benefit from changing job opportunities.

The theory divides the returns to education into two parts, the "individual" and the "social". While the individual return of the theory is represented by an individual income level, the social return is the increase in national income and economic development of society with increasing productivity and income of individuals. Schultz (1966) continued his studies in this field and posited that people have a significant place in total national wealth, and when labor is taken into consideration with the value it added into total outputs, it is seen that the capacity of manpower to proliferate is much more than the total amount of all other wealth forms.

According to Schultz (1966), "human capital" "ages" over time and requires maintenance. He mentioned that unemployment causes decrease in abilities, and causes human capital to become inactive while recruitment affected by religious and national discrimination will waste investments in human capital. He noted that the reason for low-income of some individuals in society is due to their health and to low investment in their education (Schultz, 1966). In Human Capital Theory, the injustice in distribution of income in society is explained by the variety of human capital. The reason why some people have low income seems to result from the fact that they made an insufficient investment in their human capital. Nowadays, Schultz's view has been shaped as a continuous investment in "human capital" (generally financed by individuals) which is called "lifelong learning".

The aim of all activities of a "rational" person mentioned by Schultz and other neoclassic economists is to increase income. If a person's knowledge gained in school, through training in his/her professional life and through research do not increase income or do not provide financial benefits to society, then it is a complete waste of effort. Psacharopoulos (1973) first tried to measure the social and individual income that is ensured by investments in education in 32 countries while in a later study (1981) he updated the data of this research. In the second study, he performed a cost-benefit analysis, and examined the rate and relationship between the incomes of workers and their education level. At the end of these investigations by Psacharopoulos between 1958–78, he reached four important results (Psacharopoulos, 1981; Woodhall, 1987): The social rate of return to primary education was considerably higher, in most countries, than the rate of return to higher education, and that the private returns to higher education were much higher than the social returns; either private or social, the return on the investment in education is 10% more than the cost of the opportunity; individual and social returns of education in underdeveloped countries show more meaningful differences than in developed countries. On the other hand, Coleman (1988) emphasized the importance of social capital in the process of the formation of human capital. According to this, social capital of both the family and the social status group to which the family belongs directly affects the human capital of the next generation.

Human Capital Theory degrades education into a technical process focused merely on transferring knowledge and abilities. However, there is still some research which shows the continuing belief that the theory is still valid for labor markets which have undergone some significant structural changes since the 1980s and to which neoliberal policies are applied today. This is shown by the efforts to ensure all kinds of professional education programs used as tools to prevent unemployment and poverty provided by formal professional education and governmental organizations to local institutions. Although most of the programs offered by the commercial institutions do not result in direct employment, the institutions continue to spread the notion that they open the way to increased income and job placement through the professional or general education programs they offer.

Screening Hypothesis, Tail Hypothesis, the Theory of Labor Market Segmentation

Other views that try to explain the economic value of education in terms of definite premises are Screening Hypothesis, Tail Hypothesis and the Theory of Labor Market Segmentation. According to Screening Hypothesis, education does not increase performance by increasing necessary knowledge and abilities; it incorporates individuals into the system according to their abilities, it graduates them from the system or eliminates them. Different diplomas, certificates and documents give information to employers about individuals they will employ (Woodhall, 1995). According to Screening Hypothesis, employers take not only the cognitive features, but also some definite personality features into consideration while employing individuals. While people that will be employed in low-status jobs are required to be "punctual", "conformist", "able to take part in teamwork" and "can take orders", university graduates who are at the top of the professional hierarchy are required to have qualities such as "self-esteem", "multi-dimensions" and "leadership" (Blaug, 1995). These aspects are ensured in the education system through the hidden curriculum. When employers check to see if an individual has these qualities or not, they look at his/her education type and level.

According to Tail Hypothesis, efficiency is not a feature of individuals; it is a feature of jobs. As workers who can be developed are low-cost, the ones that will be employed are at the beginning of the tail. In this hypothesis, it is accepted that there is a relationship between education and income and employers line up the individuals who applied for the job from the most educated one (the ones that can be developed more easily) to the least educated one (the ones that can be developed with more difficulty) (Carnoy, 1982/1990).

According to the Theory of Labor Market Segmentation, labor markets are divided into primary and secondary. Primary markets are the ones with advanced level jobs in which modern technology is used. In these markets, more qualified labor exists. In the secondary markets, a less advanced technology is used; there are more indefinite, unsecured and undesirable jobs in these markets. There is almost no mobility between the markets. According to this theory, while workers in the primary market are well educated; the workers' education level in the secondary market is not important. On the other hand, it is noted in a research study carried out in the USA on labor markets that the educational level of workers in segmented markets can be effective in terms of crossing markets, but as this is an intrasystem process, it complicates seeing the effects of education (Aksoy, 1999). Although these theories have some critics, they were not opposed to the hypothesis of Human Capital Theory as the basis; they rather played a supplementary role to it.

"Quality" Indicators of Education According to Human Capital Theory

In the Human Capital Theory framework it is expected from the education system that it should ensure qualifications that employers require from students who are seen as potential laborers. Human Capital Theory deals with quality/qualification in education in terms of increasing production and profit besides increasing capital stock. "Quality" indicators are primarily made of values that can be quantified. According to Hanushek (2005), empirical studies on human capital are generally centered on schooling rates. Regarding the relationship between labor's increasing need for literacy and the increase in production efficiency, efforts to extend education became an issue, during the years when mass production was developed. Gannicott & Thorsby (1992) said that the interest was mostly on quantitative extension in education before it focused on "quality in education". Schooling ratio is one of the most used quantified indicators. Adult female and male literacy ratios are also accepted to be important quantitative indicators. When this ratio is almost 100%, it is thought that the country's educational qualification is high. The most common other indicators in the analysis of qualification of education are expenses per student, schooling rates, literacy rates, grade level repetition rates, passing rates, student/teacher ratio, results of international comparison tests and employment rates of graduates and their income. In the studies of Mayer, et al. (2005) on quality indicators, the indicators which are important in terms of "teachers, classes and school" are: Academic abilities of teachers, their teaching experiences in their field, other professional activities, professional development, content of classes, use of technology, size of classes, positive discipline and the academic environment.

Generally while estimating the amount of expenditure per successful student, it is seen that the expenses per student are high in countries where repeating grades and drop-out rates are high. Such estimations suggest one could increase the quality and decrease expenses per student by decreasing the number of students who repeat a grade level or drop out of school. Carnoy (1995) stated that the rate of repeating a grade level and dropping out of school does not show the level of quality in education, because these rates are not related to the quality of previous education, but they represent the appropriateness of the next level. On the other hand, distribution of repeating a grade level and dropping out of school in terms of social classes as groups is important. But these rates are generally taken into consideration as a common problem and the concept of the relationship of failure to "social class", "gender" and "disadvantaged groups" is not taken into consideration. This is put forward as an indicator that is "neutral", impartial", free from classes and groups, or belonging to the personal features and efforts of individuals.

Another indicator of quality of education that is used often is the income of graduates. It is implied that individuals who have high incomes received a "quality" education. Their productivity and performance increase with the amount of quality education and they have higher incomes when compared with others. But the number of the educated unemployed increases daily which creates doubt about the correctness of the views put forward by Human Capital Theory. On the other hand, there are some studies showing that the relationship of employment to education is not very close in terms of new economic relations (Johnston, 2007). According to Aksoy's (2007) research in employment, variables of family, and acquaintance, relationships are more important than the education level in industrial workplaces in Turkey. For instance, most of the positions that have higher incomes are given according to family and other relationships rather than education level, graduation success or productivity. As the saying goes, "It is not what you know but who you know". Nevertheless, in the neoliberal era when public responsibility is rejected, income is more connected to macro politics or an individual's "cultural and social capital" rather than "human capital".

In recent years, international comparison exams have been proposed to measure "quality" in education and the results can be seen as reasons for changing programs at the macro level. In these exams, students from different countries are tested on mathematics and science, and the success of students in these tests show the "quality" of education in these countries. Although there are international exams on literacy and level of understanding of social facts (such as PIRLS: Progress in International Reading Literacy Study, and CIVED: The IEA Civic Education Study), the exams whose results draw attention are science and mathematics exams. Students from economically developed countries usually achieve better results in these tests than those from the countries that have less economical development. There are some views that when countries invest in education, it increases the "quality in education" or economic development speeds up with the "increase in quality" (Hanushek, 2005). Economic development or increase in national income is also seen as indirect indicators of educational quality. Wößmann (2005) compared some variables of students from different countries in the far east (Hong Kong, Japan, Korea, Singapore, Thailand), who were successful in TIMSS exams in terms of their families' education level, gender and age, number of books in their houses, with their grades in international comparison exams. While the study revealed that "quality" is related to some factors besides schools, it is within the boundaries of the premise that "quality" can be measured with international exams. These evaluations through international exams result in the integration of education systems to a global system and accreditation of education systems by global institutions. While it is possible to extend "indicators of quality education" as expenses, financing sources, different levels of educational attendance, unemployment of the youth and adult population, and development in literacy, and rates of university graduation, there are problems in gathering reliable data especially in underdeveloped countries (Welch, 2000).

On the other hand, it has been noted that the priorities used as indicators of quality in education for years have been continuously imposed especially on underdeveloped countries and that they are parallel to World Bank priorities. Additionally research data have been used for supporting the politics that give way to these priorities while the results create a "self-fulfilling prophecy" (Welch, 2000; Saad-Filho & Johnston, 2007). On this point, indicators of quality in education and the basic explanation of education mentioned by Human Capital Theory have been criticized by critical-radical education theorists in addition to some economic approaches which are seen to be in the same category.

Criticisms of Human Capital Theory's Vision of Quality in Education

Explanations about education in Tail, Screening Hypothesis and the Theory of Labor Market Segmentation that are created with and after the Human Capital Theory has the same point of view has been put forward with expectations about the quality of education. The human being is addressed as "homo economicus" in all these educational economic theories. Homo economicus is a human being who values his personal benefits above everything including social benefits, whose only aim is to choose the best tools that will ensure him the greatest benefit and to make the most rational choices. In the theories mentioned above, it is assumed that the biggest goal of "a human being" is to achieve economic interest. Additionally, it is stated that if each individual thinks about maximizing their benefits, then the highest social benefit will be reached.

Critical theorists show that the education process is not as innocent as proposed in human capital and related theories and hypotheses, and instead, try to explain by normative efforts how schools should really be.

Critical theorists try to reveal social and educational realities that were overlooked by Human Capital Theory and other theories. In this way, theorists try to counter not only the theories mentioned above, but also the dominant economics theory which sees all social institutions including education and human beings as at the service of the market. Especially after the 1960s, Marxist theory had an important effect on developing critical, radical discourses and theories in education (Giroux, 1984). According to Marx (1976), what makes a person an individual is his "creative practices". If education moves away from creativity, and is used only as a tool for making money, then the individual becomes alienated from his efforts, from himself and from society as well. During the alienation process, the person becomes *objectified* rather than being the *subject of his own actions;* he comes under the domination of machines, organizations, media and other people and transforms into a being that is directed externally. This situation is in contradiction with the understanding of the "holistic person". Human Capital Theory sees the human body, mind and cognitive abilities as meta, and claim that these meta should become more effective and productive through education. Human Capital Theory breaks an individual's power over his integrity by *separating his efforts and power to exert effort.* The common starting point of critical educators is to ensure that education is seen as a process that gives individuals a critical point of view about power relations rather than the macro education approach that centers on the market and presents a "rational person" model. Spring (1997) said that it is very natural for people who aim at making radical transformations in society to have a very critical attitude towards organized education systems. He emphasizes the political, social and economic role of schools which are the main themes in critical theory.

Seeing people merely as capital, turning labor power into something that can be bought and sold in the market, making education responsible only for developing labor power are the simplest views of Human Capital Theory in the logic of capitalist study. But according to Rikowski (McLaren, et al., 2006, p. 136), the labor force is absolute for all societies in various forms depending on the social formation. Human capital and the labor force should not be considered as identical. While the form of labor forces changes regarding societies, human capital is a phenomenon which only exists in the capitalist society. If we are talking about "labor in the capitalist society", thus, it means we are referring to human capital form of labor as *de facto*.

Some responses to the criticisms of Human Capital Theory are: anything that is sold or prepared to be sold in the market is knowledge, abilities and the effort capacity of human beings rather than the person him/herself and the concept known and sold as meta is neither total wealth nor the effort itself. But the combination of effort force with effort is still a source of depression for those providing the capital (McLaren, et al., 2006, 137–140; Cole, 2005).

While Rikowski (2004, 567–568) stated that capitalism, market and its education and schooling styles should be criticized, these criticisms should be related to the satisfaction of the needs of people. Thus, education in the future should enable students to search for satisfaction of the needs of societies and people beyond the societies. These needs and separating them from desires and wishes should be included in the pedagogy.

According to Bowles & Gintis (1975), Human Capital Theory ignores the class contradictions in societies. Bowles & Gintis (1975) also criticize the fact that the social dimension of education is not taken into consideration and it is only related to production. But, they additionally mention that education cannot have a different function in a capitalist society. According to Bowles & Gintis (1976), reforms in the education system cannot be expected to remove inequalities between classes alone. As the "economic" need for well educated workers increases, inequalities in the education system will become more and more important in order to create social classes continuously from one generation to another (Bowles, 2001). But according to critical theorists, schools and the whole education system are places of conflict, and struggles will occur just as in the other places of conflict.

Althusser (1992, 2002) divided the capitalist state's institutions into "oppressive and ideological apparatuses of the state". These apparatuses complete each other. While Althusser (2002) defined school as an ideological apparatus, he emphasized "the function of re-production of education" that is ensured through schools. Children whose families are raised with capitalist values will be raised as qualified workers and interiorize the values of capitalism. In parallel with this explanation, Martell (2006) stated that capitalism needs workers, citizens and consumers that voluntarily do whatever is asked of them and accept everything they are told in the way it is told. According to Martell (2006, 3), the "creation of such a human capital is the most basic role of schools in capitalist societies".

Bourdieu & Passeron (1970/1990) stated that cultural capitals of groups that are dominant in the society are turned into cash in schools in order to protect the hegemony of these groups and cultural capital is used as a device to divide students in the society properly into classes. Bourdieu's studies, on the place of some concepts such as habitus, social class, and pedagogical activity and especially "cultural capital" in different fields, include some criticisms about liberal-neoliberal politics and Human Capital Theory that sees education only as an economic investment which is isolated from class relations (Grenfell, 2010).

Apple notes critically that the function of schools today is to distribute professional positions to children; if this happens, then the other important functions of schools will be ignored. He stated in his criticisms that schools are not the only places where hidden curriculums are experienced, vocational information is given, graduates are assigned to the job market, but they are also places that reproduce dominance relations that are significant in terms of meta production and dominant ideology (Apple, 1984/2006).

The "sociocultural transactional model of education" suggests that the definition of education should be focused on socializing and transaction rather than on economical concepts, shows that the effect of schooling and literacy in interpersonal relations indirectly result in economic mobility also. This model criticizes Human Capital Theory and education definitions based on the economy (Bartlett, 2007). In his ethnographic study over two years in Brazil, Bartlett (2007) stated that socialization, that is, learning communication and expressing oneself, is one of the important acquisitions of literacy studies. The findings of this study show that an increase in literacy abilities does not directly lead economic mobility (increase in income, new job opportunities etc.), so it is impossible to mention any autonomous "literacy effect". This study shows that social networking is a key factor for economic mobility, and schooling contributes to the expansion of social networking; the economic mobility of students and adults (with some exceptions) is related to personal relations, not to literacy. This study emphasizes the value of re-conceptualizing the meaning of education as "interaction" (Bartlett, 2007).

In underdeveloped countries (periphery of the world capitalist system), there are gender related and regional inequalities in addition to income differences in using educational rights (Ercan, 1998; Eğitim-Sen, 2005; UNESCO, 2006). In this case, decreasing the inequalities between regions and gender are accepted to be one of the primary quality indicators. Ignoring all these inequalities and taking international exams in order to reach standardization in education are the other issues that are criticized. In recent years, just as in the economic sectors, the issues of high qualification, sufficiency and success have become external and relative concepts in the education field (Aksoy, 2003).

Basic Concept and Approaches Put Forward by Critical Education Theorists

According to critical thinkers, the human being is beyond "homo economicus". Rather than merely accepting the human being as a species imbued with the ambition to possess things, critical thinkers see humans as a species involved in intellectual production, and emphasize that individuals' personal and intellectual development should be supported and they should be entitled to a *critical way of thinking*". One of the most important tools in ensuring this point of view is the basic concepts and approaches of the education process (Wulf, 2010).

Sharing concepts and meanings that can be used in transforming the discourse and language that exclude humanity and replace it with "profit", market and economy instead are accepted to be significant by critical education thinkers. After the 1980s, there has been a strong "blockade" and "hegemony" by the implementers of neo-liberal politics (eg. by the World Bank, International Monetary Fund, World Trade Organization) through their agreements on the critical concepts and discussions about education systems world-wide.

Some of the concepts and methodologies that are accepted by critical education thinkers include: Enlightenment, participation, solidarity, dialogue, social justice, equality, equity, subjectivity, emancipation, autonomy, humanization, diversity, multiculturalism, democratic education, right to education, public education, free education, culture, habitus, social classes, problem posing education, social construction of knowledge, freeing information, holistic human, power relations, real necessities of human, emancipatory knowledge as opposed to a technical-practical one, praxis, society-individual balance, production relations, social reproduction, deconstruction, oppression, discrimination, racism, sexism, gender roles, alienation, othering, market centeredness, commercialization, commodification, privatization, human capital, competition, performance, profitability, objectification, hidden curriculum, hegemony, cultural capital etc.

Rikowski (2004) said that education of the future will be anti-capitalist, and emphasized that this education system is critical; it is connected to human needs and gives priority to the freedom of human beings. Education is a process needed for the *liberation* of humans, for ensuring them to take personal responsibilities, for becoming the *subject of relationships;* in short it is needed for *humanization.*

Paulo Freire (2003), one of the pioneers of critical pedagogy, draws our attention to the fact that oppressors think that only they are the "human beings" and the others are "objects". According to Freire (2003), an education system that is shaped by market conditions sees students as the objects of production, and he stressed instead an education that centers on humanistic values. In the "problem posing education" suggested by Freire, education is not reduced to a process in which students' empty minds are filled with the teachers' own words, but instead the student is seen as the subject of the learning process which is the activity of recognition and creation. Freire also emphasized the importance of dialogue and said that the understanding level of individuals that are being educated should be respected (Freire & Macedo, 1998). As mentioned by Leonardo (2004), most of the readers of critical social theories in education are accustomed to political statements and concepts different from the ones that look at quality/qualification in education in the frame of Human Capital Theory and related theories. Leonardo cites some of these such as "pedagogy of the oppressed" (Freire, 2003), "predatory culture", "ideology and curriculum", "struggle for pedagogies", "dancing with bigotry", "globalization of white supremacy", "knowledge, power and discourse", "discourse wars", "education under siege" and "teaching to transgress" (all cited in, Leonardo, 2004). Although these concepts are known by the critical theory academics, this is a limited mass. Mayo, also attracts our attention to Freire and Gramsci with many of critical concepts and approaches which enable us to strengthen our minds against oppressive and non-humanized educational practices, especially regarding to adult education. (Mayo, 1999:2008).

Final Words

In this study the economics of education theories' views on quality of education have been discussed. We conclude that market driven quality indicators that are revealed by human capital theory and other hypotheses derived from human capital theory ignore the inequalities and injustices in society. This ignorance results in tacit support for the injustices. So in order to reach a more equal world, to be emancipatory in this world and to have a more humane education the critical educational theories' concepts of qualified education must become the main topic of the educational agenda.

The critical concepts discussed in this study lead us to conclude that true "quality education" helps students realize social injustices and motivates them to search for emancipation. Educational quality indicators based on the tenets of neo-liberalism work as a hegemonic paradigm of Human Capital Theory related to the economic role of education. This should be reviewed continuously in order to prevent alienation and to encourage education to promote humanization in a holistic manner. Education policies should reflect humanistic considerations. The duty of including more humanitarian premises in education belongs not only to administrators or politicians that determine the education policies, but also to all academicians, teachers, students, families and education unionists who can see the results of goals, practices, criteria and discussions, and who are also affected by them. Concepts and methodologies related to the critical education include dynamics that will transform the qualifications of the educational process in addition to the perception of educators about education and their own roles in it.

NOTES

[1] A Turkish version of the paper was published in 2011 as "Eğitimde Nitelik: Eğitim Ekonomisi Kuramlarinin Eğitimin Niteliğine İlişkin Kurgusunun Eleştirel Analizi". in *Eğitim Bilim Toplum*, 9(33), pp. 60–99. Permission for an English version of the study was provided by the Journal.

REFERENCES

Abalı, G. (2007). Kalitenin Göreliliği. [Relativity of the Quality]. *Abece Eğitim ve Ekin Dergisi 248*. 2–7.
Adams, D. (1993). Defining educational quality. [Defining Educational Quality]. *Educational Planning*. 9(3), 3–18.
Aksoy, H. H. (1999). Relationship between education and employment: How do employers use educational indicators in hiring? Results from a participatory observation. *Journal of Interdisciplinary Education, 3*(1), 171–187.
Aksoy, H. H. (2008). Standard ve Standardlaştırma. [Standard and Standardization]. In Başkaya, F., Ördek, A. (Ed.) *Ekonomik Kurumlar ve Kavramlar Sözlüğü. Eleştirel Bir Giriş*. Ankara, Özgür Üniversite Yayınları. 1045–1058.
Aksoy, H. H. (2003). Uluslararası Karşılaştırma Ölçütlerinin Kullanımı ve Türkiye. [Using of International Comparison Criteria and Turkey]. *Eğitim Bilim Toplum*. Winter, *1*(1), 51–60.
Aksoy, H. H. (2007). Career and training in the new economy: A study focused to small scale enterprises located in OSTIM Organized Industrial Region in Ankara/Turkey. *Educational Sciences: Theory & Practice 7*(3), 1067–1084.
Aksoy, N. (2010). Hidden commercialization in Turkish public education: corporate social responsibility and its function in commercialization of education. Paper presented at *XIV World congress of WCCES bordering, re-bordering and new possibilities in education and society*. Istanbul, June, 14–18, 2010.
Althusser, L. (1992). Louis Althusser ideology and ideological state apparatus. In Easthope, A. McGowan, K. (Eds.). *A critical and cultural theory reader*. Open University Press. 50–58.
Althusser, L. (2002). *İdeoloji ve Devletin İdeolojik Aygıtları*.[Ideology and Ideological Apparatus of State] İstanbul: İletişim Publications.
Apple, M. (1984/2006). *Eğitim ve İktidar*. [Education and Power]. (Trs. E. Bulut). Istanbul. Kalkedon. (Originally published at 1984).
Apple, M. (1989). *Teachers and texts. A political economy of class and gender relations in education*. New York: Routledge, Charman and Hall Inc.
Apple, M. W. (2011). Rightist education and godly technology: cultural politics, gender, and the work of Home Schooling. *Multidisciplinary Journal of Educational Research, 1*(1), 5–33. doi:10.4452/ remie.2011.01

Aspin, D. N., Chapman, J. D., & Wilkinson, W. R. (1994). *Quality schooling. A pragmatic approach to some current problems, topics, and issues.* Cassell Villiers House.

Ball, S., & Youdell, D. (2008). *Hidden privatisation.* Research report. Brussels: Education International. http://download.eiie.org/docs/IRISDocuments/Research%20Website-%20Documents/2009–00034–01-E.pdf (Retrieved: 13 December 2010).

Bartlett, L. (2007). Human capital or human connections? The cultural meanings of education in Brasil. *Teachers College Record, 109*(7). 1613–1636. http://www.tcrecord.org (Retrieved: 27 June, 2009).

Becker, G. S. (1962). Investment in human capital: A theoretical analysis. *Journal of Political Economy. Supplement, 70*(5), 9–49. Part 2: Investment in Human Beings.

Becker, G. S. (1993). *Human capital: A theoretical and empirical analysis, with special reference to education.* Chicago: University of Chicago Press. (Originally published at 1964)

Berliner, D. C., & Biddle, B. J. (1997). *The manufactured crisis. Myts, fraud, and the attack on America's public schools* (2nd ed.). New York: Addison-Wesley Publishing Company, Inc.

Blaug, M. (1995). Wage Labour and Education. In Carnoy, M. (Ed.) *International encyclopedia of economics of education* (2nd ed.), (pp. 44–52). Oxford: Elsevier Science Ltd.

Bourdieu, P. & Passeron, J. C. (1970/1990). *Reproduction in education, society and culture.* (Trs. from French to English R. Nice) (2nd ed.). London: Sage Publications. (Originally published at 1970).

Bowles, S. (2001). Unequal education and the reproduction of the social division of labor. In Strouse, J. H. (Ed.). *Exploring socio-cultural themes in education* (pp. 120–126). Merrill Prentice Hall.

Bowles, S., & Gintis, H. (1975). The problem with human capital theory. *The American Economic Review, 65*(2). American Economic Association.

Bowles, S., & Gintis, H. (1976). *Schooling in capitalist America.* New York: Basic Books Publishers.

Broadberry, S. N., & Wagner, K. (1996). Human Capital and Productivity in Manufacturing During the Twentiety Century: Britain, German and the United States. Van Ark, B., Craft, N. (Ed.) *Quantitative aspects of post-war European growth.* Vol. I, New York, NY: Press Syndicate of University of Cambridge. 244–270.

Carlin, W. (1993). *West German growth and institutions, 1945–90.* CEPR Conference on Postwar Growth in Oxford,. http://www.ucl.ac.uk/~uctpa36/-west%20germany%20in%20crafts%20toniolo.pdf (Retrieved:15 Dec. 2010)

Carnoy, M. (1982/1990). Eğitim ve Ekonomi İlişkisi. [Economics and Education].(Trs. N.Tural.) *Ankara Üniversitesi Eğitim Bilimleri Fakültesi Dergisi, 22*(1), 485–504. (Originally published at 1982).

Carnoy, M. (1995). Benefits of Improving the Quality of Education. In Carnoy, M. (Ed.), *International Encyclopedia of Economics of Education* (2nd ed.) (pp. 154–159). Oxford: Elsevier Science Ltd.

Cheng, Y. C., & Tam, W. M. (1997). Multi-models of quality in education. *Quality Assurance in Education, 5*(1), 22–31.

Cole, M. (2005). New Labor, Globalization, and social justice: The role of education. In Fischman, G. E., McLaren, P., Sünker, H. & Lankshear, C. (Ed.). *Critical theories, radical pedagogies, and global conflicts,* Lanham. Rowman & Littlefield Publishers, INC. 3–22.

Coleman, J. (1988). Social capital in the creation of human capital. *American Journal of Sociology, 94,* Supplement. 95–120.

De Castell, S., Bryson, M., & Jenson, J. (2002). Object lessons: Towards an educational theory of technology. *First Monday, 7*(1), 1–7 Journal URL: http://firstmonday.org/

Denison, E. F. (1962) Education, Economic Growth, and Gaps in Information. *Journal of Political Economy, Supplement, 70*(5), 124–128

Eğitim-Sen. (2005). *4. Demokratik Eğitim Kurultayı, Eğitim Hakkı .* [Democratic Education Convension, Right for Education] Vol. 1. Ankara: Eğitim Sen Publications.

Ehrlich, I., & Murphy, K. (2007). Why does human capital need a journal. *Journal of Human Capital. 1*(1), 1–7.

Ercan, F. (1998). *Eğitim ve Kapitalizm.*[Education and Capitalism]. İstanbul: Bilim Publishing.

European Commission (2000). *European report on the quality of school education sixteen quality indicators report based on the work of the working committee on quality indicators.* http://ec.europa.eu/education/policies/educ/indic/rapinen.pdf

Farenga, P. (2006/2008). Eğitimin Temelleri. [Foundations of Education]. In Hern, M. (Ed.). *Alternatif Eğitim. Hayatımızı Okulsuzlaştırmak.* İstanbul: Kalkedon Publishing, 251–256. (Originally published at 2006.)

Feenberg, A. (1999a). Whither educational technology? *Peer Review. 1*(4). Summer. http://www-rohan. sdsu.edu/faculty/feenberg/peer4.html. (Retrieved: 15th May, 2007).

Feenberg, A. (1999b). *Questioning technology.* London and New York: Routledge. Taylor and Francis Group.

Freire, P. (2003). *Ezilenlerin Pedagojisi.* [Pedagogy of Oppressed]. (Trs. D.Hattatoğlu-E. Özbek). İstanbul: Ayrıntı Publishing.

Freire, P., & Macedo, D. (1998). *Okuryazarlık: Sözcükleri ve Dünyayı Okuma.* [Literacy: Reading the Word and the World. (Trs. S. Ayhan). İstanbul: İmge Publishing House.

Gannicott, K., & C. D. Throsby. (1992). Educational quality in economic development: Ten propositions and an application to the South Pacific. *International Review of Education, 38*(3), 223–239.

Georgiadis, N. M. (2007). Educational reforms in Greece (1959–1997) and human capital theory. *JCEPS: 5*(2). http://www.jceps.com/?pageID=article &articleID=105

Giroux, H. A. (1984). Marxism and schooling: The limits of radical discourse. *Educational Theory, 34*(2), 113–135.

Grenfell, Michael. (2010). *Pierre bourdie: Key concepts* (3rd ed.). Durham, Acumen Publishing Ltd.

Hanushek, E. A., Benson, C. S., & Others (1994). *Making schools work improving performance and controlling cost.* The Brooking Institution, Washington D.C.

Hanushek, E. (2005). The economics of school quality. *German Economic Rewiev, 6*(3), 269–286.

Johnston, D. (2007). Yoksulluk ve Bölüşüm: Yeniden mi Neoliberal Gündemde? In Saad-Filho, A. & Johnston, D. (Eds.). *Neoliberalizm. Muhalif Bir Seçki.* [Neoliberalism: A Critical Reader.] (Trs. Ş.Başlı & T. Öncel) pp. 225–235. İstanbul, Yordam Publishing.

Johnson, K. A. (2003). The downside to small class policies. In Noll, J. W. (Ed.) *Taking sides clashing views on controversial educational issues* (pp. 273–276). Connecticut: McGraw-Hill/Dushkin.

Kılınçalp, N. (2007). Okul Aile Birliklerinin Etkinlikleri ve Sorunlarına İlişkin Yöneticilerinin Görüşleri. Ankara İli Altındağ, Yenimahalle ve Çankaya İlçeleri Örneği. [Activities of Parent Teacher Associations and Views of Their Administrators About Their Problems. Sample of Ankara Province Altındağ, Yenimahalle and Çankaya Districs] Unpublished Thesis of Master of Science. Ankara University Institute of Educational Sciences.

Leonardo, Z. (2004). Critical social theory and transformative knowledge: The functions of criticism in quality education. *Educational Researcher, 33*(6), 11–18.

Levin, H. M. (1995). Work and education. In Carnoy, M. (Ed.) *International encyclopedia of economics of education.* Second Edition. Oxford: Elsevier Science Ltd. 10–19.

López, R., Thomas, V., & Wang, Y. (1998). *Addressing the education puzzle: The distribution of education and economic reforms.* World Bank. http://www-wds.worldbank.org/ servlet/WDSContentServer/ WDSP/IB/2000/02/24/000094946_99031911111953/Rendered/PDF/multi_page.pdf

Martell, M. (2006). Introduction. In Martell, G. (Ed.). *Education's iron cage: And its dismantling in the new global order. Canadian center for policy alter* pp. 1–15.

Marx, K. (1976). *1844 Elyazmaları, Ekonomi Politik ve Felsefe,* [Economic and Philosophic Manuscripts of 1844] (1st ed.) (Trs. K. Somer). Ankara:Sol Publications.

Mayer, D. P., Mullens, J. E., & Moore M. T. (2005). Monitoring school quality. *Education Statistics Quarterly 3*(1). http://nces.ed.gov

Mayo, P. (1999). *Gramsci, freire and adult education: Possibilities for transformative action.* London: Zed Books.

Mayo, P. (2008). *Liberating praxis. Paulo Freire's legacy for radical education and politics.* Rotterdam: Sense Publishers.

McLaren, P., Rikowski, G., Cole, M., & Hill, D. (2006). *Kızıl Tebeşir. Eğitim Söyleşileri.* [Red Chalk: On Schooling, Capitalism and Politics]. İstanbul: Kalkedon Publications.

Postman, N. (2004). *Televizyon Öldüren Eğlence Gösteri Çağında Kamusal Söylem.* [Amusing Ourselves to Death: Public Discourse in the Age of Show Business] (Trs. O. Akınhay). İstanbul: Ayrıntı Publishing.

Psacharopoulos, G. (1973). *Returns to education: An international comparison.* Amsterdam: Elsevier.
Psacharopoulos, G. (1981). Returns to education: An updated international comparison. *Comparative Education, 17,* 321–341.
Rikowski, G. (2004). Marx and the education of future. *Policy Futures in Education, 2*(3–4), 567–568.
Saad-Filho, A., & Johnston, D. (2007). *Neoliberalizm. Muhalif Bir Seçki.* [Neoliberalism: A Critical Reader]. (Trs. Ş. Başlı ve T. Öncel). İstanbul: Yordam Publishing.
Schultz. T. W. (1962). Reflections on investment in man. *Journal of Political Economy.* Supplement. *70*(5), pp. 1–8. Part 2: Investment in Human Beings.
Schultz, T. W. (1966). Beşeri Sermayeye Yapılan Yatırım. [Investment in Human Capital]. In M. Berk., F. Gönün. & S. İlkin. (Ed.). *İktisadi Kalkınma Seçme Yazılar.* Ankara: METU Faculty of Management Sciences Publications. 406–424.
Spring, J. (1997). *Özgür Eğitim.* [A Primer of Libertarian Education].(Trs. A. Ekmekçi). İstanbul: Ayrıntı Publishing.
UNESCO. (2006). *Education for all. Global monitoring report. Strong foundations early childhood care and education.* Paris. Unesco Publishing.
Wasley, P. A. (2003). Small classes, small schools: The time is now. In J. W. Noll (Ed.) *Taking sides clashing views on controversial educational issues,* 268–272. Connecticut. McGraw-Hill/Dushkin.
Welch, A. R. (2000). Quality and equality in third world education. In A. R. Welch. (Ed.). *Third world education: Quality and equality.* London, UK. Garland Science.
Woodhall, M. (1987). Human capital concepts. In G. Psacharopoulos (Ed.) *Economics of education,* (pp. 21–24). Oxford: Pergamon Press.
Woodhall, M. (1995). Human capital concepts. In Carnoy, M. (Ed.), *International encyclopedia of economics of education,* (2nd ed.), (pp. 24–28). Oxford: Elsevier Science Ltd.
Wößmann, L. (2005). Educational production in east Asia: The impact of family background and schooling policies on student performance. *German Economic Review 6*(3), 331–353. doi: 10.1111/j.1468–0475.2005.00136.x
Wulf. C. (2010). *Eğitim Bilimi. Yorumsamacı Yöntem, Görgül Araştırma, Eleştirel Teori.* [Educational Science- Hermeneutics, Empirical Research, Critical Theory] (Trs. H. H. Aksoy, H. Ö. Aras, A. Kayahan). Ankara: Dipnot Publishing.

AFFILIATIONS

Hasan Hüseyin Aksoy
Ankara University

Aygülen Karahan Karakul
Ministry of Education Turkey

Hatice O. Aras
Technology & Design Teacher, Istanbul

Dilek Çankaya
Doctoral Student, Ankara University

PART II

EDUCATION AND DEVELOPMENT
IN A NEOLIBERAL WORLD

SUZANNE MAJHANOVICH

HOW THE ENGLISH LANGUAGE CONTRIBUTES TO SUSTAINING THE NEOLIBERAL AGENDA: ANOTHER TAKE ON THE STRANGE NON-DEMISE OF NEOLIBERALISM[1]

CONTEXT

By 2008 when it appeared as if the American and European markets would crash and that the world was on the verge of an economic depression, economists from both the left and right began to proclaim the end of neoliberalism, or at least of some of its basic features exemplified by, for example, the Washington Consensus. Nobel laureate, Joseph Stiglitz, in a 2008 interview with the *Berliner Zeitung* said "the philosophy of deregulation is dead". He added further that "Neoliberalism like the Washington Consensus is dead in most Western countries" (Stiglitz, 2008a and b). Under the circumstances, it was difficult for right wing pundits to continue to support the notion that the market is best left to its own devices and will always correct itself when problems arise. Deregulation to enable increasing trade openness had not worked. Ironically, the financial institutions that had in the boom times demanded that government stay away from the working of the market now found themselves in need of government bailouts to avoid collapse. The Western governments felt that the institutions were too big to fail fearing that if the banks and corporations were to collapse, they would take the whole economy down with them plunging the whole world into economic depression, with massive unemployment. Despite the knowledge that bailouts would ultimately have to be paid for by the tax payers, even tax averse factions held their noses and agreed to the bailouts and stimulus financing in some areas to keep the economy going. An economic depression was averted, at least in the developed North, but to prevent further deficits, austerity became the rule of the day. Strangely enough, although it was manifestly clear that it was financiers who had caused the problems by taking advantage of an overly deregulated market to implement reckless and questionable practices, yet, they somehow escaped censure, and often were even able to reward themselves for their practices, ending up wealthier than before. But working class people were suffering greatly: unemployment was rising, secure jobs with benefits were not returning, unions were bullied into bargaining away hard won rights and privileges for workers, and were even deemed the cause of the economic problems (Krugman, 2013). Disparity between the small number of extremely wealthy and the rest of the populace, seeing its standard of living plummeting has been growing steadily.

S. Majhanovich and M.A. Geo-JaJa (Eds.), Economics, Aid and Education: Implications for Development, 79–96.

It is no wonder then that there was a call for a return to regulation, a reintroduction of checks and balances and a more sober approach to economic management. And yet, five years down the road, the market and economy have not fully recovered, and the neoliberal market agenda, albeit a bit restrained seems to prevail. Economists in the US and European Union continue to express trust that the market will keep the world economy moving forward, but also push governments to impose austerity measures on the people that will see secure jobs ever harder to win, lower salaries for those with jobs, and few or no benefits. Youth in particular are struggling the hardest to find their way in these brutal, cutthroat economic times. Meanwhile the super-rich and the corporations they control continue to pull in huge profits while unemployment remains unacceptably high. Francis Fukuyama, who in "The End of History" exulted over the triumph of Western ways when Communism came to an end in Europe, now in an article entitled "The Future of History" is concerned about whether liberal democracy will prevail in a neoliberal world that is damaging the middle class. He has said: "The current form of globalized capitalism is eroding the middle class social base on which liberal democracy rests" (Fukuyama, 2012). Joseph Stiglitz, (2008b) had anticipated the problem when he observed "Today, there is a mismatch between social and private returns. Unless they are closely aligned, the market system cannot work well."

Neoliberal market fundamentalism was always a political doctrine serving certain interests. It was never supported by economic theory." Stiglitz (2013) echoes Fukuyama's concern about the faltering middle class when he notes, "there is a worldwide crisis in inequality. The problem is not only that the top income groups are getting a larger share of the economic pie, but also that those in the middle are not sharing in economic growth, while in many countries poverty is increasing. In the US, equality of opportunity has been exposed as a myth" (p. 2). This paper discusses in general the economic conditions particularly in the developing world, and how market fundamentalism despite is flaws and abject failures has managed to continue as the dominant framework. It also looks at the effect of the new world order on higher education. Finally, it suggests that language, especially the English language as the *lingua franca* of commerce has helped to cement the continuing neoliberal discourse of the primacy of the market.

GLOBALIZATION AS NEO-COLONIALISM

Globalization as seen in a benign light is associated with the breaking down of borders, the speed of communication around the world as a result of technological advances and the freeing up of markets.
As Tsui and Tollefson (2006) define it:

[I]t is typified by time-space compression, captured in the metaphor of the *global village,* and characterized by interconnectivity (…) as well as intensity, simultaneity, and instantaneity of knowledge generation, information transmission, and interaction. (…) [It] is effected by two inseparable mediational tools, technology and English (p. 1).

There is no doubt that our world is a more homogenized and more accessible place today, and that those with the technical wherewithal benefit enormously from the speed at which communication and interchanges can be made from anywhere in the world.

The new technology has made possible the outsourcing of labour so that, for example, when a person in Canada experiences a problem with a computer from an American company but assembled in China, and seeks technical assistance by telephone, she will inevitably find herself speaking to someone in India or in the Philippines, and miraculously the problem will be solved. But although this technical miracle benefits the computer owner and contributes to rising standards of living in formerly developing countries, it also has a negative effect on workers in the West who have lost their position to cheaper labour elsewhere. In this way, the dark side of globalization as an expression of economic liberalism is revealed. Bourdieu (2001) warned of this hegemonic result of globalization when he wrote:

> "Globalization" serves as a password, a watchword while in effect, it is the legitimatory mask of a policy aiming to universalize particular interests, and the particular tradition of the economically and politically dominant powers, above all the United States, and to extend to the entire world the economic and cultural model that favours these powers most, while simultaneously presenting it as a norm, a requirement (p. 84).

Of course, it is becoming clear that the dominant powers do not necessarily represent the government of the United States but rather the power represented by transnational corporations, and by organizations such as the World Bank (WB), the International Monetary Fund (IMF) and the World Trade Organization (WTO), organizations that have tirelessly put forward neoliberal initiatives through the Washington Consensus. Because the discourse of market fundamentalism under neoliberal globalization has taken hold, government involvement has drastically declined. Consequently privatization, deregulation and decentralization proceed apace to give free rein to the market. There is a sorry history of how this new version of *laissez-faire* economics has been imposed on struggling nations around the world, and the havoc resulting for the citizens of those countries (See Geo-JaJa & Mangum, 2003 and Abdi, 2012). The neoliberal project was imposed through European and US-controlled International Monetary Fund (IMF) and the World Bank. These agents of neoliberalism were able to exert their will on struggling countries in Latin and South America, in Africa as well as in former Communist bloc countries. More recently European Union countries in economic straits, Ireland, Greece, Spain and Cyprus have also had to accept harsh austerity plans in order to start to pay off their debt loads.

STRUCTURAL ADJUSTMENT PROGRAMS IN AFRICA

The draconian solution exacted by the IMF and the WB is best embodied in the Structural Adjustment Programs (SAPs) that have been imposed on debt-ridden countries since the 1980s with the stated aim of righting economic woes, repaying debts and encouraging growth, but usually with disastrous results and growing impoverishment for the populace (Geo-JaJa & Mangum, 2001, Abdi, 2012) The familiar pattern of a few, connected to transnational companies, along with the companies' directors benefitting enormously, while the general populace struggles to eke out a living in appalling conditions has been the unfortunate result of SAP imposition. When one considers what structural adjustment entails; namely, privatization and deregulation, which undermines the influence of governments, and transfers power to market interests with program conditionalities such as cuts to social programs, especially in areas of education, health and housing; currency devaluation, concentration on commodities attractive for exportation to the detriment of, local food consumable goods and services, it becomes clear that the SAP plan was never intended to better the lot of developing nations, but rather to re-colonize them and ensure that economic benefits flow to the transnational or wealthy donor countries of the G8. One of the most egregious examples was the privatization of water in Bolivia where the local populace could not afford to access their own national resource and thus were unable to water crops, and produce feed for their animals, let alone provide drinking water for their families. Is it any wonder that riots and civil unrest often ensue from imposed Structural Adjustment Programs? The Structural Adjustment Programs have been severely criticized for many years causing what has been called "a race to the bottom" for poor developing nations who experience increased dependency on the richer nations while falling into ever deeper poverty. (See Global Issues, 1998/2013:http://www.globalissues.org/article/3/structural-adjustments-a-major-cause-of-poverty)

Countries that have experienced the harsh and negative effects of a SAP include Algeria, Benin, Bolivia, Ecuador, Niger, Nigeria, Russia, Sudan, Uganda and Venezuela among others (Global Issues article on Structural Adjustment, 1998/2013). The problem of policy rhetoric versus reality with regard to SAPs around the world has been well documented, particularly for Africa. (See Geo-JaJa & Mangum, 2001). Geo-JaJa & Mangum (2003) and Geo-JaJa (2004) have focused on damage to education in Nigeria as a result of SAPs related policies of decentralization and privatization of education. As Abdi (2013) has noted about the effect of SAPs on Africa,

One can look at what SAPs have achieved for Africa in the past 30 or so years, and from any pragmatic perspective, the picture is anything but encouraging. So much so that one might not help but assume the intentions of the IFIs (International Financial Institutions) were never formulated to fulfil their rhetorical representations. Indeed, the very nature of SAPs i.e., what they are at their core, is not compatible with the basic structures and practices of African life. At their core, SAPs are one important part of globalization, but at a sub-level, they are to fulfill the requirements of the dominant neo-liberal political and economic agenda where the practices of supply side economics, in which in the context of non-interventionist and unregulated market driven relationships, supply creates its own demand (p. 354).

Indeed, even the WB and IMF eventually recognized problems with SAPs, and in 1999 replaced them with a program they called Poverty Reduction Growth Facility (PRGF). They also renamed the Policy Framework Papers as the Poverty Reduction Strategy Papers (PSRP). Unfortunately, the harmful conditionalities mandated by SAPS are still being imposed:

> [T]he PRSP process is simply delivering repackaged structural adjustment programmes (SAPs). It is not delivering poverty-focused development plans and it has failed to involve civil society and parliamentarians in economic policy discussions. *(PRSPs just PR say civil society groups, Bretton Woods Project Update #23, June/July 2001,* cited in Global Issues article on Structural Adjustment, 1998/2013).

That neo-liberal economic policy still prevails in 2013 can be seen in an item from Canada's most recent federal budget where the Canadian International Development Agency (CIDA), previously a semi-autonomous organization dedicated to overcoming inequality globally by providing aid to developing countries and mounting development projects in education, agriculture, water management, and the like has been taken over by the Foreign Affairs and International Trade Department. Now rather than addressing inequities in the developing world, the priority will be placed on potential economic benefits to Canada and private commercial interests through various projects. As Jill Allison, writing in the *Globe and Mail* puts it "CIDA, the agency meant to respond to global inequities, has been fully co-opted into the Harper government's agenda that puts the economic interests of the few ahead of the social interests of the many" (Allison, *Globe & Mail*, Letters to the Editor, March 25, 2013, p. A10). There have been justified concerns in the past about aid to Africa not meeting real needs of the countries or people, but this cynical move by Canada's government ensures that in future, the priority of aid projects in Africa and elsewhere will be on profit to corporations rather than to locally identified areas of need to assist in real development of nations.

IS EDUCATION PART OF THE PROBLEM OR PART OF THE SOLUTION?

Education has long been considered as a necessary element for social advancement and sustainable development. However, the kind of schooling one receives and the curriculum studied may or may not contribute to helping people reach their full potential and ready themselves for a functional role or place in society. Since formal schooling often acts to inculcate the values and culture of the dominant establishment powers, outliers are often badly served. The residential schools in Canada provide a particularly egregious example. The colonial rulers reasoned that by removing young indigenous children from their families and placing them in residential schools, they could assimilate them to the ruling European culture and destroy their traditions and ways of knowing which the colonizers considered to be inferior and pagan, as well as ensure that they lost their native languages. Teachers in the residential schools by and large subjected the native children to brutal treatment, and the "education" they received was meant to prepare menial workers who could serve the colonial masters. Incredibly, the last residential school in Canada only closed in 1996. Many reports have detailed the havoc wrought on indigenous people of North America, including "loss of language, grade retardation, high dropout rates, rampant physical, sexual and emotional abuse, alienation and intergenerational communication breakdown" (Binda & Lall, 2013, p. 16; see also Aboriginal Healing Foundation, 2009; Canadian Council on Learning, 2007; Royal Commission on Aboriginal Peoples, 1996; Assembly of First Nations, 1994).

Colonized peoples around the world suffered similar fates under colonial imposition of a European schooling system that was usually not at all relevant to their lives and experience, and further, was designed to train only a small percentage of the locals as elites who would carry out the bidding of the colonial masters and act as intermediaries with the local populace who would be the unskilled labourers. The practice of providing schooling in a colonial language and downplaying or ignoring local languages ensured that large numbers of students would never be able to complete schooling. It is after all, difficult if not impossible to learn concepts in a language one does not understand (See Babaci-Wilhite, Geo-JaJa & Lou 2012)

Most colonized countries in Africa gained their independence by the 1960s. And yet the school system continues largely to be modeled on the European system, the language of instruction usually a colonial one, at least in secondaryand tertiary levels. Despite years of research showing the importance of having the medium of instruction (MoI) in native, local languages (Brock-Utne, 2000, 2001), European languages still prevail as the MoI, particularly at the tertiary level, but also at the secondary and even primary levels in some cases. So firmly entrenched is the notion of the superiority of northern European education as opposed to the apparent irrelevance of local languages and cultures in a globalized world, that policy makers and parents are convinced that their children will never be able to participate and succeed in the global economy unless they have mastered its language—usually the English language. Despite failure and dropouts from the European system and clear indications that European style education is not working, oddly enough, no one seems to be suggesting alternative types of education such as Freire (1970/2000) might have championed that would focus on grassroots needs and work from the ground up rather than top down imposition. Instead, failures are blamed on the "lazy" students and poor teachers although little is done to help prepare teachers better. So people in the developing world continue to pursue an English education as recommended in our neo-liberal globalized world where the language of business, and commerce, as well as of the powerful international agencies like the World Bank is English.

Even in countries where policies were created to allow for indigenous languages or a national language other than English to be the Medium of Instruction as in South Africa and Tanzania, the results have not been promising. Local languages are used only for the first few years at the primary level after which the MoI becomes a European language, predominantly English. Tanzania had committed to making Swahili the MoI at the secondary and tertiary levels (Babaci-Wilhite, 2013) but gradually English is making inroads again as the main language of instruction under the pressure of parents and government policy makers. In South Africa, despite promising results when local languages were the MoI in the first three years of primary school, plans have not proceeded to continue the local languages in subsequent grades (Mbekwa & Nomlomo, 2013). The situation in Asia is similar. Malaysia provides an interesting example. After first doing away with the trappings of colonial education such as use of English as MoI throughout the system along with graduation requirements including Cambridge administered O- and A-level tests, and replacing them by education in the national language, Bahasa Malaysia, in 2002, the government decided to require that Mathematics and Science from primary grades onwards would be taught in English, on the grounds that subjects such as Science, Information Technology (IT) and Mathematics, important for admission and success in the global economy required competence in English. However, after years of disappointing test results, lack of qualified teachers able to instruct the subjects in English, as well as resistance from the Chinese and Tamil minority groups, the government decided to revert to the old system and end the experiment of English as MoI for Science and Mathematics in the primary and secondary levels. (See Majhanovich 2013, Babaci-Wilhite 2013). Nevertheless, English as MoI in higher education in Malaysia continues apace. Also expensive private education in English is available and draws children of affluent Malaysian parents.

The widespread imposition of SAPs and more recently the Poverty Reduction Strategy Papers (PRSP)—which were supposed to respond to the abysmal failure of the Structural Adjustment Programs—have contributed to the entrenchment of European style education programs or internationalization of education in developing countries. The SAPs required already impoverished countries to cut back on social program spending and to privatize education and other social programs wherever possible (See Geo-JaJa, 2006). Private schools have proliferated as a result following models of European schooling using European languages as the MoI. This trend works against the goals of the EFA policy, since the parents in impoverished countries cannot afford the school fees and considerable costs for uniforms, books, transportation to the school or residential fees and the like. Under SAPs governments have had to cut back funding drastically for education with the result that it is nearly impossible for public schools to function effectively. Parents want to educate their children but cannot afford the costs of private schools and so must deny some of their children, often the girls, access to school. Thus, many in the developing world find themselves caught in a situation where it is difficult if not impossible to see their children through to the end of secondary education. However, even if they succeed in getting their children to school, one has to question whether the schooling their children receive is providing them with anything relevant to their context. The high dropout rates are not surprising in these circumstances.

The true believers in neo-liberalism policies of the WB and IMF, no doubt were convinced their plans would ultimately raise the standard of living in the developing world and would integrate these countries into the global economy. But they seem to have very little understanding of education, and so it is not a surprise that the EFA goals will not be reached under their watch. In a recent volume entitled *The World Bank and Education* edited by Klees, Samoff & Stromquist (2012), the World Bank comes in for strong criticism for its disastrous record with regard to education in the developing world. Steven Klees observes, since UNESCO, because of severe funding cuts is no longer able to be an effective leader in global education policy, the World Bank has stepped in to take its place (Klees, 2012). The ideology of the World Bank is predominantly neoliberal; that is, it views development, as economic growth which will be effected by downsizing government involvement in society, through privatization, deregulation and the liberalization of the economy (Klees, 2012, p. 51). These requirements when carried out are inimical to a sound public education system. Klees states categorically the "World Bank policy [has] been an educational disaster, harmful to children around the world" (p. 50). Nordtveit (2012) echoes this harsh criticism of World Bank policies on education noting that for the World Bank, "education as a human right is not emphasized" (p. 28), and cites the Global Campaign for Education which in response to World Bank strategies for education says "the strategy focuses too heavily on private sector and market based approaches to education and on education as an instrument to serve the job market (Global Campaign for Education, p. 2, cited by Nordveidt, p. 29); Nordveidt confirms, "the World Bank is focused on economic growth, the primacy of the market, focus on processes rather than on pedagogy" (p. 29).

The World Bank with its primarily business interests and market orientation is really ill-suited to meddle in education programs, and rarely in its policy documents even touches upon issues that would concern educationists; namely schools, teachers and teacher training, class size and curriculum issues, students with exceptionalities, and the like. Instead, it uses the market agenda as the lens through which education is viewed to "solve" educational problems. As such, education is definitely a commodity, and the private sector is an organism which should partner with governments to implement the service of education and ensure that the student "clients" receive appropriate skills to meet labour market needs (Nordtveit, 2012, p. 24). Because too much privatization of national concerns and institutions is not palatable to some countries, the ploy now is to push public private partnerships (PPPs) to make it look as if nations still have some say in the matter. In a clever riff on Crouch's book *The Strange Non-Death of Neoliberalism* (2011), Susan Robertson in the volume on the World Bank and Education lays out the problem areas from privatization of education and the facilitation of Public, Private Partnerships (Robertson, 2012; see also Davidson-Harden & Majhanovich 2004, regarding issues with PPPs).

Because so much of the business world depends on "quality" control and assessments to measure quality of production, it is not surprising that the World Bank strategies for education include reliance on standardized testing and ranking of countries in the international assessments like PIRLS (Progress in International Reading Literacy Study) and TIMMS (Trends in International Mathematics and Science Study). The World Bank believes that the disappointing results of many African countries on these assessments can be overcome by more accountability measures particularly of teachers, and more assessments provided by private interests—although there is little evidence that this approach actually does anything to solve the problem. What seems lost on the WB policy makers is the human element of education. As Mark Ginsburg (2012) has noted:

> ...if one begins with a concept of teachers (or, for that matter, students) as human beings then the *process* of learning and human development becomes very relevant. From this starting point, one would be less likely to focus only on the *product* of learning, treating teachers as a material component or as commodity. If teachers were conceived of as human beings, with special attention to teachers as learners, then strategic attention by the World Bank, other international organizations, and governments would be given to how education systems and policies need to encourage and facilitate teacher learning (p. 91).

So in answer to the question "is education part of the problem or part of the solution", we have to admit that for both the developing and developed world, under the ongoing neoliberal discourse as espoused by such powerful education policy makers as the World Bank, current education practices are not contributing to solutions. Further, neo-colonialism seems to prevail, rather than liberation and a move to real democracy. The situation for education is in crisis in the developing world, but the affluent north has not remained unscathed. As Giroux (2004) has pointed out, neoliberal policies applied to education systems in the west undermine an important task of education, namely, that of preparing engaged citizens. He believes that neoliberalism has had a serious and negative impact on the language of democracy, education and the media. He urges resistance to ensure that democratic institutions be restored to their central place of importance in our society.

ENGLISH AS A HEGEMONIC LANGUAGE

Native speakers of English perhaps unconsciously claim entitlements because of their language. It often seems that it is assumed that everyone should be communicating in English. For example, in Canada, an officially bilingual French and English country, it is not uncommon when a group of Francophone and Anglophones meet, even if the Francophones outnumber the Anglophones, that the language used will be English. Francophones in Canada have accepted the necessity of speaking English to communicate with fellow Canadians outside of Quebec. Except for the province of Quebec where French is the official language, and where a series of laws have been enacted requiring proficiency in and use of French in all walks of life, English dominates elsewhere in Canada. However, if one hopes to work in Quebec, one must demonstrate a working knowledge of French, confirmed by success on a language test administered by the Office of French Language in Quebec (l'Office québécois de la langue française). Although outside of Quebec, Canadians tend to scoff at the language laws in Quebec and complain about their rigour, the Quebec population feels threatened by the power of English in today's world and has reacted with laws to protect their language and culture. Meanwhile in the rest of Canada few have bothered to become proficient in Canada's other official language and so English tends to prevail everywhere. Of course, by law, all federal agencies in Canada must be able to offer services in both official languages and it would be unlikely for anyone to be elected Prime Minister in Canada without a working knowledge of both languages.

Perhaps surprisingly, the US has never enacted a law to designate an official language (see Kubota, 2006; De Palma & Teasley, 2013). Still it is quite clear that English is really the only language tolerated. In certain states there are edicts about language. An English-only ideology pervades education policy as reflected in the laws banning bilingual education in California (1998), Arizona (2000) and Massachusetts (2002) (See Kubota, 2006). Nevertheless, when it is perceived that national security in the US is under threat from foreign interests and that knowledge of other languages is needed in a sense of "know your enemy" interest grows in training people in various foreign languages. However, the main language of communication remains English.

The fact that the powerful international financial agencies such as the World Bank and International Monetary Fund are controlled by G8 economic, strategic and political interests dictates that their working and reports will be primarily in English. And this transfers to other agencies around the world like ASEAN (Association of South East Asian Nations) and the Asian Development Bank whose working language is English. The neoliberal underpinnings of these agencies are reflected in policies they develop. For example, when Cambodia joined ASEAN in 1999, and affirmed its intentions to become a democratic state, it included in its constitution clauses committing it to a market economy and organized its economy to facilitate integration into the world economy (Clayton, 2007, p. 97).

The European Union with its 27 states—soon to become 28 when Croatia officially becomes a member in the summer of 2013—currently recognizes 27 official languages although the daily workings of the EU parliament and its policies are in English, French and German. Still two-thirds of the policy drafts are in English and its motto "One Europe" is in English only (Phillipson, 2006. See also Phillipson, 2003). Recently a German delegate and minister of the EU parliament suggested that the working language should be English only. Crystal (2003), reports that the English language has special or official status in 75 countries. The number of countries or territories favoring the use of English is growing. There are now more people who have learned English as a second language and speak it with some proficiency than native speakers of English (Majhanovich, 2013).

In the academic domain, English has made great inroads. More and more universities, based in the English speaking world are setting up off-shore campuses or partnering with universities abroad to offer programs usually in business, commerce, engineering and medicine. The language of instruction is inevitably English. Many universities in Europe and Asia that formerly offered programs in various disciplines in the national language, now also offer programs taught in English.

Academic journals, especially those highly ranked on the international index publish primarily in English. Even the UNESCO based journal, *The International Review of Education,* which includes abstracts of articles in English, French, German, Spanish and Russian, and presumably would accept articles in any of those languages, professes preference for articles in English.

Typically the language of communication at international conferences will be English even if papers in the local language are accepted as long as simultaneous translation into English or outlines of the paper in English are provided as handouts. One would think that the country hosting an international conference would be able to declare its native language as the main language of communication but that is usually not the case these days.

The pervasiveness of English confirms its status as the *lingua franca* of the world. The connections of neoliberal organizations to the multilateral agencies that use English as their working languages confers a certain neoliberal slant to many of the products produced as policies or academic courses and articles emanating from the off-shore universities. This element will be discussed in the next section. For non-English native speakers trying to find a place in a world that demands English as the language of communication, there are considerable challenges. Unsurprisingly, many resent the "free ride" English native speakers have when publishing in scientific journals (van Parijs, 2007). In our globalized world, academics face pressure to publish in English in highly ranked academic journals. Non-English speakers must overcome the hurdles of writing in Standard English often to cultural or methodological norms alien to their context. This challenge speaks to issues of equality (Flowerdew, 2007). It also confirms the neo-colonial, hegemonic nature of English today.

Yukio Tsuda (1997) details the negative consequences that arise as a result of the dominance of English: " (1) linguistic inequality to a great disadvantage of the speakers of languages other than English; (2) discrimination against the non-English speaking people and those who are not proficient in English; and (3) colonization of the consciousness of the non-English-speaker, causing them to develop linguistic, cultural, and psychological dependency upon, and identification with the English, its culture and people." (p. 22)

As an example of linguistic inequality he looks at international conferences where because of the gap in proficiency in language between native and non-native speakers, the English speakers tend to monopolize discussions and marginalize the others through speed of delivery and use of idiomatic speech unfamiliar to the non-English-speaking audience. He cites Takahashi's (1991) observation that "native speakers of English in the English dominated conferences use their linguistic advantage to magnify their powers so that they can establish [an] unequal and asymmetrical relationship with non-English speakers and thus push them out of the mainstream of communication" (Takahashi , 1991, pp 188–89, translated from Japanese and cited in Tsuda, 1997).

As a native English speaker who has attended international conferences presenting papers in English, probably at a pace faster than my audience could readily grasp, I plead guilty to causing confusion, but it was not done intentionally. The requirements of presenting findings of a complicated project in 15 or 20 minutes necessitate a rapid delivery. There is a certain 'jargon' that is expected in academic communications. Still, Takahashi has a valid point and English presenters at international conferences should be more sensitive to the linguistic capabilities of their audience. The advent of power point presentations that summarize the talk along with handouts to support the address should mitigate the problem somewhat. However, the issue remains of the advantage afforded to native English speakers in such congresses and their often taken for granted assumptions that it is the responsibility of the locals to rise to the necessary level of competence in English to make sense of the presentations, not the duty of the English presenter to try to accommodate the non-English speakers.

Tsuda further laments the "colonization of consciousness" as a result of the dominance of English. This results in the devaluation of local cultures including artistic representation, traditional education practices, local literatures and languages. Africa has certainly suffered from this effect of English dominance (See Ngugi, 1981, Babaci-Wilhite, Geo-JaJa & Lou, 2012). In place of local culture, the influence of Anglo-American culture is becoming pervasive.

Lest one think that Tsuda's arguments are overstated, one only needs to look to the growth of English academic programs at the tertiary level world-wide, the numbers of academic journals published in English as well as international conferences for all disciplines with English as the medium of communication. The list continues to grow.

A particularly disturbing example of English hegemony and colonialism in the academic world can be found in Korea. In an article entitled "Neoliberalism as Language", Piller and Cho (2013) present the unfortunate case of an elite university in Korea, the Korea Advanced Institute of Science and Technology (KAIST) which, motivated by the desire to make their institution more competitive in the world market had chosen to make English the only MoI, amazingly even extending this requirement to the learning of foreign languages such as Russian or Chinese that had to be taught through the medium of English! This is but one example of academic restructuring in Asia in a rush to internationalize. The human toll has been high with a rise in suicides both among faculty members and students. The extreme difficulty of working in a foreign language in which they were not proficient and in which they were unable to attain competency led to their acts of despair.

This recalls the case of local Cantonese speaking teachers of English in Hong Kong schools and colleges who were required to pass demanding proficiency tests in English and in English pedagogy in order to retain their licences to teach. Native speakers of English, many of whom had no particular preparation to teach English as a foreign language (unlike their Hong Kong teaching peers) were exempt from the assessments (Van Deven, 2006, So, 2003)

In the case of KAIST the restructuring included English as the MoI to make it possible in the guise of internationalization to accept non-Korean students. However, as has been pointed out, English MoI rather than reflecting a move to the international that validates diverse languages and cultures, actually represents "the transfer of the US model of academic capitalism to another national context" (Kauppi & Erkkilä, 2011 cited in Piller and Cho, 2013, p. 31), and of course involves the neoliberal impetus toward marketization and corporatization of universities (Piller and Cho, 2013, p. 31). Under the new structure, KAIST blatantly adopted the neoliberal mission to focus on science and engineering with the aim of supplying superbly qualified workers to industry at low cost. Piller and Cho identify this as a transformation of higher education "from the service of the common good to a capitalist enterprise" (p. 32).

A key point of Pillar and Cho's argument is that the push for English as MoI in higher education in Korea and elsewhere is actually language policy in the service of global neocolonialism. As Heller (2010) and others have argued, language, namely the English language, is central to the neoliberal order (cited in Piller and Cho, p. 28). In the next section I turn to a discussion of how the English language supports and sustains neoliberal policy.

ENGLISH LANGUAGE AS AN ANCHOR FOR NEOLIBERALISM

At the beginning of the paper, I discussed the perseverance of neoliberal policies despite their demonstrable failures worldwide, and contribution to growing inequality between a small cadre of the very wealthy and a decline of the middle class including a growing number of the impoverished. An argument can be made that the English language has contributed to the continuation and indeed entrenchment of this faulty economic paradigm. It certainly has contributed to neo-colonialism in African former colonies where under imposed Structural Adjustment Programs, European-style education with English as the MoI has proliferated. The devaluing of indigenous languages and knowledge production has been a sorry outcome (see Babaci-Wilhite, Geo-JaJa & Lou, 2012).

As mentioned above, linguists such as Heller and others (2010) have traced the commodification of language. An examination of the discourses used in current policies for higher education institutions, for primary and secondary education and fiscal policies for nations shows language imbued with the tenets of neoliberalism. Where once educators would vigorously dispute that education is a commodity to be bought and sold on the world market, now it seems taken for granted and normal.

In the past students engaged in higher education for enlightenment and intellectual growth. Now it seems that the goals of education have narrowed. As noted by Abelmann et al (2009 cited in Piller and Cho, 2013) regarding student identity:

The new model student is an autonomous student-consumer who is responsible for managing his or her own lifelong creative capital development.... contemporary college students are able to narrate their human capital development while obscuring the structural workings of college rank and family capital. The hubris of this new generation works against a more broadly social imagination because it acclaims individuals who do not conform to collectivist demands.

Arguments for the goal of education as a means to liberate human beings, teach them critical thinking skills and realize their human potential are giving way to more instrumental, utilitarian, and yes, neoliberal notions. Institutions of learning are now supposed to function to train workers to enter and serve global markets, to prepare students for jobs. Other more esthetic goals are highly criticized as being irrelevant in today's world. The language of the market has insinuated itself into all areas of daily discourse. We speak of the importance of developing the "brand" of our institutions; universities compete for a "target market" of student "clients" and wish to stake out their position in the "knowledge economy". This reflects the powerful influence of globalization on the internationalization of education and homogenization of language What university administration would dare to omit from its mission statement claims of provision of quality, perhaps world-class education? Everyone, even young secondary students are urged to prepare "business" plans outlining the courses they will be taking, chosen to help them develop the skills needed to participate in the global market.

It appears that economics new-speak has 'colonized' other fields so that now the language describing these domains all begins to resemble the language of the market and must reflect product and potential for profit making. Hasan (2003) as cited in Holborow (2006) has observed how the English language has been affected in the new order.

She talks of 'glibspeak' [which] consists of turning the semantics of ordinary English upside down and globalizing new concepts which are friendly to the ideology of capitalism...she observes that political words such as *equality, freedom, liberalization,* and *non-discrimination* are redolent with ideological shifts. She also charts the process of 're-semantization' by drawing attention to the ideological meanings which have attached to *globalization* only recently— like 'lower costs of production', 'international expansion of companies' and appropriate take-overs' (Hasan, 2003, 437 cited in Holborow, 2006, p. 90).

The importance of the English language worldwide as a co-opted partner in the neoliberal globalization project cannot be underestimated. Of course, in the reality of internationalization, provision of English instruction has become a most lucrative business. Teachers of English need to be aware of ethical implications of the product they offer. As has been argued by Piller and Cho (2013) among others, the primacy of English, particularly the English of neoliberals in policy can have the effect of suppressing dissent, particularly among those less proficient in the language. Tsuda is justified in his suspicions of the colonizing effects of globalization on non-English speaking nations.

Of course, one could not recommend the cessation of English language teaching to non-English speakers around the globe. That would disadvantage them even more. English IS the current *lingua franca* of the modern world particularly in the areas of business commerce, ICT, science and engineering and social policy. As I have stated before,

> Although in a globalized world it would be unwise and even patronizing of native English speakers to suggest to education policy makers in developing nations that they should not promote opportunities to learn English, on the other hand, they should reflect on the reasons behind the phenomenal spread of English, and focus on English programs that best prepare citizens for situations where English is needed. Furthermore, those who are mandating English knowledge in their populace should consider realistic expectations for mastery as well as methods and approaches that would be the most appropriate for learning English for various purposes. It is in no one's best interest simply to mandate knowledge of this international language without planning for implications in teacher training, in curriculum development, effects on the current education system and issues of equality and social justice. One has to ask whose interests are being served. (Majhanovich, 2013, p. 250).

The implications for those charged with teaching English are enormous (see Babaci-Wilhite, 2012). Kumaravadivelu (2006) sees the current situation of globalization as essentially a neo-colonialization project abetted by the English language. He observes, "whether they know it or not, and whether they like it or not, most TESOL professionals end up serving the profit motives of global corporations and the political motives of imperial powers (p. 23). His solution, like that of others concerned about this uncomfortable state of affairs, is teachers' awareness, and attention to curriculum to allow for reflection and resistance by those who have been co-opted into the globalization project. Perhaps only then can some kind of balance return and the worst excesses of neoliberalism be undone.

CONCLUSION

Neo-liberalism seems to remain the order of the day despite its many failures, and its deleterious effects on democratic society, particularly in the developing world. How has such a destructive economic policy been able to retain its stranglehold on a suffering world? It would seem that Bourdieu (2001) was correct in his judgment that neoliberalism has managed to pass itself off as the required norm which cannot be resisted. It has been argued in this paper that the English language used in articulating the policies of neoliberalism has assisted in inculcating neoliberalism into the human psyche as the only way to act. Language is powerful and the language of neoliberalism is persuasive. And yet, doubts are arising. As long as it was only the developing world that suffered under neoliberal policies, it seemed that the problem lay not so much in the policies but rather with the countries themselves that just could not adjust to the necessary means to correct their failing economies and become profit making enterprises. The suffering masses would just have to make do and work harder. However, now that the innate problems of a neoliberal approach are affecting the developed West and North as well, and are driving down the middle class on which, as Fukuyama has stated, democracy rests, perhaps policies will change. Perhaps the situation has reached the tipping point where attention will move away from the primacy of the market to concern for the well-being of society as a whole. One can only hope.

NOTES

¹ With acknowledgement to C. Crouch (2011). *The strange non-death of neoliberalism.*

REFERENCES

Abdi, A. (2013). Intensive globalization of African education: Re-interrogating the relevance of structural adjustment programs (SAPs). In Y. Hébert, & A. Abdi (Eds.) *Critical perspectives on international education.* Rotterdam: Sense Publishers.

Abelmann, N., Park, S. K., & Kim, H. (2009). College rank and neo-liberal subjectivity in South Korea. The burden of Self-Development. *Inter-Asia Cultural Studies, 10*(2), 229–47.

Aboriginal Healing Foundation (2009). *Response, responsibility and renewal: Canada's truth and reconciliation journey.* Ottawa: Author.

Allison, J. (2013). Letter to the editor, the *Globe and Mail.* March 25, 2013, p. A10.

Assembly of First Nations (1972). *Indian control of Indian education.* Ottawa: Author.

Babaci-Wilhite, Z. (2013). A study of escalating debates on the use of a global or local language in education: Tanzania and Malaysia. In D. B. Napier & S. Majhanovich (Eds.) *Education, dominance and identity* (pp. 121–132). Rotterdam: Sense Publishers.

Babaci-Wilhite, Z. (2012). A human rights-based approach to Zanzibar's language-in-education policy. *World Studies in Education 13*(2), 17–33.

Babaci-Wilhite, Z., Geo-JaJa, M. A., & Lou, S. (2012). Education and language: A human right for sustainable development in Africa. *International Review of Education 58*, 619–647.

Binda, K. P., & Lall, M. (2013). Decolonizing indigenouos education in Canada. In D. B. Napier & S. Majhanovich (Eds.) *Education dominance and identity* (pp. 11–27). Rotterdam: Sense Publishers.

Bourdieu, P. (2001). *Contre-feux 2: Pour un movement social européen,* (p. 84). Paris: Raisons d'agir.

Brock-Utne, B. (2000). *Whose education for all? The recolonization of the African mind?* New York: Falmer Press.

Brock-Utne, B. (2001). Education for all—in whose language? *Oxford Review of Education 27*(1), 115–134.

Canadian Council on Learning (2007). *Redefining how success is measured in first nations, Inuit and métis learning.* Report on Learning in Canada, 2007. Ottawa: Author.

Clayton, T. (2007). *Language choice in a nation under transition: English language spread in Cambodia.* New York: Springer.

Crouch, C. (2011). *The strange non-death of neoliberalism.* Cambridge: Polity.

Davidson-Harden A., & Majhanovich, S. (2004). Privatisation of education in Canada: A survey of trends. *International Review of Education 50*, 263–287.

De Palma, R., & Teasley, C. (2013). Constructing Spanish: Discourses of language hegemony in Spain. In D. B. Napier & S. Majhanovich (Eds.) *Education dominance and identity* (pp. 101–118). Rotterdam: Sense Publishers.

Flowerdew, J. (2007). The non-Anglophone scholar on the periphery of scholarly publication. *AILA Review* 20, 14–27.

Freire, P. (1970/2000). *Pedagogy of the oppressed*. New York: Continuum International Publishing Grp.

Fukuyama, F. (2012). The Future of history. Can liberal democracy survive the decline of the middle class? *Foreign Affairs* http://www.foreignaffairs.com, accessed March 2, 2013.

Geo-JaJa, M. A. (2006). Educational decentralization, public spending, and social justice in Nigeria, *International Review of Education*, *52*(1–2), 129–153.

Geo-JaJa, M. A. (2004). Decentralization and privatization of education in Africa: Which option for Nigeria? Special Issue of *International Review of Education, 50*(3–4), 309–326.

Geo-JaJa, M. A., & Mangum, G. (2003). Economic adjustment, education and human resource development in Africa: The Case of Nigeria. *International Review of Education, 49*(3–4), 293–318.

Geo-JaJa, M. A., & Mangum, G. (2001). Structural Adjustment as an inadvertent enemy of human development in Africa. *Journal of Black Studies, 32*(1), 30–50.

Ginsburg, M. (2012). Teachers as learners: A missing focus in "learning for all." In S. Klees, J. Samoff & N. Stromquist (Eds.) *The world bank and education* (pp. 83–93). Rotterdam: Sense Publishers.

Giroux, H. (2004). *The terror of neoliberalism: Authoritarianism and the eclipse of democracy*. Boulder, CO: Paradigm Publ.

Global Campaign for Education (2011, January 17). *Response to the world bank sector Strategy.* www.ifiwatchnet.org.

Global Issues http://www.globalissues.org/article/3/structural-adjustment-a-major-cause-of-poverty. Accessed April 12,2013.

Hasan, R. (2003). Globalization, literacy and ideology. *World Englishes 22*(4), 433–48.

Heller, M. (2010). The commodification of languages. *Annual Review of Anthropology 39*, 101–114.

Holborow, M. (2006). Ideology and language: Interconnections between neo-liberalism and English. In Edge, J. (Ed.), *(Re)locating TESOL in an age of empire* (pp. 84–103). Houndsmills, Basingstoke, Hampshire: Palgrave Macmillan.

Kauppi, N., & Erkkilä, T. (2011). The struggle over global higher education: Actors, institutions and practice. *International Political Sociology 5*(3), 314–26.

Klees, S., Samoff, J., & Stromquist, N. P. (Eds.) (2012). *The World Bank and Education. Critiques and Alternatives*. Rotterdam: Sense Publishers.

Klees, S. (2012). World bank and education: Ideological premises and ideological conclusions. In S. Klees, J. Samoff & N. Stromquist (Eds.) *The world bank and education,* (pp. 49–65). Rotterdam: Sense Publishers.

Krugman, P. (2013). The jobless trap. *New York Times* Op. Ed article, April 21, 2013.

Kubota, R. (2006). Teaching second languages for national security purposes: A case of post 9/11 USA. In *(Re)locating TESOL in an age of empire* (pp. 119–138). Houndsmills, Basingstoke, Hampshire: Palgrave Macmillan,

Kumaravadivelu, B. (2006). Dangerous liaison: globalization, empire and TESOL. In Edge, J. (Ed.), *(Re)locating TESOL in an age of empire,* (pp. 1–26). Houndsmills, Basingstoke, Hampshire: Palgrave Macmillan,

Majhanovich, S. (2013). English as a tool of neo-colonialism and globalization in Asian contexts. In Y. Hébert, & A. Abdi, (Eds.) *Cultural perspectives on international education* (pp. 249–261). Rotterdam: Sense Publishers.

Mbekwa, M., & Nomlomo, V. (2013). Voices from the classroom: Teacher and learner perceptions on the use ofthe learners' home language in the teaching and learning of school mathematics and science. In. D. B. Napier & S. Majhanovich (Eds.) *Education, dominance and identity* (pp. 133–149). Rotterdam: Sense Publishers.

Ngugi wa Thiong'o, J. (1981). *Decolonizing the mind: The politics of language in African literature.* London: James Carey.

Nordveidt, B. H. (2012). World bank poetry: How the education strategy 2020 imagines the world. In S. Klees, J. Samoff & N. Stromquist (Eds.) *The world band and education* (pp. 21–32). Rotterdam: Sense Publishers.

Phillipson, R. (2003). English for the globe or only for globe-trotters? The world of the EU. In Mair, C. (Ed.), *The politics of English as a world language,* (pp. 19–30). Amsterdam-New York: Editions Rodopi B.V.

Phillipson, R. (2006). Language Policy and Linguistic Imperialism. In Ricento, T. (Ed.) *An introduction to language policy: Theory and method* (pp. 346–361). Oxford, UK: Blackwell Publishing.

Piller, I., & Cho, J. (2013). Neoliberalism as language policy. *Language in Society,* 42, 23–44.

Robertson, S. (2012). The Strange non-death of neoliberal privatization. In S. Klees, J. Samoff & N. Stromquist (Eds.) *The world bank and education* (pp. 189–206). Rotterdam: Sense Publishers.

Royal Commission on Aboriginal Peoples (1996). *Report of the royal commission on aboriginal peoples.* Ottawa: Queen's Printer.

So, M. (20003). *When the tables are turned: the LPAT for English Teachers in Hong Kong.* Unpublished Masters Thesis, University of Western Ontario.

Stiglitz,J.(2008a). Interview with the *Berliner Zeitung,* October 9, 2008. (http://nyc:indymedia. orgen/2008/10/100813.shtml. Accessed March 2, 2013.

Stiglitz, J. (2008b). The End of Neo-liberalism? *Project Syndicate.* http://www.project-syndicate.org/ commentary/the-end-of-neo-liberalism, Accessed March 2, 2013.

Stiglitz, J. (2013). "The Post-Crisis Crises" *Project Syndicate.* http://www.project-syndicate.org/ commentary/global-warming—and-structural-change-by-joseph-e—stiglitz. Accessed March 2, 2013.

Takahashi, J. (1991). Kokusai Kaigi-ni Miru Nihonjin-no Ibunda Koushu. In J. Takahashi et al (Eds.) *Ibunka-eno Sutoratejii* (pp. 181–201). Tokyo: Kawashima Shoten.

Tsuda, Y. (1997). The Hegemony of English and Strategies for Linguistic Pluralism: Proposing the Ecology of Language Paradigm. In L. Smith & M. Formen (Eds.) *World Englishes 2000* (pp. 21–31). Selected Essays. Honolulu HI: College of Languages, Linguistics and Literature. Univ. Of Hawaii and East-West Center.

Tsui, A. B. M., & Tollefson, J.W. (2006). Language policy and the construction of national cultural identity. In A. B. M. Tsui & J. W. Tollefson (Eds.) *Language policy, culture, and identity in Asian contexts,* (pp. 1–21). Mahwah, NJ: Lawrence Erlbaum Assoc.

Van Deven, T. (2006). *The native-english teaching program in Hong Kong, China: A critical ethnography.* Unpublished doctoral thesis, University of Western Ontario.

Van Parijs, P. (2007). Tackling the Anglophones' free ride. *AILA Review,* 20, 72–86.

AFFILIATION

Suzanne Majhanovich
Faculty of Education
Western University
London, Ontario, Canada

CHRISTINE DAYMON & KATHY DURKIN

THE ECONOMIC CAPTURE OF CRITICALITY
AND THE CHANGING UNIVERSITY
IN AUSTRALIA AND THE UK

INTRODUCTION

The implications of neoliberal forms of globalization for national economies, states and individual lives have been the topic of major public debates over a number of years. Their hegemonic influence has been described as 'an economic capture of the social' (Banerjee 2007: 146) because of the extent to which free market forces, as spread through globalizing flows, have become normalized and even normative in regulating and evaluating the public sphere and the quality of social lives around the world. To date, relatively less attention has been paid to the effects of these phenomena on education although a handful of influential scholars have pointed to the toxicity of the neoliberal agenda and its associated pedagogical model for democratic society (Freire 1998, Fallis 2007, Giroux 2009, Olssen 2004, Torres 2009). They claim that the role of education as central agent responsible for the production of democratic norms and values has been diminished by the relatively recent focus on education as a means of national competitive advantage. For example, in the UK, Australia and the USA, education is now seen as the key to national prosperity and global, economic competitiveness. With universities in many countries emphasising the advantages of learning for the development of professional competencies and employability, higher education appears to have firmly embraced the economic imperatives of globalization and the self-interested trappings of neoliberalism which have been described by Lauder et al (2006) as market competition, efficiency, and greed as a source of social progress. These are at odds with the skills and predispositions required for active and conscious participation in democratic society which include a commitment to community, care, justice and civic engagement, as well as the possession of a critical conscience (Olssen 2004). The effects of this shift in the university's role from serving the ideals of democracy to obeisance to the demands of the economy have rarely been studied qualitatively at the level of the classroom.

We argue that it is through investigating the extent to which a critical conscience is valued in tertiary teaching and learning that we can gain insights into the effects of macro-level forces on the internal functioning of the university. To this end, our chapter presents an examination of student and lecturer experiences of critical thinking, a skill at the core of a critical conscience which is essential if 'citizens [are]

S. Majhanovich and M.A. Geo-JaJa (Eds.), Economics, Aid and Education:
Implications for Development, 97–114.

to participate in a modern, democratic society; critical thinking enables citizens to make their own contribution to society in a critical and aware manner' (Ten Dam and Volman, 2004, 375). Critical thinking is likely to be compromised when the neoliberal agenda is foregrounded in the activities of the university.

THE CHANGING UNIVERSITY

Historically protected from and averse to the forces of consumption and economic success, the university has long served the ideals of democracy and the public good, promoting and representing these through its responsibilities as critic and conscience of society while at the same time being accountable to its citizens. Although higher education grew out of a commitment to applied knowledge and professional education, traditionally this was combined with a fierce dedication to educating critical and ethical citizens (Cole 2009). Today, the democratic purposes of the university appear to be corroding, and the 'social contract' (Fallis 2007) between the university and the society that supports it is under great stress. Economic pressures, the encroachments by governments and corporate entities on scholarly practice, and the changing priorities of the university itself have led to a form of 'academic capitalism' (Slaughter and Rhoades 2004) whereby higher education has become more 'business'-like in structure, orientation and practice. As a result, the university is increasingly characterized by the utilitarian, career-fixated attitudes of students (Giroux 2009; Zell 2001), the use by academic administrators of business tools and terminology to assess and quantify teaching and learning (Simon and Banchero 2010), the employment of marketing techniques to brand its 'products' and manage its reputation for prestige and competitive advantage (Fairclough 1993; Hearn 2010; Wedlin 2008) and the acceptance by many academics of the need to become 'knowledge entrepreneurs' whereby their research is monetised (Hearn 2010, 212).

As the modern university struggles with or accedes to the colonising forces of neoliberal globalization, it risks marginalising its democratic function and its associated role of developing individuals with a critical conscience who are equipped for active, responsible engagement in society as open-minded, flexible thinkers. Instead of designing curriculum to provide 'the modes of critical discourse, interpretation, judgment, imagination, and experiences' (Giroux, 2009: 671) that enable [students] to engage actively in society or to 'question the market as the hegemony it has become' (Gibbs, 2001: 93), the university focuses instead on corporate relevance, thus narrowing the aims of education and compromising educational principles, values and goals related to critical and democratic citizenship and the transformation of society (Ball, Bowe and Gewirtz 1994). For example, in critiquing forms of management education, Reed and Anthony (1992: 601) state that a focus on business-related, functional and technical skills 'crowds out any sustained concern with the social, moral, political and ideological ingredients of managerial work'. To overcome this, Samra-Fredericks (2003) argues for lecturers to have a 'critical sensibility' in order to draw students' attention to the social and moral issues and unintended effects of taken-for-granted practices and reasoning in the discipline of management.

CRITICAL THINKING

Although there are disagreements between academic disciplines about the meaning of critical thinking (Egege and Kutieleh, 2004), being critical is generally associated with evaluating the logic of another's argument, being sceptical of and challenging conventional wisdom, and recognising this as never value-free (Mingers 2000). Tsui (2002:743) defined criticality as an ability to 'identify issues and assumptions, recognise important relationships, make correct inferences, evaluate evidence or authority, and deduce conclusions'. Ennis (1987) identified a number of critical thinking skills that can be broadly categorised as questioning, evaluation, analysis, reflection, inference and judgement, these skills being evidenced in the organisation and logic of an argument. Facione et al (1995), building on Ennis' work, identified seven characteristics of critical thinking: truth-seeking; open-mindedness; analyticity; systematicity; critical thinking self confidence; inquisitiveness; and maturity of judgement.

Critical scholars have encouraged the teaching of critical thinking for enabling a re-examination of knowledge and practice, including taken-for-granted, largely unchallenged goals and assumptions (Caproni and Arias, 1997), and a problematizing of knowledge itself. When engaging critically, students need to 'ask difficult questions that sometimes have no clear answers, to look at moral and economic imperatives of managerial practices, and to live with ambiguity and anxiety' (Caprioni and Arias, 1997: 301). Critical thinking is evident in robust academic inquiry, having its source in dialogical debate and academic argumentation. As such, it is closely associated with what Olssen (2004) terms 'contestation' (p. 278), a pre-condition for democracy. Olssen states that, 'A government will be democratic to the extent that people can contest whatever it decides' (p. 279); democratic society is one that is debate based, accepting of conflict and alert to different points of view. Torres (2009) advances this idea when he claims that without critical thinking skills citizens cannot participate actively in society, choosing instead to align with professional and economic values. Further, when citizens are unable to question societal norms and conventional practices because of their lack of critical ability, then there are no advocates to challenge and resist the hegemonic forces of neoliberal globalization, and thus disadvantage and discrimination are perpetuated. Critical thinking, therefore, is a crucial component of democratic citizenship, enabling students to make an active contribution to the transformation of society (Glaser 1985).

METHODOLOGY

With a focus on the skill of critical thinking, we set out though qualitative research to reveal how the effects of the globalized neoliberal agenda are evidenced in higher education in the UK and Australia. We concentrated on the postgraduate level on the assumption that the tension between academic rigour, democratic ideals and corporate relevance was likely to be more pronounced because many students were part-timers who were experienced participants in the market economy through their current work roles.

We conducted sixty-three in-depth interviews with students and their lecturers in two universities, one longitudinal study taking place over four years in a British university, with an extension of this study being carried out over one semester in an Australian university. Participants included postgraduate home students (British and Australian), and international students, the latter comprising the majority of the cohorts in both universities. Forty-five postgraduate students were interviewed, thirty-three in the original, longitudinal phase of the study in the UK and twelve in a second phase in Australia. Eighteen lecturers were interviewed, ten in the UK and eight in Australia. Each in-depth interview lasted forty to sixty minutes. The samples were achieved through a combination of purposive and self selection, and the sample size was deemed sufficient to achieve data saturation within the constraints of time and resources. Public relations and marketing courses were targeted in both case sites to ensure commonality in the degree content. Because our data are associated with a particular context, it is possible that our results would have differed if we had interviewed students and lecturers involved, for example, in the humanities or natural sciences. For this reason, our results need to be treated with caution.

Through in-depth interviews and qualitative document analysis of unit learning guides, we focused on two overriding research questions:

What is the value placed on critical thinking by those teaching university postgraduate courses and by postgraduate students?

How is criticality taught and learnt at the postgraduate level?

We recorded and transcribed all the interviews, analyzing them together with the data from the document analysis. We undertook multiple iterations of the following steps: searching manually for common themes in the data, openly coding these, extracting patterns in the data and developing broader categories, such as relevance of critical thinking development to personal lives/careers, challenges in teaching criticality, factors influencing acquisition of critical thinking skills, and interpreted these within the framework of neoliberal globalization. We had already identified inductively some early themes and categories in the British data before the Australian study began and we sought to compare and contrast these with the Australian data. We subsequently found the same patterns to be evident in both data sets, with few distinctions. We then obtained corroboration from the literature for the observed relationships which enabled us to develop a set of propositions.

In the following section, we support our findings with evidence from quotations, each representing the views of more than a single individual whose words we selected to illustrate the common opinions of multiple interviewees (except where specifically noted in the text). On the whole, in attributing quotations to interviewees, we have used the universal term of 'lecturer' or 'student'. However, where it is important for illustrative purposes to identify the interviewee's nationality, we have done so – not to highlight cultural stereotypicality – but to clarify the interviewee's viewpoint and thus aid the reader's interpretation.

Engaging with Critical Thinking

Defining critical thinking: differences and uncertainty

Students and lecturers define critical thinking differently and for many it is an ambiguous concept. On entry to postgraduate courses, many students had minimal, if any, engagement with academic critical thinking, and therefore had little understanding of what it entails. Notably, many international students acknowledged the existence of culturally relative differences in academic learning, as illustrated in the comment of a Chinese student:

[In China], it's not really what you are supposed to do. Asking the 'whys? whats? hows? and wheres?' is not done.

Yet lecturers noted that the problem is not confined to international students. For example:

Asian students are not used to questioning things, but our home students can't do it either. They can talk a lot, they can make their point, but they can't rationalise things. They never had to in school, so they're not used to it. (Lecturer).

Although such challenges are well documented with regard to international students (e.g. Ryan 2010), lecturers in our research observed that most students, whether home or international students, experienced difficulties notably because of the paucity of critical thinking skills' development at the undergraduate level.

For some students, critical thinking was 'just another set of rules' that needed to be learned and followed in order to pass a course. Others engaged in what Paul (1982:23) describes as 'weak critical thinking' where they argued one side of an argument, refuting alternative views, without understanding how to synthesise perspectives into a convincing, well evidenced critical argument.

At first I thought it meant I had to challenge everything, but I didn't really understand what 'challenge' meant. I thought I had to just give my own opinions based on my common sense. But later, I realised that I needed to find evidence to support my opinions, but I didn't know how to (synthesise) others' opinions into my argument.

I thought it meant to say something opposite to what the author thinks, or to say there is something wrong with his theory. So, criticising the authorities.

Even by the time I did my dissertation, I hadn't really grasped it – I have done some critical thinking in the dissertation, but I don't understand it 100%.

These impoverished notions of criticality and argumentation continued to remain relevant for many throughout the whole period of study, indicating the lack of support to develop their skills further, or their unwillingness to grapple further with the concept.

To some extent, students' negative, bewildered or instrumental attitudes are an outcome of the different views and positions of lecturers towards critical thinking and its value in education. Less than half of the public relations and marketing communications lecturers who participated in the study had a well-developed sense of the possible meanings and applications of criticality (although there were proportionally more lecturers in the British university with a good sense of criticality because staff had been exposed there to training sessions and staff team discussions on criticality in learning and teaching). Others were unable to distinguish and describe the characteristics of critical thinking, or to articulate strategies for teaching and encouraging its practice. This suggests a neglect by some to engage in critical examination of their own pedagogy. Some lecturers wondered if they as well as their colleagues had failed in their ability to identify and nurture this important skill, as illustrated in the following quotation:

Argumentation is the unmentionable word when it comes to training lecturers. It's just assumed. Everybody thinks they know about it, but no-one talks about it. Some colleagues do not have a consciousness of what critical argumentation means, and therefore cannot articulate this to the students; other colleagues do have this consciousness and can share their good practice. (Lecturer)

In contrast to those unable to define or demonstrate their engagement with critical thinking, other students and lecturers clearly understood and valued the concept for the intellectual freedom it offered to generate alternative insights on their topic of study or teaching, or into their own, contextualised lives.

Critical thinking develops you personally. You don't accept everything at face value; you tend to question things more. It becomes part of you. (Student)

You problematise things in your mind and see different perspectives and angles, and how you can intellectualise and approach problems in a more complex way. This is really good, this is what academic life does for you – it helps you THINK. (Student, our capitals to express the participant's emphasis)

Lecturers who were proficient in defining and applying the concept, understood it to include purposeful and evaluative reading, writing, oral debate, and reflection, all skills that could be taught and encouraged in seminars as well as through assessed work.

Using sources from other disciplines encourages thinking outside the box – exposing students to different perspectives, approaches and debates. Part of critical thinking is being able to change one's mind, always being open to new information, raising questions, reflecting on and re-visiting issues, to see if one's perspective has changed. Part of this learning process is the lecturer giving feedback to students so that both skills and confidence in critical thinking increase together. (Lecturer)

This participant had observed a marked change in students' learning behaviour when she actively encouraged critical thinking in class discussions. After this training, students became more motivated to ask questions, and to do pre-reading in order to take an informed and active role in class discussions.

Critical thinking, therefore, appears to be a confusing concept that some students and lecturers do grasp and employ, but which others fail to articulate, and, in the case of students, choose to shun, or only partially apply even after completing a masters program. To some extent, impoverished notions of criticality may be due to a number of factors including a lack of engagement by students with argumentation at the undergraduate or foundational level; a lack of support for skills development during postgraduate studies; and possibly more importantly due to the ambiguous or diverse understandings (whether positive or negative) that are conveyed by lecturers themselves.

The Value of Critical Thinking: Differences and Tensions

There was little consensus of opinion across the research participants regarding the value of critical thinking, with disagreements and/or a lack of awareness concerning its democratic role and/or its relevance to the workplace.

With regard to the notion that critical thinking is a socially desirable trait that enables full citizen participation in the democratic process, many students, especially those from abroad who had lived under authoritarian and repressive regimes, prized the freedom of expression that they associated with study in British or Australian universities. They had expected this in Anglophone postgraduate study and regarded it as a major motivator for their choice of study in these countries, as Egege and Kutlieleh (2004) also noted in their research. Their appreciation of the worth of critical thinking (even if they expressed the concept in different words) inspired some students in our study to step out and risk rehearsing their newly acquired skills: being sceptical about the conventional, exploring and arguing alternative notions of truth. A Croatian student echoed the views of some international students when she stated that:

Here you have absolute freedom to think whatever you want, you just have to argue it. I like that intellectual freedom.

Critical thinking therefore was valued by some students for its association with social and cultural engagement in democratic issues and this view was supported by some lecturers, but not all. Instead, the majority of public relations and marketing lecturers regarded career advancement and, more broadly, economic wealth, as the most significant consequences of an ability to think critically. This view correlated with that of mature students with work experience. For most of them, a critical conscience was aligned with career enhancement where the ability to read and listen sceptically but sensitively, in order to understand and evaluate different points of view, and to critique, debate and self-reflect from an informed stance were all attributes that would enable them to progress professionally. In their view, critical thinking enabled communications executives to 'think outside the box' and appreciate 'the bigger picture' surrounding an issue or problem, to 'look a lot more critically' at whatever lands on the desk, and therefore to develop more convincing, evidence-based professional arguments 'by drawing on different sources of information and comparing and contrasting them' (Student). Skills in criticality, therefore, were considered to motivate good decision-making at work, enabling often contradictory information to be analyzed, evaluated and prioritised so that decisions could be made 'with confidence' and opinions formed on the basis of sound evidence. Such skills were considered to be obligatory for an accelerated career.

In contrast to those who perceived the acquisition of critical thinking skills as beneficial for corporate or civic engagement, some students considered them either irrelevant for careers in communication and marketing, or a 'waste of time' because their home cultures did not condone criticality as endorsed by Anglophone cultures. Those in this group with previous work experience recalled how the communication function was driven by tight deadlines and the constant demands of the media. Therefore:

There was not "the luxury, the time to weigh arguments, to think about different perspectives. We were expected to produce very simple messages and solutions, very quickly and make quick decisions. (Student).

Comments exemplified by this quotation highlight functional distinctions within work, i.e. early career roles may involve little problem solving, and therefore there may be less call for critical thinking than at more strategic and managerial levels.

The cultural unacceptability of critique and challenge in the workplace was a concern for some international students:

I can't use critical thinking in the industry back home because they will feel that I am challenging and arguing with the managers, and it will seem rude and offensive. (Taiwanese student)

Similarly, in South Korea, according to a student from that country, those who had studied abroad had a reputation of 'being difficult to work with'; they could appear offensive and disrespectful especially to older colleagues who might feel personally insulted when their ideas were challenged or when improvements were suggested by younger people who had studied abroad. Even in the UK, according to a British marketing lecturer, some industries did not encourage innovative thinking because 'people who think critically can be a source of problems: they may question the authority's existing systems'. Fears about appearing disruptive in the workplace, then, may not have been confined to those anticipating careers solely in Asia.

Cynicism about the value of critical thinking in the workplace included the concern that the concept itself may not be translatable to a different language. An Iranian student stated that: 'When I want to translate critical thinking into my language, it doesn't make sense. So I ask myself, is it a universal skill?'. In many countries with communist and authoritarian regimes, criticism has a negative connotation: 'We grew up with our parents teaching us "don't criticise other people's opinions", (Korean student). This prohibition would apply more keenly toward those in authority, or those who had officially published papers or books.

Perceptions about the cultural inappropriateness of critical thinking and the surfeit of potentially unwelcome consequences for returning students led some to dismiss these intellectual skills as irrelevant for life and work. This prevented them from experimenting with critical thinking. However, when required to demonstrate critical thinking in course assessment (and not all assignments did require this), some students may have appropriated such skills in order to achieve postgraduate goals. In such cases, these skills were likely to be rejected on returning home:

Here I know I have to think; I have to use my brain. But in Taiwan, I just follow everyone else. I don't need to think. (Student)

In effect, the perceived irrelevance and the cultural unacceptability of critical thinking deterred many postgraduate public relations and marketing communications students from developing expertise in criticality. The issue was further complicated by second language and communication challenges. Yet student lack of interest in developing critical skills for professional careers was likewise evident in many home students. Lecturers commented on students' lack of appreciation for developing critical skills:

I try to teach critical thinking, but when I mention it to students they start rolling their eyes. Students who respond to critical thinking are in a small minority – the majority either hate it or have no clue about it. The thing that concerns me most is that they don't have a habit of questioning 'why?'. Everything is focused on getting jobs at the end, rather than developing a broader base of skills.

Many students, therefore, focused on passing assignments but did not see the need to reflect critically on what they had learned. They became 'acquisitive' instead of 'inquisitive' learners (Lauder et al, 2006). Together, these issues have triggered a dilemma for marketing and public relations lecturers whose ambitions for their students' intellectual development may be in collision with students' more pragmatic, vocational goals.

Although no academics expressed the view that critical thinking might not be relevant, a content analysis of unit learning guides associated with courses in public relations and marketing communications in the sampled British and Australian universities revealed that not all units actively encouraged dialogue and unmitigated questioning, the crossing of interdisciplinary borders or the embracing of critique and possibility (Giroux, 2009). While unit learning objectives in the British university tended to be more explicit about the requirement for criticality, this provided in some cases only a cursory nod to the development of skills in the evaluation of scholarly ideas. On the whole, the content of public relations and marketing communications courses in both universities emphasised the achievement of practical skills, models and business-related solutions that were informed primarily by textbook chapters rather than wider, more scholarly reading. The key learning objectives of the following postgraduate course in the Australian university, for instance, bore little relationship to high skills development:

> This course is designed for applicants wanting to develop a greater depth of knowledge in the marketing field. It enhances the ability of marketing executives to anticipate demand for projects by analysing the behaviour of competitors and customers. Students design, organise and control marketing strategies to reach a target market.

Within the same program, a unit in public relations sought to enable students' to:

> Identify an organisation's key publics or stakeholder groups and predict their behaviour; identify and analyse ethical issues affecting organisational/ stakeholder relationships; apply specialised PR concepts to real life business situations; prepare a public relations plan; differentiate between the role of PR and other major business disciplines, especially marketing.

To some extent, the apparent intellectual paucity of such courses may have been influenced by lecturers' haziness about the nature of critical thinking or their hesitance to employ critical thinking because of their own vulnerabilities in teaching the concept. However, the evidence also indicates that despite the espousal by many lecturers of the importance of scholarly rigour and the development of critical intellectual capacity, some did not promote this because they acceded that practical, work-based competences were more immediately valued by employing organisations.

In summary, multiple perspectives exist about the importance or otherwise of critical thinking, ranging from its value to personal and professional development, its crucial role in enabling engaged citizenship in a democratic society, to its lack of relevance in any capacity especially that related to the workplace. A combination of students' and staff attitudes cohered around each of these perspectives.

Challenges to Teaching Criticality

As previously indicated, some lecturers were not able to articulate a clear understanding of what critical thinking entailed, nor to describe how they would endeavour to teach or encourage it. This suggests that even though they might have espoused the need to teach criticality, they themselves did not engage in critical reflection of or in their own pedagogy.

Those who were actively committed to the promotion and teaching of critical thinking implied that universities' emphasis on employability and market competition was having a detrimental effect on the quality of education:

At this university we've shot ourselves in the foot because we try too hard to align ourselves with industry. We don't really encourage students to think critically. So that while we are producing job-ready graduates who can hit the ground running, about two years down the line they hit the wall because they can't really think independently. As soon as they are promoted a little and asked to make decisions, to research something, to decide on the best option, to benchmark things, they won't be able to do it. This is driven by industry on the one hand, and also by the students because they want that first job. But we try too hard; industry doesn't even want this; they'd be happy for us to stretch students more. (Lecturer)

In disapproving of the university's proximity to industry, this lecturer considered that the supposed corporate-relevancy of postgraduate courses did little to prepare students for the world of work where their credentials might assist their employability but would do little for their longer term careers. In this, the university did a disservice to both students and themselves. However, despite his dissatisfaction with the present system, this lecturer failed to associate the development of critical thinking with the development of skills related to the participation in and the transformation of democratic society. Other lecturers considered that:

It is very narrow-minded for universities to think that because industry doesn't require critical thinking, then we don't have to teach it.

Despite convictions about the importance of critical thinking in higher education, these lecturers considered that the promotion of critical thinking in higher education had become so problematic that they were waning in their enthusiasm for teaching it. There was a reticence to emphasise critical thinking in teaching because this would necessitate 'lots of effort' and 'an unacceptable investment of time' in helping students grasp the principles of critical thinking, in light of the lack of motivation by some, the evident challenges facing many international students, and increasing class sizes.

Not many students appreciate critical thinking, because it is not something you can buy off the shelf. It's an ongoing, continuous struggle – you have to acquire a new habit of making informed decisions. But it's not popular. (Lecturer)

I've had to minimise the critical thinking element for my classes because of large class sizes which make individual feedback impossible. (Lecturer)

To motivate and enable students, lecturers agreed that detailed comments on each piece of assessed coursework was essential if students were to grasp the principles of critical thinking, but 'it is impossible to provide this' when so many students had little, if any, prior experience of these principles, and class sizes were increasing, due to inter alia the massification of higher education.

Recognising that the problem might be insurmountable, some marketing and public relations lecturers opted instead to deliver 'customer service' by providing students with full information and direction to achieve high grades without needing to critically evaluate the material, or engage in a rigorous, intellectual pursuit of truth. In this way, they taught to meet students' consumerist expectations.

> Students today are trained to be spoon-fed, where everything is given to them, and the marking guide is very explicit and spelled out. (Lecturer).

> For many of our assignments we were spoon-fed. The lecturers pointed us in the direction they wanted us to go in, told us what information we needed. So we didn't really need to critically think. (Student)

Some lecturers claimed that assignment guidelines had become like checklists, to ensure that students knew exactly what needed to be included and could 'follow a formula' to achieve good marks. Students were encouraged to rely on prescriptive model answers that left little or no room for thinking creatively, even though lecturers acknowledged that 'there's no such thing as a model answer in industry' and that 'model answers encourage rote learning'. The result was that:

> Theoretical frameworks and tools are not critiqued in courses, and pre-described frameworks are relied on. Case studies are used but whether critical thinking is encouraged or not depends entirely on the level of discussion generated in class. (Lecturer)

While some lecturers in public relations and marketing continued to exert their pedagogical convictions, at the same time they were confronted and challenged by university policies, corporate imperatives and student demands to prioritize practical, professional skills at the expense of theoretical and conceptual engagement. Others were more sanguine or instrumental, bowing to these consumerist expectations.

DISCUSSION AND CONCLUSIONS

The data reveal that there are few distinguishable differences between the British and Australian universities with regard to understandings about critical thinking. However, among those teaching postgraduate courses in marketing communications and public relations, or those about to enter the home or global contemporary labour market, these understandings are multiple and complex. For some, the notion of critical thinking is a perplexing or ambiguous one, difficult to articulate and therefore a practice to be avoided. The understanding of others is partial, their employment of 'weak critical thinking' (Paul 1982) indicating their engagement in a limited form of argumentation which is insufficient to demonstrate the acquisition of higher order skills. Staff and students whose grasp of criticality is well developed, are in the minority. For them, critical thinking involves problematizing issues, gleaning alternative insights from the employment of multiple perspectives on contextualised issues and events, and being capable of argumentation including at a conceptual level. Within the discipline of public relations and marketing communications, then, the data indicate that there are no common understandings about the meaning of critical thinking.

With regard to the value or otherwise of criticality, this is perceived diversely. On the one hand, it is held to be important for personal and professional development. On the other, it is seen by some to have a fundamental role in motivating civic participation in a democratic society. Thirdly and in contrast, it is viewed as not at all relevant for employment in a global labour market. The views of both students and academics are associated with each of these. Some interviewees, mostly students, see little value in acquiring critical thinking skills because of their perceived irrelevance to future careers, or because their home or professional cultures do not encourage criticality. What they want (and believe they need) above all, are vocational tools for employment. In a highly competitive, global labour market, they want to achieve advanced credentials, but they fail to see the relevance of critical thinking as an essential life skill for enabling creative and entrepreneurial endeavour in a knowledge economy, and more importantly its relevance for the development of democratic competency. The majority of students of marketing communication and public relations appear to be content to be customers of education, with education understood as a commodity. However, there remains a significant number who want to be challenged and stretched intellectually at university and who are not content with a narrow education focused on workplace-related skills.

In focusing on critical thinking because it is a crucial component of the 'critical conscience' and therefore an essential competency for democratic engagement, our study has revealed some of the effects of neoliberal globalization on the functioning of the university at the level of teaching and learning. We posit that the impact of neoliberal globalization on teaching is most evident in the increasing tension that lecturers experience between the need to develop intellectual capacity, and a critical conscience, and the requirement to acquire practical, professional skills. Teaching strategies to deal with this tension differ and appear to be changing. Some lecturers continue, despite challenges from university policies, corporate input into education and student demands for practical or professional skills, to promote and teach critical thinking because of its perceived value as core to postgraduate development. Nevertheless, they often experience stress in their endeavours to resist the introduction of university policies and practices designed to achieve economic-driven efficiencies and corporate imperatives. Others succumb to the consumerist demands of students for the standardization of materials, practical skills and learning buttress goals of competitive advantage. In effect, these lecturers follow an instrumental, vocational approach that in the long run is likely to reduce intellectual confidence, creativity and sensitivity to alternative perspectives. The root of these different teaching strategies may lie, firstly, in the diverse meanings held by lecturers of critical thinking and its value in education, or to the extent of resistance or acceptance by lecturers to neoliberal imperatives.

That only a minority of lecturers and students we interviewed appreciated the value of critical thinking not only for productivity but also for its capacity to reveal inequalities, and to facilitate critical and civic engagement in wider social and cultural issues is but one indicator that corporate relevancy as an ideal is flourishing in the modern university. Instrumental teaching strategies which do not engage students with critical thinking, as outlined above, also indicate that the university's democratic functions are withering, if indeed they existed in the first place in the universities where we conducted our research.

Our empirical findings support much of the conceptual arguments around the notion that the global macro forces of neoliberalism are increasingly colonizing the modern university, changing its essential nature, corroding its democratic purposes, in favour of producing graduates who are worker-consumers instead of citizen-subjects (Watkins 2008).

Our findings indicate that course design and content is changing to reflect economic and competitive imperatives. We posit that as this process continues, universities will develop courses that combine modules based primarily around market incentives, and this will lead to a loss of disciplinary coherence and further loss of critical orientation in courses.

To some extent, one might argue that the university is simply a victim of the economic pressures of the advanced capitalism that is associated with globalization and neoliberalism, but our study indicates that the university may be actively generating and contributing to those pressures, not least through the development of students who eventually will become participants in a corporate realm that perpetuates those same pressures. Therefore, with Fallis (2007:415) we argue that it is time now for the university to reconsider its corporate trajectory and make changes by reconsidering its responsibilities to democratic life and accepting the roles of critic and conscience of democratic society. It could begin this process by promoting critical thinking throughout the university and also thoroughly embedding it into all aspects of its teaching and learning activities. As Tenant et al have claimed:

> Promoting a 'critical' engagement is the key –which allows the possibility of questioning existing practices rather than simply aligning oneself with institutional priorities, goals, visions and ways of doing things. (2010, 12)

Strategies might begin with professional development for lecturers. Critical thinking could be made the specific focus of in-training sessions where dedicated space could be given to discuss practices which have proved effective in embedding critical thinking into teaching programs. These sessions could involve the collaborative sharing of good practice, resources and exemplars. Assignment and exam questions could be collaboratively discussed amongst lecturers to ensure they demand an element of criticality. For instance, previous research suggests that taking essay exams rather than multiple choice exams appears to be positively related to students' self-reported growth in critical thinking, and therefore it may be necessary to reconsider the form of assessment throughout courses. New staff could be encouraged to develop their own teaching practices through mentoring as well as peer observation of criticality-rich lessons which would enable them to see in action how critical debate and questioning in the classroom can be encouraged.

To encourage students' critical thinking, lecturers might introduce a range of alternative, or even contradictory, theories and models for students to evaluate with regard not only to their applicability to the contemporary workplace, but also to civic engagement and the democratic sphere. As classrooms become more multi-cultural, lecturers might stimulate interactions amongst students in order to encourage understanding of how different epistemological beliefs and informal theories-in-use can offer useful, alternative ways of dealing with a variety of scenarios and problems. In addition to inviting visiting speakers from public, private, and third sectors (such as charities and activist movements) to reflect on the value of criticality for career progression, lecturers might involve students in debating with guest speakers the implications of professional and corporate activities, such as the potential hegemonic effects on cultures and communities. Research methodology courses could place an emphasis on the critical analysis of research papers, for example by assessing the trustworthiness of findings in light of both the evidence presented to support them, and other published research with contrasting results.

This study is limited in its focus on postgraduate students in one distinct field of study at two universities. We are mindful of Naidoo and Jamieson's (2005) point that because organisational cultures mediate the effects of neoliberal globalization, the experiences of universities and staff and students differ. Further, they note that globalization is playing out differently in different societies and therefore the generalizability of our argument can be only partial. Nevertheless, our investigation straddles universities in two countries and also draws on extant arguments related to the processes and implications of globalization, neoliberalism, criticality and higher education in 'liberal' societies. Therefore, we suggest that these findings and key questions may be transferred with caution more widely to the tertiary sector in order to contribute insights into the colonizing effects of neoliberal globalization on the democratic purposes of the university, with consequences for how present and future citizens are prepared for active participation in the societies to which they belong.

REFERERENCES

Ball, S., Bowe, R., & S. Gewirtz. (1994). Market forces and parental choice. In S. Tomlinson (Ed.), *Educational Reform and Its Consequences* (pp. 17–39), London: Rivers Oram Press/Institute for Public Policy Research.

Banerjee, S. B. (2007). *Corporate social responsibility: The good, the bad and the ugly.* Northampton, MA: Edward Elgar.

Caprioni, P., & Arias, M .E. (1997). Managerial skills training from a critical perspective. *Journal of Management Education 21*(3), 292–308.

Cole, J. R. (2009). *The great American University: Its rise to preeminence, its indispensible national role, why it must be protected.* New York: Public Affairs.

Dozier, D. M. (1992). The organizational roles of communications and public relations practitioners. In J. E. Grunig (Ed.), *Excellence in public relations and communication management* (pp. 327–355). Hillsdale, NJ: Lawrence Erlbaum.

Egege, S., & Kutieleh S. (2004). Critical thinking: Teaching foreign notions to foreign students. *International Education Journal* 4(4), 75–85.

Ennis, R. (1987). A taxonomy of critical thinking dispositions and abilities. In J. Baron & R. Sternberg, R. (Eds.) *Teaching thinking skills: Theory and practice*, (pp. 9–26), New York: Freeman.

Facione, P. A., C. A. Sanchez, Facione N. C., & J. Gainen. (1995). The disposition toward critical thinking. *The Journal of General Education 44*(1), 1–25.

Fairclough, N. (1993). Critical discourse analysis and the marketization of public discourse: The universities. *Discourse and Society* 4(2), 133–168.

Fallis, G. (2007). *Multiversities, ideas, and democracy.* Toronto: University of Toronto Press.

Freire, P. (1998). *Pedagogy of Freedom: Ethics, Democracy, and Civic Courage.* Lanham, MD: Rowman and Littlefield Publishers.

Gibbs, P. (2001). Higher education as a market: A problem or solution? *Studies in Higher Education* 26(1), 85–94.

Giroux, H. A. (2009). Democracy's nemesis. The rise of the corporate university. *Cultural Studies, Critical Methodologies 9*(5), 669–695.

Glaser, E. M. (1985). Critical thinking: Educating for responsible citizenship in a democracy. *National Forum, 65,* 24–27, cited in Ten Dam, G., & M. Volmer. (2004). Critical thinking as a citizenship competence: teaching strategies. *Learning and Instruction, 14,* 359–379.

Hearn, A. (2010). "Through the looking glass". The promotional university 2.0. In M. Aronczyk & D. (Eds), *Powers blowing up the brand. Critical perspectives on promotional culture,* (pp. 195–217). New York: Peter Lang.

Lauder, H., Brown, P., Dillabough J-A., & Halsey, A. H. (2006). Introduction: The prospects for education: individualization, globalization, and social change. In H. Lauder, P. Brown, J-A. Dillabough & A. H. Halsey, (Eds.) *Education, globalization and social change,* (pp. 1–70). Oxford: Oxford University Press.

Mingers, J. (2000). What is it to be critical? Teaching a critical approach to management undergraduates. *Management Learning, 31*(2), 219–237.

Naidoo, R., & I. Jamieson. (2005). Empowering participants or corroding learning? Towards a research agenda on the impact of student consumerism in higher education. Reprinted In H. Lauder, P. Brown, J-A. Dillabough & A. H. Halsey, (Eds) *Education, globalization and social change,* 2006, (pp. 875–884). Oxford: Oxford University Press.

Olssen, M. (2004). Neoliberalism, globalisation, democracy: Challenges for education. *Globalisation, Societies and Education 2*(2), 238–273, reprinted in *Education, Globalization and Social Change,* 2006. H. Lauder, P. Brown, J-A. Dillabough & A. H. Halsey (Eds.) 261–287, Oxford: Oxford University Press.

Paul, R. (1982). Teaching critical thinking in the 'strong' sense : A focus on self-deception, world views and a dialectical mode of analysis'. *Informal Logic Newsletter 4*(2), 2–7.

Paul, R. (1994). Teaching critical thinking in the strong sense. In K. S. Walters (Ed.), *Re-Thinking Reason: New perspectives in critical thinking,* (pp. 181–198). Albany, New York: Suny Press.

Reed, M., & A, P. (1992). Professionalizing Management and Managing Professionalization. British Management in the 1980s. *Journal of Management Studies 2,* 591–613.

Ryan, J. (2010). 'The Chinese learner': Misconceptions and realities. In J. Ryan & G. Slethaug, G. (Eds), *International Education and the Chinese Learner,* (pp. 37–56). Hong Kong, Hong Kong University Press.

Samra-Fredericks, D. (2003). A proposal for developing a critical pedagogy in management from researching organizational members' everyday practice. *Management Learning 34*(3), 291–312.

Simon, S., & S. Banchero. (2010). Teaching role reduced to a balance sheet. The Australian, November 3, 30–31.

Slaughter, S., & G. Rhoades. (2004). *Academic capitalism and the new economy: markets, state and higher education.* Baltimore, Maryland: The Johns Hopkins University Press.

Ten Dam, G., & M. Volmer. (2004). Critical thinking as a citizenship competence: teaching strategies. *Learning and Instruction, 14*, 359–379.

Tenant, M., McMullen & Kaczynski, D. (2010). *Teaching, learning and research in higher education. A critical approach.* New York: Routledge.

Torres, C. A. (2009). *Education and neoliberal globalization.* New York: Routledge.

Tsui, L. (2002). Fostering critical thinking through effective pedagogy. *The Journal of Higher Education* 73(6), 740–763.

Watkins, E. (2008). *Class degrees: Smart work, managed choice, and the transformation of higher education.* New York: Fordham University Press.

Wedlin, L. (2008). University marketization: The process and its limits. In L. Engwall & D. Weaire. (Eds.) *The university in the market* (pp. 143–53). Portland Press: London.

Zell, D. (2001). The market-driven business school. Has the pendulum swung too far? *Journal of Management Inquiry 10*(4), 324–338.

AFFILIATIONS

Christine Daymon
Murdoch University, Australia
Kathy Durkin
Bournemouth University, UK

BETHSAIDA NIEVES

SYSTEMS OF REASON(ING) IN THE IDEA OF EDUCATION REFORMS FOR ECONOMIC DEVELOPMENT: THE PUERTO RICAN CONTEXT

INTRODUCTION

This study focuses on problematizing the systems of reason in the globalization discourse of education reform for economic development. The objective is to analyze Puerto Rican education reforms in terms of developmental policies relating to the social constructions of human capital in linguistic, economic, and biopolitical terms. The primary question guiding this study will be: *Is the drive towards globalizing higher education and research for the knowledge economy becoming another tool of governmentality?* In answering this question, the author examines how language is historically and currently used as a rationale for constructing 'the citizen' and 'the child' within education reforms of Puerto Rico. Specifically, the relationship between language education, economic development, and biopolitics is examined. In addition, the biopolitical implications of producing an education system specifically designed for a knowledge economy is discussed.

BACKGROUND

As a commonwealth striving to become a competitor in the knowledge-based economy, Puerto Rico strives to remain adaptable to the shifting technological, economic, and scientific global trends. However, concerns that current curricula and paradigms in higher education are not able to meet the challenges have encouraged Puerto Rican education administrators to create and implement reforms to meet and surpass global competitors. The competitive advantage of the reforms, I believe, is less about the economy, and more about the political economy. In this sense, the focus on productivity and efficiency becomes less about economic development, and more about education reforms for managing the security, territory, and population of the state.

The idea of education reform for economic development draws on a discourse of globalization. Whether globalization is referenced as a translation, transformation, or transmogrification of ideas, the conveyance of discourses between cultural contexts changes form as they move between the local and the global. Such "traveling" discourses between regional and global systems of governance both reveal and

S. Majhanovich and M.A. Geo-JaJa (Eds.), Economics, Aid and Education:
Implications for Development, 115–124.
© *2013 Sense Publishers. All rights reserved.*

conceal how subjectivities and nations are formed. For the purposes of this chapter, globalization as a discourse used in education reforms for economic development is examined from a theoretical perspective with the intention of applying it to a specific geographical context, which is Puerto Rico. The attempt is not to define what education reform for economic development means for Puerto Rico, but instead, to problematize ways of 'knowing' and 'understanding' the historical development of the idea of education reform for economic development both in and out of the Puerto Rican context. Examining the systems of reason(ing) embedded in education reforms for economic development helps us understand historical rationales for governing the child, and the citizen.

LANGUAGE EDUCATION, ECONOMIC DEVELOPMENT, AND BIOPOLITICS

For over a hundred years, the language education narrative has dominated Puerto Rican education reforms. The 2009–2010 and 2010–2011 Consolidated State Performance Reports for Puerto Rico indicate that approximately 40–45% of students tested at or above proficiency level for reading/language arts and science. During the 2011 *Puerto Rican Education Summit: Investing in Our Future*, held in San Juan, Puerto Rico, language proficiency was central to preparing Puerto Rican students for the global competitive economy of the 21st century. This narrative of language proficiency as a basis for economic development, however, is not new. Historically speaking, *governmentality* was to become a way of thinking and acting, in trying, "to know and govern wealth, health and happiness of populations" (Rose & Miller, 1992, p. 174). Relating this concept of governmentality to Puerto Rico, the question to consider is: Does the drive towards globalizing higher education and research for the knowledge economy become another tool of governmentality? Specifically, does an historical overview of education reform for economic development reveal aspects of governmentality?

At the turn of the twentieth century, language education policy reforms served as a tool of intervention by United States policymakers in the newly established colony of Puerto Rico. MacDonald (2004) points out, "During the period of the Foraker Act [1900–1917], five different commissioners held office, each introducing different policies concerning the scope of English language instruction in the schools" (p. 98). Each incoming commissioner of education changed the official language of instruction in Puerto Rican schools thereby making the language acquisition of both Spanish and English difficult for students. Commissioners of Education rationalized language education policies as necessary for both economic development and human progress. For example, Major General Guy V. Henry, the military governor of Puerto Rico in 1899, maintained that English would be the language of instruction in Puerto Rican schools (Solís, 1994. p. 51; García Martínez, 1976, p. 59). During the same year, U.S. functionary Victor S. Clark organized the School Laws of the Island of Puerto Rico and recommended changes to both school district and public instruction laws (Osuna, 1949). English language instruction, closely linked to the idea of education reform for economic development, remained part of the language education rationale of Puerto Rico. Clark's words printed in the *Teachers' Manual for the Public Schools of Puerto Rico* (1900) would foreshadow the shifting language policies in Puerto Rican education, and the enduring discussion that English would be the language of economic development and human progress:

The justification of the study of the two languages lies in the fact that one is the mother tongue of the great majority of the pupils of this island and is doubtless destined to be the household tongue of the people for many years to come. To exclude its study is to allow it to degenerate into a vulgar and ungrammatical patois. Which, while it would not loosen its tenacious hold upon popular sympathy, would cease to be an active force in the culture and enlightenment of the people. The other language is destined to be the business and political language of this Island, and should be taught in order that the rising generation may have the same advantages in a business, professional or political career as their compatriots of the mainland. (Clark, 1900, p. 70; Navarro, 2002, p. 49).

Samuel McCune Lindsay, Commissioner of Education of Puerto Rico, argued for English language instruction to promote economic development. In Lindsay's (1900) *Report of the Commissioner of Education for Porto Rico,* he writes:

Every effort has been made to encourage the study and use of the English Language. This has been done in the interests of the people of Porto Rico [sic], whose future commercial prosperity depends upon their adoption of the English language as the prevailing speech throughout the island. (Report of the commissioner, 1900/1902, p. 29).

Although Commissioner Lindsay insisted that learning English did not mean the neglect of the Spanish language, he contextualized English language learning in economic terms:

[T]he one common language of social, political, and business intercourse will be the English tongue, common not only to all parts of our national territory but to large sections of the civilized world. We cannot do our duty by the children of Porto Rico [sic], in preparing them to earn a living and to take their place, in public life, in the business world, and in private occupations in the future unless we teach them thoroughly to know the English language. (Report of the commissioner, 1900/1902, p. 30).

The 1902 Official Languages Act made English and Spanish the official languages of government and education in Puerto Rico until 1991, when it was overturned and Spanish became the official language of Puerto Rico (Barreto, 1998, p. 119). In 1993 bilingual education became law, and has been in place until the present day.

Superficially, the limit of language education reform for economic development is that a systematic and standard method for policy implementation was never fully developed. Moreover, the rapid successions of changing language education policies would have a debilitating impact on language learning, as students would achieve fluency in neither Spanish nor English. More fundamentally however, the limiting factor of the language education for economic development argument is that language education reform became a site for political maneuvering and machinations of governmentality, rather than a site for thinking about how to educate students. Language, power, and knowledge relationships were fused into one purview for seeing the 'normal/abnormal' world, which was one in which the Puerto Rican child's language was neither normal nor acceptable for the global economic arena. Power relationships became hidden within the discourse of language education reform for economic development, and discourses of education and reform transmogrified into discussions of human progress.

Currently, Puerto Rico's economy is undergoing a transformation from an industrial based economy to a knowledge based one. Puerto Rico's education system is therefore refocusing its curriculum design to include scientific and technological research and development, entrepreneurship, privatization, and innovation. During the 2011 *Puerto Rican Education Summit: Investing in Our Future*, educators, administrators, students, and parents, as well as government and business stakeholders gathered to both celebrate the recent successes in Puerto Rican education and plan for the future. While recent successes in infrastructure, investments, and bureaucratic reforms were celebrated, all had an eye towards the increasing future student test scores and teacher accountability (Duncan, 2011). The most recent test scores, while not demonstrative of all that a student represents, do show that there is much room for improvement in how and what is taught in Puerto Rican schools (Nieves, 2012):

Percentage of Students Scoring at or Above Proficient 2009–2010
(based on US dept of ed report)

Grade	Mathematics	Reading/Language Arts	Science
3	65.3%	52.2%	Non-testing grade
4	48.3%	39.5%	66.1%
5	37.2%	40.4%	Non-testing grade
6	9.0%	46.5%	Non-testing grade
7	5.8%	32.8%	Non-testing grade
8	7.4%	39.1%	22.6%
HIGH SCHOOL	3.8%	34.9%	39.1%
AVERAGE	25.3%	40.8%	42.6%

Low student test scores, and lack of professional development and accountability for teachers is a major challenge for Puerto Rican schools.

Complicating the already difficult teaching and learning circumstances is the debate over the Bilingual Generation pilot program advocated by former Governor

Percentage of Students Scoring at or Above Proficient 2010–2011
(based on us dept of ed report)

Grade	Mathematics	Reading/Language Arts	Science
3	65.5%	53.6%	Non-testing grade
4	52.1%	44.3%	68.4%
5	40.0%	44.4%	Non-testing grade
6	10.5%	48.4%	Non-testing grade
7	6.8%	37.4%	Non-testing grade
8	8.7%	45.2%	26.7%
HIGH SCHOOL	7.9%	37.5%	46.4%
AVERAGE	27.4%	44.4%	47.2%

of Puerto Rico, Luis Fortuño. The Bilingual Generation program set to run from 2012–2022, "aims to graduate a 100 percent English-Spanish bilingual class from secondary schools by 2022" (Marcano, 2012). As noted in the above chart, the 2009–2010 and 2010–2011 test scores for English language reading proficiency were, on average, between 40–45% for all grades tested. The Bilingual Generation program, begun in August 2012, is intended to raise those figures of 40–45% to 100% by High School graduation (Marcano, 2012). The objective of the pilot program is to teach Math and Science in English, and all other courses in Spanish (HS News Staff, 2012). Ultimately, students will be able to use their bilingual language skills to successfully participate in the knowledge economy, as evidenced by beginning the bilingual program in the subjects of Math and Science. There is, however, much debate over the Bilingual Generation pilot program. With English language education seen as a force of Americanization by some, an instrument for joining the global knowledge economy by others, the narrative of education reform for economic development for Puerto Rico continues to be hinged on bilingual language development.

A third area influencing this discussion of education reform and economic development in Puerto Rico is the biopolitical implications. When Foucault (1978) first introduced the term, 'biopolitics' in *The History of Sexuality* and *The Birth of Biopolitics* 1978–1979 lectures (2008) he defined it as a technique of governing by the state over its population. In contemporary views of biopolitics, the governing of the individual is no longer a sovereign power of the state. Instead, the individual self-regulates and chooses to do so based on information obtained through science and economics. Several researchers have sought to problematize and further redefine Foucault's concepts of biopower and biopolitics. For example, Žižek (2004) defines biopolitics as, "the politics of the administration of life" (p. 509). In borrowing from Bröckling, Simons (2006) defines biopolitics as the " 'intersection between a politicization and economisation of human life' " (p. 524). Closer in definition to both authors Kort (1989) defines biopolitics as, "exponents of the biobehavioral approach to the study of political processes and institutions" (p. 105). For the purposes of this study, I will use Foucault's definition of biopolitics, with the perspective that language education reform becomes the technique of governing by the state over its population. In the case of Puerto Rico, there is a paradoxical relationship between biopolitics and education. The biopolitical will of the state is driving education reform for economic development in Puerto Rico's education system today, but the state is also at the mercy of biopolitical developments driven by the market.

When Foucault introduced the term of biopolitics, he noted that in order to understand biopolitics, one had to understand liberalism (Foucault et al., 2008). Liberalism, according to Foucault, is to be analyzed as a principle and method of the rationalization of the exercise of government, a rationalization which obeys – and that is what is specific about it – the internal rule of maximum economy" (Foucault et al., 2008, p. 318). The internal rule of maximum economy, in part, called for the constant production of freedom. Within the liberal art of government, freedom was used to regulate, to produce and to organize bodies (Foucault et al., 2008). Foucault also correlates biopower and capitalism, which is an area several scholars have seen as the modern day crisis of globalization, leadership, human rights, education, etc. With regards to biopower and capitalism, Foucault (1978) notes:

This bio-power was without question an indispensible element in the development of capitalism; the latter would not have been possible without the controlled insertion of bodies into the machinery of production and the adjustment of the phenomena of population to economic processes. But this was not all it required; it also needed the growth of both these factors, their reinforcement as well as their availability and docility; it had to have methods of power capable of optimizing forces, aptitudes, and life in general without at the same time making them more difficult to govern (p. 141).

Foucault continues to argue that while capitalism was one instrument of the state used to ensure production, it was the anatomo- and bio- politics as a technique of power that sustained economic processes. In other words, although capitalism was considered to be part of the institutions of power, anatomo- and bio- politics of schools, families, armies, police, etc., sustained them (Foucault, 1978, p. 141). In the Puerto Rican case, language education reform can be viewed as a biopolitical technique of power sustaining economic processes. As a commonwealth nation, Puerto Rico's education, governing structure, and economic viability are tied to the United States. In order to sustain itself, Puerto Rico must also sustain its ties in each of these areas to the U.S.

The discussion also pivots on the point that the market drives biopolitical developments. Collin & Apple argue that biopolitics and biopolitical production in relation to neoliberal projects aimed at deregulation, competition, and privatization, put citizens in direct demands of economic markets (Collin & Apple, 2007). They call for researchers to draw from post neo Marxist and post structural theories as a way of clarifying how biopolitics is affecting education in the Global Age. Lemke (2001) like Collin & Apple (2007) also views capitalism in terms of the optimization of the human body in relation to work and to the self, and for creating new forms of social organizations and topographies for understanding the growing needs of biocapital production. Within this understanding, Lemke argues that analyzing biopolitics as a form of governmentality requires a micro- and macro- understanding of politics in order to unpack the relationships between globalization, the semantics of ideologies, and economic structures of production. He states, "This enables us to shed sharper light on the effects neo-liberal governmentality has in terms of (self-) regulation and domination" (Lemke, 2001, p. 203). If considering Puerto Rican education reforms for economic development, a case can be made that the market has driven language education reforms since 1898.

Another layer to this discussion of biopolitics as a type of governmentality in education reforms for economic development is Giroux's (2008) discussion of neoliberalism. Giroux challenges the concept of the entrepreneurial self by arguing that the rationale of neoliberalism is one in which the state gains more power, not less. In this sense too, it can be argued that education reforms for economic development becomes a type of governmentality because the market dictates what the student should learn. Neoliberalism, according to Giroux, is, "a political-economic-cultural project, [that] functions as a regulative force, political rationale and mode of governmentality" (p. 589). He argues that biopolitics is a way of creating stronger ties between the state and corporations because when citizens become entrepreneurial actors; the state is able to promote market values. Individuals and groups displaced by the market are seen as disposable. These displaced individuals, according to Giroux, are viewed by a new hyper-neoliberal state as impediments to market free trade, consumerism and neoconservative ideals. Considering the Puerto Rican case, those who are bilingual are not an economic impediment to the state. The call by Giroux is to stop using, "politics as an act of war and markets as a measure of democracy" (p. 192). Instead, he demands that democracy must prevail in light of the totalitarian essence of the markets, however, "even the "complex" contemporary [democratic] societies still rely on the basic divide between included and excluded" (Žižek, 2004, p. 514). In which case, the "bioeconomy" driven by biopolitics still continues to problematize the ethical notion of who is included, and who is excluded in terms of education, economics, and politics. For Puerto Rico, those unable to learn English and participate in the knowledge economy are excluded and eventually become politically, economically, and culturally displaced.

CONCLUSIONS

Viewed from the aforementioned perspectives, education reforms, economic development, and biopolitics can play a significant role in how globalizing higher education and research for the knowledge economy becomes another tool of governmentality. In this study, the case for biopolitics as a type of governmentality has been examined. First, the complex interplay of language policies and economic development was examined. Then, the discussion of economics and biopolitics was discussed. Finally, it was argued that based on this study, it can be argued that the drive towards globalizing higher education and research for the knowledge economy is becoming another tool of governmentality; however, there are additional aspects to consider. On November 6, 2012 Puerto Ricans living in Puerto Rico voted in a plebiscite that may determine its commonwealth status. On the first portion of the plebiscite, fifty-four percent of all Puerto Rican voters rejected the current commonwealth status, and on the second part of the plebiscite, sixty-one percent of all voters chose U.S. statehood (Castillo, 2012). Moreover, five percent of voters opted for independence, and thirty-three percent for sovereign free associated state (Patterson, 2012). Problematic to the wording of the second part of the plebiscite was that it did not include the current commonwealth status on the list of options. As a result, many voters left the second question blank and the validity of the plebiscite results have come under severe scrutiny. In response, the Obama administration has requested that $2.5 million of its 2014 budget be used to conduct a new plebiscite for Puerto Rico (Caribbean Business, 2013). It would be the first plebiscite funded by the United States Federal Government, and the vote could determine Puerto Rico's political status. The U.S. Congress, however, will ultimately decide whether or not Puerto Rico will become a state. If Puerto Rico were to become a state, the language issue would be central to education, government, and business practices. Spanish is currently the official language of each arena, but as the 51st state, the official language would likely become English. If so, the system of education that is currently in Spanish would need to change, thus raising questions over the language/languages of instruction, testing, and fluency. Furthermore, Puerto Ricans would gain the right to vote for the U.S. president and have official voting rights in the U.S. Congress and U.S. Senate, thus having the potential to impact future educational policy and governance for Puerto Rico. In the meanwhile, the politics of knowledge and social change will continue to rest on the idea that the mastery of English and Spanish will optimize the economic, political, and cultural life of Puerto Rican citizens.

NOTES

[1] Data obtained from following report: http://www2.ed.gov/admins/lead/account/consolidated/sy09–10part1/pr.pdf

REFERENCES

Barreto, A. A. (1998). *Language, elites, and the state: Nationalism in Puerto Rico and Quebec.* Westport, Conn: Praeger.
Caribbean Business Online Staff. (2013, April 10). *PR status plebiscite in Obama budget.* Retrieved from http://www.caribbeanbusinesspr.com/news/obama-budget-has-$2.5m-for-pr-plebiscite-83109.html
Castillo, M. (2012, November 8). Puerto Ricans Favor Statehood for First Time. Retrieved from http://www.cnn.com/2012/11/07/politics/election-puerto-rico/index.html

Collin, R., & Apple, M. W. (2007). Schooling, literacies and biopolitics in the global age. *Discourse: studies in the cultural politics of education. 28*(4), 433–454.

Duncan, A. (2011, October 11). *The road ahead for Puerto Rico.* Retrieved from http://www.ed.gov/news/speeches/road-ahead-puerto-rico

Foucault, M., & Senellart, M. (2008). *The birth of biopolitics: Lectures at the Collège de France, 1978–79.* Basingstoke [England]: Palgrave Macmillan.

Foucault, M. (1991). Governmentality. In Burchell, G., Gordon, C., & Miller, P. (Eds), *The foucault effect: Studies in governmentality with two lectures by and an interview with Michel Foucault,* (pp. 87–104). Chicago: University of Chicago Press.

Foucault, M. (1978). *The history of sexuality.* New York: Pantheon Books.

García Martínez, A. L. (1976). Idioma y política: El papel desempeñado por los idiomas español e inglés en la relación política Puerto Rico-Estados Unidos. San Juan de Puerto Rico: Editorial Cordillera.

Giroux, H. (2008). Beyond the biopolitics of disposability: rethinking neoliberalism in the New Gilded Age. *Social Identities. 14*(5), 587–620.

Government, Washington, D.C. (2012). *Consolidated state performance report: Parts I and II for State formula grant programs under the elementary and secondary education act as amended by the No child left behind act of 2001.* For reporting on school year 2010–2011: Puerto Rico. U.S. Dept. of Education: Washington, D.C.

Government, Washington, D.C. (2011). *Consolidated state performance report: Parts I and II for state formula grant programs under the elementary and secondary education act as amended by the no child left behind act of 2001.* For reporting on school year 2009–10. Puerto Rico. U.S. Dept. of Education: Washington, D.C. Retrieved from http://www2.ed.gov/admins/lead/account/consolidated/sy09-10part1/pr.pdf

HS News Staff. (2012, August 8). *Puerto Rico's bilingual education program begins.* Retrieved from http://www.hispanicallyspeakingnews.com/hispanic-education/details/puerto-ricos-bilingual-education-program-begins/17687/

Kort, F. (1989). Review: Biopolitics as political theory. *Politics and the Life Sciences. 8*(1), 105–107.

Lemke, T. (2001). 'The birth of bio-politics': Michel Foucault's lecture at the Collège de France on neoliberal governmentality. *Economy and Society,. 30*(2), 190–207.

MacDonald, V.-M. (2004). *Latino education in the United States: A narrated history from 1513–2000.* New York: Palgrave Macmillan.

Marcano, I. (2012, July 17). Fortuño's Plan for English Proficiency in Puerto Rico. Retrieved from http://www.coha.org/fortunos-plan-for-english-proficiency-in-puerto-rico/

Navarro, J.-M. (2002). *Creating tropical Yankees: Social science textbooks and U.S. ideological control in Puerto Rico, 1898–1908.* Latino communities. New York: Routledge.

Nieves, B. (2012, April 19). The Past, Present and Future of Puerto Rican Education. Comparative and International Education Society Newsletter, *CIES Perspectives, 1*(158), 12–13. http://www.cies.us/newsletter/april%202012/CIES%20-%20Spring%202012%20Newsletter.pdf

Osuna, J. J. (1949). *A history of education in Puerto Rico.* Rio Piedras, P.R: Editorial de la Universidad de Puerto Rico.

Patterson, D. R. (2012, November 24). *Will Puerto Rico be America's 51st State?* Retrieved from http://www.nytimes.com/2012/11/25/opinion/sunday/will-puerto-rico-be-americas-51st-state.html?pagewanted=all

Puerto Rico., Clark, V. S., & Puerto Rico. (1900). *Teachers' manual for the public schools of Puerto Rico.* New York: Silver, Burdett. Retrieved from: http://www.archive.org/stream/teachersmanualfo00puer#page/70/mode/2up/search/justification

Puerto Rico. (1900). *Report of the Commissioner of Education for Porto Rico for 1900-.* Washington: Govt. Print. Off. Retrieved from: http://openlibrary.org/books/OL20500545M/Report_of_the_Commissioner_of_Education_for_Porto_Rico

Rose, N., & Miller, P. (1992). Political power beyond the state: Problematics of government. *The British Journal of Sociology, 43*(2), 173–205.

Simons, M. (2006). Learning as Investment: Notes on governmentality and biopolitics. *Educational Philosophy and Theory 38*(4), 523–540.

Solís, J. (1994). *Public school reform in Puerto Rico: Sustaining colonial models of development. Contributions to the study of education*, no. 60. Westport, Conn: Greenwood Press.

Žižek, S. (2004). From politics to biopolitics. . . and back, *The South Atlantic Quarterly. 103*(2/3), 501–521.

AFFILIATION

Bethsaida Nieves
Department of Curriculum and Instruction
University of Wisconsin-Madison

HU RONGKUN, QIAN HAIYAN & ALLAN WALKER

DECENTRALISATION, MARKETISATION, AND QUALITY-ORIENTATION

Major Pursuits of Basic Education Reforms in China from 1985 to 2010

This chapter aims to present the major pursuits of basic education reforms in China from 1985 to 2010. It includes three sections. The first section briefly analyses the international educational context that has greatly influenced reforms in Chinese basic education. The second section depicts the backgrounds of the reforms. The third section focuses on specific education reform and policies directly shaping the present educational context.

INTERNATIONAL EDUCATION CONTEXT

In the past two decades or even much earlier[1], globalization has been a term widely used to describe

... the intensification of worldwide social relations which link distant localities in such a way that local happenings are shaped by events occurring many miles away and vice versa. (Held, 1991, p. 9)

The process blurs national boundaries, shifts solidarities within and between nation-states, and deeply affects the constitution of national and interest-group identities (Morrow, &Torres, 2000). Governments throughout the world are eager for more cooperation with other nations in order to enhance their economic competitiveness (Mok, 2003). New approaches to maximising productivity and effectiveness have been sought for the purpose of improving the efficiency and effectiveness of public service (Dale, 1997).

As a consequence, neo-liberal ideology has been rapidly recognised as a solution and has gained an international advocacy. The turning-point happened in the years 1978–1980 when 'neoliberalism' was adopted by the newly-elected Thatcher and Reagan Governments[2] in the UK and the US, followed by a group of developed countries such as Australia, New Zealand, and Canada (Harvey, 2005). Accordingly, the neo-liberal doctrines[3] took the place of the Keynesian welfare regime, which prevailed in the third quarter of the 20th century (Panic, 1995), and dominated most recent globalisation discourse and policy.

Hence, there has been a fundamental change in the relationships among the state, the public sector and the market. The role of the government shifted from

S. Majhanovich and M.A. Geo-JaJa (Eds.), Economics, Aid and Education: Implications for Development, 125–142.

'provider of welfare benefits' to 'builder of market' (Sbragia, 2000). Strategies of marketisation, devolution, choice and privatisation were implemented in most Western communities (Henry *et al.*, 1999). The responsibilities of the state were increasingly shared by other actors, including the market, the family, the third sector and individuals (Peters *et al.*, 2000; Rhodes, 1997; Salamon, 2002).

Such a trend has caused dramatic changes to the character and functions of education in most countries around the world (Mok, 2003, p. 3). Burbules and Torres (2000, p. 15) explicitly state that

> In educational terms, there is a growing understanding that the neo-liberal version of globalisation, particularly as implemented (and ideologically defended) by bilateral, multilateral, and international organisations, is reflected in an educational agenda that privileges, if not directly imposes, particular policies for evaluation, financing, assessment, standards, teacher training, curriculum, instruction, and testing.

Central to the reform is decentralisation[4]. Despite the diversified strategies and outcomes visible in different countries, educational decentralisation has been a common initiative for governments around the world (Mok, 2003). It aims to dismantle centralised educational bureaucracies and to create improved educational systems entailing significant degrees of autonomy on educational institutions to unleash their initiative, creativity and productivity and accomplish quality education (Hanson, 1998; Power *et al.*, 1997). With that purpose, school based management has been widely adopted as a mode of school autonomy, which is perhaps the most common reform initiative worldwide over the past decades (Moos, & Møller, 2003).

Meanwhile, marketisation and privatisation[5] have become the most popular policy strategies for reforming educational institutions (Mok, 2005; Mok, & Currie, 2002). More types of agencies other than the state are allowed to engage more in education (Dale, 1997). The importance of parental choice and competition between various forms of provision has been stressed, and an 'education market' or 'quasi-market' has emerged in the West (Bridges, & McLaughlin, 1994; Le Grand, & Bartlett, 1993). During the process, many management practices used in market sphere or private sector have been introduced into school administration (Lindblad *et al.*, 2002). Schools are encouraged to manage through output controls, explicit standards and goals of performance, clear targets and indicators of success, preferably in quantitative forms (Dempster, 2000; Blackmore, 2004). The role of the state has gradually shifted from a direct provider of educational service to an umpire and a regulator of the market (Chan, 2002; Sbragia, 2000).

This does not mean a weakening of the state power. In fact, the state's control on school education has actually tightened in virtue of a process of recentralization or centralised decentralisation (Mok, 2003). For example, the state can regulate the operation of school education *via* a recentralised curriculum and an emphasis on accountability (Mcinerney, 2003; Moos, & Møller, 2003); by the establishment of certain regulatory mechanisms and/or assessment/quality assurance systems, the state can determine where the work will be done and by whom, and steer the development of educational institutions indirectly (Massen, & van Vught, 1994; Neave, 1995; Whitty, 1997).

In the era of globalisation, this wave has influenced the education reforms and policies occurring in individual nation states around the globe (Lindblad et al., 2002; Papagiannis et al., 1992). Due to the distinct social and educational contexts, however, the specific measures and impacts are not uniform in different countries (Mok, 2003). The following section displays the unique background of Chinese basic education reforms.

BACKGROUNDS OF CONTEMPORARY CHINESE EDUCATION

Social Background

As one of the most important countries in the 21st century, China had not actively communicated with the outside world until the late 1970s when the 3rd Plenum of the 11th Congress of the Chinese Communist Party decided to reorient China toward the market and implement 'reform and opening-up' policy (Yergin, & Stanislaw, 1998). Before that, China had generally isolated itself from the Western capitalist economy with a highly centralised 'planned economic system' where everything was under the state control and state-owned-enterprises dominated nearly all domestic economic sectors (Starr, 2001). Through adopting the reforming policy, the idea of the market economy was introduced from the West to establish the 'socialist market economy' in the country (Mok, 1997b; Yergin, & Stanislaw, 1998).

This shift coincided with the turn to neo-liberalism in Western countries (Harvey, 2005). The importance of the market and free enterprise was gradually recognised (Yergin, & Stanislaw, 1998; Hayhoe, 1996) and relevant reforms emerged in agriculture and industry[6]. More efforts, such as edging into the World Trade Organization, have been made to integrate its economics into the global business system (Lejour, 2000). Many Western notions, e.g. effectiveness, performance and competition, penetrated into Chinese economic system and broke 'the eating-out-of-the-big-pot egalitarianism' and 'iron-rice-bowl' ideology[7] that had originated from the previous planned economy (Harvey, 2005).

With the shift in its economy, the Chinese government has carried out a series of administrative reforms since the early 1980s (Pittinsky, & Zhu, 2005; Starr, 2001; Tsao, & Worthley, 1995). All these reforms focus on the decentralisation and transformation of governmental functions, aiming to promote the process of constructing democratic politics, transform governmental functions and enhance administrative efficiency (Zhang, & Zhang, 2001). The government has gradually shaken off the bonds of the planned economic system and turned itself from an 'omnipotent government' into a 'limited government' that would pay more attention to providing public products and service (Zhang, & Zhang, 2001). People began to reflect on the traditional 'hierarchy' ideology underling the Chinese administration

127

system and be aware of participation, competition, equity and responsibility (Zhang, & Zhang, 2001; Starr, 2001).

However, the society of mainland China still exhibits strong Eastern cultural elements. Unlike the rule-based capitalistic society[8] in the West, Chinese society is founded on social relationships and interlocking social networks that comprise overlapping networks of people linked together through differentially categorised social relationships (Fei, Hamilton, & Wang, 1992). The philosophy of this society favors an aesthetic construction toward virtue rather than the foundational, metaphysical reality in Western societies (Lessem, & Palsule, 1997). Action is determined by a nominalist consensus about what is acceptable and what 'we' can work with (Lowe, 2003, p. 7). During the economic transformation, the traditional culture seems to be suppressed but it actually plays an important role in the seemingly westernised society (Liu, 2003; Starr, 2001).

At the same time, political control always features the transformation of this society. The government still takes too many responsibilities and tries to play the role of social intermediary (Harvey, 2005). What has emerged in China is a particular kind of market economy that increasingly incorporates neoliberal elements with authoritarian centralised control (Harvey, 2005). In this sense, the present Chinese society can be described as a mixture of Western values system, traditional culture and mainstream political ideology.

Within the broad social context, contemporary Chinese basic education has been undergoing a process of transformation towards decentralisation and marketisation (Mok, 1999). The initial round of basic education reforms in China generally aimed to change the basic education system that existed before 1985.

Basic Education System Before 1985

From 1949 to the late 1970s, the Party-state[9] set up a centralised education system (Ngok, & Chan, 2003). This educational system featured three characteristics: politicalisation in setting educational goals and curriculum, high-level centralisation in educational administration, and exam-orientation in school education.

First, politics and political ideology played an important role in setting education goals and curriculum. All decisions or actions about education made by the Chinese Communist Party (CCP) were mainly determined by its contribution to the goal of building China into a powerful socialist country (Yang, 2003). In a word,

> Education must fill its political role, must serve the proletariate politically and also must be united with productive labor, and finally it must be carried out under the leadership of the Party. (CNIER, 1983, p. 213)

Hence, the major tasks of education was the training of a 'red and expert'[10] (*youhong youzhuan*) working class intelligentsia to achieve the four modernisations (CCPCC, & SC, 1958). Training talent with the socialist ideology became the upmost aim of

Chinese schooling. The focus on political ideology reached its height during the Cultural Revolution (1966–1976) (see Cleverley, 1991).

Second, the government established a highly centralised educational administration system. All educational establishments were placed under the leadership of the central education authority[11]. Provinces, autonomous regions, and centrally administered municipalities placed education departments under the direction of local governments. In line with the directives or regulations issued by the central authority, these departments directly attended to local educational administration, involving ordinary administration, teaching staff arrangements, equipment, and financial management, etc. Counties, cities, and municipal districts had their educational bureaus taking care of administrative work in secondary and elementary schools. With the hierarchical framework, the state assumed nearly all responsibilities for schooling.

Meanwhile, the centralised system was tightened through an ideological control and a cadre (*ganbu*)[12]-based personnel system at the school level (Huang, 2005; Lin, 1993). Each elementary and secondary school had a Party branch or committee, headed by the secretary, who was appointed by a higher level communist authority. Important matters had to be submitted to the school Party committees or branches for decision. Most school leaders appointed by local authorities served as both party secretary and principal, the chief administrator of the school. They had nominal official ranks[13] which were usually determined by the status of their schools and, in turn, determined their income (Huang, 2005; Yang, 2004). In this way, schools came under the control of the Party and the government.

Third, the key school system and national College Entrance Examination (CEE) system aggravated the exam-orientation in school education. Because of the limited resources in the early years of the new China, policy-makers determined to reserve quality educational resources for students who were identified as priorities of the socialist construction. As a result, a small number of schools were selected, re-organized, funded, and transformed into 'key schools' (*zhongdian xuexiao*) (Yuan, 1999). These schools, whose main purpose was to prepare the most promising students for higher education, were usually assigned more financial resources, better teachers, and students with higher scores on competitive entrance tests.

At the same time, the national CEE system, reinstated after the Cultural Revolution (1966–1976), intensified 'exam prepping' to an extreme. It was seen as almost the only way and the most effective way of selecting intellectually qualified candidates for higher education (Kwong, 1983, Yang, 2003) and as an approach to achieving social and economic mobility (Niu, 1992). In order to pass the exam, students had to first enter a key school – if a student could not enter the key school during the whole period of basic education, it would be unlikely for him or her to be admitted to a university (Kwong, 1983). Thus, the whole basic education system in China became highly competitive and test-oriented. Teachers made their students focus on examination materials and rote learning; the school administration extended school hours, assorted and placed students into different tracks, overloaded students with extra assignments, and devoted the senior years to examination preparation (Liao, 1993; Niu, 1992; Yang, 2003).

Against the social and educational background mentioned above, the next section specifies the primary reform efforts made in basic education between 1985 and 2010, which largely reshaped the basic education system in contemporary China.

BASIC EDUCATION REFORMS IN MAINLAND CHINA FROM 1985 TO 2010

As the market reforms and the 'open-door' policy were implemented in the late 1970s, the post-Mao Chinese leaders increasingly realised the significance of education for China's economic development and social progress. But the existing educational system was woefully inadequate to contribute to the new economic opportunities (Hawkins, 2000, p. 443). Thus, in May of 1985, the CCPCC convened a conference and released a general policy[14] initiating the reform in education. From then on, the central authority promulgated a series of educational policies driving the education reforms in order to make schooling better serve the needs of the Chinese labor market and economic development and promote China's global competitiveness (Hawkins, 2000).

Being affected by strong market forces and the global neo-liberalist ideology, these reform policies have fundamentally reshaped China's educational system in terms of orientation, financing, curriculum and management (Agelasto, & Adamson, 1998). Two major focuses stand out successively from these changes. From the mid-1980s to the early 1990s, the transformation mainly targeted aligning the educational system with the newly emerging market economy through the process of decentralisation and marketisation (Hawkins, 2000). With the reform deepening, quality education has become the paramount pursuit driving the change in China's schooling since the early 1990s. These two aspects are explained in the following section.

Reshaping Educational System for Market Economy

From the mid 1980s to the early 1990s, the reform aimed to reshape the educational system and correct the over-centralisation of political power and bureaucratism to meet the needs of the emerging market economy (Chu, 2008; Pepper, 1993; Shi, & Zhang, 2008). The specific measures centred on diminishing the Party's influence on administrative matters, reducing the state's participation and rigid governmental control over schools, devolution of authority to local levels and increasing the place of the market in providing education. These led to a series of fiscal, structural and management reforms in China's education.

First, a more decentralised funding system for basic education has been gradually established. Since the '*Decision of the Chinese Communist Party Central Committee on the Reform of the Educational System*' (CCPCC, 1985) made the first step to devolve financial responsibility to lower levels, educational officials at the county, township and village level began to pursue alternative sources to fund basic education. The *Compulsory Education Law* explicitly stipulated that local authorities assume responsibility for compulsory education (NPC, 1986). These reform documents suggested six basic methods for funding precollegiate education: subsidies provided by central authorities (the main source), urban and rural educational surcharges levied by local governments, tuition for non-compulsory education and incidental fees collected from students, income from school-run enterprises, contributions from industry and social organisations, donations from community organisations and individuals, and the establishment of educational funding (see Wang, 2009).

In 1995, the *Education Law* established legislatively this funding system which blends central and local governmental financial support along with various alternative channels in the public and market spheres (NPC, 1995). Accordingly, principals of higher quality schools can raise additional school revenue from school-run businesses and fees paid by some 'choice students'[15] (*zexiaosheng*). Although the bulk of the funding still comes from state resources, the role of the central government has been considerably reduced (Hawkins, 2000).

Second, the structure of basic education has experienced a market-oriented change. There were two major measures. One was to diversify educational services. The new policy began to actively encourage and fully support social institutions and citizens to establish schools according to law and to provide guidelines and strengthen administration (CCPCC, 1993). Hence, a variety of non-governmental or semi-private schools have emerged and competed with the government schools in pre-collegiate education (Tsang, 2001). The other one was to promote vocational education to cultivate talents for the market economy because this type of education was believed to be better than general education in training young people for employment in industry (Tsang, 2000). Therefore, the senior secondary education was changed from the predominance of general education to an equal mix of general education and vocational education (CCPCC, 1985).

These steps not only helped the government to narrow the gap between limited educational resources and the public need of education, but also promoted the introduction of competition and market mechanism into Chinese educational system (see Hawkins, 2000; Mok, 1999; 2003). As a result, an 'internal market' or 'quasi-market' has slowly developed in the Chinese educational system (Chan, & Mok, 2001; Mok, 1997a, 1997b). With the process, self-financing students emerged as customers in the education marketplace and some related issues, such as school choice[16] and arbitrary charges levied by schools, began to appear in Chinese basic education (Chan, & Mok, 2001; Tsang, 2000; 2001).

Third, much more administrative power of school education has been devolved to lower levels. With the policy towards decentralisation and marketisation, the state has gradually retreated from direct control over school management and deliberately increased the responsibility and administrative power of lower authorities and school leaders. As a result, local governments could define the school-entry age, school staff commitments and duties, teachers' salaries, duration of basic education and structure of nine-year compulsory education, and determine school curricula and textbooks, as well as supervise the operation of school education (Hawkins, 2000).

131

At the school level, the adoption of the principal responsibility system drew a distinct line between the duties and responsibilities of a principal and those of a Party secretary and enabled school principals to run schools with much more autonomy. Under this system, a school has both a principal and a party secretary. Principals are in charge of the school's daily administration and can make decisions independently on such matters as student admissions and teacher assignments without consulting with the Party secretary (Delany, & Paine, 1991). Party secretaries' responsibility is to make sure that school leaders follow CCP's educational policies and organise various activities for Party members (SEC, 1991).

By virtue of the reform initiatives in this period, education was closely related to the nation's economic development. The central government gradually changed its approach to managing education, from direct control to indirect monitoring and supervision through legislation, funding, planning, and advice on policies. Local authorities and various social energies and resources were motivated, mobilized and channeled to provide educational services. The previously highly centralised educational system has undergone the processes of decentralisation and marketisation (Ngok, 2007).

However, the reform did not make much change with respect to the political and ideological control over schools and the exam-orientated tradition of Chinese education. School principals were included in the cadre system and thus worked like governmental officials (Qian, 2008). Ideology-based moral education continued to be given top priority in both personnel administration and school education, which was predominated by the uniform curriculum formulated by the central government (see Yuan, 2007). The key school system continued and the high selective CEE still overarched the entire phase of basic education.

Furthermore, new issues emerged. For example, district disparity grew with the process of decentralisation (Wang, 2009). In the rich areas, the local governments could provide sufficient financial support for basic education, whereas many schools in poor and rural areas could hardly get enough funds to pay teachers, purchase instructional materials, and improve school facilities (Tsang, 2002). The competition for quality educational resources not only led to two chronic problems: a one-sided pursuit of promotion rates to a higher level of schooling and the academic overloading of students (Yang, 2003), but also caused some corruption in education – unqualified students are accepted to a higher level of schooling or a key school though '*guanxi*' – back door, personal relationship, or kinship (see Yuan, 2007).

All these were harmful for the development of basic education in China. Policy-makers began to think about how to improve the educational system. As a consequence, improving educational quality became the major goal of the reform initiatives in the next stage.

Improving Schooling for Quality Education

Since the early-1990s, the notion of quality education, originally as an antithesis to 'examination-oriented education', was proposed as a guiding principle of basic education reform. This term was first officially used in the *Advice of the Chinese Communist Party Central Committee (CCPCC) on Further Reinforcing and Improving Moral Education in Schools* in 1994 (CCPCC, 1994). In 1998, achieving quality education was formally set as a goal of the education reform (MoE, 1998). In 1999, quality education received 'full-scale promotion' (CCPCC, 1999). A series of reforms have been initiated in terms of school classification, the curriculum and examination system and the personnel system. Senior secondary education became a field which has captured considerable attention under the banner of quality education.

Exemplary school system. One of the early measures was to adopt an 'exemplary school' system to replace the previous 'key school' system. The new system is designed to identify quality education practices within all kinds of high schools, whether previously key or ordinary schools, so that the exemplary schools can exert their influence and lead the other schools towards better schooling. In 1994, the State Council (SC) explicitly posited that

By the end of 20th century ... nationwide priority is given to build about 1000 experimental, exemplary high schools (see SC, 1994).

In the next year, the State Education Commission (SEC) reconfirmed the strategic importance of developing exemplary schools on the basis of the previous key school system and emphasised that all levels of government and educational administration as well as all social circles should further prioritise and enhance the development of exemplary high schools by increasing resources input, improving school conditions, and motivating the exemplary schools (SEC, 1995).

Hence, a bunch of exemplary or model high schools, many of which were original key schools, have been established and developed by the local authorities all over the country, especially in Beijing, Tianjin, Shanghai and the east coastal provinces, where the local governments are able to provide adequate resources to support the construction of exemplary schools. As required, these schools have made some breakthroughs or extraordinary achievements in promoting quality education and have met the high-standard criteria for the physical environment and equipment of the school (SEC, 1995). To some extent, the exemplary high schools, taking the place of the former key schools, represent quality educational resources and outcomes in contemporary China.

Curriculum and examination reforms. Accompanying the change in school classification, a profound transformation has taken place in the school curriculum and examination system to reduce students' workload and change the examination orientation of Chinese basic education. A new curriculum outline, *Compendium for Curriculum Reform of Basic Education (trial edition)*, was published in 2001 and amended in 2002 (see Feng, 2006; Lo, 2000). This new framework aims to shift the basic education curriculum:

– from a narrow perspective of knowledge delivery in classroom teaching to a perspective concerned with learning how to learn and develop positive attitudes;

- from isolation among subjects to a balanced, integrative, and selective curriculum structure;
- from imparting out of date and extremely abstruse content to teaching essential knowledge and skills relevant to students' lifelong learning;
- from students' passive learning to developing their capacities to process information, obtain new knowledge, analyse and solve problems, as well as communicate and cooperate with others;
- from exclusively viewing the function of curriculum evaluation to be identification and selection to paying attention to the other functions, i.e., the promotion of student growth, teacher development, and instructional improvement; and
- from a centralised curriculum control to three levels of control system: central government, local authorities, and schools. (Feng, 2006)

Consequently, a new type of comprehensive course (*zonghe kecheng*), which combines the contents of several subjects, has been introduced into basic education. A three-level curriculum system has been formed, including national curriculum, local curriculum and school curriculum. Accordingly, schools today are supposed to develop their own school-based curriculum (*xiaoben kecheng*) according to their unique characteristics or the unique demands of local communities (MoE, 2001a).

These innovations were first implemented at the level of compulsory education in 38 pilot districts in 27 provinces in 2001 and then expanded to the whole nation in the following three years (Song, 2002). In light of the positive effects[17] and informative experiences collected in the prior phases, a new round of curriculum reform for general high schools started in four provincial districts in 2004. By 2009, the wave had engulfed 24 (of 31) provincial districts of China. In a word, high school education is emerging as the centre of the latest curriculum reform in Chinese basic education.

Accordingly, two major exams conducted in the senior secondary education, the municipal-level High School Entrance Exam (HSEE) and the national-level CEE, were changed to match the orientation of the curriculum reform. As the scores of these two entrance examinations are the most important determinants of admission to high schools and colleges, they always act as a key 'lever' to adjust school instruction (Feng, 2006; Qian, 2008). Thus, the reform continued to aim to reduce the exam-orientation of drilling and teaching. In 2002, the MoE first officially stipulated that: within the nine-year compulsory education system, students are enrolled on a catchment area basis[18]; the HSEE should consider students' overall quality and individual differences and change the total-score-based admission; besides the score on the exam, admission can be determined according to the records of student growth, social practice and social public service activities, sports and arts activities, and integrated practice activities (MoE, 2002).

As to the CEE, the expanding of university enrolment since 1999 somewhat alleviated the pressure. From the beginning of this millennium, the exam time[19], frequency[20] and subject areas[21] have all been adjusted to reduce the competitive nature of the exam and the attendant burden imposed on high school students. Meanwhile, the original centralised exam system was gradually replaced by provincial determination of exam contexts[22] (Shi, & Zhang, 2008). And the government has gradually delegated the power of enrolment to individual higher education institutions[23]. In October 2009, Peking University, one of the top universities in China and a world-renowned institution, proposed to add 'nominations from secondary school principals[24]' to the original CEE system. In 2010, the university will pilot the initiative in thirteen provincial districts, including Beijing and Tianjin, to recruit extraordinary students with well-rounded qualities or certain forte(s).

Personnel reforms. Another approach to improving school education was to change the school personnel system. The reform mainly concerns two groups of people: principals and teachers. Both of them have experienced a change in terms of the management system and professional development.

For school principals, more initiatives have been made to strengthen their professional role as school leaders. A professional ranking system, career ladder system (*zhiji zhi*) with a new pay scale for principals was proposed in 1993 and first tried out in two districts (Jing'an and Luwan) in Shanghai in 1994. Following that, the system came into effect in one district in Beijing in 1996. After the innovation had been piloted in many cities[25], the state council decided to actively promote the career ladder system nationwide and empower local authorities to design their own implementation schemes (SC, 2001). Although different, the specific systems set up in different districts of China are all designed to abolish the official rank of principals (i.e., the cadre system), separate the functions of government from school affairs, and form an open, fair, competitive and merit-and-competence-based selection and reward mechanism to facilitate principals' professional growth and ultimately promote quality education (Huang, 2005). The *Implementation Advice on Deepening Personnel System Reform in Primary and Secondary Schools* (MoP[26], 2003) restated the decision of abolishing the official rank system, promoting engagement hiring system for principals and implementing a tenure system in schools.

For teacher management, more autonomy has been given to school principals in teacher recruitment and promotion. According to *Implementation Advice on Deepening Personnel System Reform in Primary and Secondary Schools* (MoP, 2003), the teacher hiring system will be completely adopted in primary and secondary schools. Individual schools can recruit new teachers, interview candidates and submit a list of qualified candidates to the local education bureaus for approval. Furthermore, a performance-based system of professional ranks and rewards has been required to be implemented in schools (MoP, 2003). By virtue of the system, teachers can be promoted or rewarded in light of their performance. To promote the three-level curriculum system, a number of national professional training programs have been designed for school principals and teachers and school-based professional training has been emphasised (Feng, 2006). Professional development has become an essential component of school human resource management.

Compared with the structural reform in the preceding period, these ongoing actions towards quality education reflect the efforts made by Chinese government to resolve the chronic problems embedded in the Chinese basic educational system. Through these initiatives, basic education in China today is directed towards more emphasis on school accountability for teaching and learning, on student-centred teaching and learning, on local and school realities, on individual needs and all-round development of students, and on teachers' and principals' professional qualification and development.

In conclusion, Chinese educational system, like those in many Western societies, has been reshaped by a series of neo-liberal reforms conforming to changes in Chinese society. The economic development and societal transformation in China have posed a variety of new issues and challenges to its education system, which constitute a contextual demand for education reform. The ongoing education reforms are an active response to the demand and aim to better support and promote economic and societal development in China.

NOTES

[1] According to Morrow and Torres (2000), there are as least three basic views with respect to the origins of globalisation. Some have asserted that it develops with the origins of human civilization that is more than five centuries old. A more influential theory links it with the origins of capitalism, culminating with the emergence of a global economy in the 16th century. A third perspective that exploded in 1990s considered it a more recent phenomenon that dates from the mid-twentieth century or perhaps the last two decades. Here the focus is not the origin of the phenomenon, but rather its effects on global education environment.

[2] Margaret Thatcher was elected Prime Minister of Britain in 1979. Ronald Reagan was elected President of the United States in 1980.

[3] Two core principles are honoured by the neoliberal doctrines: the superiority of markets over politics in providing for human needs, generating prosperity and enhancing personal freedom, and the need to defend individuals' market rights, including property rights, the right to assert one's inequality and the right to choose from a diversity of goods and services in the market place. (See Faulks, 2000, p. 75)

[4] Decentralistion refers to both devolution and deconcentration (see Bryant &White, 1982; Stevens, 1994).

[5] In broad terms, privatization points to the reduction of state intervention and the transfer of responsibility for production from the state to the non-state sector; marketization signifies the development of market mechanisms and adoption of market criteria within the public sector (Mok, 1997a, 1997b).

[6] The reform started from agriculture with the adoption of a 'household responsibility system', which ensures that each family is responsible for the land it tills. In the mid-1980's, the reform began to focus on restructuring state-owned-enterprises (SOEs) in order to make them more responsive to the requirements of market and competition. (See Yergin and Stanislaw, 1998; Hayhoe, 1996).

[7] The two idioms refer to the system of guaranteed llifetime employment in state enterprises, in which the tenure and level of wages ae not related to job performance" (Qian, 2008, p. 23).

[8] The system relies on verifiable public information and accepted legal processes.

[9] The term 'Party-state' is used to describe China's political system which is dominated by the CCP (Starr, 2001).

[10] This term was used to define a cultured, socialist-minded worker who is developed in an all-round way, both politically conscious (i.e., red) and well educated (i.e., expert) (see CCPCC & SC, 1958).

[11] The Ministry of Education (MoE) was first established in 1949 by the government. In 1970, the MoE was abolished and a Leading Group of Science and Education was set up within the State Council. In 1975, the MoE was reinstated but replaced by the State Education Commission (SEC) in 1985. In 1998, the SEC was renamed MoE (see Xiong, 2006).

[12] 'Cadre' (ganbu) is a formal appellation of the governmental officials in China (Huang, 2005).

[13] For example, a principal of a provincial/municipal key high school had an official rank generally equal to that of the mayor of a county; a principal working in a county/district key school, had a rank equal to that of a deputy mayor.

[14] i.e., the *Decision of the Chinese Communist Party Central Committee on the Reform of the Educational System (CCPCC, 1985)*.

[15] Normally, students receiving basic education, especially the nine-year compulsory education, are required to attend schools in their district of residence. But parents still can pay a fee for their children so that they can enter some public schools in other districts and/or with higher entry threshold, or non-government schools (see Tsang, 2000; 2001).

[16] See footnote 24.

[17] Three years after the implementation of curriculum reform, there has been a positive tendency in learning and teaching processes in the pilot districts (MoE, 2004).

[18] The nearby enrolment was reconfirmed by the *Compulsory Education Law* revised in 2006.

[19] In 2003, the CEE began to be held on June 7–9 instead of July 7–9.

[20] In 2000, the CEE began to be held twice a year (spring and summer) instead of once per year (summer) in pilot areas. Today only Shanghai still follows this policy.

[21] Since 2002, the CEE has been restricted to four subject areas in a model of 3+X. Within the model three subject areas are required, i.e., Chinese, Math, and English, and candidates are allowed to choose one or more additional subjects from the following: Physics, Chemistry, Biology, Politics, History, and Geography; this decision was made in light of the requirements of a specific college. Before the reform, six subject areas would be tested according to the broad major division the examinees prefer. For students wishing to major in the arts, the exam involved Chinese, English, mathematics, geology, history, and politics. For science majors, the exam covered Chinese, English, mathematics, physics, chemistry and biology.

[22] The exam content can be determined by the provincial authorities individually or collectively.

[23] The 2003, the government started a pilot program of 'independent enrolment of universities', involving 22 higher education institutions nationwide. These universities could control 5% of the planned quota to recruit qualified candidates.

[24] According to this plan, secondary school principals, who are qualified to recommend students to Peking University, can nominate outstanding students according to the quota. The number of this type of candidates is no more than 3% of the total number of the students that the university plans to recruit. The nominated and qualified candidates can directly participate in the interview, and are exempted from the independent enrolment examination held by Peking University. If they pass the interview, they can be admitted with a much lower score than the normal admission score (see OSRoPU, 2009).

[25] E.g. Shenyang, Dalian, Zhongshan, Guangzhou, Guiyang, Zhucheng.

[26] The Ministry of Personnel (MoP) was merged into the Ministry of Human Resources and Social Security in 2008).

REFERENCES

Agelasto, M., & Adamson, B. (1998). *Higher education in post-mao China*. Hong Kong: Hong Kong University Press.

Blackmore, J. (2004). Restructuring educational leadership in changing contexts: A local/global account of restructuring in Australia. *Journal of Educational Change, 5*, 267–288.

Bridges, D., & McLaughlin, T. H. (Eds) (1994). *Education and the market place*. London: Falmer Press.

Bryant, C., & White, L. G. (1982). *Managing development in the third world*. Boulder Co: Westfield Press.

Burbules, N. C., & Torres, C. A. (2000). *Globalization and education: Critical perspectives*. New York & London: Routledge.

Chan, D., & Mok, K. H. (2001). Educational reforms and coping strategies under the tidal wave of marketisation: A comparative study of Hong Kong and the Mainland. *Comparative Education, 37*, 21–41.

Chan, Y. C. (2002). Policy implications of adopting a managerial approach in education. In K. H. Mok & K. K. Chan (Eds.) *Globalisation and education in Hong Kong* (pp. 243–258). Hong Kong: Hong Kong University Press.

China National Institute for Educational Research (CNIER). (1983). *The chronology of educational events of the people's Republic of China* (中华人民共和国教育大事记). Beijing: Educational Science Publishing House. (in Chinese)

Chu, H. (2008). A brief review on the basic education administration system reform over past 30 years in our country (我国基础教育行政管理改革30年简评). *School Administration* (中小学管理), *11*, 4–8. (in Chinese)

Cleverley, L. (1991). *The schooling of China* (2nd ed.). North Sydney: Allen & Unwin Pty Ltd.

Dale, R. (1997). The state and governance of education: an analysis of the restructuring of the state-education relationship. In A. H. Halsey, H. Lauder, P. Brown & A. S. Well (Eds.) *Education: Culture, economy, society* (pp. 273–282). Oxford, England: Oxford University Press.

Delany, B., & Paine, L. W. (1991). Shifting patterns of authority in Chinese schools. *Comparative Education Review, 35*, 23–43.

Dempster, N. (2000). Guilty or not: the impact and effects of site-based management on schools. *Journal of Educational Administration, 38*, 47–63.

Faulks, K. (2000). Political sociology: A critical introduction. Edinburgh, Scotland: Edinburgh University Press.

Fei, X. T., Hamilton, G. G., & Wang, Z. (1992). From the soil: The foundations of Chinese society (乡土中国). *A translation of Fei Xiaotong's Xiaotong Zhongguo*. With a Translation and Epilogue by Gray G. Hamilton & Wang Zeng. Berkeley and Los Angeles, CA & London, England: University of California Press.

Feng, D. M. (2006). China's recent curriculum reform: progress and problems. *Planning and Changing, 37*, 131–144.

Hanson, M. E. (1998). Strategies of educational decentralization: Key questions and core issues. *Journal of Educational Administration, 36*, 111–128.

Harvey, D. (2005). *A brief history of neoliberalism*. New York: Oxford University Press.

Hawkins, J. N. (2000). Centralization, decentralization, recentralization: Educational reform in China. *Journal of Educational Administration, 38*, 442–454.

Hayhoe, R. (1996). *China's universities, 1895–1995: A century of cultural conflict*. New York and London: Garland.

Held, D. (1991). *Political theory today*. Stanford: Stanford University Press.

Henry, M., Lingard, B., Rizvi, F., & Taylor, S. (1999). Working with/against globalisation in education. *Journal of Education Policy, 14*, 85–97.

Huang, W. (2005). Primary and middle school principal: From the executive pose to the managerial profession (中小学校长：从行政职务到管理职业). *Theory and Practice of Education, 4*, 19–23. (in Chinese)

Kwong, J. (1983). Is everyone equal before the system of grades: Social background and opportunities in China. *The British Journal of Sociology, 34*, 93–108.

Le Grand, J., & Bartlett, W. (Eds.) (1993). *Quasi-Markets and Social Policy*. London: Macmillan.

Lejour, A. (2000). China and the WTO: The impact on China and the world economy. Paper prepared for the *Annual conference of global economic analysis*, Melbourne, Australia, June 20–30.

Lessem, R., & Palsule, S. (1997). *Managing in four worlds: From competition to co-creation*. Oxford: Blackwell.

Liao, G. (1993). Thoughts on the current college-university entrance examination and the general middle school graduation examination. *Chinese Education & Society, 26*, 83–96.

Lin, J. (1993). *Education in post-mao China*. Wesport, CT & London: Praeger Press.

Lindblad, S., Johannesson, I. A., & Simola, H. (2002). Education governance in transition: an introduction. *Scandinavian Journal of Educational Research, 46*, 237–245.

Liu, S. (2003). Culture within culture: Unity and diversity of two generations of employees in state-owned enterprises. *Human Relations, 56*, 387–417.

Lo, L. N. K. (2000). Educational reform and teacher development in Hong Kong and on the Chinese Mainland. *Prospects, 30*, 237–253.

Lowe, S. (2003). Chinese culture and management theory. In I. Alon (Ed.), *Chinese culture, organizational behavior, and international business management* (pp. 3–26). Westport, CT: Praeger Publishers.

Massen, P., & van Vught, F. (1994). Alternative models of governmental steering in higher education: an analysis of steering models and policy-instruments in five countries. In L. Goedegebuure & F. van Vught (Eds), *Comparative policy studies in higher education* (pp. 35–63). Utrecht: Lemma.

Mcinerney, P. (2003). Moving into dangerous territory? Educational leadership in a devolving education system. *International Journal of Leadership in Education, 6*, 57–72.

Mok, K. H. (1997a). Marketization of education in the Pearl River Delta. *Comparative Education Review, 41*, 260–276.

Mok, K. H. (1997b). Privatization or marketization: Educational development in post-mao China. *International Review of Education, 43*, 547–567.

Mok, K. H. (1999). Education and the market place in Hong Kong and mainland China, *Higher Education, 37*, 133–158.

Mok, K. H. (Ed.) (2003). *Centralization and decentralization: Educational reforms and changing governance in Chinese societies*. Hong Kong: Comparative Education Research Centre, University of Hong Kong.

Mok, K. H. (2005). Globalization and educational restructuring: University merging and changing governance in China. *Higher education, 50*, 57–88.

Mok, K. H., & Currie, J. (2002). Reflections on the impact of globalization on educational restructuring in Hong Kong. In K. H. Mok & D. Chan (Eds.) *Globalization and education: The quest for quality education in Hong Kong* (pp. 259–277). Hong Kong: Hong Kong University Press.

Moos, L., & Møller, J. (2003). Schools and leadership in transition: The case of Scandinavia. *Cambridge Journal of Education, 33*, 353–370.

Morrow, R. A., & Torres, C. A. (2000). The state, globalization, and educational policy. In N. C. Burbules & C. A. Torres (Eds.) *Globalization and education: Critical perspectives* (pp. 27–56). New York & London: Routledge.

Neave, G. (1995). The stirring of the prince and the silence of the lambs: the changing assumptions beneath higher education policy, reform and society. In D. D. Dill & B. Sporn (Eds.) *Emerging patterns of social demand and university reform: Through a glass darkly* (pp. 54–71). Oxford: IAU Press.

Ngok, K. (2007). Chinese education policy in the context of decentralization and marketization: Evolution and implications. *Asia Pacific Education Review, 8*, 142–157.

Ngok, K., & Chan, K. (2003). Towards centralization and decentralization in educational development in China: The case of Shanghai. In K. H. Mok (Ed.), *Centralization and decentralization: Educational reforms and changing governance in Chinese Societies* (pp. 81–98). Hong Kong: Comparative Education Research Centre, University of Hong Kong.

Niu, D. (1992). *Policy education and inequalities: In communist China since 1949*. Lanham: University Press of America.

Office of Student Recruitment of Peking University (OSRoPU, 北京大学招生办公室). (2009). *Peking University's implementation plan for 'Nominations from secondary school principals'* (北京大学关于试行"中学校长实名推荐制"的实施方案). Retrieved January 10, 2010, from http://www.gotopku.cn/data/detail.php?id=4913.

Panic, M. (1995). International economic integration and the changing role of national governments (pp. 51–78). In Ha-Joon Chang & R. Rowthorn (Eds.) *The role of the state in economic change*, Oxford: Clarendon Press.

Papagiannis, G. J., Easton, P. A., & Owens, J. T. (1992). *The school restructuring movement in the USA: An analysis of major issues and policy implications*. Paris: UNESCO.

Pepper, S. (1993). Educational reform in the 1980s: A retrospective on the Maoist era. In M. Y. Kau & S. H. Marsh (Eds.) *China in the ear of Deng Xiaoping: A decade of reform* (pp. 224–278). New York: M. E. Sharpe.

Peters, M., Marshall, J., & Fitzsimons, P. (2000). Managerialism and educational policy in a global context: Foucault, neoliberalism, and the doctrine of self-management. In N.C. Burbules, & C.A. Torres (Eds.) *Globalization and education: Critical perspectives* (pp. 109–132). New York and London: Routledge.

Pittinsky, T. L., & Zhu, C. (2005). Contemporary public leadership in China: A research review and consideration. *The Leadership Quarterly, 16*, 921–939.

Power, S., Halpin, D., & Whitty, G. (1997). Managing the state and the market: "New" education management in five countries. *British Journal of Educational Studies, 45*, 342–362.

Qian, H. (2008). *The secondary school principalship in China: Leading at the cusp of change.* Unpublished doctoral dissertation, The Chinese University of Hong Kong, Hong Kong.

Rhodes, R. A. W. (1997). *Understanding governance: Policy networks, governance, reflexivity and accountability.* Buckingham: Open University Press.

Salamon, L. M. (2002). *The tools of government: A guide to the new governance.* Oxford: Oxford University Press.

Sbragia, A. (2000). Governance, the state, and the market: what is going on? *Governance, 13*, 243–250.

Shi, Z. & Zhang, X. (2008). Education reform: Experience from China. *Journal of Beijing Normal University* (Social Science), *5*, 22–32. (in Chinese)

Song, X. (2002). *The focal issues in pilot districts of curriculum reform: An interview with Zhu Muju,* Deputy Director, Office of Basic Education, Ministry of Education. Retrieved January 10, 2010, from http://library.jgsu.edu.cn/jygl/gh02/lwj/3935.htm.

Starr, J. B. (2001). *Understanding China: A guide to China's economy, history, and political structure (Revised and Updated Edition).* New York: Hill and Wang.

Stevens, K. (1994). A framework for the analysis of shared decision making in rural New Zealand Schools. Paper presented at the *International conference held by the rural education research and development centre,* Townsville, Australia.

The Chinese Communist Party Central Committee (CCPCC), & the State Council (SC). (1958). *Instructions of the Chinese communist party central committee and the state council on educational work* (中共中央、国务院关于教育工作的指示). Retrieved January 10, 2010, from http://news.xinhuanet.com/ziliao/2005–01/05/content_2419375.htm. (in Chinese)

The Chinese Communist Party Central Committee (CCPCC). (1985). *Decision of the Chinese communist party central committee on the reform of the educational system* (中共中央关于教育体制改革的决定). Retrieved January 10, 2010, from http://news.xinhuanet.com/ziliao/2005–02/06/content_2554936.htm (in Chinese)

The Chinese Communist Party Central Committee (CCPCC). (1993). *Outline of educational reform and development in China* (中国教育改革与发展纲要). Retrieved January 10, 2010, from http://old.hnedu.cn//fagui/Law/12/law_12_1044.htm. (in Chinese)

The Chinese Communist Party Central Committee (CCPCC). (1994). *Advice of the Chinese communist party central committee on further reinforcing and improving moral education in schools* (中共中央关于进一步加强和改进学校德育工作的若干意见). Retrieved January 10, 2010, from http://www.moe.edu.cn/edoas/website18/15/info3315.htm. (in Chinese)

The Chinese Communist Party Central Committee (CCPCC). (1999). *Decision of the Chinese communist party central committee and the state council on deepening education reform and promoting quality education in an all-round way* (中共中央国务院关于深化教育改革全面推进素质教育的决定). Retrieved January 10, 2010, from http://www.cycnet.com/zuzhi/ywdd/files/014.htm. (in Chinese)

The Ministry of Education (MoE). (1998). *Action plan for revitalizing education towards the 21st century* (面向21世纪教育振兴行动计划). Retrieved January 10, 2010, from http://www.moe.edu.cn/edoas/website18/70/info1226904382825770.htm. (in Chinese)

The Ministry of Education (MoE). (2001a). *Compendium for curriculum reform of basic education (trial edition)* (基础教育课程改革纲要) (试行). Retrieved January 10, 2010, from http://www.edu.cn/20010926/3002911.shtml. (in Chinese)

The Ministry of Education (MoE). (2002). *Circular on active promotion of the assessment and examination system reform in primary and secondary schools* (关于积极推进中小学评价与考试制度改革的通知). Retrieved January 10, 2010, from http://www.moe.edu.cn/edoas/website18/05/info405.htm. (in Chinese)

The Ministry of Education (MoE). (2004). *Third evaluation report of curriculum reform in compulsory education* (义务教育课程改革第三次评估调查总结报告). Retrieved January 10, 2010, from http://www.eps.bnu.edu.cn/news/Article/Class3/Class17/200602/1764.html. (in Chinese)

The Ministry of Personnel (MoP). (2003). *Implementation advice on deepening personnel system reform in primary and secondary schools* (关于深化中小学人事制度改革的实施意见). Retrieved January 10, 2010, from http://www.moe.gov.cn/edoas/website18/49/info5649.htm. (in Chinese)

The National People's Congress (NPC). (1986).*Compulsory education law of the people's Republic of China* (中国人民共和国义务教育法). Retrieved January 10, 2010, from http://learn.tsinghua.edu.cn/flfg/js/yiwujiaoyufa.htm. (in Chinese)

The National People's Congress (NPC). (1995). *Education law of the people's Republic of China* (中国人民共和国教育法). Retrieved January 10, 2010, from http://learn.tsinghua.edu.cn/flfg/js/jiaoyufa.htm. (in Chinese).

The State Council (SC). (1994). *Advice of the State Council on implementing the Outline of Educational Reform and Development in China* (国务院关于《中国教育改革和发展纲要》的实施意见). Retrieved January 10, 2010, from http://www.jnsms.com/edu/code/ggfz.html. (in Chinese)

The State Council (SC). (2001). *Decision of the state council on reform and development of basic education* (国务院关于基础教育改革与发展的决定). Retrieved January 10, 2010, from http://www.edu.cn/20010907/3000665.shtml. (in Chinese)

The State Education Commission (SEC). (1991). *Post qualification and position requirement for a principal in the national middle or primary school* (*trial edition*) (全国中小学校长任职条件和岗位要求) (试行). Retrieved January 10, 2010, from http://gx.pudong-edu.sh.cn/ReadNews.asp?NewsID=462. (in Chinese)

The State Education Commission (SEC). (1995). *Circular on the assessment and acceptance of 1000 exemplary general high schools* (关于评估验收1000所左右示范性普通高级中学的通知). Retrieved January 10, 2010, from http://www.hxedu.gov.cn/ReadNews.asp?NewsID=615. (in Chinese).

Tsang, M. C. (2000). Education and national development in China Since 1949: Oscillating policies and enduring dilemmas. *China Review 2000*, Hong Kong: Chinese University Press.

Tsang, M. C. (2001). *School choice in the People's Republic of China*. Occasional paper, June, Teachers College, Columbia University.

Tsang, M. C. (2002). *Intergovernmental grants and the financing of compulsory education in China*. Memo, June, Teachers College, Columbia University.

Tsao, K., & Worthley, J. (1995). Chinese public administration: Change with continuity during political and economic development. *Public Administration Review, 55*, 169–174.

Wang, W. (2009). Equity and adequacy in education finance: An analysis of compulsory education finance reforms and regional disparities in China (中国义务教育财政改革与地区差异分析：教育财政的公平与充足). *Journal of Public Administration, 2*, 101–125. (in Chinese)

Whitty, G. (1997). Marketization, the state and the re-formation of the teaching profession. In A. H. Halsey, H. Lauder, P. Brown & A. S. Wells (Eds.) *Education: Culture, economy and society*. Oxford (pp. 299–310). England: Oxford University Press.

Xiong, W. Z. (2006). On problem of the name of state administrative organ (国家行政机关名称问题探究). *Administrative Law Review, 3*, 22–27. (in Chinese)

Yang, D. P. (2003). A slow sunrise: challenges confronting China's modern education in the 20th century (艰难的日出：中国现代教育的二十世纪). Shanghai, China: Wenhui Press. (in Chinese)

Yang, G. S. (2004). Actively Explore, Adventurously Practice, and Accelerate the Establishment of Principal Career Ladder System (积极探索，勇于实践，加快建立校长职级制度). Retrieved January 10, 2010, from http://www.edu.cn/20010830/209975.shtml. (in Chinese)

Yergin, D., & Stanislaw, J. (1998). *The commanding height: The battle between government and the market place*. New York: Simon and Schuster.

Yuan, G. F. (2007). An analysis of national educational assessment policy in the People's Republic of China and the United States. Unpublished doctoral dissertation. Cleveland State University, Cleveland, OH, US.

Yuan, Z. G. (1999). *On Chinese educational policy transformation: Case studies on equality and efficiency of key-point middle schools in China* (论中国教育政策的转变:对我国重点中学平等与效益的个案研究). Guangzhou, China: Guangdong Educational Press. (in Chinese)

Zhang, C., & Zhang, M. (2001). Public administration and administrative reform in China for the 21st century. Paper presented at the *ASPA on-line virtual conference*, Panel #44 of ASPA 62nd Annual Conference, Newark, NJ.

AFFILIATIONS

Dr. Hu Rongkun
Faculty of School Leadership Training and Research,
Beijing Institute of Education

Dr. Qian Haiyan
Department of Education Policy and Leadership
Hong Kong Institute of Education

Dr. Allan Walker
The Joseph Lau Luen Hung Charitable Trust Asia Pacific Centre for Leadership and Change & Department of Education Policy and Leadership
Hong Kong Institute of Education

HELENA MODZELEWSKI

NARRATIVE AS AN EDUCATIONAL TOOL FOR HUMAN DEVELOPMENT AND AUTONOMY

A Case Study with Homeless Single Mothers in Uruguay

INTRODUCTION

There is broad agreement that political literacy is probably the most important issue in the quest for strong democracy (Barber, 1984).[1] However, there is also agreement that schools alone cannot provide the student with an education in democratic values because it is in fact the family that is the primary moral educator of the child. Parents are children's first moral teachers. In addition, while children change teachers almost every year, they tend to keep the same parent throughout their formative years. This parent-child relationship also involves a very important emotional aspect because this relationship can cause children to feel either loved and worthy or unloved and unworthy (Honneth, 1996; Nussbaum, 2005). These feelings can stay with a person for the rest of his/her life. Additionally, the degree to which parents are able to teach their children to respect their authority is also thought to lay the foundation for future moral growth (Damon, 1990; Herman, 2008; Kochanska et al, 2005). Therefore, paying attention to parents, in addition to schools, is an issue of utmost importance in the building of strong democracy.

In the developing countries where most children are born in homes with incomes below the official poverty level, many of the factors that influence the development of values are absent (Cortina & Pereira, 2009). Poverty naturally coexists with other important family risk factors such as inadequate health care, the inability to provide a stimulating learning environment in the home, chronic exposure to violence, and poor parental mental health.[2] How can we advance towards strong democracy in the developing countries if, apart from focusing on the schools, parents' political literacy is not emphasized as well?

CONTEXT

In Montevideo, capital of Uruguay, hundreds of homeless people depend on night shelters provided by the State. These shelters consist of large houses owned by the State, where homeless people can stay the night, but have to leave in the morning. Some of these people have found themselves homeless only recently, because of particular economic circumstances, but others were born in that situation, know no

S. Majhanovich and M.A. Geo-JaJa (Eds.), Economics, Aid and Education:
Implications for Development, 143–156.

other life and thus cannot see a way out. This is a terrible handicap for democracy because these people represent a growing population of citizens who have not been able to acquire the basic capabilities that would let them lead a life with minimum respectable characteristics, let alone the capabilities necessary to decide on what is best for their community, to participate and to vote.

Concerned with this problem, in 2006 the Ministry of Social Development called on non-governmental organizations (NGOs) to apply for funds in order to develop projects aiming at different solutions. NGO *Centro para el Desarrollo de Intervenciones y Estudios Socioculturales* ("Center for the Development of Sociocultural Studies and Policies"), applied and was granted funds for a Daytime Activity Center for homeless single women with children (Cortina & Pereira, 2009).

Why focus on this population in particular? According to Martha Nussbaum (2000), an appallingly great number of women in the world lack the necessary social, affective and economic support in order to carry out the fundamental functions of a human life. They experience malnourishment more frequently than men, and are more vulnerable to physical violence and sexual abuse. They have fewer opportunities to become literate and even less access to professional or technical education. Nussbaum goes on to say that on accessing the labor market they face obstacles such as intimidation from their own families, salary discrimination and sexual harassment, often without effective legal resources. Overwhelmed by their lives, coping with both remunerated jobs and full responsibility for their children and homes, they usually lack opportunities for entertainment or the cultivation of imaginative and cognitive faculties. Such social and political circumstances, as Nussbaum (2000) points out, translate into unequal human capabilities (pp. 1–4).

However, as Amartya Sen has indicated countless times, women are a substantial factor when it comes to reducing poverty. According to Sen (1999), since women are the ones that care for the children, they become the model for future citizens, as well as usually being the ones who manage the family's economic resources. Some social policies focusing on women have resulted in a better quality of life for the whole family and a decrease in infant mortality rates. An example of this is the Indian State of Kerala (Sen, 1999, pp. 193–202).

Nevertheless, one of the problems of the implementation of such policies is the preferences that the very women express. Martha Nussbaum (2000, p. 112) points out that often, existing preferences are not good references for social policies, because their genesis is mixed with circumstances outside the subjects' control.

One of the assumptions underlying this work is the existence of specific kinds of preferences, the *adaptive preferences,*[3] which spring from the persistent frustration of expectations. This frustration may shape preferences in such a way that the subjects experience a desire for some circumstances in their life that do not seem rational, whereas they reject possibilities leading to changes in their situation (Vigorito et al, 2010).

Consequently, the main aim of the Daytime Activity Center mentioned above was to provide these women with tools that could give them the chance to see their own lives in a different way, thus motivating them to look for ways to change their homeless condition. As a result, this could provide their children with the example of an autonomous[4] life, which the children could then internalize.

The Daytime Activity Center operated between January 2007 and December 2010. It was open 365 days a year from 9 a.m. to 6 p.m., and housed sixty people (women and children) at a time. The most interesting aspect of this case study was its results: whereas in other State shelters or drop-in centers for the homeless in Montevideo people tend to settle down and consider of these places as home, in this Daytime Activity Center 60% of the total number of guests chose to look for steady jobs,[5] find their own place to live, and leave. This may have meant that the educational activities carried out in the Center aiming at the reconstruction of these women's autonomous identity worked significantly well.

In this article I shall first present why, according to Sen's capability approach, it is important to work with women to achieve social changes. Second, the concept of adaptive preferences will be presented as the main obstacle in the target population's decision-making. Third, the notion of rational emotions will be explained as the way out of the problem of how to educate emotions. Next, the methodology used in this case study will be justified by explaining the narrativity of emotions, which makes them feasible to aim at through the use of narrative, and by presenting the importance of working with others – the other women in the group or the educator. Finally, the case study will be approached through the description of a specific example whose positive results were particularly enlightening.

THEORETICAL FRAMEWORK

As has been already pointed out, this work is based upon Amartya Sen's capability approach and his conviction that women are a significant factor when reducing poverty is concerned. Sen's capability approach serves as a normative framework for welfare assessment.[6] From this framework, it is possible to determine: i) when a person is in a better or worse social position, ii) what poverty is, iii) what the best ways for development are, and iv) what measures should be taken in order to realize justice. The growing importance of this perspective mainly originated from Sen's remarkable participation in the debate on distributive justice that started after the publication of *A Theory of Justice* by John Rawls (1971). In this discussion, the capability approach brought together a range of ideas that were usually excluded from traditional approaches to the economics of welfare. The main focus of the capability approach is on what individuals can do, thus introducing a dimension to the evaluation of well-being called "capability".

Sen (1999) assimilates the concept of capability to the freedom a person has of achieving his/her goals. In consequence, in assessing how well a person is or what should be done to support someone in the pursuit of his/her life plan, the emphasis must be moved from resources such as income, to the meaning these resources carry for the individual. Resources are essential for anyone to realize his/her life plan, but the capability approach evaluates their impact on individual freedom. From this perspective, poverty becomes less dependent on the resources someone has, and is associated with other circumstances such as the education that someone has received, his/her propensity to disease or how the values of his/her community affect his/her decisions. Since from this perspective women are usually less free than men, it is Sen's position that they should be particularly focused on by social policies.

As caretakers for children, women tend to be the model for future citizens. They are usually the ones who manage the economic resources of the family as well, so good practices learnt from their mothers are transmitted to future adults –and citizens. Some social policies focusing on women have given rise to a better quality of life for whole families and to decreasing infant mortality rates. The Indian State of Kerala is an example of this (Sen, 1999). Taking into account India's particularly impoverished situation, Kerala stands out as extraordinary. In addition to its remarkable literacy rate, Kerala has the lowest infant mortality rate in India and quite a low fertility rate. Apart from this, Kerala's growth rate has not only kept pace with the national average, but also at times ranked among the highest in the country.

The "Kerala secret" remains a matter for speculation and debate among development experts. Part of the explanation may be as follows. In the first place, Kerala was historically a matriarchal society; a tradition with which the social policies carried out recently did not clash. These social policies, as Amartya Sen points out, have included a focus on basic education, basic health care and equitable land distribution. These policies were focused especially on women, who are not only mostly literate, but also greatly recognized in their property rights, which is perhaps favored by the traditional matriarchal society mentioned above.

However, Kerala does not stand out for its income levels, which clearly shows that it is not necessarily higher income that is needed to combat marginalization, but rather something related to education, the development of capabilities and the subversion of values. As a matter of fact, even material needs are defined within the exercise of one's capabilities; that is to say, in order to be able to know how to change someone's life, it is necessary to know what is wrong with it, what he/she really needs. Poverty is a very general concept that cannot be grasped straight away; the conceptualization of it—to understand why someone is poor, what aspects of his/her life should be changed in order for him/her to combat his/her own poverty— may require the exercise of political freedoms and civil rights, because it certainly requires discussion and exchange. For example, basic income, without any kind of cultural reference or reflection, can be spent in a totally ineffective way. As Sen espouses:

> Political and civil rights, especially those related to the guaranteeing of open discussion, debate, criticism, and dissent, are central to the processes of generating informed and reflected choices. These processes are crucial to the formation of values and priorities, and we cannot, in general, take preferences

as given independently of public discussion, that is, irrespective of whether open debates and interchanges are permitted or not. (Sen, 1999, p. 153)

As Katherine Simon (2001) points out, to be a citizen is not just to hold a legal status in relation to a particular State; rather it is to possess the capacities and have access to the opportunities to participate with others in the determination of one's society. It can be gathered from the above statement that although it is important to focus on women when thinking about social policies, to only provide them with things such as income, health and civil rights—and simply hope that they make use of them—is not enough. Something else must take place, some kind of education in the use of these elements that women can gain or lose in the twinkling of an eye if they are not autonomously able to make use of them. That is the reason why Sen says that preferences cannot be taken as given; to handle money in a careless way, to pay little attention to one's own health and to decide not to send one's children to school are not simply "preferences". They are tendencies acquired over the course of one's life that are learned, and therefore can also be unlearned.

Consequently, Martha Nussbaum (2000, p. 112) says that one of the problems with the implementation of social policies is the preferences expressed by the very women at whom these policies are aimed. This is because many existing preferences are not good references since their genesis ·is mixed with circumstances outside the subjects' control. As a matter of fact, it has been demonstrated that *adaptive preferences* (Elster, 1983; Nussbaum, 2000) spring from the persistent frustration of expectations, which shape preferences in a way that makes the person experience an irrational desire towards some circumstances in his/her life, at the same time he/she rejects opportunities that would help him/her change his/her situation. The challenge is, then, to find a way to dismantle such preferences by, in Harsanyi's (1982, p. 55) words, getting to the core of these women's "true preferences" in order to help these women realize on their own what is really better in order for them to lead their lives autonomously. It is their preferences that have to be changed.

As already mentioned, the frustration generated by desiring something that cannot be obtained ends up favoring a preference towards the conditions the person already has. It is evident that these adaptive preferences come from *frustration*, which is an essentially emotive reaction towards a certain state of affairs. This emotive reaction explains the fact that, for example, a person living in extreme poverty, or a battered wife, does not take any action in order to change his/her situation. Being emotive, this reaction does not conform with our intuitions about the rationality of human behavior.

However, emotions in general, and these emotions in particular, are far from irrational, in spite of the insistence by the dominant rationality on labeling them as such. It is precisely because of this kind of emotive rationality that it is possible to change adaptive preferences, as I will try to explain below.

In the following pages I am going to develop the idea that emotions can indeed be rational, as well as discuss a suitable method for re-educating them. This is Nussbaum's (2000, p. 15) "narrative method", which was applied to this case study.

147

METHODOLOGY

In order to make the methodology intelligible, first it is necessary to explain what I mean by "emotive rationality". Rationality has traditionally been seen as linked to models of impartiality and invulnerability. Emotions, along with poetry, have been left aside when considering the elements that should take part in State institutions. In looking for an alternative, Nussbaum strongly criticizes this new "common sense", dominant in our modern age, which states that pure reason and calculation are capable of solving every problem. She primarily goes against Rational Choice Theory, with its utilitarian roots, which, through the *Law and Economics* movement led by Richard Posner, affirms that it is only possible to consider someone's choices as rational in the normative sense if it can be demonstrated that such choices have been made according to the utilitarian concept of rational maximization and do not reflect the influence of emotional factors. This position has ended up being so attractive that it has colonized almost every aspect of human life, including morality. Consequently, under the influence of these ideas, morality tends to be considered as a system of objective and impartial "principles to be grasped by the detached intellect" (Nussbaum 2005, p. 1), whereas emotions are understood as motivations that can either support or subvert our choice to follow a certain principle.

In contrast, Nussbaum (2005, p. 1) considers emotions as "intelligent responses to the perception of value", thus including them "as part and parcel of the system of ethical reasoning". In this conception, emotions are not given a privileged place of trust in moral philosophy, as they may be no more reliable than any other set of beliefs. However, it is recognized that emotions cannot be ignored, as they often are.

Nussbaum (1997) assumes that the contrast between emotion and reason has been taken for granted in public discourse, but beyond this contrast, there is an error or insufficiency in the definition of what emotions are, as well as confusion between the descriptive and the normative uses of the term "reason". In fact, even if the definition of "reason" might be conceived of without emotional elements such as compassion or gratitude, this does not imply that, normatively, the excluded elements should be treated as dispensable.

As an example, she mentions the instructions given to a jury in a particular court case in the State of California in 1986. When the jury was about to make a decision, they were warned against letting themselves be led by sentiment, sympathy, passion, prejudice or public opinion (Nussbaum, 1995). A good jury, it was said, shall come as close as possible to a purely rational decision.

However, it is possible to refute all main objections made about the consideration of emotions. In the first place, emotions are usually claimed to be unthinking energies that simply push the person around. Nussbaum (2005) rejects this position by saying that emotions cannot be unthinking as they are *about* something: they have an object. That is to say, my fear is not simply the physical reaction of trembling or heart-leaping; it is provoked by an object that I fear.

148

Secondly, emotions are said to be dissociated from judgment, and thus irrational. Again, the author discharges this objection by saying that the emotion's object is, in addition, an *intentional* object. Fear that someone I love could die not only has this person as an object, but also speaks volumes about the person, about myself and about our relationship. It shows how much the person means to me, which could be translated into a very complex judgment, such as: "Many times I crave company; this person's company is particularly pleasing to me; this person is important to me; therefore I would suffer if she died". This complex stream of thought involves very dense, rich perceptions of the object, such as memories and imagined events in the future. Therefore, emotions are far from dissociated from judgment. In fact these judgments are not only statements about the present ("I love this person"), but mainly about the past ("She helped me when I was down; we had a lot of fun together last summer"), thus constituting the narrative structure of emotions. This is important in order to fully understand the methodology used in this case study, which I shall discuss below.

Based on this conception of "rational emotions", Martha Nussbaum attempts to understand the causes by which a person reaches the circumstances he/she finds him/herself in at a particular point in his/her life that have consequently generated adaptive preferences; the method she has developed is called the "narrative method" (Nussbaum, 2000). She states that in order to understand the reasons why a person has developed adaptive preferences it is necessary to get acquainted with the narrative that the person constructs regarding the circumstances that have led to his/her current situation in his/her life.

The explanation for this is quite simple. All human beings build their identities and their relationships with others around a narrative core that can be compared to the plot of a story (the Aristotelian *mythos*). It is different from examining an inanimate object: in order to know whether a table is a table, I need to perceive its characteristics and know the definition of a table –quite a static process. In order to know whether a friend is a friend, I need to know the narrative of the events that have created the bond between us – a dynamic process. Narratives, however, can be constructed in different ways around the same events, so that the same event can be perceived as having different causes depending on the subjective point of view from which it is observed. Psychoanalysts know this very well; therapy is an instance of re-narration of certain events in a patient's life. In Nussbaum's (1990b, p. 204) words, it all boils down to escaping the "self-stereotyping" that the subject has made of him/herself, thus being able to avoid behaving in accordance with this self-assigned stereotype.

Likewise, adaptive preferences can be understood as an emotional reaction towards frustration; people tell their own stories in a way that justifies their lack of achievement. In fact, frustration appears when experiencing some *cognitive dissonance*, which can be defined as an uncomfortable feeling caused by facing or holding two contradictory and simultaneous ideas. The ideas may include attitudes, beliefs and the awareness of one's own behavior (Festinger et al, 1966).[7] It is

149

human nature to want to achieve a certain coherence or internal consistence in one's own opinions and attitudes. This desired coherence could be assimilated into the particular way in which humans connect the events in their lives as a kind of plot or *mythos,* as mentioned above. Under this perspective, inconsistencies or cognitive dissonances can be fought by fixing the plot so that the new narrative organization restores coherence. That is why Nussbaum needs narrative in order to find the causes of the development of this psychological phenomenon.

Therefore, Nussbaum uses the narrative method to comprehend why a person develops adaptive preferences, although she does not put it forward as a restorative method.[8]

Conversely, in order to help someone *out* of adaptive preferences, the hypothesis used in this case study is that it is necessary to give the person the opportunity to retell his/her own story in order to trace back the string of events, emotions and beliefs that have shaped a certain outcome. What is new about this case study is the fact that, while Martha Nussbaum uses the narrative method in order to *explain* the reasons why a person develops adaptive preferences, in this case study the narrative method has been applied so as to *revert* this development.

The fact that this re-telling of these women's stories takes place in a group if done orally, or with a "teacher" or "coordinator" as the audience if written, is crucial. The reconstruction of a person's life story cannot be formulated in a monological way; it is necessary to carry it out in front of others, or rather *through* others (Mead, 1934; Taylor, 1992; Ricoeur, 1992; Honneth, 1996), who play a key role in the process of the constitution of identity. This has led these authors, among others, to affirm that identity is constituted dialogically, as a response to relationships with others through which the person conceives of him/herself as a welcome member of society – or not. Recognition, thus, becomes a crucial element of such relationships, and the absence of recognition brings about instances of violence or exclusion (Honneth, 1996). That is the reason why the peer group or the educators play such an important role in this case study.

Now that this theoretical introduction to the methodology has been completed, it is possible to present the steps taken in order to help these women out of their adaptive preferences. These involve getting the women to trace their lives back to the causes and helping them understand the sources that have led them to become homeless. The steps taken were the following:

1. The educators generated cognitive dissonance in the women by introducing information and group discussions that were intended to make the plot of their lives difficult to sustain without a change.
2. The women were encouraged to re-tell their own stories in groups or write their own stories during an optional literary workshop.
3. The educators introduced the women to artistic works about people who have had similar experiences (short stories, excerpts from novels, scenes from films). This opened the women's horizon towards other possible responses to similar situations.

150

4. The educators responded to additional spontaneous needs of the women, like the need to write down their own stories or the need for more information. Paper and pen were provided and all their questions were answered.

A CLOSE-UP ON THE EXPERIENCE: THE OPTIONAL LITERARY WORKSHOP

I thought of the literary workshop for the first time when I heard from the other educators that one of the women had asked for a copybook to use after the meetings and had started to write beautiful stories or reflections about her life. "Children, that's all I have made in my life..." read one of her stunning writings. I personally had only been involved in articulating the theoretical framework of the whole project up to that point, when I decided to start the literary workshop for those who explicitly wished to write.[9] As mentioned before, the Center had started working in 2007, and story-telling had already been used for different purposes, but it was not until mid 2008 that the literary workshop was explicitly conceived of and implemented.

The first meeting was compulsory for all the women that were present in the Center at that moment, to give them the "chance" to try it out and not let them say they were not interested, as they tended to do. We were sitting around a big table where they usually have lunch, ideal for the purposes of the workshop, as they could write on it. I had chosen maternity as the first topic, as I knew it was something all of them shared and I did not want to start working on something controversial. I brought some excerpts from a Spanish translation of the novel *The Millstone*, by Margaret Drabble, and worked specifically on the title: why did they think that title was chosen, if the main subject was maternity? They immediately started chatting, addressing each other, or me, about the difficulties of being a mother. Some denied finding it a burden; others got angry at this denial, accusing those who claimed this of being "hypocritical". When I felt that the goals of the warm-up stage had been achieved, I handed out sheets of paper and pens and asked them to write about how they experienced maternity. Some of them were at a loss for what to do: should they write down a thought, a story, or a poem? Any of those, I answered. At home I went through the nine pieces that had been handed in. One of the women had made a drawing of herself with her child, holding hands. Another had told me about tender mischievous incidents. The one that caught my attention most read: "When our children are born, we die..." That was sufficient material for discussion during the following meeting, between reading it aloud, carrying out group discussions and eventually asking them to write down similar experiences. A similar procedure was followed for different themes such as memories of their own childhood, past and present emotional relationships and dreams of the future, among others.

The changes presumably provoked by this process were slow, far from definite, and difficult to measure. Only four women became steady members of the workshop, while others started and stopped, which made the results difficult to estimate.

But some changes were observed in the way these mothers treated their children, or in the relationships that developed between these women. There was a clear example of a piece of narrative that made a significant change in the life of two of these steady members: Silvana and Erika, two pretty assertive-looking twenty-five-year-old girls. When we had started talking about emotional relationships, most of the women had said they had nobody to fall back on and that they did not need anybody either. This was Silvana and Erika's case. Both of them pointed out that they were in their current homeless situation because they could not look for a job, as they had nobody to leave their children with when they were not at school. However, they seemed proud of their isolation, as if they were showing off how independent they were. This was a clear example of adaptive preferences. To be unable to look for a job because one has nobody to leave one's children with hardly implies independence. Some cognitive dissonance had to be introduced, urgently. They had to realize they needed other people; that with no relationship to fall back on they were not independent, but incomplete.

Therefore, it took two meetings of talking about the topics of love and friendship before they were ready to write something. We discussed the definition of trust and the problems that are to be expected in every relationship, as well as the fact that having problems does not mean the relationship necessarily has to come to an end. When the moment came to write something down, Erika wrote about something unrelated, whereas Silvana left the room with an excuse. However, some weeks later, when we were discussing something totally different, Silvana asked me if she could now write about her relationship with Erika. I nodded. The outcome was surprisingly engaging, right from the title: "Erika, my mate, my friend, my sister". Then she told the story of how they had met on the street, as they were both looking for somewhere to sleep since they had very recently become homeless. The story was warm and gave out a glow of hope, as if the sun had risen at last on such a gloomy reality. Later, Silvana told me that she had given the piece of writing to Erika to read, who had thanked her and told her she felt the same. A couple of weeks later, both Erika and Silvana were looking for jobs. Erika found a job first, as a janitor at a State enterprise,[10] and Silvana took care of Erika's children while she was at work.

My point is that a simple piece of narrative meant an important change in the lives of these women. The narrative of her relationship with Erika that Silvana rebuilt let both of the women's emotions emerge. Along with these sentiments came trust, which they needed the most. When the experience of the Center came to an end in December 2010, they were both on their way to finding steady jobs and a place to live on their own. This was a benefit not only for them, but also for their children, who had been almost condemned to growing up depending on the State and having no other family than their mothers. By December 2010, these children had a working parent in the family as a role model and a kind of "step-aunt" and "step-cousins" as well. This, I had made evident to them after reading another story that Erika wrote about a typical day in her life. "Mum" said my son, "is Silvana coming to pick us up from school today?" "No," said I, "Mummy is coming today". I read this piece aloud and told the whole attentive group of five women: "This reminds me of a typical family, where Granny or Aunty picks up the kids from school while Mummy is at work". Erika and Silvana looked at each other and smiled. They had a family at last. This should not be expected to last forever. Other problems may arise and these women may fall apart. But this was a very important step in their lives; they realized they could trust someone, look for a job and dream of a better future. This meant a lot in the desert of their lives.

CONCLUSIONS

In this way, a feasible solution to the problem of adaptive preferences was reached by working on the emotions, conceived as rational, that support their narrative structure. This narrative structure, when made explicit, reveals circumstances that have led to adaptive preferences as a reaction to emotive failure. Narratives heal this emotive failure and disrupt the self-stereotyping that makes these people behave accordingly. In Silvana and Erika's case, they realized that the reason that had them stuck with their children and no job was not the fact that they were independent women, but their lack of trust in other people; they also realized they had someone to trust close at hand. Narratives make people see themselves in a different, new way, thus showing alternative courses of action, re-opening their possibilities of finding their own way out of a situation that is hardly "preferable".

The results of this work suggested the following:

a. It is possible, from the area of education, to pull down the self-stereotypes that keep many people self-marginalized from society and, specifically, from democratic life,

b. It is never too late because this process can be carried out with adults, making it possible to work with the parents, thus contributing to democratic education initiatives that the children may be receiving at school, and

c. Educators *can* make a difference, because autonomy is not acquired on one's own, but rather within a group. This makes the guidance of trained staff (teachers, psychologists, social workers, etc.) extremely useful. These educators should be prepared to introduce cognitive dissonance in these people's lives in order to make them open to critical thinking, giving them the chance to take control of their own lives and eventually become active members of society.

NOTES

[1] I understand the concept of "strong democracy" as defined by Barber (1984). According to Barber, representative or "thin" democracy is grounded in a perspective of individualistic rights that weakens the role of citizens in democratic governance. On the other hand, in a strong democracy citizens govern themselves by participating in political, economic and social decision making, instead of delegating their power and responsibility to representatives. It is in the context of strong democracy that the expression "political literacy" takes the greatest importance, my conception of which is the ability to participate in public debates, understand and respect diversity, and dissent on the basis of human dignity and equality.

2   In fact, in his capability approach, Amartya Sen (1999) defines poverty as the combination of these factors, within which income is only one and certainly not the most important.

3   As denominated by Elster (1983) and Nussbaum (2000).

4   My conception of autonomy coincides with Dewey's idea of autonomous self, which implies communication, cooperation and coordination of one's own interests with those of the community (Dewey, 1930). That is why the work with significant others is one of the main pillars of this research.

5   This population tends to survive on a monthly cash transfer and other public social assistance programs, and they are also usually engaged in very unstable activities and temporary jobs which do not contribute to the Social Security System, which prevents them from being entitled to other social benefits, such as escrow funds.

6   In this account of the capability approach I follow Pereira (2013).

7   The most famous literary example of cognitive dissonance is Aesop's fable, *The Fox and the Grapes* in which a fox sees some high-hanging grapes and wishes to eat them. Unable to reach them, he persuades himself that the grapes are probably not worth eating as they are not ripe yet. The most famous case in the study of cognitive dissonance was described by Leon Festinger and others in the book *When Prophecy Fails* (1966). It focuses on a group of people who were expecting the imminent end of the world on a certain date. When the prediction failed, the group did not disintegrate, but rearranged the original prophecy to fit into the new reality.

8   Nussbaum does put forward a constructive use of narrative in Nussbaum (1990a, 1997, 2010) but does not develop an explicit methodology for working on adaptive preferences.

9   At this point it is important to highlight that Uruguay's literacy rate is 98%, the highest in Latin America, which makes this activity more than feasible even when working with a population of these characteristics.

10   As of 2005, the Uruguayan Ministry of Social Development provides people from poor homes with temporary jobs and training, provided that they enroll and express their willingness to participate. The program is called *Trabajo por Uruguay* ("Work for Uruguay").

REFERENCES

Barber, B. R. (1984). *Strong democracy: Participatory politics for a new age.* University of California Press.

Cortina, A., & Pereira, G. (2009). *Pobreza y libertad. Erradicar la pobreza desde el enfoque de Amartya Sen.* Madrid: Tecnos.

Damon, W. (1990). *Moral child: Nurturing children's natural moral growth.* New York: The Free Press.

Dewey, J. (1930). *Human nature and conduct: An introduction to social psychology.* New York: The Modern Library Publishers.

Elster, J. (1983). Sour grapes. *Studies in the subversion of rationality.* Cambridge: CUP.

Festinger, L., Henry Riecken, & Stanley Schacter. (1966). *When prophecy fails: A social and psychological study of a modern group that predicted the destruction of the world.* New York: Harper Torchbooks.

Harsanyi, J. C. (1982). Morality and the Theory of Rational Behaviour. In Amartya Sen and Bernard Williams (Ed.), *Utilitarianism and beyond,* 39–62. Cambridge: CUP.

Herman, B. (2008). *Moral Literacy.* Cambridge, M.A.: Harvard University Press.

Honneth, A. (1996). *The struggle for recognition: The moral grammar of social conflicts.* Cambridge: Polity Press.

Kochanska, G., Aksan, N., & Carlson, J. J. (2005). Temperament, relationships, and young children's receptive cooperation with their parents. *Developmental Psychology, 41,* 648–660.

Mead, G. H. (1934). *Mind, self, and society.* Chicago: University of Chicago Press.

Nussbaum, M. (1990a). Narrative emotions: Beckett's genealogy of love. In Martha Nussbaum (Ed.), *Love's knowledge* (pp. 286–313). New York: Oxford University Press.

Nussbaum, M. (1990b). Perception and revolution: The princess casamassima and the Political Imagination. In Martha Nussbaum (Ed.), *Love's knowledge* (pp. 195–219). New York: Oxford University Press.

Nussbaum, M. (1995). *Poetic justice*. Boston: Beacon Press.
Nussbaum, M. (1997). *Cultivating humanity: A classical defense of reform in liberal education*. Cambridge MA: Harvard University Press.
Nussbaum, M. (2000). *Women and human development*. Cambridge: CUP.
Nussbaum, M. (2005). *Upheavals of thought*. Cambridge: CUP.
Nussbaum, M. (2010). *Not for profit: Why democracy needs the humanities*. Princeton University Press.
Pereira, G. (2013). Poverty as a Lack of Freedom. In Christoph Luetge (Ed.), *Handbook of the philosophical foundations of business ethics*, 709–719. Heidelberg: Springer.
Rawls, J. (1971). *A theory of justice*. Cambridge, MA: Harvard University Press.
Ricoeur, P. (1992). *Oneself as another*. Chicago: University of Chicago Press.
Sen, A. (1999). *Development as freedom*. Oxford: OUP.
Simon, K. G. (2001). *Moral questions in the classroom: How to get kids to think deeply about real life and their schoolwork*. New Haven: Yale University Press.
Taylor, C. (1992). *Multiculturalism and the politics of recognition*. Princeton NJ: Princeton University Press.
Vigorito, A., Pereira, G., Burstin, V., Fascioli, A., Modzelewski, H., Reyes, A., & Salas, G. (2010). *Preferencias adaptativas. Entre deseos, frustración y logros*. Montevideo: Fin de siglo.

AFFILIATION

Helena Modzelewski
Department of History and Philosophy of Education
Universidad de la Republica (Uruguay)

PART III

THE AFRICAN CONTEXT

MACLEANS A. GEO-JAJA

EDUCATION LOCALIZATION FOR OPTIMIZING GLOBALIZATION'S OPPORTUNITIES AND CHALLENGES IN AFRICA

Indigenous knowledge is an integral part of the culture and history of local community. We need to learn from local communities to enrich the development process James D. Wolfenson , President of the World Bank (cited in Gorjestan 2000).

INTRODUCTION: GLOBALIZATION AND ECONOMIC DECLINE

With decreasing diversity in societies in the world today, the dramatic impact of globalization on education has resulted in deprivation of opportunity that enhances human capabilities, as well as human development challenges. Globalization has led to internationalization of higher education in Africa, but countries do not have the resources to meet the exploding demand without compromising quality or equity. As the market-logic of globalization – neoliberal capitalism- continues to devalue and degrade all aspects of indigenous knowledge production as an integral part of the development process; one consequence has resulted in a clamor for social justice, self-determination, and opportunities for localizing globalization.

Indigenous knowledge, an important part of community reproduction, is the large body of local knowledge and skills developed within/outside the formal educational system utilized in a broader manner with great potential to be used universally. Flavier, et al (1999:479) highlight indigenous knowledge as science that is user-derived, not scientifically derived, and its use complements and enhances the gains made by modern-day innovations. Ellen Bielawski described and noted indigenous knowledge as follows:

> Indigenous knowledge is not static, an unchanging artifact of a former way of life. It has been adapting to the contemporary world since contact with "others" began, and it will continue to change. Western science in the North is also beginning to change in response to contact with indigenous knowledge (1990:8).

Indigenous knowledge embedded in culture and unique to a given location or society is an important part of socialization and internationalization of opportunities. But there is more at stake here, as current education rarely teaches students to be

S. Majhanovich and M.A. Geo-JaJa (Eds.), Economics, Aid and Education:
Implications for Development, 159–182.

self-reflective about the communities in which they live, focusing instead on a desire for economic security. Indeed, it is socio-economic insecurity, and deprivation that predominates numerous standardized packaged international recommendations and policies. Thus, matters of equity and rights are removed from schooling, just as matters of socio-economic security are not fundamental features contained in the orthodox development roadmap.

The purpose of this paper is to promote these tenets that are consistent with the basic philosophy of self-development and sovereignty recognized by the Universal Declaration of Human Rights (1948) and the International Convention on Economic, Social and Cultural Rights (ICESCR 1966), which commit states to promote and protect a wide range of economic, social and cultural rights, including rights relating to an adequate standard of living. Following these declarations, other Conventions and international agencies all have underscored the sanctity of the right to enjoyment of the benefits of cultural freedom and indigenous knowledge (Geo-JaJa 2013; Babaci-Wilhite et al 2012; Tomasevski 2001:12–15). These authors argue that these social obligations are both individual and collective social responsibilities hence learning from local communities to enrich development should be a concern for globalization. Also included among other interests to be addressed is the impoverishment and stratification of society by globalization practices. To be more succunct, reference can again be made to the work of Katarina Tomaševski. Under the subtitle "Schooling can be deadly", she claims that translating what rights-based education means from vision to reality "requires the identification and abolition of contrary practices" (Cited from the United Nations Permanent Forum on Indigenous Issues (UNPFII 2012:15). In globalization, which emerged from what is called the Washington Consensus, the disparity between rich and poor in the world has reached unprecedented levels, along with opening Africa to world markets, both of which undermine fulfillment of the commitments adopted by the World Summit for Social Development 1995. This informs a critical discussion of the on-going contestation of further broadening globalization. Consequently, the new wave of globalization has far-reaching implications on education as values and identities are no longer shaped locally in the classroom. In addition, while inequality has risen in developing Asia, emerging Europe, Latin America, the Newly Industrializing Economies (NIE), and social well-being among all income groups in Africa has declined over the past two decades, inequality has only converged in the North due to trade openness. Geo-JaJa and Zajda (2005) and Tikly (2004) commented that one of the most essential aspects of globalization was that it brought disempowering economism into education, making it increasingly subordinated to fit international manpower needs. As noted by Stanley Aronowitz deemphasizing critical and broader pedagogy engagement, a mode of intervention that offered self-reflection and shaped leaners consciousness has downgraded the local needs and the development of communities (Aronowitz 2008).

How this has evolved still remains a topic of debate, but this problem often frustrates attempts of localized development. Most importantly, the absence of a humanized globalization in perpetuating and legitimizing social division and economic decline in society draws people away from indigenous knowledge production, and the North away from socially responsible customs. The reality is that today in many countries in Africa, the choice of indigenous knowledge in education policy disregards both the Science and the rights of language choice by implementing a non-local, non-indigenous language for instruction in schools (Babaci-Wilhite 2012). Scientifically speaking, this does not form a basis for rights-capability based educational development, nor does it bring social justice or quality in education. These negative feedback effects directly or indirectly affect the independence or privilege "extension" between social, cultural, political, and economic rights that results in process freedom or opportunity freedom in global societies. The foremost concerns are the implications regarding the effectiveness of education and the impediments to making knowledge meaningful in order to make it transformative. It is time to recognize the wealth of African knowledge and to promote its languages in education. The use of local languages and a culturally sensitive approach play important roles in the maintenance and regeneration of indigenous innovation (Babaci-Wilhite and al. 2012). This would make a significant contribution to African development on its own terms and for the benefit of the majority of Africans.

Another purpose of this chapter is to examine: (a) globalization trends on education across Africa and (b) provide a new roadmap for rethinking education, as well as ways to humanize globalization. Managing globalization to minimize development disadvantages is also a key concern in this chapter. The chapter is structured as follows: Section 1 sets out the essential meaning of globalization in development, in light of the fundamental changes in the effectiveness of learning in schools. Section 2 outlines the dimensions and characteristics of globalization. This section also argues against the proposition that economic and education "openness" is a price Africa must pay for convergence. In the next section, exposed is the fact that neoliberalism is paying insufficient attention to liberating education from economism. This seems not to be able to address the economic and human challenges of Africa. The last section questions the consistency of globalization to the objective of giving voice and widening choices that are core processes for enlarging capabilities. I engage in this chapter, with the hope of contributing to the discourse on impediments to learning in school systems caused by globalization. It is vitally important to recognize the reasons for that, and so as to enable the author and readers to think what should be the guiding principles for a new strategy of social justice and responsibility in development.

What Globalization Does and What It Does Not Do – A Background

The evidence to be provided will demonstrate that schooling and other forms of education, particularly localized knowledge conditions could foster social integration, which significantly contribute to the complexity of convergence. Therefore, it is imperative to understand that this self-contained "black box" in globalization must prepare learners to challenge globalization not to foreclose education as a practice for freedom. This is often hidden in education aid as a foreign policy. This interplay of education under globalization has led to (i) producing distressed individuals that are unprepared to confront challenges or who lack faith in society and their future; and (ii) aggravating disempowerment and dislocation of the poor. Globalization resulting in dissipating commitments to economic freedom, led Geo-JaJa and Zajda (2004) to question the sincerity and bias of neoliberal reform in education. However, despite "invisible" hands, the issue of significance is whether globalization in its grounded neoliberalism contributes to decrease in education, widespread deprivation, and societal impoverishment (World Bank 2006).

Or does it feed on developing human capabilities that gives people the ability to participate in social, cultural, economic and political life in dignity? To answer the latter in the affirmative depends on if appropriate attention is given to localization of curriculum over just access to schooling. According to Cheng (2000), how education should respond to the trends and challenges of globalization will remain a major concern for its relevance in policy-making for decades. More specifically, Green (1999); Ayyar (1996); Brown & Lauder (1996); Henry et al. (1999), commented that globalization has led to considerable convergence of different reform initiatives. They also show that less evidence exists of any systematic convergence at the structures and processes levels, as educational development is impacted differently in many parts of the South.

This requires the recognition that the delivery language should be the language spoken and used in the community, thus promoting equality and social dignity. In a wider approach, education construction ought to be shaped in the context of social, political, cultural and economic dynamics within and across societies. This means respect for the cultural and sovereign rights of nations. It is vitally important to note that neocolonialism or market liberalization imposing norms of the external that are restrictive and oppressive to diversity has either intensified or created new forms of deprivation and insecurity. We may avoid this undesired outcome when people, rather than goods are at the Centre of globalization resulting in broad-based patterns of sustained inclusive quality growth and sustainable development. This underlines the importance of the cultural dimension and the growing compleimentarity between culture and local tangible and intangible resources for the creation and/or regeneration of a shared vision of local societal development – equal freedom from the control by others, as well as equal opportunity to pursue a sense of self dignity. Localization refers to the transfer, adaptation, and development of related values, knowledge, technology, and behavioral norms — the implementation of institutional autonomy, school-based management and community-based curriculum (Wang 2006; Altbach 1999; James 1994).

As the relationship between localization and globalization in education is dynamic and interactive, localizing globalization in education can create more value for local development if local creativity and adaptation can be induced in a process of transformational change. This supports four scenarios of delocalization of education in globalization that include "totally isolated", "totally globalized", "totally localized" and "both highly localized and globalized". In a nutshell, localization is that process of bringing the global into the context of related local knowledge and values – local relevance and legitimacy decentralization for self-determination in education – through curriculum with localized content based on cultural, economic, political, social, and learning aspects of society (Altbach 1999; Wang 2006). In this discourse, teachers and classrooms are no longer alienated from the dynamism of the local community, as they are no longer bound by standard knowledge imposed by the central authority. The key point is that education reform should maximize education relevance to local development and bring in community support, collaboration in learning, and teaching. Shaping the qualities of learners in the classroom for active learning and self-actualization are the de-robotized and liberated teachers who are informed of changing local communities and international contexts. Some examples of practices of localization include community involvement in education, public-institutional collaboration, decentralization of institutional management, and a new education paradigm that maximizes opportunities for learners to benefit from a broader education curriculum and culture (Wang 2006). Local development needs to be valued, local knowledge including local languages need to be preserved, and children need to be prepared for the world in a language that promotes understanding (Babaci-Wilhite 2012).

Despite scientifically-based evidence, in order to make any change possible, one would need to question both the causes and the effects of such harmful language and educational policies that currently exist at every level, from government officials and policy makers down to the local participants in education. In referring to the close linkage between global education and globalization, the smallest perturbation of the system has long-term repercussions. Furthermore, I can assertively present the following outcomes:

i. strong mismatches and discrepancies prevail between the actual changes occurring in education as a result of globalization;

ii. proposed reforms and structured efforts that stifle growth are part of a framework for educational policies having some consistency with the trend of globalization.

The perceived impacts of globalization compromise what is happening in the classroom, the school, or the quality of education seen as an integral part of the culture and life of society – a significant resource that contributes to increasing efficiency, effectiveness and sustainability of the development process. According to Nicolas Gorjestani, the Chief Knowledge Officer, Africa Region of the World Bank, "recognition of indigenous knowledge and institutions as a vehicle to increase efficiency of development programs and the sustainability of development efforts, requires harnessing this only asset the poor have over control for mutual learning and adaptation" (2000). Furthermore, in the African classroom the spread of European social structures and institutionalized forms of cultural transmission, and the neglect of indigenous knowledge, encompassing broader pedagogy has turned teachers into robots as they teach to a prescribed curriculum. However, it is imperative to rethink the curricula, teaching methodologies and pedagogy associated with mainstream schooling, based on a worldview that does not adequately recognize or appreciate indigenous notions of an interdependent universe and the importance of place in their societies. Consequently, the challenge now is to reconnect traditional education to a sense of dignity and its attendant cultural practices for self-determination. In this vein, schooling that requires knowledge convergence demands devising a system of education that respects the epistemological and pedagogical foundations provided by both indigenous and the global cultural traditions. It is imperative; therefore, that we come at this juncture to see and understand the world in its multiple dimensions and varied perspectives, rather than viewing the world at the expense of a single worldview and knowledge system. In short, it is no wonder that formal education structures in the South have been found wanting to mitigate social development and educational poverty given the imposition of the incongruities and complexities of specialization, standardization, compartmentalization, and systematization that are inherent features of the North, which are often in direct conflict with social structures and practices in the South. (See Barnhardt & Kawagley 2005).

The above facts lead me to contend that increasing incorporation of indigenous knowledge in development roadmaps, in facilitating a culturally appropriate development framework, and avoiding the commodification of education will help to balance development, socialization and internalization for sustainable resource use and convergence. In other instances the non-leveraging of indigenous knowledge is a shortcoming of education in globalization in building capacity or for enlarging education opportunities to empower the locals to apply their own knowledge to address critical problems. In particular, the practice of globalization that is consistent with marketization and internationalization of education, which has fundamentally changed the ways that education in the South is structured, delivered and managed as the only answer for all nations convergence is difficult to comprehend. This idea of the supremacy of the market is now challengeable since globalization in hollowing out indigenous knowledge and the State from genuine policy initiatives has bound or confined education, teachers and national sovereignty. With the contestable promotion of globalization with all its limitations, we can assertively name it as the reinvigoration of colonialism or a corollary of global capitalism's self-interest.

Conceptual Issues: Measuring Globalization and that Which is Behind it?

Globalization is a broad concept casually used to describe a variety of phenomena that reflect increasing economic interdependence or political power relationships between the centre and the periphery. As is demonstrable through the literature, to different scholars, the conceptual understanding of globalization may be different. Accordingly, I will confine my discussion on the more narrowly defined components of globalization: measuring education inequality based on its fit to local needs,

164

based on well-being, and depositing "knowledge" to society. In this stance, the most appropriate variable for capturing enlarging opportunities is arguably the type of education consumed (see Babaci-Wilhite et al. 2012).

According to Cheng (2000), globalization is the transfer, adaptation, and development of values, knowledge, technology and behavioral norms across countries and societies in different parts of the world. In the belief in radical educational restructuring, success depends on the extent to which policy makers and governments take school realities into focus, rather than being driven by the political imperatives of the North, which has little to do with classroom realities. These are some of the roadblocks hampering positive provision of rights, efficiency and efficacy in education (Babaci-Wilhite et al. 2012). For others, this promises prosperity for countries that practice trade liberalization and economic deprivation for countries that do not.

For Roland Robertson, with whom globalization theory is most closely associated, globalization is an accelerated compression of the contemporary world and the intensification of consciousness of the world as a singular entity (Robertson 1992: 132). The clearest attempt to produce a general mapping of globalization across disciplines was offered by Amartya Sen, the economist, philosopher and human development doyen, who in his Ishizaka lecture noted that there is no single, all – encompassing definition of globalization. Instead, it has become a broad heading for a multitude of global interaction, ranging from the expansion of cultural influences across border to the enlargement of economic and business relations throughout the world (Sen 2002). The demand for the world to move towards "unicity" or "global unicity", the growing "oneness" of the world as a homogenous socio-cultural piece plays an increasingly significant role of globalization not defined in human terms, and influences socio-economic restructuring by imposed mimetic pressure on education to reforms to curricula. For this influential Nobel Laureate whose work is consistently informed by the notion of development as freedom, the above definitions are curiously in order, perhaps, because they allow us to conceptualize the process of 'globalization' at multiple levels.

Highlighted is the prominent role of globalization trying to make the world a single place by virtue of the power of a set of globally diffused ideas and pedagogy that render the uniqueness of societal and ethnic identities and traditions irrelevant except within local contexts and in scholarly discourse. In short, central to them is that education is seen as an instrument to facilitate growth rather than focusing more on transmitting values and an attitude supportive of nation-building or society building. This is the only way globalization can create the ground for political or systemic legitimation in Africa. One can even argue that the prominent role of globalization in education policy making is by way of external socio-economic and social political changes. In this chapter, globalization is the acceleration of a trend that has continually influenced society and institutions, particularly education, over the past century, i.e. the 'liberalization of exchanges' and the 'increasing interdependence of societies'.

Globalization and its Distributional Effects in Africa

What do I mean by the 'Distributional Effects of Globalization'? Why pay attention to the question? What do distributional effects of education in globalization mean? The term "distributional effects of globalization" means the effects of globalization on the economic, political, cultural and social distribution in a nation. The distributional effect of education in globalization might be negated when curricula frameworks and teaching and learning materials that promote values and human rights and education for the world of work are not put in place. However, the most important feature of education in globalization concepts is the propagation and promotion of economic superiority among different countries. To this end, what is most surprising is that the distributional changes went in the opposite direction from that suggested by the Bretton Wood Institutions. While globalization was expected to help develop the underdeveloped South, who are presumed to be disadvantaged in the knowledge economy compared to the technologically advantaged North, instead the South has only experienced parallel evolution of social inequality and a decline in education (Geo-JaJa and Yang 2003; Geo-JaJa and Zajda 2005; Winters et al. 2004).

The difference between desired and undesired globalization matters, as it can be seen as a significant process which could contribute to the increased efficiency or effectiveness of education, and the sustainability of development. The difference between globalist and anti-globalist on globalization's positive or negative results is also distinctively different. Neither party has ceded any ground either on their position on the influence of globalization on education and its adjustability to markets and cultural values. The question is, will a globalized system of education characterized by stratification and dominance of external knowledge production be able to contribute to sustainable growth and better income distribution? In the long run, will the expansion of mass, low-quality higher education spell trouble for the goals of high economic growth?

This matters not only in terms of achieving contextual convergence, but it also matters in terms of people losing connections with their communities – they become disempowered and exploited or excluded from political integration, such as centre (the North) versus periphery (the South) relationships (Frank 1969). Underpinning this linkage of globalization and education is the interconnectedness of the internationalization of sustainable development but with an additional emphasis on an indigenous knowledge based approach to education. It is understood that this relationship that raises questions about the connectivity between State-led development and the globalization-led growth points to the coercive reforms and learning about the wider world as the means through which the North exercised control over the South. In the past two decades with the massification and internationalization of education leading to the problem of lowering of education standards, particularly with the Structural Adjustment Programs (SAP) imposed belt-tightening in public expenditures, the importance of quality assurance is downgraded. In the long-term these processes of low quality education spell doom for the goal of equity and growth convergence. Clearly such formulation of education cannot adequately address the issues of equal access to, quality and equity in education. Is there no better alternative? Probably a better approach for fulfillment that meets the 4-A scheme designed by Katarina Tomasevski requires that education must be available, accessible, acceptable, and adaptable. She will further note that the success of any education roadmap should be "assessed by the contribution it makes to the enjoyment of all human rights" (Tomaševski 2004:5). What this quality schooling means is that schools must cater to the best interests of each child in developing and transmitting their curriculum. I will assert that to meet the need for right to education and right in education might be actualized if the contribution of the capabilities approach is not replaced by a rights framework, but rather a more promising roadmap to combine the two essential frameworks, which have elements of "threshold" and "duty-bearers" (see Geo-JaJa 2013 forthcoming).

The North and the coercive international organizations had pledged to eliminate these forms of unequal power disparities and work towards economic and income-distributional convergence. But, unfortunately, the real driver of this pledge is mainly an instrument for reproduction: for the North to reproduce identity and open economies for trade, by way of pedagogy convergence and the internationalization of education. Its global perspective and standards situated in globalization lead to the wider context of dependency growth. On the contrary, I believe that success in challenging inequity, injustice and unsustainable development requires commitment to humanizing globalization – broadening curriculum and incorporating pedagogic approaches that aligns well with the local-international agenda. All these factors in maximizing opportunities tend to guarantee the highest standard of inclusive sustainable development.

Quality education here is based on enlarging freedom of opportunity meaning we need to rethink education as the practice of freedom and self-identity. Quality education ensures or extends the requirements for right to education to rights in education. It envisions pedagogy as a practice for freedom and local identities and teacher freedom as essentials for spiritual enlightenment and inclusive human development. This is beyond the current classroom, with a transfer of ideologies packaged in the Global North, where any vestige of critical thinking or creativity and imagination quickly migrates to sites outside the schooling culture. Teachers are increasingly reduced to 'robots' and are deskilled, unable to pay attention to each individual learner or teach lessons that are in conformity with the learner's idiosyncratic nature and natural development. For instance, in this regime of Learner-centred teaching, the teacher is to study and learn about the dynamism of the learner and society. In this instance, the issues of how local values and cultures and identities are reproduced are the grounds of the local classroom. Moreover such a classroom ensures that the learner is given the opportunity to think local first, before their role as critical world citizens. Precisely for the author, as education is not natural and in conjunction with the values of reason, this approach ensures that the teacher must not interfere with the learner's nature, which is a reflection of the sacred and education's sovereignty from commodification. Importantly, with regards to the consistency of such form of education with the inalienable basic right to education, the work of Katerina Tomasevski must be considered. She had aptly remarked that "indigenous knowledge is an integral part of the culture and history of a local community. We need to learn from the local community to enrich the development process (Tomaseski 2004:54). This construct of the classroom demands that whatever education was available to leanersit must be adapted to the best interests of each child and society. Against the regimes of educational colonialism and internationalization of curriculum that has little relevance to the local context but are organized around globalization and instrumentalized knowledge over the priority of social responsibility.

On the contrary, I do argue that education in the broader sense as a practice for "Larger Freedom" expands human capacities necessary for self-reflection and discovery, and particularly human agency and, hence, the possibilities for self-determined development. In summary, I propose that education should deemphasize its focus on living in an interdependent world and empower people to work towards critical agency and a just and sustainable world.

In the broader education framework strengthened by all critical elements of teaching and learning, people are not in any moral danger if they are given freedom; moreover, external cultures should not change the roles of communities. Internationalization or globalization should not make locals prioritize education for the global rather than for the local (see McGinn 1996). In accordance to this framework that interlinks social responsibility and internationalization with localization, a conceptually local context of development now becomes significant as instrumental norms in understanding distributional effects of globalization in education – rights in education (see Forthcoming Geo-JaJa 2013).

At the same time, while I do not want to moralize, while globalization might be necessary for growth propelled by trade liberalization, it is not an effective mechanism to bring about convergence or desired well-being. The South is coerced and pressured to conform to educational structures inevitably designed to service the interest of the North, thus breeding increasing dependency (see Altbach 2002). Furthermore, to Altbach, the implication of commodification of education and the General Agreement on Trade in Service (GATS), the latter in particular which provides unfettered access to world markets to the North has significant potential underpinnings – education now as an internationally tradable commodity might be inappropriate and irrelevant for the South. As countries no longer have the ability to control elements of the curriculum or as other key elements of education delivery are lost, no longer can education be seen as a commodity purchased by consumers to build knowledge. Skills for the market place can be seen as effective mechanisms for self-development but there is more to education as a means for improving competitiveness or stigmatization of communities. Hence, the questioning of the reproduction of an increasing quantity of wasted humans because of the divergence imperative on sustainable development. The evidence provided led to my apprehension over the prominence given to globalization as the only hope for Africa. Rather than assume the mantle of false questioning, I call into question further pursuit of impractical neoliberalism, which gives insufficient attention to a rights-capability framework as previously explicated (see Geo-JaJa 2013 forthcoming; Babaci-Wilhite et al. 2012; Geo-JaJa and Mangum 2003; Sen 1999). The function of Learner-based curriculum construction is that it will engage nations in a veritable inner struggle for their own resurgence. This is how the much longed-for qualitative leap towards a particular mode of agency and effective actualization of Africa's potentials will become a reality, rather than just an idea.

Economic Consideration in Globalization: Structural Adjustment in Education

Much of the focus on the role of education in globalization has been in terms of adjustment policies of the World Bank and other international lending organizations in low-income countries. Due mainly to economic considerations, such policies involve cuts in social spending, particularly in education. This invasion of the education sector by economic concerns entails several consequences: to some extent the efficiency and equity of education which depends on the nexus of teaching and learning and other basic public services must now meet new requirements of efficiency and profitability and be structured to meet global economy skill needs who also act like demanding clients.

The push for economic consideration or privatization of public services leads to very depressing well-known outcomes: increased segmentation and resources inequity between different types of educational institutions, a decrease in access to quality education, as well as a general drop in the quality of education. However, as Joel Samoff (1994) noted, observers have reported that structural adjustment policies often encourage an emphasis on inappropriate skills and reproduce existing social and economic inequalities, leading actually to lowered enrollment rates, and a misalignment between educational need and provision. As part of the impetus toward efficiency in expending resources, the use of cross-national school effectiveness studies represents a new form of racism by apportioning blame for school failure on local cultures and contexts. But I will also mention the capability of economicism to contribute to or enhance inclusive sustainability development in Africa if the developmentally enriching role of indigenous knowledge is merged into main stream development discourse. Non-reliance on the role of indigenous knowledge in the development of local sustainability or the facilitation of a culturally appropriate development program is a core drawback of globalization.

Globalization and Education Localization: Disadvantages of Globalization

Of the multitude of complex issues of education which have to be described and analyzed is quality or relevant education. A right to education neither captures nor does it address this important concept. I propose that the obligation for quality education which includes both individual and collective elements, is not recognized in global economic, fiscal, or education strategies, but is imperative. The Commission For Africa (CFA) captures the spirit of quality education by incitingly defining the role of education as follows:

Education is a fundamental human right. It is a means to the fulfillment of an individual. It is the transfer of values from one generation to the next. It is also critical for economic growth and healthy populations. ... The case for education is overwhelming – both in terms of fulfilling human security and as an investment with very high returns (CFA 2005: 181).

Underpinning the above quote is the interconnectedness of education and globalization, globalization and sustainable development with inclusive rights. All of these have implications for understanding social responsibility and a broader view of the wider context of the interconnectedness of social justice and education in the South, particularly indigenous education in Africa. The issue of how instrumentality within education includes the independence of social responsibility and the complex cultural identity recognizes that human life is conditioned not determined. Cheng (2000) and Brown (1999); in their respective analyses give a thought-provoking view of globalization with a complex interplay of social justice and opportunities for knowledge sharing, self-social values, and promoting functioning livelihood. Importantly, for the argument developed here, this issue of redistribution and recognition of local social responsibility of globalization will continue to have significant drawbacks and will create serious negative impacts on development, particularly in education and cultural decolonization (Green et al. 2007). In sum, it is argued that the acceleration of globalization has altered the scale of social justice, and the question of social justice and dependency of the South since the end of the Cold war needs revisiting.

Other potential negatives of globalization are the overwhelming political influence of the North on the South and the rapid increasing destruction of the indigenous knowledge base. In fact, the overwhelming of local knowledge or its disappearance in globalization, replaced by external knowledge has led to decreased contribution of education to local development (see Babaci-Wilhite et al. 2012).

Further, with globalization and the current agitation for decentralization in education, further eroding the role of the State has led to the lack of trust in the public sector and the delegitimization of the State's action. In this vein, with the obvious dangers of economism in education in a minimalist State, establishing a counterbalance of State power to formulate and implement educational policies may be a highly desirable strategy for recolonialization/repenetration of the South. These assertions inform the desire to look in the next section at what drives Globalization.

What Drives the Globalization Processes?

Apprehension expressed over the prominence given to globalization as the only hope for Africa is driven by determined negative outcomes. I also tend to not believe that integrating into the market economy is a price Africa must pay to counter serious unbalanced development. If this is the price of globalization, I argue to the contrary and against reactionary policies so costly to human beings, which interpret power within the confines of production, distribution and consumption of knowledge in market-driven conditions. The Washington Consensus – neoliberal – framework that does not respect culture and humanity with regard to the multiple dimensions of 'larger Freedoms' will continue to deepen Africa's already fragile exploited economy. Restoration of options of development welfarism – access to public goods as inherent rights of citizenship, against the Washington Consensus campaign against welfarism is a necessary condition. It is therefore, recommended that any plausible well-being strategy should target broad social, cultural and political rights that focus on intrinsic norms.

In considering the African challenge, the key feature that ought to be stressed is not the internationalization of education or the efficiency of markets in globalization, but rather it should be a focus on how indigenous education can be mainstreamed into the curriculum, especially with the coming of internationalization in schooling, to achieve relevant education with a focus on socially responsible well-being and development. This is a notion of education and development visions that are imposed as universal. Moreover, it means that the act of the global, the principle of fusing all the different world cultures or economies into one world, has only come to exclude the Global South. The form and content of the logic, is always a matter of a market-driven roadmap of neoliberal capitalism. This particular logic is delinked from the centre construction of a multidisciplinary approach to a self- development framework.

The multifaceted nature of globalization captured in the approach I espouse, is expected to lead to a revival of local knowledge and will reinvigorate traditional economic systems as the vehicle of resuscitating Africa back to immediate post-colonial embodiment. The Neocolonialist framework witnessed in structural adjustment, privatization, and now neoliberal-globalization presumes the superiority of one world culture, knowledge system, and language over growth of a purely State welfarism. This has failed Africa. In other published works, I have questioned the deliverability of such thinking, as it negates the appreciation of broad social and economic rights. These measures that appropriately drive effectiveness, equity, and voice of the people, as active agents of inclusive development at all times trumps trade openness as the only hope for Africa. For instance, at the highest level of integration, trade openness or marketization of education are not defined in rights or sovereignty terms, which seek to create a more structural and holistic approach to social change.

What definition of Globalization measures up? Globalization involves the assimilation and re-articulation of people to constructed international or local circumstances. Globalization can also be considered a process of hybridization of ideas, values, knowledge, and identity. Saad-Filho and Johnson (2005:2) put it very succinctly in stating that "globalization is nothing more than the international face of neoliberalism: a worldwide strategy of accumulation and social discipline that doubles as an imperialist project". Can it not then be interpreted that it is globalization by concentrating wealth and power in the hands of the already developed countries that brings about sameness to the surface appearance of modernity.

To be more concise, I will define this phenomenon as the economic, political, and societal forces pushing local education towards increasing internationalization or that which also pushes international education into hegemonic localization. In a nutshell I see education in globalization, as the "shrinking" of indigenous knowledge in the world, and a switch from consciousness of the local to the global knowledge pedagogy. Thus, achieving an equitable distribution of the added value of indigenous knowledge base in the legacy of the new colonialism to serve the higher purpose of humanity is a challenge. Joseph Stiglitz narrowly defined globalization as "the removal of barriers to free trade and the closer integration of national economies", but did argue strongly against "neoliberal globalization in leading to social spending cuts that created and worsened global crises" (Stiglitz 2002).

Phenomenal processes of globalization in introducing a new dimension of internationalization or marketization in education exclude people from the power and opportunity to fight against human injustices or for rearticulating hope against powerlessness. For the South it has reduced autonomy in matters of economic and cultural development as it harmonizes policy regimes into convergence. Underlying this is the view that trade and military power determines political balance or the strategic withdrawal of the State. In other words, the politics of 'structural adjustment' conditionalities or that of internationalization of education which circumscribe the State position are conducive to the process of globalization. This is the process in which World Bank/IMF frameworks crystallized into the ideological formulations of neo-colonialism, which grudgingly relegated the idea of convergence or autonomous development to the background, resulting in the triumph of capitalism.

It must be noted as well that an overbearing military is a basic driver of the North foreign policy and is inextricably intertwined with globalization. For Andersen, Harr and Tarp (2006), a dominant military is used as a foreign policy mechanism for market penetration, as well as for vote bribery at the United Nations (Arndt et al. 2006; Berthélemy 2006).

Learning and Schooling in Globalization. This section is focused on how globalization can directly or indirectly influence the process of education. In a more recent publication with Babaci-Wilhite and Lou (See Babaci-Wilhite et al. 2012), we articulate how schooling in globalization developed as an anti-oppressive education that is consistent with active learning pedagogies that foster critical thinking and student-centred teachings that shape self-development for Africa. Education in broader globalization is said to have such major implications for the ownership and transmission of knowledge, which would determine learning to be, learning to learn, learning to do, and learning to live together. While such an approach distinguishes itself from that which does not engage the global education agenda that prevents investing, mapping of or depositing "knowledge, values and cultures" to society, it assigned less priority to indigenous knowledge. In short, as earlier suggested, "Local conditions matter not because economic principles change from place to place, but because those principles come institution free and filling them out requires local knowledge" (Rodrik 2003:29), Furthermore Babaci-Wilhite (2012) states that indigenous knowledge should be included in the curriculum as well as indigenous languages that are critical to the preservation and development of indigenous knowledge. Consequently, widespread and indisputable in the literature is that both local and global issues; should be an essential broader part of local curriculum for quality learning, as they are considered implicit to rights in education. Africans will not achieve social justice nor will they achieve human rights in education until it is acknowledged that local languages, identity and culture are to be respected and highly prioritized in the local curriculum (Babaci-Wilhite and Geo-JaJa 2011). Reconstruction of education must be understood as a source of inspiration for locals. Those who are concerned with the effects of an instrumentalist focus of education in globalization need to address the issues of 'access', 'quality', 'relevance', 'equality'; and 'efficiency' of education.

What are Schools for? Creating a Place for Indigenous Knowledge in Education

Due to the rapid development and change in nearly every aspect of the world brought on by globalization, people begin to accept education in itself as an important value or goal (Chapman et al 1996). The complexity of this thing called school is expected to help students to learn how to learn and help teachers to learn how to teach. Schools are also facilitators of teachers' professional development, in serving as a place for systematic learning, teaching, and disseminating knowledge, and as a center for systematically experimenting and implementing educational changes and developments (Cousins 1996). Schools provide a service for different educational needs of the community, disseminate knowledge and promote psychological development to this and next generation. If this is true, it is argued that the key to learning is for teachers to promote psychological development and help learners feel a sense of ownership and responsibility by giving learners appropriate choices. With the empowerment of choice and control over their learning, they will bond with the school and society. If education as a means of empowerment and a human right is denied, mankind is deprived of opportunity, which in itself represents poverty and ignorance. Without romanticizing empowerment, it is here defined as the ability of people to actively exercise a desired influence over the outcomes of education and development processes of their choice. This has dampened early optimism that surrounded education as salvation or education as synonymous with promoting human and social progress.

Education, when seen as an investment to enhance human capabilities and to promote economic self-sufficiency can help to minimize living in poverty and economic and cultural polarization. These bold missions can be met in all parts of the world only when globalization offers the prospects of repackaging the way power is exercised and the politics of reform conditions. It is imperative that teachers know about the social context of poverty and enlarging opportunities and freedom (See Sen 1999). For Tilak (2005:58) a strong and inclusive education system is necessary to serve (a) itself as development, as 'freedom,' as a 'capability,' as a human right, and as human development, as a key dimension of sustainable development – as an end, and (b) as a means of sustainable development from economic, social, cultural, and political points of view. In this vein, solutions to social and economic challenges to the local require education forms and a balanced edifice of an education system focused on human development, human capital, economic growth as well social justice and social responsibility.

In fact, education in contributing to the legitimization of the language of the local provides extreme examples of internal development consistent with linguistic, social and human rights. Obviously, economism or globalization's demand for unique human capital or in putting greater emphasis and value on external knowledge and ideas has not allowed for localization. This affliction has often undermined understanding of cultural realities of the local. According to one set of reasoning, this process is comparable with deprivation conceived as powerless, voicelessness, vulnerability and dependency.

One of the shortcomings of globalization, in modifying the role of education suggests that the role of indigenous knowledge and language varies according to socioeconomics and the level of State intervention in the education market in the interest of equity. Crucially, then, reliance and dependence on superimposed education reforms in globalization is mired down by socio-cultural and political instability just as colonialism is associated with economic and geo-political interests that are direct reflections of the State of non-development in the South (Frank 1969). The imposition of globalization curriculum together with the *lingua franca* of English or another powerful European language has allowed the dominance of the North to consolidate their control of macro-economic policy of the South.

The dislocation of education and development of the South or the assault of globalization on language of choice or in questioning of local identities and particularisms constitute development and education poverty. As a consequence of this, the casual interpretation of these factors that constitute quality education as a crucial and sufficient condition for social and economic regeneration is contestable (see Azaridis and Drazen 1990). In this regard, it became necessary to call for a rethinking, reconstruction and new approach to the neoliberal globalization process that include integration of the indigenous (economic, social, political or linguistic) into the global systems, for a broader umbrella of education (instrumental plus intrinsic) focused on an active and participatory instructional approach. These are the factors that shape and unveil opportunities of hope for rights in education – quality education to all – regardless of gender, location, language or ethnic origin.

Strong reservations have been expressed regarding neoliberalism that has abruptly uprooted indigenous education and condemned it as barbaric and primitive.

Africa must now come to transit from a traditional system of delivery with excessive attention paid to memorization, to a Learner-centred education – with more active and participatory teaching-learning strategies.

As education in globalization and its internationalization has resulted in conformity, disempowerment and legitimating ideologies of the North, education has not only produced instrumental knowledge congenial to fostering education poverty, but has also manipulated alternative education discourses within a framework suited to globalization's goals. Without any doubt, education has lost its critical edge in promoting social development as it is now nothing more than a mechanistic process to oil the industrial complex that erodes the moral capacity of the global knowledge and economy. As commented by Tilak (1996) for India, and Torres (2001:115) in Latin America, for education to remain the main element in globalization driven by geopolitical interests, schooling for Africa will need to take a new varied form. Here, Michael Ernest Sadler, writing over a century ago, rightly poses objections to international 'cherry-picking':

In studying foreign systems of education Sadler noted that we should not forget that:

> factors outside the schools matter even more than the factors inside the schools, and govern and interpret variable measures inside ... No other nation, by imitating a little bit of German organization, can thus hope to achieve a true reproduction of the spirit of German institutions ... All good and true education is an expression of national life and character ... The practical value of studying in a right spirit and with scholarly accuracy the working of foreign systems of education is that it will result in our being better fitted to study and understand our own (Sadler 1900:50).

We disdain globalization as a new hegemonic power relationship of extensive networks with vested interests in global type knowledge and a hastened penetration of the South. This can be associated with dynamics of decreasing sovereignty, destabilization and/or dependency through compromised quality education, as demonstrated in Figure 1 below. According to evidence from the wider literature, Asian countries whose governments invested in quality education (the top half of Figure 1) have successfully globalized (Green et al. 2007; Tikly et al. 2003). Further, the pathway taken in the campaign for globalization in education determines the vice of the transformation of "modernity" into Africa, which has come to be the dynamics of economic or education poverty or the development of underdevelopment by the agents of development (see Frank 1969; Ake 1996:111; Geo-JaJa and Mangum 2003).

Argued in broader terms, globalization with its asymmetric relationships between the North and the South develops the developed at the expense of the developing, as the socio-economic and educational structures of African countries are subordinated via globalization to foster the skill and knowledge interests of wealthy nations. I stress one more time that under globalization, education policy should be embedded

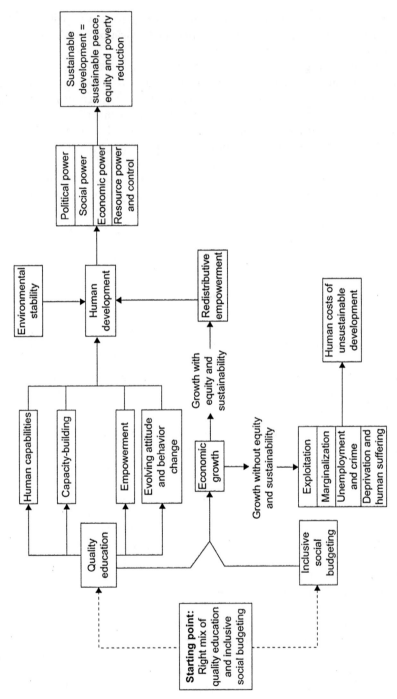

Figure 1. Education in Globalization for African Sustainable Development.¹(Source Geo-JaJa Forthcoming Unpublished).

in local culture and sustained by ideas and values, and customs of local and world views. Consequently, there can be no doubt of their major contributions to the totality of social investment interventions and the mobilization of social and political capital for sustainable livelihoods or for ensuring the rights in education which is a matter of justice, voice and economic equity.

To close this section, the Bottom half of Figure 1, shows that education under globalization for African sustainable development has brought three important developments: massification without quality, commodification and decreasing adaptability to indigenous needs. The top-pathway is an illustration of humanistic education: a critical element of teaching and learning for political, social, economic, and for voice and choice – self-discovery (the Top-Pathway). Accordingly, while rooting itself in negating anti-local orientation or anti-development measures brought on by globalization in the form of capability deprivation, cultural distortions, and the internationalization of indigenous knowledge, it deepens citizens' participation in the promise of globalization. Against this regime of local understanding, countries must not seal learners off from global knowledge, despite the fact that the transplanted education of the North with its presumed supremacy as the broad "toolbox" of globalization has substantiated its promises to the global community while undermining the local.

Summary and Concluding Observations

At a time when education has become an instrument of disempowerment, powerlessness, and unpromising mode of conformity, coupled with the divergent quality and inequality of education, globalization's imperative for actualization of the Top-Pathway of Figure 1 is questionable. Rather, the promise of convergence has only materialized to be consistent with the outcomes illustrated in the Bottom-pathway of Figure 1. More is at stake here than just education and economic poverty, skill reproduction security, and sovereignty. In schooling, the supremacy of the broad "toolbox" of neoliberalism has made pedagogy into a practice of disempowerment. That which should encourage transformational development instead is now subordinate to the corporatization and internationalization of education; teachers are now reduced to deskilled classroom robots as they do not have any control over what they teach in the classroom. Accordingly, despite the bold market-driven logic of the World Bank/IMF imposed throughout the continent, an honest evaluation of such reforms acknowledges that, the lacunae of globalization has only brought on an increasing economic downward trajectory in Nigeria (Geo-JaJa 2006; DfID 2007), a declining standard of living in Tanzania (Tikly et al. 2003; Duygan and Bump 2007) and creation of shrinking access to education with equivalent shrinking of quality of life for Ghana. Under such circumstances, education in Africa reflects the fear of giving the learners freedom to study what they want, when they want, how they want, and if they want, thus questioning the probability of schooling enabling learners to be self-reflective and empowered in the world.

As commented by Altbach (2002), it is a matter of urgency that the current conceptualization of education driven by neoliberal globalization, which has forced countries with different academic needs and resources to conform to structures inevitably, designed to serve the interest of external economies and academic institutions undergo a paradigm shift in content. Summing up, while there is much that is wrong with globalization as currently contextualized, the process still has unrealizable multiple benefits to addressing the changing face of development and human insecurity, the multi-dimensionalities of poverty and inequality. The implication of the State in sustainable development is possible only when the nature of globalization in both pedagogy and curricular content take into consideration local traditions, learning styles, and the impact of cultural norms and values on knowledge for development policies.

The overall view of globalization put forward in this chapter sees globalization as containing both opportunities and threats for national development by the dangers and the role of international agencies in sector wide approaches to planning and development. Advocating for a 'localized path' in globalization is in line with the livelihoods of the South and for the motive of fostering glocalization economic competitiveness, which are culturally and politically-driven. Such a construct nature of globalization will expand opportunity for freedom and ensure sustainable socio-economic rights, with a broader scope of teaching both the instrumental and the intrinsic in education, both mutually reinforcing self-reflection and social change. Thus, advocated is that the impact of a teacher should be assessed by the contribution the teacher makes to the leaner's enjoyment of "Larger Freedom" and to enable the leaner to understand the local and the larger world. I close the chapter by questioning if education in globalization without the full involvement of the State and civil society can play its constitutive and instrumental roles in development?

NOTES

[1] Source: Geo-JaJa (2013).

REFERENCES

Ake, C. (1996). *Democracy and development in Africa.* Washington D.C.: Brookings Institution.
Altbach, P. G. (Ed.). (1999). *Private prometheus: Private higher education and development in the 21st century. Contributions to the study of education no. 77.* Connecticut: Greenwood Press.
Altbach, P. G. (2002). Knowledge and education as international commodities. *International Higher Education, 28,* 2–5.
Andersen, T. B., Harr, T., & Tarp, F. (2006). On US politics and IMF lending, *European Economic Review 50,* 1843–1862.
Arndt, C., Jones., S., & Tarp F. (2006). Aid and development: The mozambican case. Discussion Paper 06–13, Department of Economics, University of Copenhagen (forthcoming, In S. Lahiri (Ed.) *Frontiers of economics and globalization: Theory and practice of foreign aid,* Elsevier.
Aronowitz, S. (1998). *"Introduction," Paulo Freire, "pedagogy of freedom",* Lanham: Rowman and Littlefield.
Aronowitz, S. (2008). *Against schooling: For an education that matters,* Boulder, Colorado: Paradigm Publishers.

Ayyar, R. V. V. (1996). Educational policy planning and globalisation. *International Journal of Educational Development, 16*(4), 347–354.

Azaridis, C., & Drazen, A (1990). Threshold externalities in economic development. *Quarterly Journal of Economics, 105*, 501–526.

Babaci-Wilhite, Z., & Geo-JaJa M. A. (2011). A critique and rethink of modern education in Africa's development in the 21st century. *Papers in education and development* (ped) (pp. 133–153). Number 30- journal of the school of education. University of Dar es Salaam: Tanzania,

Babaci-Wilhite, Z. (2012a). An analysis of debates on the use of a global or local language in education: Tanzania and Malaysia. In D. B. Napier & S. Majhanovich (Eds.) *Education, dominance and identity* (Vol. 3, pp. 121–133). Rotterdam: Sense Publishers.

Babaci-Wilhite, Z. (2012b). A right based approach to Zanzibar's language-in-education policy. Special Issue on Right based Approach and Globalization in Education. *World Studies in Education Journal, 13*(2), 17–33.

Babaci-Wilhite, Z., Geo-JaJa, M. A., & Shizhou L. (2012). Education and language: A human right for sustainable development in Africa. *International Review of Education, 58*(5), 619–647.

Barnhardt, R., & Kawagley, A. O. (2005). Indigenous knowledge systems and Alaska native ways of knowing. *Anthropology and Education Quarterly, 36*(1), 8–23.

Berthélemy, J. C. (2006). Bilateral donors' interest vs. recipients' development motives in aid allocation: do all donors behave the same? *Review of Development Economics, 10*, 179–194.

Bielawski, E. (1990). Cross-cultural epistemology: Cultural readaptation through the pursuit of knowledge. Edmonton: Department of Anthropology, University of Alberta.

Brown, P., & Lauder, H. (1996). Education, globalization and economic development. *Journal of Education Policy, 11*(1), 1–25.

Brown, T. (1999). Challenging globalization as discourse and phenomenon. *International Journal of Lifelong Education, 18*(1), 3–17.

Commission for Africa (2005). Our Common Interest: Report of the Commission for Africa, March.

Chapman, J., D., et al. (1996). (Eds). Introduction and overview. In *The reconstruction of education. Quality, equality and control* (pp. 1–17). Cassell: London.

Cheng, Y. C. (2000). A CMI-Triplization Paradigm for Reforming Education in the New Millennium. *International Journal of Educational Management, 14*(4), 156–174.

Cousins, B. (1996). Understanding organisational learning for educational leadership and school reform. In K. Leithwood (Ed.) *International handbook of leadership and administration* (pp. 589–652). Dordrecht, The Netherlands: Kluwer.

Department for International Development (DfID) (2006). '*Making governance work for the poor*' (White Paper 3), London: DfID.

Department for International development (DfID) (2007). Nigeria, Country Profiles: Africa.

Duygan, B., & Bump. J. B. (2007). Can trade help poor people? The role of trade, trade policy and market access in Tanzania. *Development Policy Review, 25*(3), 293–310.

Flavier J. M., De Jesus A., & Navarro S. (1999). Regional program for the promotion of Indigenous Knowledge in Asia. In Warren D. M., Slikkerveer L. J., & Brokensha D. (Eds), *The cultural dimension of development: Indigenous Knowledge Systems*. London: SRP, Exeter.

Frank, A. G. (1969). The development of underdevelopment, *Monthly Review 18*(4), 17–31.

Geo-JaJa, M. A., & Yang, X. (2003). Rethinking globalization in Africa. *Chimera, 1*(1), 19–28.

Geo-JaJa, M. A., & Mangum, G. (2003). Economic adjustment, education and human resource development in Africa: The case of Nigeria. *International Review of Education, 49*(3–4), 293–318.

Geo-JaJa, M. A., & Zajda, J. (2005). Rethinking globalization and the future of education in Africa, In Zajda, J. (Ed.), *International handbook of globalization, education and policy research*, Amsterdam: Kluwer Academic Publishers.

Geo-JaJa, M. A., & Zadja, J. (2004). Education and inequality globally: Comparing educational outcomes. In J. Zadja (Ed.), *International book series on globalization and comparative education research, Volume 5*. Amsterdam: Kluwer Academic Publishers.

Geo-JaJa, M. A. (Forthcoming 2013). *Culture and rights in donor aid: Does it really matter for inclusive development in Africa?* Unpublished.

Geo-JaJa, M. A. (2006). Educational decentralization, public spending, and social justice in Nigeria, *International Review of Education, 52*(1–2), 129–153.

Gorjestani, N. (2000). Indigenous knowledge for development opportunities and challenges, The World Bank. This paper is based on a presentation made by the author at the *UNCTAD Conference on Traditional Knowledge in Geneva*, November 1. www.worldbank.org/afr/ik/ikpaper_0102.pdf

Green, A. (1999). Education and globalization in Europe and East Asia: convergent and divergent trends. *Journal of Education Policy, 14*(1), 55–71.

Green, A., Little, A., Kamat S., Oketch, M. & Vickers, E. (2007). *Education and development in a global era: strategies for 'successful globalisation'.* London: DfID.

Henry, M., Lingard, B., Rizvi, F., & Taylor, S. (1999). Working with/against globalization in education. *Journal of Education Policy, 14*(1), 85–97.

James, E. (1994). Public-private division of responsibility for education. In T. Husén & T. N. Postlethwaite (Eds.) *The international encyclopedia of education* (2nd ed., Vol. 8). Oxford, England/New York: Pergamon/Elsevier Science.

McGinn, N. F. (1996). Education, democratization, and globalization: A challenge for comparative education. *Comparative Education Review, 40*(4), 341–357.

Robertson, R. (1992). *Globalization: Social theory and global culture,* California: Sage Publications

Rodrik, D. (2003). '*Growth strategies' NBER working paper 10050,* Cambridge, MA: National Bureau for Economic Research.

Sadler, E. M. (1900). How can we learn anything of practical value from the study of foreign systems of education? address of 20 October. In J.H. Higginson (Ed.), *Selections from Michael Sadler: studies in world citizenship* (pp.48–51). Liverpool: Dejall and Meyorre.

Saad-Filho, A., & Johnston, D. (Eds.) (2005). Neoliberalism: A critical reader. Ann Arbor, MI. Pluto Press.

Samoff, J. (Ed.) (1994). *Coping with crisis: Austerity, adjustment, and human resources.* London: Cassell.

Sen, A. (1999). *Development as freedom.* New York: Anchor Books.

Sen, A. (2002). Globalization: past and present, *Ishizaka lectures,* 18 February 2002.

Stiglitz, J. A. (2002). *Globalization and its discontents,*W. W. Norton & Co., New York.

Tikly, L. (2004). Education and the new imperialism. *Comparative Education, 40*(2), 173–198.

Tikly, L. Lowe, J., Crossley, M., Dachi, H., Garrett, R., & Mukabaranga, B. (2003). *Globalization and skills for development in Rwanda and Tanzania.* London: DfID.

Tilak, J. B. G. (1996). Education in India: Towards Improving Equity and Efficiency. In V. L. Kelkar & V. V. Bhanoji Rao. (Eds.) *India: Development Policy Imperatives.* New Delhi: Tata McGraw-Hill.

Tilak, J. B. G. (2005). *Post-elementary education, poverty and development in India,* National Institute of Educational Planning and Administration, Post-Basic Education and Training, Working Paper Series - N° 6 Centre of African Studies, University of Edinburgh.

Tomaševski, K. (2001). *Human rights in education as prerequisite for human rights education,* Right to Education Primers No. 4, Raoul Wallenberg Institute/Swedish International Development Cooperation Agency, Stockholm, 2001.

Tomaševski, K. (2004). *Economic, social and cultural rights. The right to education.* Report submitted by the Special Rapporteur Katarina Tomaševski. Economic and Social Council, Commission on Human Rights, Sixtieth session Item 10 on the provisional agenda. E/CN.4/2004/45. 26 December 2003.

Torres, C. A. (2001). Education in Latin America and the Caribbean: A theoretical discussion of citizenship, Democracy and Multiculturalism. *International Social Sciences Review, 2*(2), 219–240.

UNPFII (2012). Indigenous children's education and indigenous languages expert paper written for the *United Nations Permanent Forum on Indigenous Issues.*

Wang, L., McCulloch N., & A. McKay (2006). Globalization and curriculum studies: Tensions, challenges and possibilities. *Journal of the American Association for the Advancement of Curriculum Studies 2*(1). http://www2.uwstout.edu/content/jaaacs/vol2/in dex.htm

Winters, L. A., McCulloch, N., & A. McKay. (2004). Trade liberalization and poverty: The evidence so far. *Journal of Economic Literature, 42*(1), 72–115.

World Bank (2006). *World development report 2006 – Development and the next generation.* World Bank, Washington, DC. http://econ.worldbank.org/wdr

AFFILIATIONS

Macleans A. Geo-JaJa, Ph.D.
Professor of Economics and Education/Fulbright Senior Specialist Fellow

David O. McKay School of Education
Brigham Young University, 306P MCKB
Provo, Utah 84602–5092
(801) 232–3130

TINGTING YUAN

THE RISING 'CHINA MODEL' OF EDUCATIONAL COOPERATION WITH AFRICA: FEATURES, DISCOURSES AND PERCEPTIONS

A NEW LOGIC OF 'AID'?

Challenging the Orthodox 'Aid'

Globalization and the economic growth of some developing countries are not new issues. Moreover, when globalization takes the form of a knowledge-based economy, education is increasingly becoming a crucial factor in the contemporary neo-liberal market of the world (Robertson, 2007, p. 19). Educational practice is embedded in economic activities as well as political competition and is also present within the complexity of international relations.

'Aid' is an international concept that emerged in the West towards the end of the Second World War and was first seen with the establishment of the International Bank for Reconstruction and Development, more commonly known as the World Bank, and the International Monetary Fund (IMF) in 1944. These organizations were designed to provide a more stable economic situation and create freer trading conditions throughout the world (Garrett, 1994, p. 1). From this emergence of these institutions it is not hard to understand why 'aid' is also called development assistance, and this demonstrates that aid means 'help' with respect to economic development. This leads to several questions that should be considered: is 'development' a normative term and if yes, who set this norm? Is there a model of development?

Traditional aid mechanisms are mainly based on the Western oriented modernization process. The fundamental logic of aid is based on the logic of 'catching up', which has set a paternal and hierarchical donor-recipient relationship since the 1950s. The American economist Walt Whitman Rostow (1960) introduced five stages of economic growth experienced by countries with investment, consumption and social trends at each stage, during the process of modernization; he argued that the most important stage is centered upon the 'taking off' stage when the norms of economic growth are well established and ready for regular growth.[1] Modernization theory explains how 'low-income countries could improve the living condition of their populations by a set of prescriptive policies to encourage economic "taking off"' (Robertson et al., 2007, p. 11). Although it is hard to define the Western model of aid as 'aid' has taken various forms during the past six decades, the underlying logic associated with Western donors has been quite consistent. It assumes that

S. Majhanovich and M.A. Geo-JaJa (Eds.), Economics, Aid and Education:
Implications for Development, 183–198.

developing countries need 'help' to 'catch up' with the developed countries that represent the model to be attained, where the process is 'developing' to 'developed', and this goal is supported by aid. Within this process, education plays the role of creating 'modern' individuals, and 'unlocks the door to modernization' (Harbison & Myers, 1964, p. 3).

Conditionality is one of the most distinctive mechanisms of orthodox aid although this has been amended in many ways over the years.[2] As described by Mosley et al. (2003, p. 1), the nature of conditionality, particularly as applied by the World Bank and IMF, is changing in response to perceived failings in enforcement. At the same time a number of 'emerging donors' particularly members of the BRIC countries (Brazil, Russia, India and China) are challenging this main mechanism of aid and are instead strongly declaring aid without strings but for mutual benefits. As Woods (2008, p. 1217) describes:

> While established donors are still clinging to an economic policy conditionality about which their development partners are sceptical, the emerging donors are keen to lend and give aid without these kinds of specific economic conditions. They package their aid in a strong rhetoric of respect for the sovereignty of other governments.

In the context of engaging actively in global economic competition, China has caused increasing discussion with respect to its cooperation with Africa, as it is fundamentally challenging the notion of 'aid'. According to Welle-Strand (2010, p. 11), '...emerging donors provide foreign aid on different terms, in different sectors, through different organizational structures, and with different goals than do the traditional donors'. Welle-strand considers 'four main ways' in which China challenges the current foreign aid paradigm:

> The donor-recipient relationship is challenged by a partnership of equals; The modes of provision are challenged by China's focus on aid that is mutually beneficial; The use of conditionalities is challenged by China's insistence on sovereignty and non-interference in domestic affairs; Multilateralism is challenged by China's preference of going the major foreign aid projects alone (Welle-strand 2010, p. 3).

Old Relationships with New Strategies

According to Woods (2008, p. 1206), 'in recent years, in the face of increases in aid from these countries, western commentators have become more anxious and vociferous about the emerging donors and their impact on the pattern of aid provision'. In fact, some of these emerging donors are not 'new' donors. Looking back in history, from 1963 to 1964, the Chinese Premier Zhou Enlai and Vice-Premier Chen Yi toured ten African countries and while in Ghana and Mali, the Premier put forward the 'Eight principles of Chinese economic and technological aid' (Yu,

1988, p. 853). The 'Eight Principles' of aid, which was probably the Chinese earliest policy in terms of aid to Africa, declared at the very beginning the idea of a 'mutual' relationship.[3] This is China's conception of 'aid': a reciprocal relation between two sides without considering either hierarchy or condition. It was built on ideology oriented solidarity among the Third World during the 1950s to 1970s, and gradually moved towards economy oriented cooperation among the developing countries in the current globalization.

The educational aid, also regarded by Chinese government as 'educational cooperation', is an important part of China-African relations. Historically, according to Li (2007), over the last 50 years, China has forged cooperative relations with respect to education with 50 African countries. This cooperation has expanded from the initial simple exchange of students to the current multi-level educational cooperation, covering various fields and taking different forms. As a new developing country, which was founded in 1949, China began to dispatch teachers and students to African countries such as Egypt and Morocco and this continued except during the period of the Cultural Revolution (Centre for African Studies of Peking University, 2005, p. 2). By the end of the 1980s, 43 African countries had sent 2,245 students to China. And following the Cold War with the disappearance of the client states, these relations were strengthened. Not only have the numbers of exchanged students and discharged teachers increased, the degrees awarded have also been extended to master's and doctoral level. It is noticeable that training classes have been held since the end of the 1990s, which cover the fields of educational administration, agriculture, computer skills, medical applications, and so on (ibid, p. 43).

As mentioned, there has been a transformation from ideology based aid to economic led aid. The most impressive progress has been with the 'new type of strategic partnership' featuring 'political equality and mutual trust, economic win-win cooperation and cultural exchanges' which have become more prevalent in the 21st century (FOCAC, 2006). From 2000, with the Forums on China-Africa Cooperation (FOCAC) which are held every three years, and claim 'pragmatic cooperation' and 'equality and mutual benefit' between China and Africa, the educational cooperation between the two continents has also entered a new age. The year 2006 was declared 'the year of Africa' in Chinese diplomatic history. The Chinese government released China's African Policy (Ministry of Foreign Affairs of the PRC, 2006) in January and held the Beijing Summit (the 3rd FOCAC) in November, invited leaders from 48 African countries. Just one year before the Beijing Summit, the educational ministers from China and 17 African countries in the 'Forum for Sino-African Education Ministers', jointly signed the Beijing Declaration in November 2005, which reaffirmed education as a prerequisite for achieving national prosperity. Specifically these countries achieved consensus for the following issues (Ministry of Foreign Affairs of the PRC, 2005):

- Regard free and compulsory primary education as a basic human right;
- Prioritize the development of education, and provide sufficient and equal opportunities to education with a view to providing lifelong education for all;

185

- Improve the equality of education and offer more opportunities for access to education as well as promoting the application of information and communication technology in education;
- Recognise the significant relevance of education for economic development in the process of pursuing economic development and eliminating poverty;
- Establish prudent vocational education policies in order to confront the challenges of unemployment, the structural adjustment of economies as well as the demands of technology;
- Develop higher education, enlarged enrolment and improving educational quality and training high-quality talent to meet the demands of economic development.

According to the above agreements, it is notable that the first consensus is very much in agreement with the UN's Millennium Development Goals (MDGs) which call for universal primary education (UPE). The agreements which focus on lifelong learning and Education for All (EFA) as well as reducing poverty through education are also very much aligned with the aims of the UN. And the discourse that is focused on 'the relevance of education to economic development' is even similar to the language used by the World Bank. However as King (2007, p. 343) has pointed out, although this forum was 'piggy-backed on the High Level Meeting on EFA, it struck out on its own', focusing more on the 'prudent policies for vocational education and technical education, as well as…encourage [ing] higher education and cultural diversity.'

These issues were emphasised again with promises written in FOCAC reports. According to the FOCAC Sharm el Sheikh Action Plan (2010–2012), by 2012 the Chinese Government would: build 50 China-Africa friendship schools; propose implementation of the 20+20 Cooperation Plan for Chinese and African institutions of higher education in order to establish a new type of one-to-one inter-institutional cooperation model between 20 Chinese and 20 African universities (or vocational colleges); admit 200 middle and high level African administrative personnel to MPA programs in China; increase the number of scholarships offered to Africa to 5,500; and train 1,500 school headmasters and teachers and continue to promote the development of Confucius institutes (FOCAC, 2009).

Generally, the main approaches of Chinese educational aid can be summarized as follows: (1) The Chinese Government Scholarship scheme; (2) short-term training; (3) cultural exchanges; (4) Confucius Institute; (5) school building and donation; (6) teacher secondment; and (7) university cooperation (Yuan, 2011a).

These approaches do not just belong to a Chinese model, and are as similar to Western approaches (such as actions by British Council) which also include scholarships, training and language learning. However, the most important Chinese characteristic which is also recognized by the participants of the fieldwork, is the different donor-recipient relationship (which is particularly different from previous colonial relations) and the common goals that are shared with African countries (particularly lead by the recipients' desire to benefit from China's experience). Chinese educational institutes in this process are the providers and organizers for delivering knowledge in a practical and diplomatic way. The following section will describe the specific case of Tanzania.

EXAMINATION OF THE 'CHINA MODEL' IN TANZANIA AND CHINA

Fieldwork was undertaken from July to November 2008 in Tanzania and China, with the goal of exploring different people's perceptions towards the China-Africa relationship in education. This included using a semi-structured interview to collect information on the perceptions of people who were working with aid practice (Tanzanian and Chinese officials in the Chinese embassy in Dar es Salaam, Ministry of Education of Tanzania, and Ministry of Finance of Tanzania) and people who have received aid (returning African students funded by Chinese governmental scholarships). Field investigation in China was undertaken in three Chinese universities that organized trainings sponsored by the Ministry of Education and the Ministry of Commerce of China. Overall 35 interviews were taken in five cities in Tanzania (Dar es Salaam and Arusha) and China (Beijing, Tianjin and Jinhua).

Based on the findings from the fieldwork in Tanzania and China, some of the key issues of this 'China model' can be summarized. The following four sub parts will reveal the overall image, the two main approaches (scholarship and training) and a historical basis of this 'China model'.

Building Relations through Education, Rather than Aid Education

Firstly it is crucial to give an overview of the Chinese model of educational aid. It has been found from both practice and discourse that Chinese educational aid in Africa is not just for 'education'. This is not difficult to understand. Education is increasingly embedded in the complexity of the global political economy. It has been seen as a central idea in the modernization theory and is 'a key means through which individuals in developing societies...become "modern"' (Dale, 2010). Today, economic globalization is increasingly linked to education through the term 'knowledge economy' (KE) – where 'knowledge' takes over from 'production' as the key driver and basis of economic prosperity (Dale, 2005, p. 146). Based on these factors it is pertinent to ask what China expects from its educational practice. Since China has declared its relationship with Africa as a 'win-win' situation, what China 'wins' through education should be examined.

Official language describes this educational practice to be a 'diplomatic mission'. For example, According to the Chinese Scholarship Council (CSC), a non-profit institution affiliated with the Ministry of Education, the Chinese Government Scholarship Program is 'established by the Chinese Ministry of Education in accordance with educational exchange agreements or Memorandum of Understandings signed between the Chinese government and governments of other countries, organizations, education institutions and relevant international organizations to provide both full scholarships and partial scholarships to international students and scholars'. The scheme supports

187

students who come to study in China on undergraduate and postgraduate programs, Chinese language training programs, as well as general scholar and senior scholar programs (CSC, 2009; 2011). Applicants can apply for these scholarships through 'dispatching authorities, institutions or the Chinese diplomatic missions' (ibid, 2011). The Tanzania case also provides an example of this aim of education. Rather than 'help' African countries to develop education, it is China's aim to 'gain' mutual benefits. This has led to China's discourse being focused on 'cooperation' rather than 'aid'. In Tanzania, the educational cooperation is a part of two countries' 'Cultural Agreement' signed by the two countries in 1992. This agreement emphasizes the responsibilities of two sides which include:

- Exchange visits, and study and lecture tours by teachers, scholars, and specialists;
- Granting scholarships to each other's students according to their needs and possibilities;
- Facilitating the establishment of direct contacts and cooperation between institutions of higher learning in the two countries;
- Encouraging the exchange of textbooks and other materials between the educational institutions of the two countries;
- Encouraging and facilitating attendance by scholars or specialists from each other's country at international academic meetings held in the other country (Government of the United Republic of Tanzania and the Government of the PRC, 1992).

It is interesting to note that, wherever possible, the countries seem to be describing two-way practice:

During the years 2005 to 2007, the Chinese side offered one hundred government full scholarships to Tanzania each year. The Tanzanian side offered China five government scholarships in 2006, and four government scholarships in 2007 (Embassy of the PRC in the United Republic of Tanzania, 2008).

Education, from this perspective, is being used to work towards a broader reciprocal relationship between China and Africa, and is embedded within a number of strategies that form part of China's diplomacy (Yuan, 2011b, p. 126). This mutual beneficial style – a fraternal expression – is different from the orthodox aid relationship, which sets a paternal relationship between donors and recipients. However, this does not necessarily lead to effective equality and quality in the practice of education. The next part of this study illustrates the perceptions on both sides regarding Chinese scholarships from the returning students.

Globalised Scholarships? – Attractiveness and Discontentedness

As previously described, China has an interest in higher education and scholarships for African students. It has a history of more than 50 years of receiving African students, and the number has significantly increased in recent years. The researcher managed to meet individuals who have studied in China before. At the time of the field work in Tanzania, the returning students that were interviewed were working as government officials, lecturers or in national companies. A number of them were young lecturers teaching in the Dar es Salaam Institute of Technology (DIT) which has an agreement with Chinese embassy with respect to scholarships. These activities are described in the articles of the 1992 Cultural Agreement between China and Tanzania. In the interview the returning students were asked to describe their feelings about their experience of living and studying in China.

The feedback from the students revealed that the Chinese Government Scholarships have become very popular in Tanzania. As described by the Deputy Principal of Dar es Salaam University College of Education (DUCE):

I will say that the relationship is growing, I mean, more Tanzanians are going to China. The image of Chinese university is changing. Because at some point people think going to China is very different than western countries, but now, it is also good.

This reflects that students actually are thinking and comparing the quality of education rather than the politics behind the scholarships. Some of the young students do not understand the so called 'win-win' or 'mutual beneficial' relations between China and Africa. Therefore, when this is discussed in China and the West, they will often say 'oh, that is the politics' and turn to other details of their experience. What they care about is whether they can get sufficient funding, whether their family members can also be looked after by the Chinese universities, and whether they can get a good job following their overseas study. Some of the opinions expressed by these students are described below:[4]

(a) A contradictory feeling of the overall experience and specific learning elements. When discussing the advantages and disadvantages of the study in China, the former students expressed happiness about their opportunities to go to China, and suggested that they would be willing to go again for higher degrees such as a PhD, or would consider sending their children to China in the future. When asked about the importance of degrees in China, they all gave positive answers – 'Yes, definitely', and one of the reasons is that they considered that there is something that can be learnt as well as opportunities to be gained from this fast-growing country.

Geo: We learnt a lot in China and from China. Now it is very important that we use what we have learnt to teach and research...Yes we always ask, why can China be so successful in this era, so it is important to study in China. Tanzania is learning from China how to develop the country, and the Chinese are hardworking people.

Amb: Many Chinese companies are now in this country. Most of them are engineering companies. The parliament building was built by a Chinese company. So maybe for us it is a good opportunity to study there as our

189

government opens a lot of business and receives things such as this scholarship agreement from China. Now we have relations in many fields.

On the other hand, when these students express dissatisfaction it is usually related to the degree length, the funding amount, teaching standards, and communication. Firstly, the three-year master's degree (even though a small number of universities have initiated two year programs already) is a contradiction in that it is a good chance to undertake further research, but it is too long for a master's degree.

> Gus: With respect to advantages and disadvantages, the disadvantage is that the master's degree in China is too long. You know a master's in UK only takes one year. But in China some of us needed one year to study Chinese, and 3 years to study for a master's degree. Altogether it will take 3–4 years.

The language seems to bring a series of problems to these students. Compared with western education, Chinese lecturers are not very good at speaking English, while communication with other Chinese people (staff and students) in the university was reported to be a problem. Moreover one of the findings was that the Tanzanian students wanted to learn more, but the university treated them as foreigners and demanded from them far less.

> Geo: Actually for me degrees at the same level in the West and East are just the same, but the problem is the language. The teaching and study is okay, but the only problem is the language. When you have difficulties or problems you do not understand, and someone comes to help you, he or she cannot explain the issue to you very well.

> Gus: According to my experience, the language caused some problems. When the teachers are going to teach the foreign students, they are slightly shy and not very confident. Nevertheless they know how to teach...however their evaluation is also different. Because you are a foreigner, they will just say, ok. But when you are Chinese, the teacher will be stricter.

> Amb: They will think that because you are a foreigner you do not need to know this. So we cannot get the same level of knowledge as the Chinese students.

While China is actively engaging in the global market of international education, it seems there are also a number of lessons to learn; and one of the issues to consider is how to provide an integrated life for foreign students and provide a quality education and related assessment standards which are equal to those offered to Chinese native students.

(b) Different views by older and younger graduates. The above discussion about the details of Chinese higher education have mostly been undertaken by young African lecturers who went to China in recent years since the 1990s. However it is quite interesting to see how the perceptions expressed by the older returning students who

attended university education in China in 1960s and 1970s differ compared to younger students. The older Tanzanian graduates in the interviews seldom complained about any of the disadvantages of their experience in China. They did not report feeling dissatisfied with the money, language, or the lecturers. They were more passionate when talking about their experiences in China compared to the younger students.

In terms of language, these older graduates did not feel that there was a problem, and felt that they had integrated well with the Chinese students. The difference between the older and younger African students is that the older students had to study Chinese. However as a result of enrolling an increasing number of foreign students, the Chinese universities started to teach their foreign students in English. Although the aim was to become internationalized, the English level of the Chinese lecturers was not sufficient. However, this was not a problem for the older students who were taught in Chinese.

Robert: I was probably in the earliest group that went to study in China, in the 60's, and we learnt Chinese very well. At least I learnt very good Chinese, but that was a long time ago.

Moti: I got a scholarship in 1977 when I finished high school in Tanzania, and I was chosen by Ministry of Education to go to China. I went to Beijing and studied Chinese for one year, and then studied electrical engineering at Shanghai Industry University for 4 years. Yes the university study was all in Chinese and we had room-mates who were also Chinese. So it was like one foreigner with one Chinese and we could get help. For us it was so integrated. It was not difficult because we were living together. I was very happy with my study in China. I didn't see any disadvantages at all.

Although it cannot be said that the previous education was better or more suitable for African students, these opinions reflect some realities: there was a smaller number of African students in China, and they are likely to have studied Chinese well and integrated with Chinese culture better. They have more affection towards China than the younger Tanzanians. On the other hand, these different opinions are based on the different historical stages of China, a time before the opening-up policies were implemented in 1978 and a time before the deeper marketization of education in today's China.

Training University Leaders and High-level Officials: Transforming the Experience
Other than the government scholarship scheme, short-term training is becoming increasingly popular between China and other developing countries, and this is especially true in recent years for higher institutional leaders and officials. As of the end of 2006, China had held 2,500 training classes for individuals from 150 countries around the world, and 80,000 people had been trained in over 150 subjects including economics, management, agriculture, law, education etc. More than 150 Chinese universities, research centers and professional training institutions contributed to

this training (Department of Aid for Foreign Countries, Ministry of Commerce, 2007). As a special way of educating people in certain professional fields in the short term, training offers opportunities for understanding Chinese culture and learning Chinese developmental experience and is likely to have promoted good relationships between China and other developing countries. In China, fieldwork has been conducted in Zhejiang Normal University (ZJNU), Tianjin Normal University (TJNU) and Tianjin University of Technology and Education (TUTE) who have been undertaking short-term training for people from Africa with the support of the Ministry of Education of China. Zhejiang Normal University, as a key research base in China for African education, has been providing training and holding forums for African university presidents.

According to an interview with the Cultural Counselor of the Chinese embassy in Tanzania, China funds the whole journey and training, including the ticket and accommodation, the staff and the lectures, as well as some visiting organizations. The period of the training normally is two to three weeks, which is suitable for professional people. In terms of educational training, the Ministry of Education authorizes most of the activities, which are usually organized by a specific university in China. There are also other training plans conducted by the Ministry of Commerce.

The training courses are strongly linked to how China has been practicing education in recent years. Lecturer Wang at the TUTE introduced their courses in vocational education to African university administrators. The seminar topics of the training included: 'curriculum and teaching reforms of vocational education: based on a direction of employment', 'vocational education in developing countries: a comparative view', 'Educational development in China', 'vocational skill certification in China', 'administration models of vocational institutions in China', and 'developing vocational education in China'. In addition, there are some opportunities to visit historical places and to go to primary, secondary or vocational schools in China.

The principal at DUCE Misa described her experience of three weeks training in Zhejiang, China:

> I visited China last year. It was in response to an invitation to our Ministry of Education. Zhejiang Normal University organized everything. There were people from different African countries that participated in the training. We visited 3–4 universities. I spent 3 weeks there. We got to know more about educational development in China. Generally we were informed about Chinese educational systems, the changes that have taken place in China, and provided with further information about educational development in China, such as how enrolment has been increasing.

This is a process of viewing and learning about a successful experience directly. The Chinese experience for them is more pragmatic and they could identify some similarities. As Misa explained:

> Yes it is useful. It is good to know what others are doing. We learn from others by sharing opinions. It is helpful to alter your own institute's programs.

For example we learnt about some foreign language programs that I was also thinking about implementing... We need cooperation with Chinese universities, and we need to learn from them.

In ZJNU the organizers showed their course reports for training from 2004–2006. The documents, drafted by organizers, are more like statements about the success of the training:

The two-sides had extensive discussions based on each side's experience, methods and difficulties of administration... This has promoted future cooperation in the educational field for China and Africa (2004 summary).

We arranged face-to-face communication between our university students and the African participants-the Cultural Saloon which allows the participants to become integrated into the atmosphere of Chinese university culture...is getting to be a bridge between the lives of China and African young people (2006 summary).

The reports are not only summaries of training, but also advertisements of Chinese universities and China. As mentioned by Yan, a director of the International Cooperation Office at TJNU: the practice implemented for African learners has also had the effect of spreading the university influence and reputation worldwide. The training is educational but also political.

This is a way of 'sharing experience to let you learn', a method which is significantly different from the Western way of 'giving direction to let you catch up'. China does not criticize or comment on how African people have done, but rather shares opinions and experience with them for common developmental goals such as vocational education.

Historical Difference Perceived: A Non-colonist 'Brother' Facing the New Age

After examining the two main approaches of scholarship and training, this part does not directly consider education. Instead, since comments on Chinese-African relationships are usually related to trade, resources and sovereignty, and people seldom talk about educational practice without consideration of Chinese 'ambition', part of my interview questions were also linked to how African people look at China, especially compared with the West. As previously described, although not caring much about politics, the returning students recognized that China is different from previous colonists. It also demonstrates that these students could hardly forget about colonial history.

John: I get something from you, and you get something from me...Yes it is win-win, and it is ok! But in the colonial times, they [the colonists] used to take everything. It was not equal. When they came and invested, they made agreements to take more, and they gave a little. They made you not independent.

They made you become more and more depend on them. It was not good. They would set conditions, conditionalities... So I am not happy about that.

Geo: We are getting something from China, and China is also getting something from me. Another thing, there are two kinds of history here, West-Africa, and China-Africa. The West colonized the continent so they know much more about Africa than the Chinese. China knows about us because of international policy, so it is different from western countries. Now they come and help, and they also get something from us because we have a lot of natural resources... China does not have a colonial relationship with us. We are getting a win-win situation. So that is why the Chinese are more welcomed.

The interviewees held similar attitudes towards colonial history. This is also a significant reason why China can set a different model. As a member that has risen-up from the Third World, China does not have a colonial relationship with Africa. It plays the role of sharing experience and offering exchange rather than providing prescriptions. The Tanzania case is even stronger on this historical basis. The friendship between Chinese Chairman Mao and the Tanzanian President Nyerere, and the TAZARA railway that runs from Tanzania to Zambia, built by China in the 1960s are probably the most impressive examples of the previous socialist relationship between China and African countries. In Dar es Salaam, there is still a gravestone commemorating 69 Chinese experts and workers who died in China's aid projects for Tanzanian national constructions (Xinhuanet, 2009).

However, a 'brother' history may not provide everything in a changing relationship, as current African students are concerned about their individual opportunities rather than politics; and there are also a number of donors such as the Nordic countries that are not colonists either. Maintaining the role of non-colonist and socialist friend does not mean that China can be a successful donor in the future. For example, with national reforms Tanzania received more aid and also trade opportunities which were not just from their previous socialist brother but many Western countries. In his interview, the Chinese ambassador in Tanzania confirmed that the FOCAC series especially Beijing Summit definitely brought China into a new age of its relationship with Africa:

We [the West and China] are all giving rising investment to Africa. Where should we be going? Africa is an aim, and the Beijing Summit was of very strategic importance...We are win-win. This win-win is a kind of mutual needs under a new situation...It is not the same brother relationships as before, but more economic benefits and market plans are being added.

In terms of specific aid approaches and modalities, the ambassador added that the current aid would consider more carefully about the recipients' urgent needs rather than what donors are willing to provide, and it would not pursue the Western models:

For our aid project, the advantage is, we can control the whole process, such as building the national sport stadium or the hospital or the schools...Normally our speed is incredible…But we have some other problems. In very few cases, we built the things they did not need, and another problem is, how to maintain the product…Western donors may have realized the problem during the recent years, and started to give direct financial support. But China will still maintain this approach at the moment, and see if we can make it more scientifically.

All these perceptions regarding history and current developmental and educational issues demonstrate that China has 'dual' advantages such as being a developing country as well as never having been a colonist (not hierarchical). China also has disadvantages as a developing country in that it still needs domestic development that restricts its ability and competitiveness of being a donor. Historical factors can only be one of the bases for building China-Africa relationships, but what is the proper role of education? And how can China improve a sustainable educational practice with Africa within this new strategic relationship? These are still questions facing contemporary China.

CONCLUSION

Finally, it can be concluded that there is a distinctive but also problematic Chinese model of 'aid':

– It is different from Western aid in its fundamental logic – in that it is not about how to help others to be like 'us' (the donors), but about how to exchange benefits through one supporting the other. Within this process, education does not just serve educational development, but also has an impact on broader diplomatic issues;
– It has its own characteristics of establishing relations and focusing on the transformation of developmental experience through both formal university education for degrees and short term training;
– It has problems in the practice of higher education – this leads to further uncertainties regarding whether Chinese educational aid can provide good quality education to the developing world competitively in the global era;
– China's non-colonial relationship with Africa in the Third World was recognised by most of the interviewees; this is set as a basis for the contemporary win-win relationship.

The Chinese government adopts the proverb that says, 'give someone a fish and you feed them for a day, but teach them to fish and you feed them for a lifetime' (Department of Aid for Foreign Countries, Ministry of Commerce, 2007). Governmental scholarships and training represent potentially strong approaches for continuingly producing knowledge that is based on the Chinese experience and for linking educational leaders and other officials between the two sides. They are not only teaching and learning how to 'fish', but also sharing the 'fish'.

Can China, representing some differences as examined in this study, bring some effective 'architecture' to the orthodox notion of foreign aid? This study concludes with words from King (2007, p. 346), who said that we 'need not take China into a western or Japanese style donor, but if China is to continue to be true to the Eight Principles of Foreign Aid, there may well be ways in which its aid pledges can be implemented which build upon those foundations of mutuality, equal benefit and self-reliant development, and avoid the many pitfalls of traditional donor-recipient relations.'

NOTES

[1] This has been called the 'Rostovian take-off model', and certain concepts developed by him have been become central to modernization theory. The five stages are: traditional societies, preconditions to take-off, take-off, drive to maturity, and age of high mass consumption.

[2] One of the trends is that 'conditionality' may not happen under some aid reforms. UK Department for International Development (DFID)'s white paper in 2009 stated that, 'the old Washington Consensus – with its advocacy of structural adjustment and a one size fits all approach to policy making – failed because it was imposed from the outside and was not tailored to country circumstances.' In May 2009 DFID issued a new guidance note to staff on implementing its conditionality policy which appears to be backtracking on their 2005 commitment not to use economic policy conditionality. The note was not supposed to change the 2005 policy which stated that DFID 'will not make our aid conditional on specific policy decisions by partner governments' (DFID, 2009).

[3] An outline of the 'Eight Principles' are: (1) Emphasise equality and mutual benefit; (2) Respect sovereignty and never attach conditions; (3) Provide interest-free or low-interest loans; (4) Help recipient countries develop independence and self-reliance; (5) Build projects that require little investment and can be accomplished quickly; (6) Provide quality equipment and material at market prices; (7) Ensure effective technical assistance; (8) Pay experts according to local standards (Chin and Frolic, 2007; 4).

The most significant features of the 'Eight Principles' are 'mutual' and 'non condition'. This was emphasised again in 1996, in China's 'Five Point Proposal' for China-Africa relationship with the term of 'non-intervention', declared by President Jiang Zemin. However the sovereignty issue was sometimes argued as a political 'condition'. According to China's African policy (2006), 'the one-China principle is the political foundation for the establishment and development of China's relations with African countries and regional organizations' (Ministry of Foreign Affairs of the PRC, 2006).

[4] All of the interviewee names used in this chapter are pseudonyms in order to protect anonymity and privacy. Consent forms have been obtained from the officials whose job titles were mentioned.

REFERENCES

Centre for African Studies of Peking University (2005). *China Africa education cooperation* (in Chinese). Beijing: Beijing University Press.

Chin, G. T., & Frolic, B. M. (2007). *Emerging donors in international development assistance: The China case.* Ottawa: The International Development Research Centre.

CSC (2009). *Chinese government scholarship scheme.* Available online at: http://en.csc.edu.cn/Laihua/1 1678d1ad1114276a296ca1f3da38f99.shtml (accessed 10 August 2011).

CSC (2011). *Notice to international students studying in China.* Available online at: http://en.csc.edu.cn/ Laihua/dd6ed814b3074388b197734f041a42bb.shtml (accessed 10 August 2011).

Dale, R. (2005). Globalisation, knowledge economy and comparative education. *Comparative Education, 41*(2), 117–149.

Dale, R. (2010). Revisiting mechanisms of external influence on educational policies. Paper presented at *the La Educación para Todos en América Latina Seminar.* Barcelona, 20–22 October.

Department of Aid for Foreign Countries, Ministry of Commerce of the PRC (2007). *National foreign aid training conference held in Beijing on 26th July* (in Chinese). Available online at: http://lb2.mofcom. gov.cn/aarticle/zc/chineseeconomic/200805/20080505523932.html (accessed 12 December 2010).

DFID (2009). *The DFID white paper and the world bank: Missing the point?* Available online at: http:// www.brettonwoodsproject.org/art-565120 (accessed 10 January 2011).

Embassy of the PRC in the United Republic of Tanzania (2008). *Cultural relation between China and Tanzania*. Available online at: http://tz.China-embassy.org/eng/ztgx/whjy/t422282.htm (accessed 13 June 2009).

FOCAC (2006). *Declaration of the Beijing Summit of the forum on China-Africa cooperation*. Available online at: http://www.focac.org/eng/ltda/dscbzjhy/DOC32009/t606841.htm (accessed 2 March 2008).

FOCAC (2009). *Forum on China-Africa Cooperation Sharm el Sheikh Action Plan (2010–2012)*. Available online at: http://www.focac.org/eng/dsjbzjhy/hywj/t626387.htm (accessed 2 December 2009).

Garrett, R. M. (1994). Aid and education: The ecology of aid, in: R. M. Garrett (Ed.), *Aid and education: Mending or spending?* Bristol: Centre for International Studies in Education.

Government of the United Republic of Tanzania and the Government of the PRC (1992). *Cultural agreement between the government of the United Republic of Tanzania and the government of the People's Republic of China*. Dodoma.

Harbison, F. H., & Myers, C. A. (1964). *Education, manpower and economic growth*. New York: McGraw-Hill.

King, K. (2007). The Beijing China-Africa Summit of 2006: The new pledges of aid to education in Africa. *China Report, 43*(3), 337–347.

Li, B. (2007). *On the issues concerned with China-Africa educational cooperation*. Available online at: http://www.cctr.ust.hk/materials/conference/China-Africa/papers/Li,Baoping-Eng.pdf (accessed 6 June 2008).

Ministry of Foreign Affairs of the PRC (2005). *Sino-African Education Minister Forum issues Beijing Declaration*. Available online at: http://www.fmprc.gov.cn/zflt/eng/zt/zfjybzlt/t223750.htm (accessed 20 April 2009).

Ministry of Foreign Affairs of the PRC (2006). *China's Africa policy*. Available online at: http://www. fmprc.gov.cn/eng/zxxx/t230615.htm (accessed 15 April 2009).

Mosley, P., Noorbakhsh, F. & Paloni, A. (2003). *Compliance with world bank conditionality: Implications for the selectivity approach to policy-based lending and the design of conditionality*. Available online at: http://www.nottingham.ac.uk/economics/credit/research/papers/CP.03.20.pdf (accessed 1 January 2008).

Robertson, S. (2007). 'Remaking the world': Neo-liberalism and the transformation of education and teachers' labour. In L. Weis & M. Compton (Eds.) *The global assault on teachers, teaching and their unions*. New York: Palgrave.

Robertson, S., Novelli, M., Dale, R., Tikly, L., Dachi, H., & Alphonce, N. (2007). *Globalisation, education and development: Ideas, actors and dynamics*. London: DFID Publications.

Rostow, W. W. (1960). *The stages of economic growth. A non-communist manifesto*. Cambridge: Cambridge University Press.

Welle-Strand, A. (2010). Foreign aid strategies: China taking over? *Asian Social Science, 6*(10), 3–13.

Woods, N. (2008). Whose aid? Whose influence? China, emerging donors and the silent revolution in development assistance. *International Affairs, 84*(6), 1205–1221.

Xinhuanet (2009). *President Hu visited the cemetery of Chinese experts in Tanzania* (in Chinese). Published on 16 February. Available online at: http://news.xinhuanet.com/newscenter/2009–02/16/content_10824580.htm (accessed 5 May 2010).

Yu, G. T. (1988). Africa in Chinese foreign-policy. *Asian Survey, 28*(8), 849–862.

Yuan, T. (2011a). China's aid modalities of human resource development in Africa and an exploration in Tanzania: Differences and recognitions. Paper presented at Development Studies Association-European Association of Development Research and Training Institutes Annual Conference. York, 19–22 September.

Yuan, T. (2011b). 'Diploma' serves 'diplomacy'? Politics of Chinese government scholarships in Tanzania", *NORRAG Newsletter, 45*, 126–127.

AFFILIATION

Dr. Tingting Yuan
Faculty of Education,
Liverpool Hope University, UK

JONAH NYAGA KINDIKI

EDUCATIONAL POLICY REFORMS
IN AFRICA FOR NATIONAL COHESION

INTRODUCTION

One of the roles of education is to help in advancing a global partnership for development as a major Millennium Development Goal (MDG). The first and common dominant international discourse on education and development is that education is of significant benefit both to the individual and society. This can manifest itself through economic benefit in the form of human capital theory where education increases the employment skills, productivity and earning power of individuals and hence contributes to economic growth. Or, according to modernisation theory, education can be of social benefit in the form of the development of more 'modern' social attitudes towards, for example, science, gender equality and the desire to achieve. Also, education might contribute politically by developing the values and behaviours required for a suitable political culture that will help to sustain a democratic political system (Harber & Davies, 1997). It is these arguments that are used to justify the enormous effort to provide universal primary education for all as witnessed in the major international conferences at Jomtien in Thailand in 1990 and Dakar in Senegal in 2000.

The second, less heard, discourse, is that of education as reproduction. While seemingly opening up opportunity for all and contributing to the development of an economic and social system based on open competition, achievement and merit, in fact, the education system merely serves to reproduce things as they are. Children from poor backgrounds go to poor schools and then into poorly paid, low status jobs or unemployment. A small number of children from poor backgrounds succeed and this provides the appearance of a meritocratic system whereas in reality it merely serves to mask the role of education in perpetuating and reproducing inequality. In Africa, for example, political elites utilise expensive private schools to help retain the privileged positions of their families (Boyle, 1999).

The third discourse, not heard about much at all until relatively recently, is the negative role of education where schooling not only reproduces society fundamentally as it is but also actively makes the lives of individuals worse and harms the wider society. This is because schools both reproduce and cause violence. Not only do they fail to protect pupils from different forms of violence in the wider society but they actively perpetrate violence themselves. This negative role of education is the focus of this paper. However, this is not to say that that theories and arguments on

S. Majhanovich and M.A. Geo-JaJa (Eds.), Economics, Aid and Education:
Implications for Development, 199–222.

the positive role of schooling in development are invalid. There is certainly truth in them but the point being made here is that, despite dominating international policy debates on education, they only tell part of the story.

RESEARCH OBJECTIVES

The main objective of this paper is, first, to examine the two less heard about discourses of the negative roles of education that schools reproduce and cause violence. The education system seems to merely serve to reproduce things as they are and this can be bad for national cohesion and development. Second, the paper discusses various types of ethnic violence in Africa, their patterns and effects on education. Finally, the paper explains how educational reform can work to reduce these different types of violence before suggesting types of education which can promote national cohesion and development in Africa.

Research Design and Methods

An in depth exploration of the scholarly literature and *ad hoc* interviews with secondary school students, teachers, parents and members of the society were used to collect data which were theorized in this paper and discussed thematically in the subsequent pages.

SCHOOLS REPRODUCE AND CAUSE VIOLENCE

Schooling can be bad for development because of its negative role of reproduction and causing violence. Even though schooling may not necessarily be doing harm, it may not be doing any good. The main argument here is that schools are often responsible for violence by omission that is by failing to protect pupils from harm.

The academic literature for example by Boyle (1999) on access to education in developing countries recognises that the poor quality schooling in many parts of Africa is a deterrent to enrolling pupils in schools. As elsewhere in Africa, school enrolments remain low particularly in rural and slum areas and even where for example, free primary or subsidized secondary education has been introduced there is high enrolment and overcrowded classrooms hence necessitating dropouts and once again low enrolments. In order to maximise the benefits of education, an economic approach to its planning has to be accepted. For example, if only qualified graduates of a particular terminal level of education are considered qualified for the labour market after an examination or if the dropout and repetition rates are high, then the expenditure on education is not commensurate with the benefits, whether these are social or economic. It is within this framework that educational planning for national development looks into quantitative aspects of development, that is, linear expansion and the qualitative aspect that is quality of education offered in schools. In the past, education development tended to concentrate on the increase in the numbers of children going to school, that is, enrolments, rather than the quality of education they received (Mutua & Namaswa, 1992). This conviction is supported by many studies around the world. For example, a study by UNICEF (2012, p. 4, 42,) on the State of the World's Children identifies access to high quality education as one of the main social determinants of urban health and development. However, negative schooling perpetuated in schools can be bad for development. For example, crime and violence affect hundreds of millions of children in schools in Africa. Some are targets and others participate in or witness such acts as assault, mugging, communal conflict and murder. In addition to the obvious direct harm they cause, crime and violence can undermine children's faith in adults and the social order hence contributing negatively to development. This also relates to poor academic performance and higher school drop-out rates, anxiety, depression, aggressions and problems of self control. Also the denial of access to quality education is anti development because it leads to poor academic performance and unemployment which contribute to children living in impoverished conditions in their adulthood (UNICEF 2011, p. 7). Therefore quality education is central to enabling children to reach their full potential. Quantitative or increased attendance can also create its own complications, as the sudden surge of students may lead to overcrowding and poor quality education. Quality education implies ensuring schools work in the best interests of the children (UNICEF, 2010, p. 11, 20, 66).

Also, a Department for International Development (DfID)/Save the Children study of schooling in India, Mali, Palestinian camps in Lebanon, Liberia, Mozambique, Pakistan, Mongolia, Ethiopia and Peru stated that while many people put their faith in schools to offer children a better chance in life, for some, 'The local schools are of such poor quality that it is developmentally healthier for children not to be in them. The school systems are run by inflexible bureaucracies – if children face difficulties in attending because of the constraints of their lives, that is their problem, not one for the school system to sort out. What is taught in school is often incomprehensible -in a language children have never heard and unrelated to their lives. Teachers are harsh, unmotivated and unmotivating. Children drop out, having learnt little' (Molteno, *et al* 2000, p. 2, Babaci-Wilhite et al, 2012).

In India, a study concluded that for many parents and children the combination of expense, large classes, unmotivated and absent teachers, an overburdened and meaningless curriculum and an oppressive pedagogy are deeply alienating and account for many of the difficulties of enrolment and retention. It is not so much a problem then of school dropouts, the term often used in the literature on education and development, as school 'push outs' (Alexander, 2000, p. 99). This opinion with regard to whether the education system in Kenya provides quality education was confirmed in the *ad hoc* interviews by one respondent, who stated categorically that,

The Kenyan system of education has served the country well although like any other, it has been seen to have some limitations. Graduates at various levels of the education system are unemployed hence encouraging wastage. The quality of education should be improved to mirror what is available in the job market.

Corruption also plays a part. As a recent book on corruption in schools and universities put it, there is no lack of data illustrating the diverse forms that corruption can take in the education sector (Hallak & Poisson, 2006). As the Hallak and Poisson also point out, educational corruption and malpractice undermines one of the potentially positive purposes of education; namely, the promotion of universal values including integrity, citizenship and ethics. The author of this chapter was interested in investigating whether corruption and tribalism in schools contributed to violence and one respondent said that:

Corruption and nepotism have contributed to violence in schools in Kenya. Violence is likely to be more pronounced in schools where funds are not put to the intended use as per the objectives. Also, tribalism is prevalent especially in recruitment and deployment of teaching and non-teaching staff.

A report by Save the Children in Mongolia, for example, noted that teachers had started hidden businesses forcing pupils to buy textbooks and hand-outs, and were charging illegal fees thus preventing many from attending school. This is coupled with widespread physical and emotional violence against children by teachers in school, also a major disincentive to attend (Save the Children, 2006).

TYPES OF SCHOOL VIOLENCE IN KENYA

Generally, school violence is regarded as any form of violent activity or activities inside the school premises. It includes bullying, physical abuses, verbal abuses, brawls, shooting and so on. Bullying and physical abuses are the most common forms of violence that are associated with school violence. However, extreme cases such as shooting and murder have also been listed as school violence. Most of the time school violence consists of small groups of people fighting amongst themselves. There is no one specific cause known for school violence and it has been shown that this is a multi-faceted problem (Harber, 2004).

However, school violence is on the rampage in the present day world where students tend to develop an arrogant attitude very easily. A good example is the U.S. Department of Education reported that at least 10% of the schools in the entire United States of America are faced with problems associated with violence and in these schools there is at least one serious case of crime other than thefts or physical attacks. One of the very famous incidents that need special mention is the Columbine High School massacre in the year 1999. Also, a recently published study on 'the teacher as the victim' in the Czech Republic showed that 10% of secondary public school teachers are considering quitting their jobs because of harassment by students (NSSC1, 2013).

Although there are many types of violence both reproduced and perpetrated in schools in industrialised countries there are specific types of school violence in Africa. In Africa, the two less heard about discourses of the negative roles of education that schools both reproduce and cause violence are reflected in the wider society which mostly takes the form of tribal or ethnic conflict. That means education systems seem to merely serve to reproduce the society and schools as they are and this can be bad for national cohesion and development. Pupils at school regularly experience bullying, sexual, tribal and racial harassment from their peers but schools often fail to protect them. Also, HIV/AIDS is prevalent in many communities in Africa yet schools and teachers have been reluctant to teach about it because of fear of, and lack of training in, teaching controversial issues in the classroom. The existence or prominence of particular types of violence in schooling in Africa as elsewhere will depend on the social and cultural context of schools, though it is often the nature of schooling itself that permits this to happen (Harber, 2004, p. 45–58; Harber, 2007).

THE PATTERNS OF ETHNIC VIOLENCE IN AFRICA

The patterns of ethnic violence in different parts of Africa are complex and many factors contribute to it. Ethnic violence takes intra-ethnic, inter-ethnic forms and even transcends international borders. Africa is compounded by violent, sporadic and often unpredictable warfare between tribes fighting each other for self-centred ulterior motives. Why do I say so? I say so because tribes would justify warfare against each other as long as it is serving their self-centred social, economic and political ulterior motives. Each tribe sees itself as doing the right thing. Some of the causes of ethnic violence include political injustice and incitements, intensified cattle rustling, proliferation of illicit small arms, inadequate policing and state security arrangement, the diminishing role of the traditional governance system, competition over control and access to natural resources such as pasture and water, land issues, ethnicity and economic factors including increasingly high levels of poverty, compounded by irregularity in economic development, rapid population growth and unemployment. Violent ethnic animosity is also exacerbated by marginalization under previous colonial governments as well as political and developmental isolation after independence.

A good example of tribal self-centred ulterior motives in Kenya is the sporadic bandit attacks and cattle rustling in the Arid and Semi Arid Lands (ASAL) areas of Kenya. Another example is where occasionally tribes attack each other as was reported in a local daily newspaper that three people were killed in fighting over water and pasture in a ethnic violence between two tribes at the border of Mwingi and Kyuso districts in Kenya. The two groups came into violence after disagreeing over the control of watering points and grazing fields. The herders, mainly pastoralists from the North Eastern province of Kenya, had been driving their livestock into the area in search of water and pasture (Mutua, 2008).

Many children in areas affected by ethnic violence in Africa are out of school because of insecurity and the fact that they are displaced from their traditional homes. Peace and security are primary components of conflict resolution. The attainment of educational goals of teaching and learning cannot be realized in situations of conflicts, insecurity and ethnic tension (UNESCO, 2010, UNICEF, 2012).

EFFECTS OF ETHNIC VIOLENCE ON EDUCATION IN AFRICA

Violent conflict between tribes is not a new phenomenon in Africa. It has been present even before the coming of the colonialists and continues to the present. The colonial governments in Africa used violence to maintain law, order and exercise their rule but failed. The independent African governments trivialized the existence of violence between different communities as non-consequential to the national interest. With this negligence, ethnic violence is posing a real threat to provision of education in Africa.

The recent pre-2007 election propaganda and the post–election violence in Kenya reflect a similar situation in conflict prone areas in Sub-Saharan Africa. For example, in past years, many developing countries have been plagued by war and violent unrest. At the end of the Second World War in 1945 the world declared itself ready to address four major challenges of humanity including poverty, hunger, disease and ignorance instead of concentrating too much on arsenals of war. But internal armed conflict is in every continent of the world. Unfortunately, the African continent is leading in armed internal conflicts. In situations of war, the civilian population is increasingly affected. For instance, we could cite the Soweto massacres in South Africa where the police shot and killed some 1000 innocent children during the 1976/1977 uprising (Harber & Davies, 1997, p. 16–19). In Kenya, during the period December, 2007 to January 2008, after the general elections, ethnic violence broke out with the result that over 1300 people were murdered and shot and over 350,000 others were displaced.

Ad hoc interviews carried out for this paper revealed that ethnic violence that rocked Kenya after the general elections in 2007/2008 affected student learning, as one respondent replied,

Getting teachers to teach in some schools after the 2007/2008 tribal violence was difficult as some sought transfers to areas they thought were safer. Lack of teachers at the beginning of first term in 2008 affected the teaching and learning process in many schools. Students took time to get accustomed to the situation.

It is widely believed that armed conflicts are caused by ethnic rivalries in Africa. This is not necessarily true because at the heart of these conflicts is the way the government manages its business in the new global society which is moving toward recognition of a multicultural, pluralistic global system. Underlying these conflicts are issues of governance, devolution, of power from the highly centralized and personalized system of governance to a decentralized one which ensures the right to effective participation in the economic and political life of a country, equitable share of the benefits of development among the ethnic groups in a multi-ethnic state and reducing inequality and ethnic social disparities (Benneth, 2009, p. 1).

Prevention of armed conflicts in Africa ultimately requires radical reforms in social, economic and political arenas including schools. At the same time the issue of ethnicity in Africa cannot be underestimated in the explanation of armed conflicts. Ethnicity is a reservoir of turbulence in a world where power, wealth and dignity are unevenly and illegitimately distributed within and among nations. Leaders of ethnic groups resort very readily to ethnicity in their search for political power. These leaders often express their objectives in terms of 'advancing the interest of our people' or protecting ourselves from another ethnic group in order to give their ambitions legitimacy (Benneth, 2009, p. 1).

In many instances in Africa, the major beneficiaries of such aspirations perhaps are the elites but the whole ethnic group becomes associated with these aims since they are pursued in the name of entire group. Once this cycle starts and conflict begins to be waged in the groups' name, fear and further animosity pervade the whole group since all members become perceived as the enemy by those against whom the conflict is being waged. In addition, ethnic violence is further fuelled by pre-existing ethnic prejudices. The search for a culture of peace should therefore begin with the analysis of two potential sources of conflict which political elites can take advantage of.

These are ideological conflicts which occur when social inequality between classes becomes the dominant reality which sparks off civil strife, governance and authority conflicts, triggered by concern for the distribution of power and authority in society. Second, is racial conflict, brought about as a result of diversity of races and the impact of discrimination in a given society; identity conflicts concern situations where ethnic religious, tribal or linguistic differences play a more pronounced role as well as environmental conflicts which are broadly resource- based conflicts over land, the control of rivers or the protection of forests (Benneth, 2009, p. 2).

This is an evocative reminder that politically instigated ethnic violence in Kenya since the 1990s is a recurring theme. Local ethnic violence appeared to be deliberately inflamed for political reasons occurring in different parts in Kenya (Allen, 1998). Clearly, such long–term violence in any society can create a culture of violence, which is difficult to eradicate overnight.

Although there is a culture of violence in society, schools themselves can perpetuate it. Schools can be the site of active violence towards students in four key ways, namely: corporal punishment, sexual violence, racial violence and examinations. Corporal punishment is a form of violence institutionally sanctioned in many schools around the world. It is incompatible with the United Nations Convention on the Rights of the Child (WHO, 2002). Although corporal punishment is officially banned in countries like Kenya and South Africa, it is still widely used (Nelson Mandela Foundation, 2005). Also authority and order in schools have consistently been associated with violent imposition; a major factor in its global spread was colonialism, particularly British colonialism.

Sexual violence is also perpetuated by schools where boys are expected to be tough, assertive, sexually predatory and ready for life in a rough-and-tumble world but females should be delicate, passive, sexually pure and sheltered (Leach & Mitchell, 2006, p. x; see also Bellamy, 2003). Moreover, in some cases in sub-Saharan

Africa, and Ghana in West Africa, some teachers abuse their authority to demand sexual favours from girls in exchange for good grades, preferential treatment in class or money. Such teachers are rarely expelled from the teaching profession, at most being transferred to another school (Tengi-Atinga, 2006). A study by Brohi &Ajaib (2006: 12) of 300 secondary school girls in Pakistan revealed that girls were sexually harassed by teachers. Girls regularly experienced comments, lewd suggestions, and inappropriate physical contact from teachers. Although they were uncomfortable with their experiences; they were protective of their schools. They gave excuses for the misdemeanours of others because they feared that their families might remove them from school if they knew more about what happened, a very real possibility according to the authors.

Racial violence occurred in the apartheid education system in South Africa, during the Rwandan genocide, as well as elsewhere in the world in Bosnia, Herzegovina and Kosovo; Israel and Palestine; Turkish and Greek Cyprus and India and Pakistan (Harber, 2004, Chap. 6., Bayliss, 2004, Bush & Saltarelli, 2000: 10).

Thus, in Rwanda, education contributed to and exacerbated the resentment and hostility between the two groups that began during the colonial period and finally erupted in the genocide of 1994 in which some 800,000 Rwandans, most of them Tutsis, died in 100 days. Teachers from the Hutu ethnic background commonly denounced their Tutsi pupils to the militia or even directly killed them themselves. Indeed, the role of schooling in this genocide poses some very serious and important questions about why and how we educate in all societies.

As two commentators on the Rwandan genocide put it,

> The role of well-educated persons in the conception, planning and execution of the genocide requires explanation; any attempt at explanation must consider how it was possible that their education did not render genocide unthinkable. The active involvement of children and young people in carrying out the violence, sometimes against their teachers and fellow pupils, raises further questions about the kind of education they received (Retamal & Aedo-Richmond,1998, p. 16).

Examinations exaggerate cultural traditions of fierce competition within schooling and this has been exacerbated by neo-liberal market reforms. In developing countries the competition for scarce places in secondary and higher education, with their assumed links to the middle and upper levels of the labour market, has become exacerbated by cutbacks in public provision of education caused both by poor economic performance and by World Bank imposed structural adjustment programmes based on neo-liberal economics (Samoff, 1994; IJED, 1996). Traditions of fierce competition within schooling are visible in the school curriculum in Kenya which is overcrowded and examination oriented. Due to the work load emanating from such curriculum, schooling is now therefore even more of a competitive assessment and selection mechanism with 'winners' and 'losers' at all levels. Yet examination results are important to many students because they are passports to different lifestyles and to teachers, parents and policy makers they are meant to measure academic success of a school. The consequence of this can be very stressful to students. Thus, students' violence may be triggered by stress associated with competitive assessment and examination processes. Such violence may cause disruptive learning and students getting involved in physical damage to school property and that of the neighbouring communities (Kindiki, 2011).

However, violence varies from one country to another and from one school to another. Violent unrest in many schools in Africa prevents them from functioning in safe and peaceful contexts because of violence in the wider society that seems to be reflected in schools. Recurring violent episodes in schools may perpetuate a culture of conflict within the school and outside, and between the school and the tribe surrounding the school. Ethnic violence in Africa has affected the provision of education as schools in these areas have been abandoned because of lack of security. Many teachers, children, parents and educational officials have deserted areas affected by ethnic violence, a situation causing elimination of any progress previously achieved through the provision of education. Evidently on the ground is the fact that the government is channelling more resources than ever before to security–related matters such as deployment of military personnel to conflict areas, building more police stations, purchase of arms, guns and ammunition at the expense of food, health and education.

PREVENTING FUTURE ETHNIC VIOLENCE AND BUILDING PEACE

The role of providing education in conflict and post conflict situations in Africa is challenging. There is need for initiating educational reform that can work to reduce these different types of violence in schools and wider society hence building peace in the future for national cohesion and development. Education could help societies in Africa, especially Kenya, to prevent future violent conflict and build a peaceful cohesive country and promote development. For example, recently, Kenyan politics adopted an urgent measure to minimise ethnic tensions by the formation of a coalition government, the government of national unity. For the first time in the history of independent Kenya and after the intervention of the international community, mainly the United States and the European Union, there was formation of a grand coalition government by three main political parties largely formed on the basis of regional and ethnic affiliation, namely, the PNU (Party of National Unity) which is mainly comprised of tribes from the Central and upper Eastern provinces of Kenya. The ODM (Orange Democratic Movement) is made up mainly of tribes from the Western, Nyanza, Rift Valley, Coast and North Eastern provinces of Kenya. Also the ODM Kenya (Orange Democratic Movement of Kenya) is made up of tribes from the lower Eastern province of Kenya. The structure of the present grand coalition government of Kenya is unique and the first of its kind in Africa.

The second country in Africa which the world is hoping might accept a unifying government is Zimbabwe. This is a government modelled on a power sharing deal but political leaders in Zimbabwe are pessimistic about this suggestion. Zimbabwe is accused by the world leaders of holding a one-candidate presidential election marred by violence. It is yet too early to establish whether coalition governments in Africa will unite different tribes or will cause them to disintegrate further. Thus, the role of providing education in post conflict situations in Africa, especially in Kenya, is a difficult one. It requires political will and commitment.

The parliamentarians have a legislative and supervisory role that empowers them to reform laws and legal rules, create new or modify existing legislation governing education in Kenya. The Education Act in Kenya was passed by parliament in 1967. This document was revised most recently in 1980. Many issues in education have changed since that time. As representatives of the people, parliamentarians in Kenya have a role to play in enacting education policies that promote peace and security as primary components of the conflict resolution debate. State stability entails promotion of rule of law, good governance, respect for human rights and fundamental freedom and access to basic necessities for all people including education (Government of Kenya (GoK) Education Act, 1968, Revised 1970, 1980, 2009, RoK (Republic of Kenya) (2002).

Today the new government of Kenya is still charting ways of governance on the drawing board especially on the issues of resettling Internally Displaced Persons (IDPs) and promotion of national cohesion. Although this is happening, the situation is still volatile. Any slight political provocation can trigger violent ethnic conflict. Therefore, there is an urgent need for the education system in Kenya to affect the role of providing education in conflict and post conflict situations since this is one of the huge challenges of the new government.

But the structure of the grand coalition government has myriads of weak points. It is arguable that Kenya needs to put in place education policies that will counteract attacks on various ethnic groups, promote peace and national cohesion. Such education policies should aim to produce non-violent citizens and a peaceful society by fostering democracy. Democracy provides the best environment for non-violent solutions of disputes and conflicts and also significantly reduces crime and anti-social behaviour amongst young people in the society.

Education might contribute politically by developing the values and behaviours required for a suitable political culture that will help to sustain a democratic political system (s) Harber & Davies (1997, p. 3) argue that,

Authoritarian regimes have been marked by civil unrest, violent repression and wars against neighbours. While democracies are not perfect, accountable and representative government minimizes internal violence and the abuse of human rights and greatly decreases the possibility of going to war without good reason. In other words democracy can help to provide a peaceful context in which school can at least function safely.

There is a need for an education policy for democracy in Africa and Kenya in particular because:

The values, skills and behaviours that form a political culture that is supportive of democracy are not inherited genetically, they are learned socially and schools must play a role in this (Harber & Davies, 1997, p. 3).

It is generally argued that democracy is promoted by patriotic citizens. When asked about the level of patriotism among the Kenyans, one respondent said that,

The level of patriotism is rather low in this country. People are selfish and are divided into different tribes. Each tribe feels that it is superior to the other one. This some times causes tribal/ethnic violence. The government should help citizens to cultivate a sense of patriotism through sensitisation of democratic education. Although the government has its limitations due to political implications, it could be possible through civic education and also through the school curriculum which inculcates a sense of belonging and ownership to the learners.

Therefore, an education policy for democracy in Africa could prevent future conflict situations because education is the process by which students could acquire knowledge, skills, values and attitudes that would help them to develop an appreciation of their cultural values (Orodho, 2002). This is translated further to mean that education is the bedrock of society's culture, civilization and a powerful tool for perpetuating socio-economic political development.

Education for democracy could be possible if the Kenyan education system addressed issues related to the quota system admission policy. In 1985, the Government of Kenya implemented a policy committing secondary schools in each district to reserve 85% of places in their schools to pupils from within the district and provincial primary schools, with the remaining 15% being reserved for students from the rest of the country. This policy is known as the quota system (Alwy & Schech, 2007: 139). The aim of the quota policy was to enhance regional equity in the provision of education. It was reasoned that the previous policy where schools could select students from anywhere based on their performance was hurting regions, which had good secondary schools but could not raise sufficient admissions from within the districts. However, the outcome of the quota system policy was devastating. While the policy could have had merit, it generally did not go as planned. The regions that did not have good schools like the North Eastern, parts of Eastern and Coastal provinces suffered as a result. Further, the creation of districts on political grounds served to show the negative impact of the policy. The political clamour for the creation of districts had not taken into account the impact it would have on secondary school admissions, since the new districts did not have good secondary schools. Consequently, the North Eastern province of Kenya has suffered as have the single constituency districts. The quota system in which students learn in their birth place has been highly criticised for promoting tribalism. Due to the dispensation of the new constitution in Kenya which was promulgated in 2010 quota system has been abolished to allow students to learn in any part of the country because it has contributed to inequalities in education and decline in educational outcomes RoK (Republic of Kenya) (2011); Amukowa, 2013; Ojiambo, 2009; Weber, 2009). Center for Comparative and International Studies.

African countries like Kenya need to have curriculum policy reform in order to meet the learners' needs fully and respond to the changing society by incorporating emerging issues in education. One way of achieving this enormous objective is to include relevant courses in pre-service and in-service teacher education, and in the induction of school head teachers. The problems and purposes of education have in general become somewhat similar in most countries; the solutions are influenced by differences of tradition, and culture peculiar to each so that the task of teachers is to 'impact the meaning of general education primary and secondary, in the light of the forces – political, social, and cultural – which determine the character of national systems of education' (Kandel, 1933, p. xi in Burns, 2009, p. 1). Teachers also need to be in-serviced on provision of education which fosters cooperation, understanding, and exchange elements (Burns, 2009).

Internationalism is an underlying motif in the building partnership in national cohesion and development. Altbach & Kelly (1986, p. 4) note that:

The improvement of international understanding in general and education in particular is a long-standing tradition in the field. There has always been and, we hope, will continue to be a humanitarian and ameliorative element that has impelled many comparative educators to become involved in international programs to improve aspects of education and to encourage increased international understanding, particularly in the schools, as a contribution to world peace and development.

When asked about learning atmosphere in schools, one respondent replied that it was neither 'enabling' nor 'conducive' because it lacked international outlook. The respondent argued that,

Internationalism is good because it minimizes tribalism, creates awareness to human rights of citizens, and promotes national cohesion, democracy as well as development. Also, it improves economy of the country and creates jobs especially in developing countries.

Thus, the literature supports that democratic countries inevitably experience real conflict with developing countries when fundamental issues such as proper utilization of donor funds have not been resolved. For example, with support from the World Bank and international community the British government demanded a refund of $78 million in aid to Kenya's Free Primary Education (FPE) programme following revelations of massive corruption (Migiro, Friday, 17 June, 2011). This is because issues related to institutional reforms in Africa are fundamental.

The education sector is affected by these reforms. If we agree that teachers are the biggest single resource, and the most potent weapon in installing both knowledge of and enthusiasm for students, then, we must carefully consider how we train them especially on the emerging issues in education (Angrist, 1998; Harris, March 12, 2008 & Doyran, 2012).

Teachers could receive training in various types of education reforms required in Africa and especially in Kenya in order to pass this knowledge to students with the aim of enhancing national cohesion. For example, the post-election violent ethnic conflict that rocked the country in January 2008 has necessitated a debate in Kenya among teachers, parents, education officials and politicians that schools could correct some of the misconceptions and prejudices created among the youth during this period. Misconceptions about issues promoting ethnic violence could be corrected through the school system. Students at all levels of education need to be prepared to overcome all forms of intolerance. The content of a national school curriculum could incorporate teaching skills that could help students begin to appreciate coexistence and begin to understand that pluralism and diversity require one to be tolerant of others (Adan, 2008; Ngare & Marete, 2008, p. 6, 4).

RESULTS

According to literature on Human Rights by Geo-Jaja (2013, forthcoming) and other scholars such as Davies (2000:3; 2002: 37–50) and Bartlett, et.al, (1999: xii) Africa should emphasise rights in education reform in order for different states to achieve national cohesion respectively. A right in education is a basic human right. Learners' right in education refer to teachers' relationships with learners, school organisation, curriculum, participation, citizenship and learners 'voice. This is an approach that promotes the opportunity for learners to negotiate from a position of strength and dignity. A right in education-based approach emphasises the concept of citizenship, active involvement and participation of learners in matters that concern them. It promotes equality, human rights and human dignity with a commitment to equal opportunities. This approach would help Africans to reflect on issues of social and moral concern and recognise how the concept of fairness can be applied to their personal and social life involving cultural critique of "equality" approach within unequal context. Thus, the results of this study are based on the evidence from the literature review and verbatim ad hoc interview reports from students, teachers, parents in selected secondary schools in Kenya and opinion leaders of the society. This paper suggests types of education which could enhance national cohesion and development in Kenya and Africa in general as follows:

1. Peace Education

UNESCO (2010) publications consider the view that conflicts are in the minds of people and it is the minds of people that the defences of peace must be constructed.

211

Peace, human rights and democracy is also highlighted as part of what children should learn in school to promote the culture of learning, and security. This dimension of understanding about peace education is manifested in UNICEF (2012) publication which also advances a comprehensive broad-based study of children rights in the world. Geo-Jaja (2013), Davies (2000:3; 2002: 37–50), Bartlett, *et.al,* (1999: xii) and Bellamy (2004) support child friendly schooling which is a rights in education based schooling. Rights in education based schooling provides education which promotes conflict resolution, gender awareness and issues of inclusion as well as protecting the vulnerable in the society, participation, peace education and living in harmony. Kenya has adopted the international commitment to provide such peace education in the spirit of making progress towards Education for All by 2015 (RoK, 2005). The Kenya government has introduced Free Primary Education and Subsidized Secondary Education programmes, initiating day secondary schools, an currently the newly elected government is promising supplying all primary school going children with laptops.

Peace education for justice and democracy helps teachers and students to resolve conflicts, clarify values, and understand diversity. Students could learn social interactions and critical thinking skills which would enable them to address issues through activities and tasks that are related to the content. Peace education is concerned with helping learners to develop awareness of the processes and skills that are necessary for achieving understanding, tolerance, and good-will in the world today. Education for peace means examining and discussing our values and attitudes towards diversity, cultural differences, tolerance, and human dignity. It also refers to developing language and social interaction skills to promote peaceful relations among people, among nations, and between human beings and the natural environment. Additionally, it includes learning to solve problems and to think critically regarding issues of violence.

* Peace education is worth introducing because our global existence depends on learning to live together without the threat of violence. Educators have a unique opportunity to promote peaceful co-existence by bringing the processes of peace-making and peacekeeping to the attention of their students in the classroom. Reasons for teaching for peace include making learners aware of the basis of violence in their daily lives. It also helps to prepare students to become good citizens of their communities, nations, and the world with skills to promote peace and human dignity on all levels of interaction. In addition, it helps to use the classroom as a microcosm of a just world order, in which the global values of positive interdependence, social justice, and participation in decision-making processes are learned and practiced.
* The implementation of peace education can be achieved in several ways. First, teachers need to include topics that raise issues related to peace and cultural understanding in classrooms. Peace education can give students basic information to help them develop positive attitudes and values related to 'peaceful' living. Also

it could be done by engaging in activities that encourage cooperation, consensus building, and reflective listening that would provide students with the skills they need to meet and resolve conflicts.

2. Political Education

Political education is vital for political socialization. Students in Africa and especially Kenya could learn about the emerging African nationalism of the 1960s, and about colonialism and its negative effects on the continent. In fact, the emergence of African nationalism was the genesis of the formation of the Organisation of African Unity (OAU) on May 25, 1963, now known as the African Union (AU). Students need to learn about the great patriots in East Africa like Jomo Kenyatta of Kenya, Milton Obote of Uganda, Nyerere of Tanzania. In central Africa patriots like Patrice Lumumba of Congo made a significant contribution as well. Also in West Africa there were prominent patriots like Kwame Nkrumah of Ghana and in North Africa Modibo Keita of Mali whereas in South Africa we have Nelson Mandela. Political education could help to build a society which is aware of their history, international diplomacy, capitalist economies such as stock exchange concepts, and the importance of freedom from colonisers as well as the dangers of tribalism in nation building. This could help in shunning tribal politics which is the main cause of violence in Africa (Oculi, 2008). For example, in the 1960s Tanzanians sang a song of work and hope, as follows: "Mwalimu (teacher) -referring to Julius Nyerere as teacher, says it can be done; play your part" Jomo Kenyatta of Kenya came up with the slogan: "Harambee" (Let us pull together). These were slogans of unity in those days and perhaps politicians and the young generation in Africa have forgotten (Benneth, 2009: 1, Harber & Davies, 1997).

3. Human Rights Education

Human rights education could include children's rights too. Education should focus on human rights, for example, the inhuman treatment that perpetrators of post-election violence meted out to fellow Kenyans. Rights are meant to protect the interests of rights holders, with interests here interpreted as concerns, plans, projects, and states of mind and being, that give meaning to our lives and are not to be confused with avoidance of pain, desire for pleasure or self-indulgent whims (Loraine, 1998).

4. Moral Education

Education for good morals will help youth to be aware of health issues such as the HIV/AIDS pandemic, drug abuse, respect for gender issues such as gender parity (equality), moral values, morality/ethics, morals, principles, social responsibility and inculcating knowledge on the aspects necessary for industrial transformation and environmental education. Moral education could be integrated in school curriculum for students. It could also be part of in-service refresher courses, seminars, initial or pre-service requirements for teacher training curriculum in Kenya. Such a curriculum for teacher training could foster issues of ethics, citizenship and integrity in the way teachers conduct themselves professionally in order to avoid unethical behaviour such as demanding sexual favours from students (UNESCO, 2010).

5. Counselling Skills Education

There is need for establishing counselling departments in all education institutions to curb the rising cases of indiscipline and disrespect. Counselling has been neglected in many schools in Kenya, leading to spiralling cases of drug and substance abuse among the youth. Counselling is more urgent given the magnitude of the recent post-election ethnic violence that disrupted learning in parts of the country. Some children face harsh conditions at home; thus, the need for teachers to provide instruction on alternatives. Teachers should desist from inflicting harsh or corporal punishment on students. Some students joining school after the introduction of free secondary education might not have been used to order and proper school behaviour; hence, the need to spend time with them to explain how the systems work. Teachers also need to be counselled alongside students as they too have become vulnerable to stress owing to pressures of life, besides being displaced by post-general election violence (Drury, 2010).

6. Conflict Resolution Skills Education

The school curriculum could be developed to include teacher-to-teacher, child-to-child and teacher-to-child conflict resolution skills. This is because the role of education in conflict resolution is indisputable. Education is a process that enables people to acquire knowledge, skills, values and attitudes necessary for developing an open mind that can appreciate socio-cultural and religious ideals. Values and knowledge are important tools for supporting societal structures such as law and order. Education is the true bedrock of the society's culture, civilization and panacea to the endemic ethnic violence in Africa. Education enlightens the inhabitants on the available resources other than age old sources; an educated tribe will also appreciate other people's ways of life which may culminate in inter-marriage that may bind the communities' friendship (Drury, 2010).

7. Sports and Athletics Education

All types of athletics and sports activities enhance cohesiveness when participants associate as teams. A good local example of how sports and athletics can promote peace in Kenya is found in the initiative of an internationally recognised athlete Tecla Lorupe who has started a school complex known as 'The Tecla Lorupe Peace Academy (TLPA). This is a complex boarding primary and secondary school, attached to a sports stadium and athletic training camp. It draws children from the Arid and Semi-Arid Lands (ASAL) of Kenya. This is a peace building institution and provides education and opportunities for talent development especially in athletics. The academy also aims at enhancing peace in Kenya and in the Greater Horn of Africa Region. In addition, it promotes peace in areas hit by conflict and civil strife. The academy seeks to use sports as a unifying factor. The academy provides opportunities for children displaced or orphaned by conflict and HIV/AIDS in the Greater Horn of Africa Region. The idea of this academy was triggered by challenges manifested by frequent cattle rustling and highway banditry among the pastoralist tribes in north western Kenya, Southern Sudan and Eastern Uganda. The first intake was in 2007 and it is hoped that this academy will transform children to focus on their education for national cohesion (Kindiki, 2011).

8. Land Issues Education

Most of the information passed on over generations, especially in regard to land issues in Kenya might have been incorrect and Kenyans especially young people need to be educated on this. Lessons on issues promoting national reconciliation and cohesion should be taught at all levels including university. The current Education Act in Kenya should be revised and aligned to the new constitution (RoK, 2011, GoK (Government of Kenya) (1968, 1970, Revised, 1980 & 2009).

9. Customary Institutions of Governance Education

Lessons could be introduced in schools in Kenya which recognise customary institutions of governance. Repeated politically instigated violent ethnic conflicts could ravage tribes because it could look as if it is institutionalized. An elaborate system and mechanisms of resolving conflicts whether intra- or inter- tribe is necessary. Traditional family ties are slowly eroding; elders in these tribes do not form a dominant component of the customary mechanisms of conflict management. The elders could be used to command authority that could make them effective in maintaining peaceful relationships and the tribe's way of life (Mweke, 2012; RoK, 2011; GoK, 2009 and MoEST, 2005).

10. Collaboration and Networking Education

The government support for introduction of lessons in schools which advocate for increased collaboration and networking between the government and customary institutions of governance should be promoted. The government could recognize customary courts whose rulings enforce law and order in the society. The government could also partner and network with NGOs involved in organizing and funding peace meetings for the affected communities. The strategies by the NGOs could include capacity building and advocacy, and building schools and sponsoring needy

215

children. The NGOs could help in the formation of Community Based Organizations (CBOs) to initiate educational development activities (Watkins, 2000: 309).

SUCCESS WITH THE IMPLEMENTATION OF EDUCATION POLICY REFORMS IN AFRICA

Strategically, Africa has achieved limited success with the implementation of educational policy reforms for national development and cohesion.

1. Peace, Counselling and Conflict Resolution Education

Africa should be able to strengthen peace, counselling and conflict education for development and national cohesion. In Kenya, successful reforms for peace education are being implemented by the Ministry of Education as it seeks to make peace education compulsory. Currently a curriculum on peace education is being developed for the integration in social studies content and also a child friendly programme has been initiated on pilot basis in primary schools. The government is emphasising the need of establishing counselling departments in all education institutions to minimise spiralling cases of drug and substance abuse among the youth. In addition, the UNHCR and UNESCO have successfully implemented peace education for refugee populations at Kakuma and Dabaab refugee camps, which are located in the harsh environment of the North Eastern part of Kenya. These areas are neglected in political matters as well as in economic development. The camps include individuals from Sudan, Ethiopia and Somalia. Peace education has been successful also in West African countries like Liberia where it has been used as a tool for post-conflict reconstruction. In Togo school curriculum has 'moral and civic education. It has been successful in other countries like Uganda, Sundan, Rwanda and Tanzania. In South Africa peace education is incorporated into the reconciliation process. Although many African countries have now realized the need for peace education, as their curricula already contained various components that could easily be labeled as belonging to this particular field its implementation has proven challenging, particularly where it has been used in a reactionary way or to 'dampen' conflict. Its successful implementation is faced with difficulties of unsustainable peace agreements, students and teacher strikes as well as human rights abuses such as gender and tribal discrimination (Drury, 2010).

2. Political, Collaboration and Networking Education

This has been successfully implemented in Kenya through establishment of District Focus for Rural Development (DFRD) and Constituency Development Fund (CDF). The provision the CDF has helped to improve school infrastructure and payment of fees for needy children. It has also helped in transition rates from primary to secondary, colleges and universities. There is improvement in retention and reduction in wastage due to dropouts. However, there are limitations of over enrolment, and overcrowded classrooms. Though faced with challenges, Kenya has made remarkable progress in promoting equitable distribution of resources and provision of job opportunities in the rural areas for development and national cohesion. This has been demonstrated in the new constitution promulgated in 2010. Activities which promote cohesion are coordinated by the National Cohesion and Integration Commission (NCIC) established in the constitution. Fair and free national elections were also held on March 2013. The new government formed by the Jubilee ruling party manifesto has pledged to supply free lap tops to all primary school children as well as strengthening education policies which support collaboration and networking (RoK (Republic of Kenya) (2011). At the regional level opportunities for partnership have created greater political regional co-operation through the establishment of the East African Community (EAC), the Economic Community of West African States (ECOWAS), the Common Market for Eastern and Southern Africa (COMESA) and Intergovernmental Authority on Development (IGAD) which promotes regional economic integration through trade and investment. The partnership with NGOs is strong. But many African governments consider NGO programmes as irrelevant to education. Some governments perceive some NGOs as unprofessional operators motivated mainly by political whims and ignoring the government. The challenge in the implementation process in many African countries is that there can be unnecessary suspicions in collaborating and networking due to differing political viewpoints (Watkins, 2000, p. 309).

3. Human Rights Education

The Government of Kenya through the Ministry of Education initiated and has successfully implemented Free Primary Education (FPE) and Subsidized Secondary Education (SSE) in order to meet the goals of Education for All (EFA) as well as Universal Primary Education (UPE) programmes which include among others access to education, human and children's' rights to and in education. In Africa, particularly Sub-Sahara region, the challenge in implementation of human rights education for development and cohesiveness is mainly focused on ggender equality, equal opportunities and access to education particularly in rural areas and informal urban settlements.

4. Moral, Sports and Athletics Education

In Kenya, Religious and Moral Education was successfully implemented in curriculum at the beginning of 1991 (UNESCO, 2010). But, the school curriculum in Africa has not given emphasis on Physical Education in order to promote sports and athletics. However, countries like Kenya and Ethiopia have been partly successful in implementing this type of education by encouraging initiation of academies for training youth talented in athletics because it promotes national development and cohesion as it is one major source of income for individuals and the societies.

217

5. Land Issues and Customary Institutions of Governance Education

Geography, History, Civics and Agriculture curriculum developers though with challenges have successfully addressed land issues and traditional governance in regard to community land rights, legal implications, ownership patterns, democracy, resource management systems and internal conflicts. Governance of communities in Africa was assured through chiefdoms, monarchies, or councils of elders. Of these, the councils of elders were the most democratic. For example, the Njuri-nceke of the Meru tribe in Kenya has throughout its history been very successful and known for justice, fairness and service to all serving as the legislative, executive and judicial organs of governance. In Nigeria, a key role is played by traditional institutions of governance in managing social conflicts in oil-rich Niger Delta communities. African curriculum developers should re-address this challenge (Mweke, 2012; RoK, 2011; GoK, 2009; MoEST, 2005).

CONCLUSION

While this study examines eeducational policy reforms in Africa for national cohesion the international economic discourse about education and development maintain that education is of significant benefit both to the individual and society. The common and specifically less heard international discourse on education and development that schools reproduce and cause violence which is bad for development begs the need for review of education policy reforms in African and in particular Kenya to go beyond the common positive outcomes of schools which concentrate on access, retention and completion rates. African governments should be able to utilize sstudents, teachers, parents and education officials as agents of educational reforms which advocate for democracy, peace, counselling and conflict resolution, awareness in local political settings, partnerships, collaboration and networking, human rights emphasizing children'S rights to and in education, inculcating moral education, sports and athletics as well as land issues and respect of customary institutions of governance which ultimately creates good citizenry. This paper concludes that national cohesion could contribute to economic development because a nation no longer ravaged by violence and internecine battles can concentrate on developing employment skills and encourage productivity that will result in greater earning power, all of which will further the economic growth of the society.

REFERENCES

Adan, J. (2008). PS tells principals to meet set targets. Promote peace, unity, karua tells heads. The Standard, Thursday, June 26. Page 6.

Alexander, R. (2000). Culture and pedagogy: International comparisons in primary education. Oxford. Blackwell.

Allen, J. (1998). "Kenya political violence spirals". [www].http://sunsite.wits.ac.za/biennale/catalog/kenya.htm). (Amnesty International, Library-Kenya, 10 June 1998).

Altbach, P., & Kelly, G. (1978). Education and colonialism. London: Longman.

Alwy, A., & Schech, S. (2007). *Ethnicity, politics and state resource allocations: Explaining educational inequalities in Kenya. Part One.* Springer. Dordrecht, The Netherlands. www.springer.com

Amukowa, W. (2013). "A call to reform secondary schools in Kenya". *American International Journal of Contemporary Research 3*(1), *January 2013. Centre for Promoting Ideas, USA.*

Angrist, J. D. (1988). "Does teachers training affect pupil learning? Evidence from matched comparisons in Jerusalem public Schools". National bureau of economic research. Cambridge. *Journal of Labour Economics, 19*(2), (April, 2001), 343–369.

Babaci-Wilhite, Z, Geo-JaJa, M. A., & Lou, S. (2012). Education and language: A Human right for sustainable development in Africa. *International Review of Education, 58*(5), 619–647.

Bartlett, S., Hart, R., Satterthwaite, D., Barra, X. & Missair, A. (1999) *Cities for children: Children's rights, poverty and urban management.* London: UNICEF. Earthscan Publications Ltd.

Bayliss, S. (2004). Fairytale texts breed hatred. *Times Educational Supplement, 14*(5).

Bellamy, C. (2003). *The state of the world's children 2004: Girls education and development.* New York: UNICEF.

Benneth, G. (2009). *Promoting a culture of peace. Higher education and the promotion of the culture of peace in Sub-Saharan Africa.* Paper Presented at the Conference on Peace Education. Nairobi, Kenya.

Boyle, P. M. (1999). *Class formation and civil society: The politics of education in Africa.* Aldershot. Ashgate.

Brohi, N., & Ajaib, A. (2006). Violence against girls in the education system of Pakistan. In F. Leach, & C. Mitchell (Eds.) *Combating gender violence in and around schools.* Stoke On Trent: Trentham Books.

Burns, B, J. (2009). Comparative and international education and peace education. School of Public Health La Trobe University, Bundoora, Australia. Paper Presented at the *Conference on peace education.* Nairobi, Kenya.

Bush, K., & Saltarelli, D. (Eds.) (2000). *The two faces of education in ethnic conflict.* Florence: UNICEF.

Davies, L. (2000). *Citizenship education and human rights education: An international overview -3.* The British Council.

Doyran, F. (Ed.) (2012). *Research on teacher education and training.* Anthens Institute for Education and Research. Athens, Greece.

Drury A. (2010). *Peace education in Kenya: Global campaign for peace education new blog human rights learning: Pedagogies and politics of peace.* http://www.peace-ed-campaign.org/newsblog/ archives/38 http://www.peace-ed-campaign.org/newsblog/

Geo-JajJa, M. A. (2013). Human rights in donor aid; Does it really matter for "own" development in Africa? (forthcoming 2013).

GoK (Government of Kenya) (1968, 1970, Revised, 1980 & 2009). *The education act, laws of Kenya, Chapter 211. Revised Edition.* Nairobi: Government Printer.

Hallak, J., & Poisson, M. (2006). *Corrupt schools, corrupt universities: What can be done?* Paris: IIEP.

Harber, C. (2004). (Ed.) *Schooling as violence: How schools harm pupils and societies.* Roultedge Falmer. Abingdon, Oxon & New York.

Harber, C., & Davies, L. (1997). *School Management and effectiveness in developing countries. The post-bureaucratic school.* London: Cassell.

Harber, C. (2007). *Another inconvenient truth: Schooling, development and the perpetration of violence.* University of Birmingham: Amsterdam.

Harris, D. N., & Sass, T. R. (March 12, 2008). *Teacher training, teacher quality and student achievement.* Working Paper 3. March 2007. National Centre for Analysis of Longitudinal Data in Education Research Madison & Tallahassee.

IJED (1996). Special edition of the *International Journal of Educational Development* on the World Bank and Structural Adjustment.

Kandel, I. L. (1933). *Studies in comparative education.* London/Bombay/Sydney: George Harrap and Co. Paper Presented at the Conference on Peace Education. Nairobi, Kenya.

Kandel, I. L. (1933) in Burns, R. J. (2009). *Comparative and International Education and Peace Education.* School of Public Health La Trobe University, Bundoora, Australia. Paper Presented at the Conference on Peace Education. Nairobi, Kenya.

Kindiki, J. N. (2011). *School effectiveness and school improvement: The context of Kenya.* Germany: Lambert Academic Publishing.

Leach, F., & Mitchell, C. (Eds.) (2006). *Combating gender violence in and around schools.* Stoke On Trent: Trentham Books.

Loraine, A. (1998). *Part III: Human rights and the rights of the child. International Journal of Children's Rights* 6(101).

Migiro, K. (Friday, 17 June 2011 11:52 AM). *Donors want their money back in Kenyan education scam.* Thomson Reuters Foundation. http://www.trust.org/item/?map=donors-want-their-money-back-in-kenyan-education-scam/

MoEST (Ministry of Education Science and Technology) (2005). Sessional *Paper No. 1 on A policy framework for education, training and research.* Meeting the challenges of education, training and research in Kenya in the 21st century. Government Printer: Nairobi.

Molteno, M. Ogadhoh, K. Cain, F., & Crumpton, B. (2000). *Towards responsive schools: Supporting better schooling for disadvantaged children.* London. Department for International Development/ Save the Children.

Mutua, K. (2008). *Three killed in fighting over water and pasture.* Saturday, Daily Nation Newspaper. June 21, 2008 page 36 Column 4 &5.

Mutua, R. W., & Namaswa, G. (1992). *Educational planning.* Educational Research and Publication (ERAP). Nairobi.

Mweke, K. (2012). The role of traditional institutions of governance in managing social conflicts in nigeria's oil-rich niger delta communities: Imperatives of peace-building process in the post-amnesty Era EEE. *British Journal of Arts and Social Sciences.* http://www.bjournal.co.uk/BJASS.aspx ISSN: 2046–9578, 5(2) 202–219. London & Colorado, Denver.

Nelson Mandela Foundation (2005). *Emerging voices* Cape Town: HSRC Press.

Ngare, P., & Marete, G. (2008). National News. Headteachers Conference. '*TSC Hardens it's stance on contracts and life skills to be taught as school subjects, small schools to be merged,* Says PS. Karua Roots for Peace. Lessons to Avert Strife'. *Daily nation, Thursday June 26.* Page 5.

NSSC1. (May 7, 2013). *School violence- A Survey. School violence, weapons, crime & bullying.* Retrieved from (http://www.nssc1.org/school-violence-a-survey.html).

Oculi, O. (2008). Barrack Obama Embodies the Post Cold War Divided for Africa. *The Daily Nation, Friday July 4, 2008.* Column 3, 18–19.

Ojiambo, P. C. O. (2009). *Quality of education and its role in national development: A case study of Kenya's educational reforms. Kenya Studies Review.* KSR Volume, Number 1, December 2009 Kenya Scholars and Studies Association (KESSA).

Orodho, J. A. (2002). *Regional inequalities in education, population and poverty patterns in Kenya. Emerging issues and direction* in population Association of Kenya, Bureau of Educational Research Nairobi, Kenyatta University.

Republic of Kenya (RoK) (2002). *Special issue. Kenya Gazette Supplement No. 95 (Acts. No. 8) Kenya Gazette Supplement Acts, 2001. The Children Act, 2001.* Nairobi: Government Printer.

Republic of Kenya (2005). *Sessional Paper No. 1 of 2005 on Policy Framework for Education, Training and Research.* GovernmentPrinters.Nairobi.

Republic of Kenya (RoK) (2011). *The Constitution of Kenya. Published by the Attorney General in Accordance with Section 34 of the Constitution of Kenya Review Act (No. 9 of 2008).* Nairobi: Government Printer.

Retamal, G., & Aedo-Richmond, R. (Eds.) (1998). *Education as a humanitarian response.* London: Cassell.

Save The Children (2006). '*Save the Children: Mongolia to Protect over 650,000 Children'* (www.politics.co.uk/press-releases/domestic-policy,children/child-abuse/save-ch)

Samoff, J. (1994). *Coping with Crisis : Austerity, Adjustment and Human Resources.* London: Cassell.

Tengi-Atinga, G. (2006). Ghanaian trainee teachers' narratives of sexual harassment: A study of institutional practices. In F. Leach, & C. Mitchell (Eds.) *Combating gender violence in and around Schools* Stoke On Trent: Trentham Books).

UNESCO (2010). *World data on education*. United Nations Educational, Scientific and Cultural Organization and International Bureau of Education: Paris.

UNICEF (2010). *State of the world's children 2010 Special Edition. Celebrating 20 years of the convention on the rights of the child*. UNICEF: New York.

UNICEF (2011). *The State of the world's children 2011 adolescence: An age of opportunity*. UNICEF: New York.

UNICEF (2012). *State of the world's children 2012: Children in the urban world*. UNICEF: New York.

Watkins, K. (2000). *Education now: Break the cycle of poverty*. London: Oxfam, GB.

Weber, A. (2009). *The causes of politicization of ethnicity: A comparative case study of Kenya and Tanzania. Working Paper No. 47, 2009*. Published by the Center for Comparative and International Studies (CIS), ETH Zurich and University of Zurich

WHO (World Health Organisation) (2002). *World report on violence and health*. Geneva: WHO.

AFFILIATION

Jonah Nyaga Kindiki
Moi University, Kenya

BETH D. PACKER

BREAKING DOWN BORDERS IN DEVELOPMENT EDUCATION

Something's Gotta Give

Despite the billions of dollars spent on development each year, a shocking 24,000 children die daily due to poverty, almost one billion people were unable to read or write at the turn of the twenty-first century (UNICEF State of the World's Children, 2008), roughly a billion people in the Global South live without acceptable access to clean water (Shah, 2010) and well over two billion have insufficient sanitation (UN Human Development Report, 2006). Yet, in 2010 the amount spent on development aid from members of the Organization for Economic Cooperation and Development (OECD) reached an unprecedented high of 128.7 billion USD (Aid statistics, 2010). Even a cursory look at the socio-economic conditions of the world's poorest nations illustrates that current development paradigms are not adequately addressing these issues.

This study attempts to break from both the latest trends and classic development paradigms by exploring a "re-localization" approach to development education and the subsequent planning and implementing of intervention policy in the Global South. Through a case study analysis of a Senegalese-American academic exchange program I argue for a shift in the framework of development education towards a model that supports locally constructed and implemented development strategies. This model brings international, regional and local actors together in acquiring theoretical and practical knowledge in development education within an entirely local context. In order to situate this approach within the current debate on development intervention policies, I preface my discussion by tracing the evolution of the various approaches to development and the need for such a paradigmatic shift. The case study will then be explored in three parts. First, I will outline the organization's educational model, which stresses exploratory learning, intercultural collaboration and increasing partnerships between academia and development practitioners. I will then present the outcomes of the program detailing its advantages as well as drawbacks. In a final discussion, I speculate on what needs to "give" in development education in order for a new paradigm to emerge.

PLAYING CATCH-UP

Since the beginning of the latter half of the twentieth century, the term "development" has been loosely employed to describe the act of improving or advancing the social,

*S. Majhanovich and M.A. Geo-JaJa (Eds.), Economics, Aid and Education:
Implications for Development, 223–238.*

political and economic systems of the global south. Classic development paradigms that emerged during the mid twentieth century in response to alarming discrepancies between the quality of life in "developed" nations and that of "underdeveloped" nations" were focused on expanding the economic growth of a country through the hegemonic "trickle down" market-oriented perspective (McMichael, 2004). These "trickle down" approaches promoted the development of a strong economy that would gradually benefit the greater society (Nederveen, 1998) and once brought "up to speed" with the rest of the world they would enjoy the same success and quality of life as their "developed" counterparts. The practical application of this model provided countries from the Global South with financing and experts to teach them how to build a strong economy through a series of projects that typically stressed the growth of industry. Potter, Bins, Elliot, and Smith (2008) discuss how decisions remained largely centralized and external expertise was conceived within a "western" framework. This classic approach, made popular during the 1950's and 1960's failed to take into account the unique circumstances and histories of aid recipient countries.

Stemming from the classic "trickle down" models, structural adjustment programs were proposed by the International Monetary Fund and World Bank during the 1970's. In this system, the World Bank and the International Monetary Fund (IMF) distributed loans to restructure the reimbursement plans of previous loans. In their book, Mohan, Brown, Milward, and Zack-Williams show that in order to receive aid, recipient countries had to comply with the conditions imposed by the lending institution, meant to ensure that loans received would be used to instate goals and policies stipulated by the lending institution (2000, p. 25). Economy-centered programs relied heavily on externally stipulated policies, which has profoundly impacted how developing countries view their own capacity to "develop". Such an approach projects an image of dependency on target countries who come to see themselves as novices in their own social, economic and political development. Growth is then perceived in economic terms and these countries are taught to realize their developmental potential by "catching up" to richer and more successful nations. As Jonathon M. Harris of Tufts University points out, externally prescribed economic growth policies have shown to breed social and economic inequalities: "the benefits of development have been distributed unevenly, with income inequalities remaining persistent and sometimes increasing over time" (Harris, 2000, p. 4). The failure of this "trickle down" market oriented approach to squelch mass poverty, despite the large sums of money invested, paved the way for more people-oriented conceptions of development and other alternative practices.

Alternative Paradigms: What Constitutes Development?

Since the 1980's, development policy has gradually moved away from the classic economic centered view of development towards alternative paradigms. Human development, participatory and grassroots models build from the ground up and focus on developing the human capacity, "especially [of] poor and marginal social groups, through their full participation in development efforts and governance processes that directly affect their lives" (Gurstein and Angeles, 2007, p. 12). The concept of human development is now a leading approach due in large part to its adoption by the United Nations Development Project (United Nations Development Project 2010). This approach is concerned with developing human capabilities and creating a successful environment to do so. Human development has brought to the forefront the importance of participation and self-reliance of local communities in the development process, typified by the participatory and grassroots bottom up models.

Such approaches aim to integrate local knowledge and socio-cultural particularities indicative of the target population in both program design and implementation. The goal shifts from teaching target audiences in developing countries how to imitate the development path of western countries to "empowering", local people by teaching them how to take charge of their own development in order to improve their quality of life. These alternative models have proffered significant changes in the way that we envision and implement development strategies (Mohan, 2001). However, target populations remain reliant on "experts" trained in paradigms that are conceived within a foreign framework to teach them how to become experts themselves in managing and directing their own development. Programs emphasizing participation and community led solutions continue to rely on foreign knowledge to guide local development, even if in the process recipients themselves become "experts".

An excellent example is the United States African Development Foundation (USADF), a leading pioneer in participatory development models. The USADF acknowledges that, "participatory development is a grounded approach to development that recognizes African communities as communities of experts who know what they need to achieve sustainable growth" (United States African Development Foundation, 2003). This model of "community led demand driven participatory development" relies on the knowledge of an external team of experts to guide local development initiatives. By introducing the idea of "local community development agents" or "trained local facilitators" it attempts to involve the community from program design to implementation, and finally evaluation. Inherent in this practice is the belief that outside knowledge is needed for a target population to respond efficiently to its own development needs. In fact, as sociologist Norman Long reveals, an essential aspect of this approach is based on "ideological underpinnings...that the injection of external inputs will provide a better solution to problems than those means that already exist, thereby opening up new opportunities and improving people's living conditions and welfare" (Long, 2001, p. 34). From this perspective, alternative paradigms limit themselves in a similar way to the classical development paradigms they so vehemently oppose: expert knowledge is transferred from an external framework to a local target population, which thwarts locally generated innovation.

Development Education Today: Introducing the Experts

Who are the experts and how are they trained? The field of international development is an increasingly popular career track worldwide (UCLA, 2013), garnering attention both in academia and the professional sector. In *Careers in International Affairs* edited by Carland and Faber (2008), Kristi Ragan notes that opportunities in the field range from "business firms, non-profits, non governmental organizations, think tanks, bilateral and multilateral donor organizations, foundations and consulting firms" (p. 321). Experts working in these domains are trained in practices associated with a specific dimension of development such as agriculture, economy, social work, gender issues, public health or a compendium of international issues and practices. In participatory and human development models, these trained experts transfer their knowledge and skills to local development agents (The ADF approach) who then guide local initiatives.

Many celebrated academic institutions in the United States, Canada and Europe offer undergraduate and graduate training to prepare for a career in international development, as do a growing number of universities in the Global South. Development curriculum at prestigious universities such as Duke University, McGill University or Columbia University emphasize the importance of gaining experience in the field as an integral aspect of the learning process. To become an "expert", students must complete a combination of classroom based theoretical coursework and hands-on experience through internships or volunteer programs (Career Opportunities in International Development, 2007). Keep in mind however the experiences students acquire continue to be within current development structures that encourage participatory, yet externally designed and planned intervention procedures. My aim here is not to enumerate diverse international development curriculums; rather I stress the extrinsic character of most development education framework, which renders existent models unable to effectively incorporate diverse local realities.

BRINGING IT HOME: INCORPORATING 'MULTIPLE REALITIES' INTO A FLEXIBLE PARADIGM

Development practices are anchored in the multiple realities of all actors involved in the process. These realities, as Long (2001) points out, comprise "differing cultural perceptions and social interests, and [are] constituted by the ongoing social and political struggles that take place between the various social actors involved" (p. 30). If development education is to nurture innovative and internally generated solutions consistent with local needs, these diverse realities must be incorporated at all stages of the process. It is time to abolish the claustrophobic boundaries that suffocate current concepts of development. To do this the Global North must relinquish its monopolistic hold on generating theory, identifying problems and implementing solutions. This is not to argue for an eradication of external aid or the abandonment of the entire development project. On the contrary, the study of development should be re-localized so that theoretical and practical knowledge is conceived and acquired within a local framework by all actors involved in the process. Traces of this notion can be found in an exploratory academic program in Senegal (which I will refer to throughout this paper as XORG) that served as a case study for this paper.

A Step in the Right Direction

In this case study I draw on an experiential educational program that was offered by the Senegalese branch of an American NGO, which I call XORG. Located in urban Senegal, XORG piloted an exploratory academic study course from 2004 to 2012 intending to shatter the North/South boundaries that divide development education. The founders aimed to demolish the symbolic and material borders that frame development education as a "Northern" led response to problems of the Global South, by designing a program that would "re-localize" the search for solutions. At the same time, their model sought to close the crater size gap that lies between academic work about development and real live implementation. Partnering with prestigious American universities, the XORG program, taught by Senegalese and International staff, joined an equal number of American and Senegalese university students in an exploratory course emphasizing innovative collaborative research and project design. All coursework was fully accredited by the American universities and counted toward the degree completion of both American and Senegalese students. XORG saw income discrepancy as one of the primary obstacles keeping expertise in the Global North. The cost of running accredited and competitive academic programs remains financially unfeasible for many institutions of the Global South who lack state and private funding to support staff, infrastructure and students' needs. In addition, many students from the Global South do not possess the financial resources to obtain an education in prestigious universities of the Global North, the powerhouse of international development careers.

Without this education they have difficulty acquiring the cultural capital to compete on the job market with students trained in these institutions. XORG saw partnering American and Senegalese students in a locally based prestigiously accredited program as the first step towards giving Senegalese students and academics the chance to dialogue with leaders in the development field. In order to offset the cost of running the program, American students paid tuition to the program similar in pricing to most quality accredited study abroad programs, which also covered the cost of Senegalese tuition. By forming tomorrow's development experts in an entirely localized context, XORG believed that they were better suited to teach a development paradigm that would take into account the multiple realities of staff, students and villagers. The twofold interdisciplinary program was divided between classroom sessions held at XORG's urban headquarters and on-site training in a rural village where theory was elaborated, revised and put into practice. Underscoring the core curriculum were the principles of intercultural collaboration, locally initiated development and the XORG model of integrating theory and practice.

From July 2008 to April 2009, I had the opportunity to work with XORG as a Program Director. I was granted access to organizational resources such as handbooks, field guides, reports, promotional material and student evaluations. My role in the organization also allowed me to participate in both the theoretical and practical portions of the program that took place in a large urban center and a rural Senegalese village. During my time in the field, I systematically observed and participated in every phase of the program. While in Senegal, I documented my observations as well as unstructured discussions that had taken place with participants and staff. In the spring of 2010, I began examining the implications of the XORG model as a new approach to development education. In addition to analyzing my own experience with the program, I conducted in-depth interviews with ten former students and three staff members, reviewed former student evaluations, final papers and project evaluations. The organization is fully aware of my status as a researcher and many former students and staff enthusiastically participated in the research process. This case analysis is the result of eighteen months of observing and collaborating with XORG.

Pedagogical Methods: Theory Meets Practice in a Localized Setting

The program was presented to students and villagers as an experiential and reflective learning process, the focus being a combination of theory and practice. The core curriculum at XORG built on action research and participatory development principles to give students the tools necessary to design and implement projects in the target village. During classroom sessions students were instructed in an overview of development theories leading up to current sustainable development paradigms. These sessions highlight historical and current development issues, both in Senegal and on an international scale. XORG instructed students in the methods of action research (a research method that merges critical reflection and theory with applied action in an authentic context), participatory rural appraisal and eco-village design (a development approach that stresses social, environmental and economic sustainability) as a starting point for initiating locally conceived development strategies. Senegalese Professors with significant experience in both academia and the professional sphere in Senegal and abroad, led classroom sessions while representatives from diverse university settings, bilateral, multilateral donor organizations and government ministries were invited to participate as "guest lecturers". These experts formed a pool of professional mentors, which students could later draw upon during the practical section of the program.

XORG promoted Action Research (AR) as an approach that provides communities with the information and tools required to examine their needs and control their own path of development (Allen, 2001). A concrete example of how action research can be applied in a development setting is through Participatory Rural Appraisal

(PRA). Students of XORG were introduced to PRA, a series of practical guidelines designed to encourage locals to carry out their own investigation of development needs and implementation of solutions (Participatory rural appraisal, n.d.). Finally, XORG trained participants in basic eco-village design, which according to XORG integrates "green infrastructural capital and traditional socio-cultural values to create a community that thrives on renewable energy sources and permaculture; local purchasing to support the village economy, local food production and distribution between neighboring villages, community lead education initiatives" (Organization Handbook, 2008). Combined, these methods were meant to provide students with a comprehensive overview of participatory approaches to development within the prevailing externally led framework. The goal of XORG was to teach students to think outside the limits of these paradigms in order to create more resilient frameworks that are contextually relevant and locally formed.

It is important to reiterate the experiential framework of XORG's curriculum, which allowed for greater flexibility in project design. This flexibility proved to be one of the most unique aspects of the program whose objective "is not to provide an abundance of technical facts and general scientific theory, or the debate generated by Western schools of thought on these topics, which is typical of most US undergraduate programs on sustainability studies" (Semester Handbook, 2008). In this respect, while the coursework did highlight sustainable development theory and strategies, it is more to give examples of what type of action is possible, rather than a prescribed course of action. Throughout the semester or quarter, "hands on" experience was alternated with classroom sessions to form a cycle of theory and practice, culminating in a two-part development project executed in the target village. The XORG program was organized in a way that allowed students to work in groups, guided by village-based mentors to design and implement a project that reflected both the needs and development vision of the target community. Each student also produced an independent research project in line with his or her own background and interests. The independent research project was required to be closely linked to the theme of the group project. The group project and independent research constitute an important step in action research training.

The semester or quarter began at XORG's urban headquarters where students were introduced to staff, their host families and received a general orientation regarding XORG and living in Senegal. About two weeks into the program, staff accompanied the students to the target village. This first visit was meant to familiarize them with the village and the local vision for community development. Students met with community members such as chiefs, mayors, school staff, associations and so on, and utilized this time to identify community interests that connected with their own educational background. The program then returned to XORG headquarters where students continued theory-based modules collaborating with staff to develop a project outline, based on participatory and action research methodology. Staff facilitated meetings with experts who were selected from XORG's mentor pool and chosen based on their qualifications and relevance to the students' projects. Mentors then assisted students in creating an effective framework and plan of action. By implicating development experts in the experiential process, XORG stressed the importance of bridging the academic study of development with practices. The distinction between academic research on development out of which theory is born and reborn, and the actual practices of development, was perceived by XORG as one of the hardest barriers to abolish. From my perspective, XORG saw this collaborative paradigm that identified local responses to local realities as both the demolition machine and the building blocks of what they would deem a new sort of partnership between theory and practice.

Midway through the program, students and staff returned to the target village to solidify teams and project themes. Students next updated and adjusted their outlines and action plans to reflect feedback and guidance from village team members. At this time, they also made note of the materials and supplementary information needed to implement the project. After the second visit, students returned to XORG headquarters where they were expected to have their project reviewed by XORG staff and program mentors. Once approval was met, they returned to the target village for a final visit and planned the implementation of their project step by step with village team members. During the implementation phase of the projects, staff members guided students in participatory methodology and assisted in gathering all information necessary to complete their projects within the allotted time frame.

Program Outcomes

Through participant observation, in-depth interviews with previous students and former staff as well as documentary analysis of primary sources, I was able to construct a picture of the outcomes of the XORG model. My findings indicate several advantageous aspects of an experiential in situ approach to the study of development that reflect XORG's goal of encouraging the experts of tomorrow to adopt a localized and flexible development model which would take into account the multiple realities involved in the process. In this section, I provide evidence of how the XORG model breaks down cultural and social borders by incorporating marginalized populations and promoting appreciation of diverse worldviews. I show how this model stimulates new ways of thinking about the development process, and encourages locally led development solutions.

Drawing on student's own reflections about their experience at XORG, it is evident that exposure to diverse cultural toolkits profoundly impacted their way of navigating the world and ultimately, their understanding of the development process itself. In order to plan and implement small-scale development projects, American and Senegalese students worked side by side with villagers to overcome polemics and obstacles rooted in differing worldviews. M., an American student explained to me during an interview "I realize now that there aren't really better ways of seeing the world, just different ways. Sometimes I got frustrated with people because they didn't do things the way that I was used to" (interview March 15,

2010). A prime example of how students learned to identify and address these issues is the library project, which was implemented in the target village. In her interview S., an American student explained that the her group wanted to "create a village library that would increase enthusiasm for reading by getting the books and putting the library physically together and getting people excited about reading and learning together" (interview March 15, 2010). During the interview S. noted that her group wanted to make the library a "fun environment but the teachers and community members [they] were working with didn't want that; they wanted more of a scholarly environment". For S. and her library group this contradicted the entire goal of their project. They gradually began to lose motivation as they saw the lack of enthusiasm for promoting learning as a fun activity a "failure" on their part to implement the project.

After several fruitless attempts to convince the villagers that this was how the project should be done, they realized their failure stemmed from trying to force their worldview on others. This realization altered the entire course of the project. According to S., the group then collaborated with villagers to create a library system that was relevant to how the villagers perceived the library's purpose as a way to "increase access to and interest in books. We wanted to bring in books in the local language and they wanted to learn French, because that is the language of higher education and work, for them it was totally practical" (interview, March 15, 2010). The group discovered that books are very expensive to buy, and rarely available to loan out. This is especially difficult for the traditionally large Senegalese family, buying books for several children, is a very costly expense. Consequently many villagers worried that their children would fall behind in school since they did not have access to the curriculum. Working within a framework that reflected local realties allowed the group to implement a contextually appropriate project. In the end, they brought in books that were consistent with the school's curriculum and they also got the children excited by having them paint and decorate the library together in a fun way. They furnished the library with comfortable chairs and also brought a few books in the local languages and "just for fun reading". Since the students have left the village, teachers have shown a growing interest in the library.

Both American and Senegalese participants leave the program with a better understanding of how culture interacts with development and what this means in the larger scope of development theory. T., an American student highlighted this process in his final paper: "any development efforts are required to have an understanding of a culture if they are to succeed. Trying to make people work in an American context does not work very well in Senegal" (interview April 3, 2010). Students observed that recognizing and working within different worldviews goes hand and hand with the concept of locally initiated and context specific development. This is best illustrated by M.'s description of the most valuable lesson he learned while in Senegal, "we come with a lot of great ideas of things they don't even need or really want. Sometimes they have priorities that don't reflect the priorities of the economists or people that have studied development in the classroom" (interview March 15, 2010).

M.'s concerns resonated with many of the American students, who insisted on the need for flexibility in development strategy. For example, A., an American student explained to me that her fieldwork "showed [her] that no matter what, development theories can only be successfully applied if they are specifically adapted to each case. Development cannot be formulaic" (interview April 5, 2010). The majority of students agreed that the most important lesson they learned from participating in the program was that development solutions must come from the people themselves and not from outside expertise. AM., a Senegalese student, summed up this point in his final paper in which he argues that the semester demonstrated that "a country can be developed only if its people really want this development" (reflection paper, spring semester 2009).

An important aspect of executing contextually appropriate development solutions is of course community participation. XORG projects carried out in target villages were meant to be an educational tool that demonstrates the benefits of community led development. In an interview with XORG Academic Director, he explained how students in the program are encouraged to join current village initiatives or choose project themes that reflect interests of the villagers. In his words:

some of the projects were already going on in the village, but students taking part in them helped dynamize them, rally support and took them to a higher level by involving more people. With the students motivating the villagers they were able to see much more physical impact in the village (interview, March 18, 2009).

The desire was for students to observe first hand, villagers taking charge of their own development, so that they would recognize from their own experience why locally led solutions are more effective and sustainable over time than externally injected intervention. Students like M. pointed out that "sometimes it's hard to admit that your project is not really working out but it is a lot better to work with the community on something they want because that will make a bigger difference" (interview March 15, 2010). Thus, they needed to adapt their goals to coincide with those of the villagers in order to carry out a successful project. Many students, like A., felt the villagers did take ownership of the projects and explained that villagers saw them "most importantly as lots of helping hands" (interview April 5, 2010). From this perspective, XORG succeeded in instilling the value of a community led approach to development, in which the expert's role should be that of a project facilitator rather than a director.

Limitations of the XORG Model

Although students received excellent hands-on training in the benefits of locally initiated projects, my analysis reveals several drawbacks of the XORG model both as a teaching tool and as a method of implementing sustainable development. In this section, I will discuss the limitations of the XORG model by employing student critiques as well as my own observations to illustrate specific limitations, in part due to financial and physical constraints as well as flaws in the implementation of the program. My aim is not to discredit the innovativeness or objectives of XORG, rather I will bring attention to specific areas, that if ameliorated would increase the effectiveness of the model.

One of the most obvious issues with this model is the fact that the projects were initiated on too small a scale to influence large policy strategies in Senegal and worldwide. The bottom line is that XORG did not possess the financial means to implement large-scale development projects, nor did the students have sufficient time to follow through with a project from conceptualization to implementation. In fact, students expressed frustration that they did not have enough time to plan and implement the project. In interviews, they described having felt rushed and forced to make arbitrary decisions rather than following the reflective and flexible process that the XORG model is designed to promote. S., who worked on the library initiative, noted disappointedly that her project didn't have the complete impact that it could have because "the main problem was that we had so little time to think or brainstorm about its design. We were a small number of people with very limited funds and an unrealistic time frame" (interview March 15, 2010). In the end, many students were disillusioned by the entire process, and are not sure that participatory grassroots development can ever be effective as a catalyst for large-scale change. S. emphasized that although a small group of teachers and educators have managed to continue the library, its doors often remained locked and many people outside the teachers, have forgotten about the project completely.

Other former students noticed that an unrealistic time frame combined with lack of financial backing inevitably limits a project's potential for sustainability and its ability to have a significant impact in the target village. One Senegalese student (L.) explained, "due to lack of time and resources, my project ended up being more like individual field-work for me, on which I wrote an analytical report at the end. There is no way that a project can be carried out properly in three weeks with no funding" (interview April 5, 2010). Without proper funding and reasonable time to carry out a project, XORG is unable to generate widespread impact in the field of development. Projects remain small-scale and centered on personal growth for those involved rather than contributing to a larger framework. Many students, like S. expressed similar reactions: "it was a good experience, I still look back on it as something that I accomplished, you know, it was a personal accomplishment but not necessarily a development achievement" (interview March 15, 2010).

It is equally important to call attention to inconsistencies observed in the transition from theory to practice. As previously noted, the strength of the XORG model lies in its intent to generate projects that support community development needs while serving as an educational tool that demonstrates first hand the benefits of locally conceived development solutions to all parties involved. The program was designed to serve as a 'living laboratory' in which participants act jointly to produce a flexible framework through which they implement contextually appropriate development projects. In practice, villagers are not significantly integrated into to the overall learning process nor adequately prepared to participate in the program. I found that most former students believed that the framework disproportionately favored the interest and worldviews of the students, namely the American students, which led to unrealistic expectations towards project outputs across the board. My observations and the documented reactions of former students show that projects failed to generate genuinely in situ responses to local needs.

Students and villagers were frustrated and disillusioned by the actual situation of the XORG program. Students envisioned implementing projects that would contribute to long-term improvement of the living conditions in the community and were disappointed when they discovered that many villagers were unclear why they were even there. Conversely, the villagers anticipated major funding to execute large-scale development initiatives. Most students agreed that villagers were not adequately prepped for their visit, which led to disjointed interpretations of project objectives. Upon completion of the library, S. noticed for example that, "people were disappointed at the amount of books we brought but I just think that they didn't understand exactly what our resources were as college students" (interview March 15, 2010). Students had expected villagers to fully embrace their interests and to guide the creation and implementation of projects. Many, like M. were discouraged by the fact that it "felt like the villagers weren't clear on what they wanted or what their expectations were from us. I don't think that they had realistic expectations of their project" (interview March 15, 2010). In the end, inadequate measures were taken by XORG to prepare target communities for participating in the program. Students were not able to achieve the level of impact they had planned, while villagers did not receive the large-scale scale aid they had hoped for.

Inadequately preparing villagers to participate in the XORG program constitutes an important oversight when translating theory into practice. Certainly if villagers do not understand the goals and expected outcomes of the program they cannot take part in the development process. Many student participants acknowledged this paradox during post program discussions adding that if they were to do their projects over again they would engage the villagers much more in every stage of the project. M. felt that his own environmentalist ideals were not necessarily appropriate in the case of his project and that they actually hindered the development goals of the village. He described this in an interview:

if I could go back I would make a large effort to cater the design and implementation to the community needs and objectives because I now believe that this would have been more beneficial to the community than the pursuit of my own goals and ideas about environmentalism and eco-tourism (interview March 15, 2010).

Thus, XORG did manage to achieve its objective of inciting experts of tomorrow to approach development alternatively from a re-localized perspective through a "learn by doing" experiential model. However, in practice, "learn by doing" translated into "learn by not doing" as students discovered the advantages of a re-localized approach not from seeing its benefits in action but from experiencing first-hand the problems with externally led development. Regrettably, villagers did not acquire the same insight, as they were excluded from much of this exploratory process.

WHERE DOES THIS LEAVE US?

I have argued that predominant externally initiated development models, no matter how participatory they may be, fail to generate development solutions that are genuinely conceived and implemented locally. The result is continued dependency on outside "experts" to teach a target audience how to plan and execute development programs that will address their local needs. As long as it is perceived necessary to stimulate development through "expert" knowledge that is acquired externally and then injected into a local community, the outcome will not fully reflect the demands of the local population. If projects do not result from the innovation or experimentation of the target population, they will never be entirely relevant to a localized and specific context. XORG's model, linking the academic study of development with localized forms of action and education, challenges program participants to reconstruct extant paradigms by generating a contextually relevant framework that is grounded in locally led solutions. In theory, such an approach breaks from predominant expert led intervention models, typically produced in a rigid western framework. XORG hoped that by "re-localizing" the training of experts and the conceptualization of paradigms, development projects would be created by the intelligence and initiative of the local population. In practice, XORG fell short of its goal due to two important factors. It continued to prescribe externally conceived solutions to local issues by excluding village participants from much of the exploratory process. Villagers were involved in the creation and execution of projects, but not in the construction of the framework in which these projects were conceived. A true "re-localization" approach would entail villagers utilizing student and staff expertise within a locally imagined framework. Secondly, the model would have a much larger impact if greater funds were secured to support the program.

Finally, villagers need to be adequately prepared for working with students and students must be prepped to have realistic expectations for their projects. This points to a need for a more circular flow of information: participants, villagers and students alike, must disseminate to the academic and professional world knowledge acquired during this experience. Until the unilateral flow of knowledge from academic and professional experts to program participants is redirected, it will be difficult for XORG's model to take root in the development world. Nonetheless, by breaking down borders in development education and demonstrating to students the many possibilities of an approach that is constructed entirely within a localized context, the XORG case suggests that another model of development is possible. Unfortunately, XORG was disbanded in the beginning of 2012, for undisclosed reasons. I speculate from prior discussions that lack of sustainable funding sources and institutional support made it difficult for XORG to operate a long-term program that fulfilled the impact they promised. In the end the XORG case illustrates that economic borders often remain the hardest to break down, as the cost of running a local quality academic program on a scale able to compete with prestigious programs of the Global North is near impossible without the resources and capital of these institutions. I see this as a lesson to both development educators and professionals of the Global North that until a new type of partnership is formed, one that would abolish once and for all the economic and symbolic borders that keep expertise in the North and problems in the South, the field of "development" will continue to chase its tail looking for "new" solutions to the same old problems. The XORG model, if embraced by the degree granting institutions of the Global North as well as by the experts trained in these institutions provides the foundation for a new way of teaching development. However, success of this model depends on how it is constructed in local contexts. It is our role as educators to help plant the seeds, then, it is up to us to step back and watch the results grow.

REFERENCES

Aid statistics – Organisation for Economic Co-operation and Development. (n.d.). *Organisation for economic co-operation and development*. Retrieved from http://www.oecd.org/dac/aidstatistics/deve

Allen, W. J. (2001). *Working together for environmental management: the role of information sharing and collaborative learning*. PhD (Development Studies). Massey University.

Bessette, Guy. (2004). *Involving the community: A guide to participatory development communication*. Retrieved from http://web.idrc.ca/openebooks/066–7/

Columbia. (2013). *Career opportunities in international development*. (n.d.).SIPA Columbia School of International and Public Affairs. SIPA. Retrieved from http://new.sipa.columbia.edu/sites/default/files/CareerOpInternationalDevelopment_0.pdf

Carland, M. P., & Faber, C. (2008). *Careers in international affairs*. Washington D.C.: Georgetown University Press.

Gurstein, P., & Angeles, L. C. (2007). *Learning civil societies: Shifting contexts for democraticplanning and governance*. University of Toronto Press.

Harris, J. M. (2000). *Basic principles of sustainable development*. Retrieved from ase.tufts.edu/gdae/.../working_papers/Sustainable%20Development.PDF.

Long, N. (2001). *Development sociology actor perspectives*. London: Routledge.

McMichael, P. (2004). *Development and social change: A global perspective*. Thousand Oaks: SAGE Publications.

Mohan, G. (2001). Participatory development. In: Desai, Vandana & Potter, Rob (Eds.) *The Arnold companion to development studies* (pp. 46–49). London, UK: Hodder.

Mohan, G., Brown, E., Milward, B., & Zack-Williams, A. B. (2000). *Structural adjustment: Theory, practice and impacts*. London: Routledge.

Nederveen Pieterse, Jan. (1998). My paradigm or yours? Alternative development, post-development and reflexive development. *Development and Change, 29*(2), 343–373.

Organization Handbook (2008). (Used by NGO in the program described).

Participatory rural appraisal (PRA) (n.d.). Retrieved from http://go.worldbank.org/AKGNZ7Z4B0

Potter, R. B., Bins, T., Elliot, J. A., & Smith, D. (2008). Geographies of Development: An introduction to Development Studies. Essex, UK: Pearson Education Limited.

Ragan, K. (2008). Careers in international development. In M. P. Carland (Ed.), *Careers in international affairs* (pp. 320–331). Georgetown University Press.

Semester Handbook (2008). (used by NGO in the program described).

Shah, A. (2010, March 28). *Poverty facts and stats. Global issues.* Retrieved from http://www.globalissues. org/article/26/poverty-facts-and-stats

UCLA. (2013). *About international development studies.* Retrieved from http://www.international.ucla. edu/idps/ids/

UNICEF. (2008). *State of the world's children 2008* (Child Survival: The State of The World's Children). Retrieved from http://www.unicef.org/sowc08/report/report.php

United Nations Development Project. (2006). *Human development report 2006.* Retrieved from http:// hdr.undp.org/en/reports/global/hdr2006/chapters/

United Nations Development Project. (2010). *Origins of the human development approach.* (United Nations Development Project Human Development. UNDP). Retrieved from http://hdr.undp.org/en/ humandev/origins

United States African Development Foundation. (2003). *The ADF approach.* Retrieved from http://www. adf.gov/approach0105pdmintro.htm

AFFILIATION

Beth D. Packer
École *Des Hautes* Études *En Sciences Sociales Paris (EHESS)*

N. ALLEKI

SKILLS MANAGEMENT SYSTEM FOR BETTER SCHOOL-TO-WORK TRANSITIONS IN AFRICA

INTRODUCTION

Nowadays international conjecture is marked by: (i) a fragile and uncertain economy due to recurrent economic crises (ii) intensification of competitiveness due to the reduction of the cycles of innovations, the intensification of the production, the saturation of consumption and the constraints of a low carbon economy (iii) the increase of long-term and youth unemployment. In this context constrained by the decrease in business opportunities and public budgets, one of the most important international challenges is designing sustainable employment policies specifically in Africa where the key social and economic indicators are alarming.

Let's take the proportion of the population below the international poverty line (population living on less than US$1 a day): except for North Africa where the percentage runs about 1 and 2%, for all other African countries, the average is 30%, the percentage is 50% for the majority and more than 50% for 40% of Sub-Saharan countries (ADB & OECD, 2010).[1] Moreover in these societies, inequalities are important; the average GDP growth for Africa is below the rate of population growth and the unemployment inactivity, deskilling and informal economy concern more and more qualified and young people.

Finally, most of the countries are characterized by governance and political instabilities. Therefore, the challenges are huge and there are urgent needs to lead labour market reforms, harness an entrepreneurial spirit, combat poverty, tackle inequalities and improve workers' situation and school-to-work transitions which have become more complex and take longer to take place. In the case of African countries, the problems caused by poor transitions should be noted because youth: (i) represent half of the population but insufficient jobs are created to meet the needs (ii) experience more unemployment even though they are more qualified, (ii) symbolize the global health of a society and its opportunity to reach sustainable economic growth.[2]

So, the crucial question is how - in an economically and politically constraining environment where the labour market regulations bring social identity crises, youth poverty and inefficiency of companies – can we improve these transitions and consequently increase youth employment? What is the explanation for poor transitions from schools to work and growing youth unemployment?

S. Majhanovich and M.A. Geo-JaJa (Eds.), Economics, Aid and Education:
Implications for Development, 239–256.

Generally, the low performance of African education systems is considered the source of mismatches and is blamed for the inadequacy of training/education leading to employment. This paper goes beyond the problem of inadequacy to interrogate the role of qualifications in regulating labour market regulations and the roles of public policies and human resources strategies in establishing the forms of the regulations of the labour markets and consequently the relationship between education (precisely formal qualifications like certificates, titles, diplomas and degree) and employment (precisely formal and informal activities and employment). In other terms, this paper studies the triptych "qualifications-skills-labour markets performance" and analyses the forms that education and employment relationships can take globally in Africa, regarding human resources management and employment public policies.

My paper is based on the following hypotheses: (i) School to work transitions are improved when management of human resources is based on skills; (ii) School to work transitions are improved when employment policies are based on the recruiting process and help employers to identify and select skills; (iii) Performing school-to-work transitions depends on the opportunities given to young people to do or to learn in a life-long perspective and depend on the capacity of employers to identify what workers are able to do and to evaluate and remunerate what they have done or learnt.

Thus, the first part of this paper gives an overview of the outcomes and functioning of education systems and their role in generating skills. The second part examines the relationship between employment/education and training to conclude on the role of qualifications in regulating labour markets. In the third and last part, some recommendations have been made to improve school to work transitions.

THE SKILLS GENERATED BY EDUCATION SYSTEMS

Regarding UNESCO databases, despite the size of the education funding deficits, many countries have achieved major advances in overcoming illiteracy, and in the provision of primary and secondary education since 2000 (UNESCO, Institute for Statistics (UIS) databases[3]).

The estimated youth illiteracy rate (an average rate for the years 2005-2008 of the percentage of people between 15 and 24 years old) is less than 10% for 13 out of a total of 26 African countries (Among a total of 54 African countries, data are available for 26 of them). The results are not as promising regarding the average illiteracy rate of people over 15 years old for the years 2005-2008. Indeed, for 10 out of 26 countries the rates exceed 40% (Benin, Burkina Faso, Liberia, Lesotho, Mali, Morocco, Mozambique, Niger, Senegal, and Sierra-Leone) while the rates for 10 out of the 26 countries are about 10-14% close to rates for European countries (Cape Verde, Congo, Gabon, Libya, Mauritius, Namibia, Sao Tome and Principe, South-Africa, Zimbabwe). This represents approximately 17 million illiterate adults or one in three adults.

Important progress in access to primary and secondary education has been made. From 1999 to 2008, an additional 46 million children enrolled in primary education in sub-Saharan Africa. Despite a large increase in the school age population, the region has increased the primary adjusted net enrolment ratio by 31% since 1999, to reach an average primary ANER[1] of 77% in 2008. In Maghreb countries on average, 88% of the primary school age children are enrolled in school. Many countries including Algeria, Egypt, Morocco and Tunisia are pushing close to universal enrolment with an adjusted Net Enrolment Ratio of 95% or above. Mauritania is the exception with enrolment rates close to 70% Significant progress has been made in the sub-Saharan African region, where the ANER rose from 59% to 77% between 1999 and 2009 (UNESCO, 2011).

Despite this progress, success of the education systems is called into question due to the following facts: (i) the proportion of children out of schools is still high: between 2008 and 2010, out of school numbers increased in Sub Saharan Africa by 1,6 million, accounting for half of the world's out-of-school children which is estimated at 61 million in 2010; (ii) Inequalities based on factors such as gender, language and location and the need to recruit an additional 1.2 million teachers are grave; (iii) the millennium development goals will not be achieved in several countries (UNESCO, 2010). That is why the World Bank introduced a new tool, a fast track initiative. It is a program which helps and grants a loan only for governments that decide to allocate 50% of the public budget in primary education. However, this instrument has induced other problems due to the fact that on the average, the system is not well regulated. Indeed regarding assessment surveys about international aid, this initiative has induced divisions between forms of education and inequitable repartition of the budget reinforcing the incoherence of the education system (NORRAG, 2009). When dysfunctions of a public system touch a majority of people, as is the case in Africa, the system is frozen and all measures that result in the reproduction of the system are open to criticism because these measures result in the reproduction of inequalities as the system can only reach its objective for a minority.

Some education issues are universal: lack of financial resources, gender inequalities in scientific and technical fields, social reproduction and unequal opportunities for minorities, disparities between cities and rural areas, the orientation of students in the fields which offer no or few opportunities, the difficulty to identify the needs of the economy and to deliver qualifications suitable with the changes of the economic needs quickly and insufficient development of alternating training and public private partnerships. So, it appears that education reforms are urgently needed especially as qualifications protect people somewhat from economic risks. Indeed, even if unemployment is high among qualified young people, they still are able to find a better life even in the informal sector more rapidly than others (ILO, 2010b).

However, we need to keep in mind that in the African context, the source of these issues is societal and they come from the absence of a human development due to the breakdowns of the economic system, above all its inability to generate an added fair value shared among stake holders. We can cite the following factors:

i. The structural weaknesses of the economy such as massive anarchical urbanisation, weak private economic dynamism, the absence of diversification of formal employment, the place of informal labour and occupations, bad working conditions in the public sector which is the major employer, the absence of mature industrialization financing by agriculture reforms, the weak rhythms of jobs creation, and others;

ii. Governance issues in the education system such as difficulties in developing and promoting cooperative policies. For instance, in almost all African countries, the social partners are not implicated in the design of education policies (absence of tripartite scientific committees and tripartite governing boards), the management of public funds are centralised so well that schools and universities do not have autonomy. All this contributes to a non-transparent management of public funds and consequently trust issues.

iii. The marginal place of African countries inside international labour segmentation and international trade.

Similarly, if technical vocational education and training (TVET) is also the poor cousin of European education systems, the situation in Africa is dramatic because: (i) the participation is almost equal to zero: for the year 2005, 40% of African countries counted participation in TVET as less than 5% among the populace. Only 20% of the countries counted a participation superior to 10% (15% in 1995); (ii) the training centres that emerged in the 1990's deliver courses that are much too rigid and standardized. Actually specifically in Africa, TVET appears irrelevant to respond to skills needs because it is not oriented to the self-employed (plumbers, builders, mechanics and accountants, etc). The majority is oriented toward white-collar jobs in the urban wage sector; its pedagogical asset, learning by doing, is not exploited as an opportunity for youth to acquire their first experiences (UNESCO – UNEVOC, 2006).

African education systems also record specific problems that do not exist anymore in European countries such as older and traditional pedagogical contents and tools (open distance learning, radio and computer-assisted education, information and communication technologies are not developed sufficiently), low investments in equipment and in infrastructures, and suspicion among teachers of authorities that does not facilitate cooperation and mutual learning of teachers with foreigners or the Diaspora; high brain drain among teachers and researchers; the fact that children of the upper class go systematically abroad to study; and finally, an absence of promotion of an African Qualifications Framework by the African Union organisation (UNESCO, 2009 & 2010).

Concern for higher education is more important as it represents the last step of initial training for individuals, produces qualifications that should bring development by integrating African economy within the globalised and knowledge economy and crystallizes the school to work transitions.

In fact, if we add the specific problems to the universal ones and to the situation of African universities, we can easily suppose that these problems are the cause of poor school-to-work transitions (Carrie, 2003). Whereas in this paper, I adopt the hypothesis that these problems structurally reproduce a vicious cycle and explain the low level of human development and the low status of the education system to influence economic growth, although the poor transition can be explained by the role of qualifications in regulating labour markets and how skills are developed and used by the employers.

The skills are a multifaceted notion. In practice, the definition often used is: potential to achieve tasks coming from the combination of: (i) knowledge; (ii) know-how; (iii) inter-personal skills (personality and behaviors), mainly acquired and developed during work experience. My definition is the following (Alleki, 2006). The skills belong to individuals even if they are integrated in a process developed collectively and which is not always successful and explains the existence of skill mismatches. This process starts during schooling and depends on both: (i) individual decisions to put into action his/her potential and (ii) interlinked labour and education environments which influence "the motivation and the satisfaction of putting potential into action " or "the satisfaction or motivation to do and succeed". In other terms, the qualifications (diplomas and degrees) can activate the motivation and satisfaction of succeeding when they guarantee access to jobs, social recognition or utility. Also, jobs can activate this motivation when human resources management recognizes the workers efforts (through for example, fair wages, good working conditions, promotions, employer-employee relationships based on trust, and so on). Finally, public policies have a proactive role in this activation as they implement the institutional and legal frameworks and standards in education and labour that permit particularly the development of learning by doing, transparency in recruitment, diminution of asymmetries of information, and the evaluation of the potential of youth.

Regarding my definition of skills, school to work transitions would be improved if: (i) companies' human resources strategies motivated and satisfied workers (ii) public policies focused on the creation of links between education and employment systems; there was transparency in recruitment and opportunities given to young people to learn by doing in a life-long perspective.

The table below shows the skills generated by education systems, especially skills linked to literacy and life skills and in part citizenship skills, skills for employment or employability and entrepreneurial and management skills.

Skills management means evaluation, accumulation and the transformation of skills. It is a complex issue because it implies developing present skills, identifying the erosion of skills and anticipating new ones. It is a challenge for a nation but also an individual act. Indeed, skills development depends on individual "motivation to do" and "satisfaction provided by doing". Therefore, the ingredients of skills development are all possibilities or the signs which activate the motivation or satisfaction to "do well". Therefore, it is a question of appreciating how the potential of individuals is used, recognised and paid through working conditions, remuneration and lifelong learning opportunities. So, managing skills go beyond managing qualifications. If the qualifications represent the formal signs of individuals abilities,

Table 1. The core skills produced in Education and Training Systems

Core skills needed by the economy	Type and level of education	Situation in Maghreb
Skills of literacy and numeracy	General secondary education	Close to being acquired by all of the new generations: (i) Poor families cannot assume requirements to go to school (enrolment, shortage of infrastructure in rural areas) without material aid. (ii) So, regarding advantages of child labour, the obligation to go to schools is not effective without financial aids in countries with high levels of poverty Weak public investments in adult education, especially for women: Bi-lingual curricula : Francophone or Anglophone curricula are completed alongside Arabic in Arabophone countries (Maghreb countries and Djibouti)
Life skills (enable people to live a full social life in the community)	General and Vocational and technical education at all levels	Transmission case by case Vocational and technical Training centres are insufficiently specialized and spread throughout the country Difficulties of the education system to enhance native languages and endogenous knowledge considered as a handicap and a way to divide the society
Social and citizenship skills	Tertiary education: general and vocational education	In general, this apprenticeship seems to be more an indoctrination than an education for critical thinking and democratic citizenship Gaps between the values and principles of the society learnt in schools and the problems of governance and practices
Skills for employment (help people to enter and to evolve in labour markets)	All forms of alternating training: General, technical and Vocational education at all levels starting with secondary schools	Dichotomy between technical and general knowledge Insufficient mobilisation of companies and governments to develop alternative training Public and private partnerships are not effective or not organised with regularity Higher education suffers from a shortage of students' mobility inside the country and inside the African continent
Entrepreneurial & management skills	All forms of alternative training	Developed for youth entrepreneurs with the mechanism of microcredit

Source: Table based on the European Training Foundation (2003), Core and entrepreneurial skills in vocational education and training from concept and theory to practical application, Torino

in practice, concrete abilities depend on components of our social identity (the feeling that we are appreciated, the sense of belonging in a society, the degree of trust in institutions and companies). That amounts to saying that reforms that consist of developing alternative training, apprenticeship and learning by doing especially in higher education which are pedagogically efficient to generate skills and which could initiate self-improvement (King & Palmer, 2006), would lose in efficiency if they do not integrate these psychological dimensions stemming from the feeling of being well appreciated. Consequently, the reforms in education should take into account how the efforts of employees are acknowledged. So, the problem here is not the production of qualifications adequate to generate skills needed by the economy, but rather how labour markets use and accumulate the potential coming from qualifications and how education systems integrate in curricula informal ingredients of this potential like indigenous and traditional knowledge, or promote national languages in higher education.

PLACE FOR QUALIFICATIONS AND SKILLS IN REGULATING LABOUR MARKETS

The macro-economic indicators are not good: the annual GDP growth (average for the years 2000-2008) fluctuates between 4% and 7% for the majority of countries (ILO, 2009, 2010, 2011).[5] There are exceptions and extremes, for instance:

i. countries that have highest annual GDP growth like Equatorial Guinea (20,3%), Angola (12,8%), Sierra Leone (10,3%) and Chad and Nigeria (8,4%)
ii. countries that have lowest annual GDP growth like Swaziland (2,5%), Burundi (2,4%), Gabon (2,1%), Central African Republic and Comoros (1,9%), Guinea Bissau (1,4%), Togo (1,3%), Eritrea (0,3%) and the exception with a negative growth of Zimbabwe (-5,5%).

The unemployment rates are rarely under 10% of the active population (low rates concern above all small countries and the average rate is around 8% in Sub Saharan Africa and 11% in North Africa). The proportion of working-age in employment is weak: 55% for women and 79% for men in Sub-Saharan countries, 22% for women and 70% for men in Northern African countries. Labour force participation is around 38% in North Africa and 57% in Sub Saharan countries on average.

Moreover, as labour markets are more and more characterized by dualism, public policies have an added challenge which is to implement policies by taking the growing inequalities in access to employment into account (Cieslik, 2008).

The low dynamics of formal job creation is explained for a great part by: (i) the under-investment in public services and in infrastructures (ii) the great difficulty to foster an entrepreneurship culture (iii) the fact that a lot of sectors in the economy tend to be informal employment like domestic services, home care, restaurant work and so on.

All these explanations suggest a need for an increase of employment and education budgets but also the budgets of public services in transportation and social affairs. This is why this structural problem is unmanageable as many governments face a trade-off between maintaining a fiscal balance and expanding government expenditures to counter the economic slowdown (ILO, 2009). Therefore, the challenge is how to manage the demand for further education and the actual high risk of social exclusion without the increase of public budgets.

In the domain of continuing training, the majority of Sub-Saharan African companies provide their own job training schemes without help from governments (Adams, & Johanson, 2004). As just a few enterprises have the size and the structure to develop continuing training, there are not enough companies offering traineeships and apprenticeships each year. Consequently, training programs financed by companies are accessible for employees with seniority as a gift to motivate them except in technical and innovative sectors demanding continuing learning and adaptation to new technologies. In the public sector, employees are not encouraged to participate in training programs because they do not have a counterpart in terms of salaries, careers or working conditions. In addition, employers do not consider continuing training as an investment in learning that can boost the labour productivity, but as an expense that increases labour costs (King, 2007).

Many characteristics of youth employment involve disregard for formal qualifications and show that unemployment goes beyond the problem of inadequacy between education and jobs and reveals a crisis of identity and a social unease.

Firstly, youth are overrepresented among the unemployed and are in precarious situations. Around the world, about 211 million youth were unemployed in 2009. 40% of them (83 million) are 15-24 years old. Added to that, there are few opportunities for mobility and the duration of structural unemployment continues to stagnate. In addition young workers are mainly low paid; unemployment affects the young more than older people. Unemployment is twice as high among youth from households in the fifth or highest income quintile compared to those in the first income quintile. Among youth, women are disadvantaged because they cumulate weaknesses like: (i) the concentration of their employment in 6 sectors including education, health, social, public services; (ii) the concentration of their employment in medium and low positions; (iii) discrimination issues related to their hitting the glass ceiling, entrepreneurship gaps and work-life balance difficulties. Globally, youth are the first victims of a deteriorated economic situation because the majority of young people are affected by public employment programs, deskilling movements and by the tendencies of African economies to respond quantitatively and not qualitatively to the growing needs of a flexible workforce (ILO, 2009, 2010, 2011).

Secondly, these negative consequences touch qualified young people more and more. In fact, on average a third of those younger than 30 years are unemployed; meanwhile they are more qualified than previous generations. Unemployment is more prevalent in urban areas and among those who have attained higher education. On average, unemployment among those with secondary education or above is three times higher than among those with no educational attainment (ILO, 2004a).

Thirdly, young people are victims of discrimination similar to ethnic minorities when entering the labour market. During their period of transition from schools to work, young people crystallize all stereotypes (a population that is not serious, unmotivated, inexperienced, unqualified, etc), according to the fact that the subjective criteria which can reassure employers (network, diplomas or experience in foreign countries) determine the recruitment. Consequently, employers are not obliged to use skills assessments or objective criteria to recruit; and this becomes a subordinate question (World Bank, 2009).

Fourthly, their jobs are characterised by low wages and bad working conditions and their skills are not enhanced through human resources strategies (ILO, 2004b & 2008). There are very few opportunities of alternative or continuing training because of the structure of the economy. There are not enough private companies with an adequate size to develop this training. Basically, human resources strategies are influenced by public and bureaucratic management and weak collective bargaining (trade unions have a symbolic role in the domain of social actions and prevention of exclusions)

Fifthly, even if some budgets are affected by employment policies and education reforms, the probability for youth to hold a formal job only thanks to their qualifications without any help coming from a network, is unlikely (DIAL, 2007). We underline the following reasons although the list is not exhaustive.

• The annual rhythm of formal jobs created is insufficient and cannot absorb the new graduates each year.
• Informal employment refers to jobs or activities where production and sales are not regulated by governments. This informal sector is important and represents a large part of youth labour. Informal activities represent on average: (i) in Sub-Saharan Africa, 70% of the non-agricultural employment and in North Africa, 43%. The average contribution of informal employment to the GDP amounts to 25%. This paper refers to various legal informal activities of self-employed workers and unpaid family workers in rural and urban areas that can be classified into the following two categories. The first one is activities which are present in the formal economy, but developed informally for both financial reasons and fall under legislative requirements such as specific qualifications or certifications to practice the professions (taxi, fast food, aesthetic, hairdressing, tourist services, retail and wholesale trade, artistic services, and more qualified jobs such as training, consulting, translation, interpreting,etc.). The second one is activities which do not exist in the formal economy or are not well enough developed, but have been created informally to satisfy needs (such as shoe-shiner, car-guarding, and street vending, home care, services in tourism, sports, telecommunications). If a large portion of informal activities is characterized by low qualifications, low salaries, high working risks and weak mobility opportunities, they are still considered as a resource for development because of their potential to create jobs, to relieve social tensions and to diminish risks of social disaffiliation and poverty

(OECD, 2008 & 2009). The due importance of informal employment among youth cannot be explained by a deficit of qualifications nor by much too rigid national fiscal legislation as it is mainly the only way to acquire a first working experience and to test their skills (Palmer, 2008).

Many labour market inefficiencies (inequalities, elitism and divisions between general and technical education, discrimination) are reinforced in the corrupt context of Africa where leaders have autocratic power and where institutions and laws have a limited effective role. Competitiveness regulators are informal and based on the potential of coalitions and negotiations that private companies can expect with the public sector; this constitutes one of the main niches of the corruption. Bad governance and corruption also influence the recruiting process and the design and implementation of public policies (Lavallée, Razafindrakoto, & Roubaud, 2008). The Index of Corruption Perception[6] in 2008 varies from 1 to 3 and above for a majority of African countries except for Botswana, Cap Verde, Mauritius and South Africa presenting an index around 5 (Transparency International, 2010).

There is a collective climate of suspicion among youth. They consider that: (i) public policies are inefficient to manage their needs; (ii) the leaders do not provide a good example since they send their children abroad to study; (iii) the recruitment is based on a vote-catching system.

This environment, as in the education area, freezes all forms of cooperation, mutual learning and exchange of practices between public and private institutions, between countries inside of the African union and with foreigners or the Diaspora.

Since the aspects of social identity depend on the governance structure, but as most of the governments are marked by corruption and cooptation and as the recognition of individual capabilities is weak and because some governments focus on control of people's behaviour; a normal functioning of the education system is impossible. As a result, a majority of young people think it is impossible to have a future inside their own country because they live in a country that reproduces inequalities and favouritism. This is reflected in many of their attitudes and beliefs: elections, relations with public administration, lack of motivation and desire to ameliorate and preserve their environment, the infrastructures or the public services.

To conclude, we can say that the current few opportunities given to youth create a crisis of citizenship. As things are, young people are more and more interested in investing in opportunistic behaviours, in informality and in the system of corruption than in investing in long term studies. This is illustrated in a World Bank report which underlines that in Sub Sahara, youth start working too early and consequently are not prepared enough to meet the demands of the labour markets (World Bank, 2009). That is why I present in the paragraph below some suggestions to improve school-to-work transitions and youth employment based on governance issues and on the accumulation of trust in individuals' capabilities inside a society: the recognition of skills acquired informally, the maturation of the alternative training and some active employment policies which can create links between education and employment. The recommendations detailed in this document, especially when they appeal to the law or adjustment macro-policies, are not relevant in critical conflict-affected countries or in countries which face urgency situations. The potential success of these recommendations is completely linked to: the quality of the political leadership, the degree of credibility and the legitimacy of governments. Youth employment policies based on financial aids tax evasion and specific contracts for youth containing financial aids contain the advantages of reducing the cost of labour and the period of youth unemployment in the short term because they do not deal with: crisis of trust, disregard for degrees and the extent of informal employment, and consequently the negative effects (opportunist and substitution effects) are important.[7]

SOME PROPOSITIONS TO IMPROVE SCHOOL TO WORK TRANSITIONS

The Legislation for Employment Protection

Legislative measures or collective agreements have the advantage of implementing a framework which can clarify the responsibilities of each stakeholder, define the rules of financing; guarantee the minimum level needed for health and security of individuals in school and in the workplace, and promote rights for education. If they are coming from negotiations with social partners, they can also boost public and private partnerships. It is indispensable to design a legal framework for the continent, a common framework of qualifications and skills, common rules of certifications, common classifications of professions and trades and common mapping of sectional skills needed (Larcombe, 2002). For example, in the domain of continuing training, legislation about co-investment and quality standards could participate to diversify the forms of training and to set up a stable financing system. Moreover, in the domain of employment, the labour laws could favour transparency in recruiting; implement so-called 'flexicurity' (a combination of flexibility and security) that can regulate dismissals and wages and prevent dangerous working conditions.

In the 1990's in developed countries, to introduce flexibility in labour markets and to boost employment, governments and social partners had to negotiate social compromises regarding the cost of labour, employment insurance, modifications to the legislation of the contracts, dismissals and working hours. During this decade, the European Union underlined, inside the employment strategy called the Lisbon Strategy, the necessity to develop flexible labour markets and promoted social compromises used in the Netherlands and Sweden as best practices and as a performing model for employment to apply to other countries. This model, called *flexicurity*, is a combination of policy approaches that include (i) flexible labour markets, (ii) generous unemployment support and (iii) a strong emphasis on activation, and is also known as the *golden triangle* of the Danish labour market policy (Madsen, 2004). Flexicurity measures include a whole set of social compromises, a combination between qualitative and quantitative flexibility and a way to stabilize employer-employee relationships because it transfers new uncertainties to employees especially when there is a social risk (bankruptcies, dismissals, and growing number of working hours,etc.). These are short term arrangements adapted to specific situations (for instance, workers accept lower pay in return for being able to keep their job). Nevertheless, also simple flexibility measures not combined to secure counterparts (part time or flexible contracts) can be included in this package. In this case, the purpose can be: (i) diminishing inequalities by offering less precariousness to workers; (ii) increasing the autonomy and multi-tasking abilities of workers by developing human capital investments (Alleki, 2010b); But in African countries, the regulations of industrial relations, the place of social partners in the design of the labour law limit the opportunities to implement these reforms. Moreover, in the African societal context, the action of the legislation is in practice limited because of the importance of the informal sector not covered by regulations and because of the poor enforcement of the law above all for youth and because of the degree of corruption. That is why public employment policies have to focus on concrete programs that permit the creation or the improvement of links between education and employment, opportunities for the development of learning by doing that can offer the satisfaction of doing.

Recognizing Skills Acquired in Informal Activities

In the informal economy, in a difficult economic context, people spontaneously develop a large and diversified portfolio of specific and general skills because they have to survive, to be able to anticipate problems, to deal with constant changes, to develop their activities or to increase their outcomes. Therefore, specific and generable skills of an entrepreneur are developed whatever the level of qualifications of the informal worker. An entrepreneur is an individual who organizes, operates and assumes the risk of creating new businesses. The primary social contribution of entrepreneurship is to escape poverty for those with little capital education or experience. Psychological factors influence an individual's likelihood of becoming an entrepreneur: extraversion, need for achievement, risk taking propensity, self-efficacy, overconfidence and creativity. The table below synthesizes a part of the skills acquired and developed in informality: the skills of an entrepreneur (Alleki, 2009).

In the domain of entrepreneurship, access to micro-credit is largely developed but assessments underline a very short duration for the businesses created. In other words, to improve the effects of micro-credit, some measures in favour of durability of business, should be initiated as: exchange of practices between self-entrepreneurs, pooling of resources and risks facilities, cost sharing instruments such as enterprise zones, trade associations for youth entrepreneurs and communicational actions like forum, challenging competitions, and awards. These measures should encourage informal entrepreneurs to recognize their skills.

Table 2. Entrepreneurial skills, helping people look for opportunities to start their businesses and improve business performance developed informally

Core skills developed by workers in difficult contexts		General and transferable skills
Category of Informal activities	Capacity to develop strategies of bypassing	Ability to take initiatives and to transform it into business ideas
		Capacity to take decisions and opportunities
Category I: informal activities which exist in the formal economy	Potential of creativity	Autonomy, independence and polyvalence
		Capacity of adaptation and dealing with uncertainty
Category II: informal activities which don't exist in the formal economy and which don't need qualifications	Ready to do anything to survive	Information processing, networking, managing transactional relationships
	Capacity to brave death and danger	Used to anticipate and deal with the vagueness of the rules and shortage of material resources
	Capacity to deal with the precariousness and the instability	Ability to manage important risks
		Ability to apply rapidly new working methods
Category III: informal activities which don't exist in the formal economy but need qualifications	Capacity to take initiatives and to innovate	Capacity to manage stress
		Capacity to negotiate
	Creativity, analytical competencies	Capacity to develop self confidence in uncertainty

International organisations have initiated some concrete programs implemented by non-governmental organisations that recognize the added value of informal workers. For example, UNESCO financed programs related to non formal education oriented to key sectors, ILO financed management and running business lessons for informal entrepreneurs, World Bank financed studies in Ghana and Cameroon to evaluate and certify skills acquired informally(Worth, 2002; Working Group for International Cooperation in Skills Development, 2003, ITCILO, 2002). These programs have the advantage of improving working conditions and the income of informal activities by supporting the skills development dynamic and they favour the development of an entrepreneurship culture. Indeed, they can facilitate the identification of new markets, new products, improving quality of goods and services and productivity (Charmes &Mohammed, 2006).

Other programs can be promoted as they contribute to the validation of skills acquired informally like: (i) simplifying administrative procedures to exercise a specific regulated profession (handicrafts, taxi services, various care and domestic services); (ii) encouraging initiatives and capabilities in specific sectors (traditional markets, local crafts and shops, agriculture) by facilitating the access to micro-credit; (iii) implementing communicational actions (forum, challenging competition, awards such as credits to participate to alternative training or guarantees for credit), facilitating mutual learning networking and exchange of practices (trade associations for youth entrepreneurs); (iv) implementing instruments of pooling resources and sharing costs (enterprise zone). All those initiatives break the informal workers' social isolation. By showing abilities and capacities of informal workers, we increase their sense of belonging as they feel non-marginalized. Moreover, the recognition or acknowledgement of all youth abilities and the promotion of their contribution to society are essential to develop respect for degrees and trust in education and employment policies.

Moreover, by doing so, we develop the links between education and employment systems on vectors like the motivation to do and the promotion of the knowledge and abilities.

Creating & Developing Intermediates of Employment

The intermediation of employment (temporary work agencies, recruitment agencies or agencies specialized in home services and care and rural activities) is not sufficiently developed. When this intermediation exists, the organisations only provide information and management of public employment aids and contracts. Intermediates are indispensable to coordinate and facilitate all forms of mutualisation and pooling of resources between Small and Medium Enterprises (SMEs) or between companies in sectors touched by higher competitive pressure or higher risks of restructuring and outsourcing.

These intermediates can also help companies to recruit young people by offering methods to assess their skills abilities. As they have information about the profile of job seekers and of vacancies, they can play a role during the recruiting process to reduce information asymmetries. So, the efficiency and interest of these agencies is related to their capacities to create bridges between companies and skills by offering a package of services to young people (vocational and job-readiness training, job search assistance, career guidance and counselling), they reduce the transaction costs linked to the identification of candidates' skills. To conclude, they can deliver to both employers and educational staff a kind of mapping of skills of young people who have left schools.

These agencies could also at the same time enhance the image and the quality of low-qualification professions by making visible all the qualifications and abilities required to hold these jobs successfully. Moreover, for low qualified professions which are essentially informal (cleaning, housekeeping, childcare, green jobs, waste treatment, home services, scholarship remedial, care services, cyber cafes, jobs in tourism, in environment and related services on health, education…), they can guarantee the quality of the services. This quality assurance can take multiple forms like training, certificates, conventions or charters. They could also distribute positive reports, communication plans and monitor training for informal workers.

These intermediates of employment should be specialized in sectors and jobs where (i) the proportion of informal job and activities as listed above is important (ii) youth are overrepresented (telemarketing, computing, local cultural, touristic and sport activities).

CONCLUSION: THE CONDITIONS FOR SUCCESS OF PUBLIC PROGRAMS: TRUST AND GOVERNANCE ISSUES

We have just seen that a non-effective skills management system due to the dysfunction of human resources strategies and public employment policies explains to a large extent the poor transitions from schools to work. Meanwhile, if public education and employment policies are reformed without giving thought to the societal constraints (the place of informal work, effective role of labour law, cost of labour, repartition of income, degree of inequalities, corruption, etc), the qualifications would not regulate labour markets and the skills mismatches would remain important. The qualifications will just play a role case by case essentially as a gatekeeper. From time to time, they will (i) offer the minimum of knowledge; (ii) determine the requirements to access certain trades; (iii) determine the remuneration. Consequently, the education system will lose a part of its efficiency, notably its crucial and structural role as the provider of resources for labour markets, adequate capabilities to the economy. But also, the jobs created will not affect economic growth and human development as a great part of them will not be recognized.

In other words, if education for all is an honourable goal it should not mask the crucial questions: what kind of education for what opportunities in labour markets and for what kind of society? This means that curricula should include emotional as well as intellectual development, and acknowledgement of individual potential to contribute to society, as well as a respect for cultural diversity, the value of 'soft' knowledge, and more accurate history. In addition, better integration of insights from psychology would contribute to understanding the need for recognition and commitments to new beliefs and emotional change.

The potential contributions to enhancing the coherence of the education system and ultimately the quality of life in Africa are enormous. Developing greater synergies between school and companies; re-aligning education to the social and cultural background of each country are some of the ingredients.

These ingredients depend on (i) the capacity of the companies to integrate within their human resources management their responsibility to developing individuals' capabilities through their skills management strategies and their participation in the financing and the design of the education system; (ii) the capacity of governments to produce an education system which (a) enhances capabilities for all through all forms of education and training for adults and youth including students and workers, and (b) allows for recognition of and good working conditions for the human development staff.

NOTES

[1] The Gini coefficients for income range from approximately more than 30% to more than 60%. The average GDP growth is around 1,6% and the average population growth is around 2,3% in 2009. For more details, see: http://www.africaneconomicoutlook.org/en/data-statistics/table-14-poverty-and-income-distribution-indicators

[2] In this paper, African countries are studied as a whole regarding their commonalities such as: historical background (invasions, colonialism) cultural issues (languages, religion, codes, arts) social situations (common values and social realities) outcomes and functioning of employment systems. The global trends about youth education and employment are comparable. To understand the regulations of national qualification systems, my theoretical framework is based on Keynesianism and Institutional economics, I also use psychological notions such as recognition, identity, belonging to a network, trust, donation, etc., to understand economic outputs and systemic regulations. My theoretical analysis presented here, using qualitative studies and surveys of international organisations or public and national institutes, has to be completed by a field study in a number of African countries. I started my empirical studies with the Algerian case in April and September 2009. For more details, see N. Alleki (2010), «La politique pour l'emploi des jeunes : des budgets importants mais une crise de confiance», *Chroniques Internationales*, Ires, March.

[3] For more details, see: http://stats.uis.unesco.org/unesco/ReportFolders/ReportFolders.aspx/ http://www.uis.unesco.org/Education/Pages/default.aspx

[4] Universal primary education is measured by the primary adjusted net enrolment ratio (ANER) measuring the proportion of children of primary school age who are enrolled either in primary or secondary school. Its value varies from 0 to 100%. An ANER of 100% means all eligible children are enrolled in school in a given school year, even though some of them may not complete it. However, if the ANER is at 100% for many consecutive years, it may imply that all children enrolled do complete at least primary school".

[5] For more details, see: http://www.ilo.org/ilostat/faces/home/statisticaldata/data_by_country?_adf.ctrl-state=rpd35izr9_77&_afrLoop=113390947434067 and http://www.ilo.org/global/research/global-reports/lang--en/index.htm

[6] Calculated by transparency international, there is a range between 10 "highly clean" and 0 "highly corrupt" and related perceptions of the degree of corruption as seen by business people and country analysts.

[7] The evaluation of employment programs and the measurement of the effects of skills on employment efficiency are still an open field of research: the research findings related to the measurement of quality and productivity in the services sector are still in progress. Reliable and valid surveys and longitudinal data and measurement methods (econometric forecasting, expert forecasts such as the Delphi method, skills audits, case studies, focus groups, sector studies, diagnosis, scenarios, observations) have to be developed. It is difficult to estimate negative effects such as opportunistic or substitution effects linked to financial public aid.

REFERENCES

Adams, A-V., & Johanson, R-K. (2004). Développement des qualifications professionnelles en Afrique subsaharienne, *Etudes régionales et sectorielles n°28820*, Banque Mondiale, Washington.

ADB & OECD (2010). *African Economic Outlook*, Paris.

Alleki, N. (2009). Social recognition of skills in informal economy. *Communication, XIXth world congress of international society for labour and social security law*, Sydney, September.

Alleki, N. (2010). La politique pour l'emploi des jeunes: des budgets importants mais une crise de confiance. *Chroniques Internationales* : Ires, March.

Alleki, N. (2006). « L'impact du modèle de la compétence sur le système de formation professionnelle continue français », *Réflexions sur la formation professionnelle et la gestion des compétences. Un état des lieux interdisciplinaire*, Ouvrage collectif, Ed. Dar El Gharb, Oran, Algérie.

Carrie, L. A. (2003). The effect of school-to-work programs on entry into non-traditional employment: Do education- and employment-based initiatives influence the transition to a stratified workforce? *Working paper,* Brown University.

Cieslik, A. (2008). Multinational firms, international knowledge flows, and dual labour markets in developing economies. *Review of Development Economics, 12*(1).

Charmes, J. & Mohammed, S. (2006). *Informalisation des économies maghrébines: Une stratégie d'adaptation à la crise du travail ou une limite aux politiques actives ?*, Eds du CREAD, Alger.

DIAL (2007). Youth and labour markets in Africa a critical review of literature. *Working paper,* DIAL, Février, Paris.

European Training Foundation (ETF) (2003). www.etf.europa.eu/web.nsf/(RSS)/C125782B0048D6F6C 1257013004A7790?OpenDocument

ILO (2004a). Starting right: Decent work for young people, *Background paper tripartite meeting on youth employment: the way forward,* October, Geneva.

ILO (2004b). In focus program on skills, knowledge and employability youth at risk: The role of skills development in facilitating the transition to work. *Skills Working Paper,* No 19, Geneva.

ILO (2008). Skills for improved productivity, employment growth and development. *International labor conference, 97th session, report V,* Geneva.

ILO (2009). *Recovering from the crisis: A global jobs pact. International labour conference provisional record 19A, 98th session,* Geneva.

ILO (2009, 2010, 2011). *Global employment trends,* January, Geneva.

ILO (2010b). "Characterized the school to work transitions of young and women: Evidence from the ILO school to work transition surveys", *Employment Working Paper* n°51.

ITCILO (2002). *Training for work in the informal sector: New evidence from eastern and southern Africa.* Hans Christian HAAN, Torino.

King, K., & Palmer R. (2006). Skills development and poverty reduction: The state of the art, Post-basic education and training. *Working paper,* n°7, Centre of African Studies: University of Edinburgh.

King, K. (2007). Education, skills, sustainability and growth: complex relations. *Communication, 9th UKFIET international conference on education and development,* Oxford.

Larcombe, G. (2002). *Emerging local employment opportunities for young people: Innovative employment & learning pathways,* Glebe: Dusseldorp Skills Forum.

Lavallée, E., Razafindrakoto, M., & Roubaud, F. (2008). Corruption and trust in political institutions in Sub-Saharan Africa. *Working Paper,* Dial: Paris.

Madsen, P. K. (2004). "The Danish model of flexicurity: Experiences and lessons", *Transfer, 10*(1).

NORRAG (2009). Network for policy research review and advice on education and training, *A safari towards aid effectiveness? A critical look at the Paris declaration & The Accra agenda for action as part of the new aid reform architecture,* NORRAG News, special issue, number 42 June, Ed. Kenneth King, UK.

OECD (2008). Informal Employment Re-loaded. Jütting J, J Parlevliet & T Xenogiani, *Working Paper* No. 266.

OECD (2009). *Is informal normal? Towards more and better jobs in developing countries,* Edited by Johannes P. Jütting & Juan R. de Laiglesia, Paris.

Palmer, R. (2008). Skills and productivity in the informal economy. Employment sector *Working Paper,* No. 5, ILO, Geneva.

Transparency International (2010). *Corruption report 2009 corruption and the private sector.* Cambridge University Press.

UNESCO – UNEVOC (2006). *Participation in formal technical and vocational education and training programs worldwide an initial statistical study.* Paris.

UNESCO (2009). *Education for all global monitoring report, "Overcoming inequality: Why governance matters",* Paris.

UNESCO (2010). *Education for all global monitoring report, "Reaching the marginalized",* Paris.

UNESCO (2011). *Universal primary education,* UIS Fact Sheet, May 2011, No. 8.

World Bank (2009). Youth and employment in Africa, the potential, the problem, the promise, *Africa development indicators 2008/09,* Washington.

Worth, S. (2002). Education and employability: School leavers' attitudes to the prospect of non-standard work', *Journal of Education and Work*, *15*(2), June.

Working Group for International Cooperation in Skills Development (2003). Vocational skills development in sub-saharan Africa, *Working Group Review*: Edinburgh.

WEBSITES UNESCO AND ILO DATABASES

http://www.africaneconomicoutlook.org/en/data-statistics/table-14-poverty-and-income-distribution-indicators/

http://www.ilo.org/ilostat/faces/home/statisticaldata/data_by_country?_adf.ctrl-state=rpd35izr9_77&_afrLoop=113390947434067

http://www.ilo.org/global/research/global-reports/lang--en/index.htm

http://stats.uis.unesco.org/unesco/ReportFolders/ReportFolders.aspx/http://www.uis.unesco.org/Education/Pages/default.aspx

AFFILIATION

Nora Alleki,
Project Leader, Ministry of Labour, Paris

NOTES ON CONTRIBUTORS

Hasan Hüseyn Aksoy is an Associate Professor in the Department of Educational Administration and Policy at Ankara University, College of Educational Sciences, Ankara, Turkey. His research interests include education and employment relationships, politics of vocational education, technology, education reforms, equity issues in education and critical/radical education. He has published numerous articles and translated several articles and books in the area. He was at the University of Cincinnati, USA as a post-doctoral fellow between 1997 and 1999, and at the Freie Universität Berlin, Germany as a visiting scholar between November 2010 and September 2011. He serves as referee and advisory board member of national and international journals and is the founding Editor of the *International Journal of Educational Policies*. He is a member of several national and international academic associations and Egitim Sen (Education and Science Workers' Union).

Email: aksoy@education.ankara.edu.tr

Nora Alleki is a socio-economist and expert in the fields of human resources management, training and employment policies. She has 11 years of working experience in monitoring public policies on employment labour and gender in the French Ministry of Labour. She is currently responsible for the service "access to employment and employability" for the department "Val de Marne". Since 2007, she has added to her work, teaching and research activities in Africa and Europe. She was an associate researcher in IRES at the time of the research reported in this volume, and published a paper about youth employment policies in Algeria in *Chroniques Internationales de l'IRES*. Globally, her research includes: (i) Regulations and financing of training systems; (ii)Employment-Education relationships and in particular school to work transitions; (iii) Youth - Women employment policies and labour markets reforms; (iv) the place of education and management of Human resources (skills management, corporate social responsibility) in development and social progress.

Email: nora.alleki@hotmail.fr

Hatice O. Aras is a "technology and design" teacher in a public school in Istanbul. She completed her Masters thesis in educational sociology and she is a doctoral student in the economics of education and planning program at Ankara University. Her research focus is on universities and the hidden curriculum. She has published articles on these topics and also worked on the translation of a book on Education Sciences. She is a member of the Education and Science Workers' Union (Egitim Sen).

Email: ozdenaras@gmail.com

Dilek Çankaya received her MA in Adult Education at Boğaziçi University, Istanbul and she is currently completing her thesis for her doctorate in the Department of Educational Administration and Policy at Ankara University, College of Educational Sciences, Ankara, Turkey. Her personal and scholarly interests focus on theoretical roots of critical pedagogy and the educational status of disadvantaged groups.

Email: dilekcankaya@gmail.com

Christine Daymon is based in Perth, Australia at Murdoch University where she leads an international project on cross-cultural learning and teaching in universities in Australia and China. She is also the director of a collaborative China-Australia research centre which investigates media and communication in Asia. With an interest in the use of ethnographic and feminist approaches to study communication and cultures, she has published widely including the co-authored book *Qualitative Research Methods in Public Relations and Marketing Communications*, now in its 2nd edition, and the co-edited book *Gender and Public Relations: Critical Perspectives on Voice, Image and Identity*, both books published by Routledge.

Email: christinedaymon@gmail.com

Kathy Durkin is a Senior Lecturer in research methodology and critical thinking. She teaches Research Principles and Practice in Masters courses in the Media School at Bournemouth University, UK. From 1997 until 2009 she ran the Critical Thinking Skills program for Masters students in the Media School to support international students in their adaptation to Western expectations of academic writing and argumentation. Her research interests lie in cross-cultural critical argumentation and debate, and her current research focuses on the marketisation and globalisation of higher education, with particular respect to critical thinking and career preparedness.

Email: durkink@bournemouth.ac.uk

Hu Rongkun is a lecturer at the Faculty of School Leadership Training and Research Beijing Institute of Education. Her research interests involve school leadership, principal leadership and training, school management, and education reforms in China. She recently published with A. Walker and Qian, H., "Principal leadership in China: an initial review" in *School Effectiveness and School Improvement*, 2012, Vol. 23(4), pp. 369–399.

Email: hurongkun662@163.com

Aygülen Kayahan Karakul is a mathematics teacher and works for the Ministry of Education. She completed her PhD in the Department of Educational Administration and Policy at Ankara University, Institute of Educational Sciences. Her research interests are education and employment relationships and critical pedagogy issues. She has published articles in several journals and translated a book on education sciences from English to Turkish.

Email: aygülen.kayahan@gmail.com

Jonah Nyaga Kindiki is Associate Professor of International Education and Policy Analysis, and current Head, Department of Educational Management and Policy Studies (EMPS), Moi University, Kenya. He holds a PhD and MEd degrees in International Education, Postgraduate Certificates in Educational Research and Study skills in Higher and Teacher Education from the University of Birmingham, UK and a Bachelor degree from Kenya. He steered the development of the EMEd (Executive Master of Education) and PhD degrees in Education at Moi University He is a member of several professional bodies, an external examiner and research with key interest in international education research.

Email: nyagajonah@yahoo.com

Steven J. Klees is the R. W. Benjamin Professor of International and Comparative Education at the University of Maryland. He did his Ph.D. at Stanford University and has taught at Cornell University, Stanford University, and Florida State University. He was a Fulbright Scholar on two occasions at the Federal University of Bahia in Brazil. Prof. Klees' work examines the political economy of education and development with specific research interests in globalization, neoliberalism, and education; the role of aid agencies; education, human rights, and social justice; the education of disadvantaged populations; the role of class, gender, and race in reproducing and challenging educational and social inequality; and alternative approaches to education and development.

Email: sklees@umd.edu

Helena Modzelewski is an Assistant Professor of Philosophy of Education at the Universidad de la República, Uruguay. Her research interests include the education of the emotions, and the contribution of literature to civic education, on which she has written a number of papers mainly in Spanish-speaking journals. She is author of *A su imagen y semejanza*, a novel on transgendered society in Uruguay that aims at contributing to the understanding of sexual diversity, consistently using literature for opening the readers'–citizens'—minds.

Email: helen_mod@hotmail.com

Bethsaida Nieves is a PhD. Candidate in the Department of Curriculum and Instruction at the University of Wisconsin-Madison. Her research interests include

International and Comparative 'Education, and Education Reform Policy for Economic Development. Her recent publications include: "Morocco's 2000 Charter for Educational Reform Policy: Language Standardizations and Fragmentations" in *Research on the Impact of Educational Policy on Teaching and Learning;* "Defining the Disabled Person: An Analysis of the Continental Plan of Action for the African Decade of Persons with Disabilities" in *Advances in Research and Praxis in Special Education in Africa, Caribbean and the Middle East.*

Email: bnieves@wisc.edu

Mario Novelli is a Senior Lecturer in International Education and deputy director of the Centre for International Education (CIE), University of Sussex. His research explore the relationship between education, globalization and international development, with a specific focus on education and conflict. He has recently published work on political violence against educators in Colombia; the securitisation of aid to education and on issues related to the new geopolitics of aid to education after 9/11. Over the last ten years he has worked on projects with a wide range of international organizations (such as UNICEF; UNESCO; Education International) and published widely in academic journals. He is currently working with UNICEF on a new 4-year program on education and peace building in conflict affected states.

Email: M.Novelli@sussex.ac.uk

Beth D. Packer is a PhD candidate in Sociology at the École Des Hautes Études En Sciences Sociales (Paris, France) in the department of Geography, Society and Development. She received a Bachelor's degree in History from California Polytechnic University San Luis Obispo and a Master's degree in Political and Cultural Sociology from the Université Paris 7. She has conducted research on international development in India and Senegal. Her current research focus is the cultural politics of women's soccer in Senegal. Beth's primary interests are critical ethnography, gender and performativity, sport, citizenship, Islam in West Africa.

Email: bethdpacker@gmail.com

Omar Qargha has worked in Afghanistan since June 2001. Before joining AFS as a Partner, Mr. Qargha successfully led the Indiana University team between 2007 and 2010 to develop national standards for teacher education universities for Afghanistan's Ministry of Higher Education. Mr. Qargha led the JBS International team between 2006 and 2007 to develop a national teacher competency and credentialing system for Afghanistan's Ministry of Education. He also served a Assistant Director for Help the Afghan Children, a grass-roots organization, from 2001 to 2006. During this time he managed school construction, developed training curriculum, and expanded the organization's programs.

Mr. Qargha holds a B.Sc in Chemistry from the University of North Florida, an MEd in Curriculum and Instruction from George Mason University, and an MA in International Comparative Education from Stanford University's School of Education. Mr. Qargha is completing his doctoral degree in International Comparative Education at the University of Maryland in College Park.

Mr. Qargha has led large program evaluation projects, including an impact evaluation of seven large projects in Afghanistan funded by the US White House. He has carried out extensive qualitative and quantitative research, published academic papers, and has presented in numerous international conferences on the topics of Afghanistan, research, and education.

Email: oqargha@gmail.com

Qian Haiyan is an Assistant Professor in the Department of Education Policy and Leadership, Hong Kong Institute of Education. Her research interests include education leadership, school principalship in China and the influence of the social and cultural context on schooling across Chinese societies. She recently published with Dr. A. Walker, "Reform disconnection in China" in the *Peabody Journal of Education,* 2012, Vol. 87(2), pp. 162–177.

Email: hqian@ied.edu.hk.

Allan Walker is the Joseph Lau Chair Professor of International Educational Leadership, Head of the Department of Education Policy and Leadership and Director of the Joseph Lau Luen Hung Charitable Trust Asia Pacific Centre for Leadership and change at the Hong Kong Institute of Education. His research focuses on expanding knowledge of school leadership in Chinese and other Asian societies and disseminating this internationally. He recently published "Leaders seeking resonance: managing the connectors that bind schools" in the *International Journal of Leadership in Education,* 2012, Vol. 15(2), pp. 237–253.

Email: adwalder@ied.edu.hk

Yuan Tingting is a Lecturer in Education in the Faculty of Education at Liverpool Hope University. She obtained her PhD degree in the Graduate School of Education at the University of Bristol. Her research interests include globalization and education, international aid for education, China-Africa cooperation and other educational issues in the context of the global political economy. She recently published "Does Western 'aid' work?—Changing discourses and logics" in *Academics in China,* 2012 (2), pp. 257–275.

Ruhksana Zia has worked as Director, Center for Learning and Teaching at Forman Christian College (A Chartered University) since 2009. She started her career as a government teacher of Higher Education in 1975. After completing her PhD in 1994 she diversified her work at the postgraduate level to include collaborations with international agencies (UNICEF, DFID, GTZ, etc.) and local NGOS. She establish a department of Development Education (with a focus on community service expanded the vision and scope of the higher education institution and intensifi research on various social issues (gender, education and development, and values education) in the context of Pakistan. (From 2001 to 2004 she represented Pakist at UNESCO (Paris). As Director of the Directorate of Staff Development she w responsible for professional development of public school teachers of Punjab (i. pre-service education with 33 colleges of education, 600 faculty. 4500 studen and in-service training of approximately 300,000 public school teachers). She h published 19 articles and edited a book in national and international publications.

Email: ziarukhsana1@hotmail.com

THE EDITORS

Macleans A. Geo-JaJa, an experienced educator and researcher is Professor Economics and Education at Brigham Young University, USA and a Visiting Profess at Zhejiang Normal University, China. He is a Fulbright Senior Specialist fellow. I combines a scholar's critical approach and the experience of an international developme adviser in his research His research analyses the underlying causes of Afric economic and education deprivations and the ways in which inclusive developme and rights in education are critically intertwined. He studied and teaches Economics Education and Development Economics, especially with a link between the academ community and the world of development practitioners. For the past several years a Fulbright Senior Specialist Fellow, he has served as technical adviser to institutio and universities in different regions of the world on capacity-building in Economics Education and the dimension of African education in globalization. He is the auth of numerous articles and book chapters on Rights in Education, Internationalizati of Education, and Globalization of Development. He currently serves as a consulti editor to the *International Review of Education (IRE)* and other journals.

Email: Geo-JaJa@byu.edu.

Suzanne Majhanovich is Professor Emerita/Adjunct Research Professor at t Faculty of Education, Western University in London, Ontario Canada. She is t Chair of the WCCES Standing Committee for Publications and the former editor the journal *Canadian and International Education.* Her research interests inclu first and second language acquisition, the teaching of English as a Foreign Langua in international contexts, globalization, educational restructuring, decentralizati and privatization of education. She is the author of numerous articles and boo and most recently has co-edited with Diane Brook Napier *Education, Dominan and Identity* (Sense, 2013), and with Christine Fox and Fatma Gök, *Borderi Re-bordering and New Possibilities in Education and Society* (Springer, 2012).

Email: smajhano@uwo.ca

CPSIA information can be obtained at www.ICGtesting.com
Printed in the USA
LVOW10s1617290614

392216LV00008B/430/P